BERLITZ®

European
PHRASE BOOK

14 key languages spoken in over 25 countries

Austria, Belgium, Croatia, Denmark, Finland, France, Germany, Greece, Italy, Netherlands, Norway, Poland, Portugal, Russia, Spain, Sweden, Switzerland, and more

Library of Congress Catalog Card Number: 73-20997

21st printing 1992

Printed in Switzerland

BERLITZ TRAVEL GUIDES

Africa
○ Algeria
Kenya
Morocco
South Africa
Tunisia

Asia, Middle East
○ China
Hong Kong
○ India
○ Indonesia
○ Japan
Nepal
Singapore
Sri Lanka
Thailand
Egypt
Jerusalem/Holy Land
Saudi Arabia

Australasia
○ Australia
New Zealand

Austria/Switzerland
Tyrol
Vienna
○ Switzerland

British Isles
Channel Islands
Ireland
London
Oxford and Stratford
Scotland

Belgium/Netherlands
Brussels
Amsterdam

France
Brittany
○ France
French Riviera
Loire Valley
Normandy
Paris

Germany
Berlin
Munich
The Rhine Valley

Greece, Cyprus and Turkey
Athens
Corfu
Crete
Greek Islands Aegean
Peloponnese
Rhodes
Salonica/N. Greece
Cyprus
Istanbul/Aegean Coast
○ Turkey

Italy and Malta
Florence
Italian Adriatic
Italian Riviera
○ Italy
Naples/Amalfi Coast
Rome
Sicily
Venice
Malta

Scandinavia
Copenhagen
Helsinki
Oslo/Bergen
Stockholm

Spain
Barcelona
Canary Islands
Costa Blanca
Costa Brava
Costa del Sol/Andalusia
Costa Dorada/Barcelona
Ibiza and Formentera
Madrid
Majorca and Minorca
Seville

Portugal
Algarve
Lisbon
Madeira

Eastern Europe
Budapest
Dubrovnik/S. Dalmatia
○ Hungary
Istria and Croatian Coast
Moscow and Leningrad
The Hermitage, Leningrad*
Prague
Split and Dalmatia
○ Yugoslavia

North America
○ U.S.A.
California
Florida
Hawaii
Miami
New York
Washington
○ Canada
Montreal
Toronto

Caribbean, Lat. Am.
Bahamas
Bermuda
French West Indies
Jamaica
Puerto Rico
Southern Caribbean
Virgin Islands
Brazil (Highlights of)
○ Mexico
Mexico City
Rio de Janeiro

Address Books
London/New York
Paris/Rome

Blueprint Guides
Europe A-Z/France
Germany/Britain
Greece/Hungary
Italy/Spain/USSR*

More for the $
France/Italy

Cruise Guides
Alaska
Caribbean
Handbook to Cruising

Ski Guides
Austria/France
Italy/Switzerland
Skiing the Alps

Europe
Business Travel Guide
Train Travel
Pocket Guide-Europe
Cities of Europe

* in preparation/○ country guides 192 or 256 p.

Contents

Preface

You're about to visit several countries in Europe and we've attempted to provide you with a useful phrase book featuring key phrases in 14 different European languages.

Our book is simple to use, since the language sections are divided into topics, from arrival to eating out, from shopping to emergencies. Each expression appears with a code to pronunciation next to it. Simply read this imitated pronunciation as if it were English, stressing the syllables that are printed in bold type. It is based on Standard British pronunciation, though we have tried to take into account General American pronunciation as well.

This European Phrase Book is made up of key extracts from 14 complete phrase books published by Berlitz. If you plan to spend a longer period of time in one country or language area, you'd be well advised to obtain a complete 192-page single language phrase book. It contains detailed travel information and tips, as well as useful phrases.

The phrases featured in each language of this book are also available in cassette form to help you prepare for your trip. The cassette is also available with a full-length phrase book at booksellers and record shops as a ''Cassettepak''.

Bon Voyage!

DANISH

Guide to Pronunciation

Letter	Approximate pronunciation	Symbol	Example	
Consonants				
b, c, f, h, l, m, n, v	as in English			
d	1) when at the end of the word, or between two vowels, like **th** in **th**is	dh	**med**	mehdh
	2) otherwise, as in English	d	**dale**	**dar**ler
g	1) at the beginning of a word or syllable, as in **g**o	g	**glas**	glahss
	2) when at the end of a word after a long vowel or before unstressed **e**, like **ch**s in Scottish lo**ch**, but weaker and voiced	g̊	**kage**	**kar**g̊er
	3) usually mute after **i**, **y**, and sometimes mute after **a**, **e**, **o**		**sige**	**see**er
j, hj	like **y** in **y**et	y	**ja**	yah

k, p, t	1) when at the beginning of a word, as in **k**ite, **p**ill and **t**o	k p t	**kaffe** **pude** **tale**	**kah**fer **poo**dher **tar**ler
	2) otherwise like **g**, **b**, **d** in **g**o, **b**it and **d**o	g b d	**lække** **stoppe** **sætte**	**leh**ger **sdo**ber **seh**der
l	always as in **l**eaf, never as in be**ll**	l	**vel**	vehl
r	pronounced in the back of the throat, as in French	r	**rose**	**roa**ser
s	always as in **s**ee	s/ss	**skål** **haster**	sgawl **hahss**derr
sj	like **sh** in **sh**eet	sh	**sjælden**	**sheh**lern
w	for Danes this is the same as **v**			
z	like **s** in **s**o	s	**zone**	**soa**ner

Vowels

Vowels are generally long in stressed syllables when followed by *at most* one consonant. If followed by two consonants (or more), or in unstressed syllables, they are generally short.

a	1) when long, like **a** in c**a**r; it can also be pronounced like **a** in b**a**d, but longer	ar*	**bade**	**bar**dher
	2) when short, like long **a**, or more like **a** in c**a**rt	ah	**hat**	hahd
	3) you will also hear, as alternatives to the above, a more or less "flat" pronunciation of **a**, which can be like **a** in h**a**t, or tend towards **e** in l**e**t; it can be long or short	ai æ	**tale** **tak**	**tai**ler tæg
e	1) when long, the same quality as **a** in pl**a**te, but longer, and a pure vowel, not a diphthong	ay	**mere**	**may**rer
	2) when short, somewhere between the **a** in pl**a**te and the **i** in h**i**t	ay	**fedt**	fayd
	3) when short, also like **e** in m**e**t	eh	**let**	lehd
	4) when unstressed, like **a** in **a**bout	er*	**gammel**	**gah**merl
i	1) when long, like **ee** in b**ee**	ee	**bide**	**bee**dher
	2) when short, like **ee** in m**ee**t	ee	**liter**	**lee**derr

o	1) when long, like **aw** in s**aw**, but with the tongue higher in the mouth; quite like **u** in p**u**t	oa	**skole**	**sgoa**ler
	2) when short, more or less the same quality of sound	oa	**bonde**	**boa**ner
	3) when short, also like **o** in l**o**t	o	**godt**	god
u	1) when long, like **oo** in p**oo**l	oo	**pude**	**poo**dher
	2) when short, like **oo** in l**oo**t	oo	**nu**	noo
y	put your tongue in the position for the **ee** of b**ee**, but round your lips as for the **oo** of p**oo**l; the vowel you pronounce like this should be more or less correct	ew	**byde** **lytte**	**bew**dher **lew**der
æ	1) when long, like the first part of the word **air**	ai	**bære**	**bai**rer
	2) when short, like **e** in g**e**t, but next to **r** it sounds more like the **a** of h**a**t	eh æ	**ægte** **værre**	**ehg**der **vær**er
å	1) when long, like **aw** in s**aw**	aw	**åben**	**aw**bern
	2) when short, like **o** in **o**n	o	**ånd**	on
ø	like **ur** in f**ur**, but with the lips rounded; can be long or short	ur*	**frøken** **øl**	**fru**rgern url

Diphthongs

av	like **ow** in n**ow**	ow	**hav**	how
ej	like **igh** in s**igh**	igh	**nej**	nigh
ev	like **e** in g**e**t followed by a short **u** as in p**u**t	ehoo	**evne**	**ehoo**ner
ou	like **o** in g**o**t followed by a short **u** as in p**u**t	ooo	**lov**	looo
øi	like **oi** in **oi**l	oi	**øje**	**oi**er
øv	like **ur** in h**ur**t followed by a short **u** as in p**u**t	uroo*	**søvnig**	**suroo**nee

* The **r** should not be pronounced when reading this transcription.

N.B. 1) Many Danish speakers put a glottal stop in or after long vowels (like the Cockney pronunciation of **t** in **wa'er**). Although it has a certain distinctive role, you will be understood perfectly well if you do not use it, so we have not shown it in our transcriptions;
2) **dd** and **gg** between vowels are pronounced like **d** in **d**o and **g** in **g**o;
3) the letter **d** is not pronounced in **nd** and **ld** at the end of a word or syllable (*mand* = **mahn**, *guld* = **gool**) or before unstressed **e** or before **t** or **s** in the same syllable (*plads* = **plahs**).

Some basic expressions

Yes.	**Ja.**	yar
No.	**Nej.**	nay
Please.	**Vær så venlig.**	vair saw **vehn**lee
Thank you.	**Tak.**	tahk
Thank you very much.	**Mange tak.**	**mahng**er tahk
That's all right.	**Å, jeg be'r.**	aw yay bayr

Greetings

Good morning.	**Godmorgen.**	goadh**mo**rern
Good afternoon.	**Goddag.**	goadh**dai**
Good evening.	**Godaften.**	goadh**ahf**dern
Good night.	**Godnat.**	goadh**nahd**
Good-bye.	**Farvel.**	fahr**vehl**
See you later.	**På gensyn.**	paw **gehn**sewn
This is Mr. ...	**Det er hr ...**	day air hehr
This is Mrs. ...	**Det er fru ...**	day air froo
This is Miss ...	**Det er frøken ...**	day air **frur**gern
I'm very pleased to meet you.	**Det glæder mig at træffe Dem.**	day **glai**dherr migh aht **treh**fer dehm
How are you?	**Hvordan har De det?**	**vor**dahn harr dee day
Very well, thank you. And you?	**Fint, tak. Og De?**	fint tahk. o dee
Fine.	**Fint.**	fint
Excuse me.	**Undskyld.**	**oon**sgewl

Questions

Where?	**Hvor?**	vor
Where is ... ?	**Hvor er ... ?**	vor air
Where are ... ?	**Hvor er ... ?**	vor air
When?	**Hvornår?**	vor**nawr**
What?	**Hvad?**	vah(dh)
How?	**Hvordan?**	vor**dahn**
How much?	**Hvor meget?**	vor **migh**erd

How many?	**Hvor mange?**	vor **mahng**er
Who?	**Hvem?**	vehm
Why?	**Hvorfor?**	vor**for**
Which?	**Hvilken/Hvilket?**	**vil**gern/**vil**gerd
What do you call this?	**Hvad hedder dette?**	vahdh **heh**derr **deh**der
What do you call that?	**Hvad hedder det?**	vahdh **heh**derr day
What does this mean?	**Hvad betyder dette?**	vahdh ber**tew**derr **deh**der
What does that mean?	**Hvad betyder det?**	vahdh ber**tew**derr day

Do you speak . . . ?

Do you speak English?	**Taler De engelsk?**	**tai**lerr dee **ehng**erlsg
Do you speak German?	**Taler De tysk?**	**tai**lerr dee tewsg
Do you speak French?	**Taler De fransk?**	**tai**lerr dee frahnsg
Do you speak Spanish?	**Taler De spansk?**	**tai**lerr dee spahnsg
Do you speak Italian?	**Taler De italiensk?**	**tai**lerr dee eetahlee**aynsg**
Could you speak more slowly, please?	**Vil De tale langsommere?**	vil dee **tai**ler **lahng**somerrer
Please point to the phrase in the book.	**Vær så venlig at pege på sætningen i bogen.**	vair saw **vehn**lee ahd **pigh**er paw **sehd**ningern ee **baw**(g)ern
Just a minute. I'll see if I can find it in this book.	**Et øjeblik. Jeg vil se, om jeg kan finde det i denne bog.**	ehd **oi**erblig. yay vil say om yay kahn **fi**nner day ee **deh**ner baw(g)
I understand.	**Jeg forstår.**	yay for**sdawr**
I don't understand.	**Jeg forstår ikke.**	yay for**sdawr** **i**gger

Can . . . ?

Can I have . . . ?	**Kan jeg få . . . ?**	kahn yay faw
Can we have . . . ?	**Kan vi få . . . ?**	kahn vee faw

DANISH

Can you show me ...?	**Kan De vise mig ...?**	kahn dee **vee**sser migh
Can you tell me ...?	**Kan De sige mig ...?**	kahn dee **see**yer migh
Can you help me, please?	**Vil De være så venlig at hjælpe mig?**	vil dee **vai**rer saw **vehn**lee ahd **yehl**per migh

Wanting

I'd like ...	**Jeg vil gerne have ...**	yay vil **gehr**ner **hai**(wer)
We'd like ...	**Vi vil gerne have ...**	vee vil **gehr**ner **hai**(wer)
Please give me ...	**Vær så venlig at give mig ...**	vair saw **vehn**lee ahd **gee** migh
Give it to me please.	**Vær så venlig at give mig det.**	vair saw **vehn**lee ahd **gee** migh day
Please bring me ...	**Vær så venlig at hente ... til mig.**	vair saw **vehn**lee ahd **hehn**der ... til migh
Bring it to me, please.	**Vær så venlig at hente det til mig.**	vair saw **vehn**lee ahd **hehn**der day til migh
I'm hungry.	**Jeg er sulten.**	yay air **sool**tern
I'm thirsty.	**Jeg er tørstig.**	yay air **turrs**stee
I'm tired.	**Jeg er træt.**	yay air trehd
I'm lost.	**Jeg er faret vild.**	yay air **far**rerd veel
It's important.	**Det er vigtigt.**	day air **vig**dee(t)
It's urgent.	**Det haster.**	day **hahss**derr
Hurry up!	**Skynd Dem!**	sgurn dehm

It is/There is ...

It is/It's ...	**Det er ...**	day air
Is it ...?	**Er det ...?**	air day
It isn't ...	**Det er ikke ...**	day air **ig**ger
There is/There are ...	**Der er ...**	dair air
Is there/Are there ...?	**Er der ...?**	air dair
There isn't/There aren't ...	**Der er ikke ...**	dair air **ig**ger
There isn't any/ There aren't any.	**Der er ingen.**	dair air **ing**ern

DANISH

A few common words

big/small	**stor/lille**	sdoar/**li**ller
quick/slow	**hurtig/langsom**	**hoor**dee/**lahng**som
early/late	**tidlig/sen**	**teedh**lee/sayn
cheap/expensive	**billig/dyr**	**bi**llee/dewr
near/far	**nær/fjern**	nair/fyehrn
hot/cold	**varm/kold**	vahrm/kol
full/empty	**fuld/tom**	fool/tom
easy/difficult	**let/vanskelig**	lehd/**vahnss**gerlee
heavy/light	**tung/let**	toong/lehd
open/shut	**åben/lukket**	**aw**bern/**loo**gerd
right/wrong	**rigtig/forkert**	**rig**dee/for**kayrd**
old/new	**gammel/ny**	**gah**merl/new
old/young	**gammel/ung**	**gah**merl/oong
beautiful/ugly	**smuk/grim**	smoog/grim
good/bad	**god/dårlig**	goadh/**dawr**lee
better/worse	**bedre/værre**	**behdh**rer/**veh**rer

Some prepositions and a few more useful words

at	**ved**	vaydh
on	**på**	paw
in	**i**	ee
to	**til**	til
from	**fra**	frar
inside	**indeni**	**inn**ernee
outside	**udenfor**	**oo**dhernfor
up	**op**	ob
down	**ned**	naydh
before	**før**	furr
after	**efter**	**ehf**derr
with	**med**	maydh
without	**uden**	**oo**dhern
through	**gennem**	**geh**nerm
towards	**imod**	ee**moadh**
until	**indtil**	**in**til
during	**i løbet af**	ee **lur**berd ahf
and	**og**	o
or	**eller**	**eh**lerr
not	**ikke**	**i**gger
nothing	**intet**	**in**derd
none	**ingen**	**ing**ern
very	**meget**	**migh**erd
also	**også**	**oss**er
soon	**snart**	snahrd
perhaps	**måske**	moss**gay**
here	**her**	hair

there	**der**	dair
now	**nu**	noo
then	**så**	saw

Arrival

Your passport, please.	**Deres pas!**	**deh**rerss pahss
Here it is.	**Værs'go.**	**vehr**sgoa
Have you anything to declare?	**Har De noget at fortolde?**	harr dee **noa**gerd ahd for**to**ller
No, nothing at all.	**Nej, intet.**	nigh **in**derd
Porter!	**Drager!**	**drah**gerr
Can you help me with my luggage, please?	**Vil De hjælpe mig med min bagage?**	vil dee **yehl**per migh maydh meen bah**gai**sher
That's my suitcase.	**Det er min kuffert.**	day air meen **koo**ferrd
Where's the bus to the centre of town, please?	**Hvor holder bussen til centrum?**	vor **ho**llerr **boo**ssern til **sehn**troam
This way, please.	**Denne vej.**	**deh**ner vigh

Changing money

Can you change a traveller's cheque, please?	**Kan De indløse en rejsecheck?**	kahn dee **in**lursser ayn **righ**sserchehg
Where's the nearest bank, please?	**Hvor er den nærmeste bank?**	vor air dehn **nair**mersder bahnk

Car rental

I'd like a car.	**Jeg vil gerne leje en vogn.**	yay vil **gehr**ner **ligh**er ayn **voa**(g)ern
For how long?	**Hvor længe?**	vor **lehng**er
A day/Four days/ A week/Two weeks.	**En dag/Fire dage/ En uge/to uger.**	ayn dai/**fee**rer **dai**(g)er/ ayn **oo**(g)er/toa **oo**(g)err

Taxi

Where can I get a taxi?	**Hvor kan jeg få en taxa?**	vor kahn yay faw ayn **tahg**sah
What's the fare to . . . ?	**Hvad koster det til . . . ?**	vahdh **koss**derr day til

Take me to this address, please.	**Kør mig til denne adresse.**	kurr migh til **deh**ner ah**dreh**sser
I'm in a hurry.	**Jeg har travlt.**	yay harr trowlt
Could you drive more slowly, please?	**Vil De være venlig at køre lidt langsommere?**	vil dee **vai**rer **vehn**lee ahd **kur**rer let **lahng**somerrer

Hotel and other accommodation

My name is . . .	**Mit navn er . . .**	mid nown air
Have you a reservation?	**Har De reserveret?**	harr di raysehr**vai**rerd
Yes, here's the confirmation.	**Ja, her er bekræftelsen.**	yar hair air ber**krehf**derlsern
I'd like . . .	**Jeg vil gerne have . . .**	yay vil **gehr**ner **hai**(wer)
I'd like a single room/a double room.	**Jeg vil gerne have et enkeltværelse/et dobbeltværelse.**	yay vil **gehr**ner **hai**(wer) ayd **ehng**gerldvairaylser/ ayd **do**berldvairaylser
a room with a bath/ with a shower	**et værelse med bad/med brusebad**	ayd **vai**raylser maydh bardh/maydh **broo**sserbardh

How much?

What's the price per night/per week/per month?	**Hvor meget koster det pr. nat/pr. uge/ pr. måned?**	vor **migh**erd **koss**derr day pehr nahd/pehr **oo**(g)er/ pehr **maw**nerdh
May I see the room?	**Må jeg se værelset?**	maw yay say **vai**raylserd
I'm sorry, I don't like it.	**Jeg synes ikke om det.**	yay **sew**nerss **i**gger om day
Yes, that's fine. I'll take it.	**Ja, det er godt. Det tager jeg.**	yar day air god day **tar**(g)err yay
What's my room number, please?	**Hvilket nummer har mit værelse?**	**vil**kerd **noo**merr harr mid **vai**raylser
Number 123.	**Nummer 123.**	**noo**merr 123

Service, please

Who is it?	**Hvem er det?**	vehm air day
Just a minute.	**Et øjeblik.**	ayd **oi**erblig

Come in! The door's open.	**Kom ind! Døren er åben.**	kom in **dur**rern air **aw**bern
May we have breakfast in our room?	**Kan vi få morgenmad på værelset?**	kahn vee faw **mor**(g)ernmahdh paw **vai**raylserd

Breakfast

I'll have...	**Jeg vil gerne have...**	yay vil **gehr**ner **hai**(wer)
I'll have some fruit juice.	**Jeg vil gerne have noget frugtsaft.**	yay vil **gehr**ner **hai**(wer) **noa**(g)erd **froogd**sahfd
a boiled egg	**et kogt æg**	ayd kogd ehg
a fried egg	**et spejlæg**	ayd **sbighl**ehg
some bacon/some ham	**noget bacon/noget skinke**	**noa**(g)erd **bay**kern/ **noa**(g)erd **sging**gerr
some toast	**noget ristet brød**	**noa**(g)erd **ris**derd brurd
a pot of tea	**en kande te**	ayn **kah**ner tay
a cup of tea	**en kop te**	ayn kob tay
some coffee	**noget kaffe**	**noa**(g)erd **kah**fer
some chocolate	**noget chokolade**	**noa**(g)erd shoagoa**lar**dher
more butter	**mere smør**	**may**rer smurr
some hot water	**noget varmt vand**	**noa**(g)erd vahrmd vahn

Difficulties

The central heating doesn't work.	**Centralvarmen virker ikke.**	sehn**trarl**vahrmen **veer**gerr **i**gger
the light/the socket the tap/the toilet	**lyset/stikkontaken vandhanen/toilettet**	**lew**sserd/**sdig**gondahgdern **vahn**harnern/toi**leh**derd
There's no hot water.	**Der er ikke noget varmt vand.**	dair air **i**gger **noa**(g)erd vahrmd vahn
May I see the manager, please?	**Jeg vil gerne tale med direktøren.**	yay vil **gehr**ner **tai**ler maydh direhg**tur**rern

Telephone—Mail

There's a call for you.	**Der er telefon til Dem.**	dair air taylay**foan** til dehm
Hold the line, please.	**Et øjeblik.**	ayd **oi**erblig
Operator, I've been cut off.	**Frøken, jeg er blevet afbrudt.**	**frur**gern yay air **blay**verd **ow**brood

DANISH

Did anyone telephone me?	**Er der blevet ringet til mig?**	air dair **blay**verd **ring**erd til migh
Is there any mail for me?	**Er der post til mig?**	air dair possd til migh
Are there any messages for me?	**Er der en besked til mig?**	air dair ayn ber**sgaydh** til migh

Checking out

May I have my bill, please?	**Må jeg bede om regningen?**	maw yay **bay**dher om **righ**ningern
We're in a great hurry.	**Vi skal skynde os.**	vee sgahl **sgur**ner oss
It's been a very enjoyable stay.	**Det har været et meget behageligt ophold.**	day harr **vai**rerd ayd **migh**erd ber**har**gerligd **ob**hol

Eating out

Good evening, sir/ Good evening, madam.	**Godaften hr./ Godaften frue.**	goadh**ahf**dern hehr/ goadh**ahf**dern **froo**er
Good evening. I'd like a table for two, please.	**Godaften. Jeg vil gerne have et bord til to.**	goadh**ahf**dern. yay vil **geh**rner **hai**(wer) ayd bord til toa
Do you have a fixed-price menu?	**Har De en "dagens middag"?**	harr dee ayn **dai**(g)ernss **mi**ddar(g)
May I see the à la carte menu?	**Må jeg se spisekortet?**	maw yay say **sbee**serkorderd
May we have an ashtray, please?	**Må vi tå et askebæger?**	maw vee faw ayd **ahss**gerbeh(g)err
some bread	**noget brød**	**noa**(g)erd brurdh
a fork	**en gaffel**	ayn **gah**ferl
a knife	**en kniv**	ayn kneeoo
a spoon	**en ske**	ayn sgay
a plate	**en tallerken**	ayn tah**lehr**gern
a glass	**et glas**	ayd glahss
a napkin	**en serviet**	ayn sehrvi**ehd**
another chair	**en stol til**	ayn sdoal til
Where's the gentlemen's toilet (men's room)?	**Hvor er herretoilettet?**	vor air **heh**rertoaahlehderd
Where's the ladies' toilet (ladies' room)?	**Hvor er dametoilettet?**	vor air **dar**mertoaahlehderd

Appetizers

I'd like some ...	**Jeg vil gerne have ...**	yay vil **gehr**ner **hai**(wer)
I'd like some assorted appetizers.	**Jeg vil gerne have forskellig hors d'oeuvre.**	yay vil **gehr**ner **hai**(wer) foss**geh**lee or**durvr**
orange juice	**noget orangesaft**	**noa**gert oa**rahng**shersahft
ham	**skinke**	**sging**ger
melon	**melon**	may**loan**
pâté	**postej**	poss**digh**
smoked salmon	**røget laks**	**rur**(g)ert lahgs
shrimps (shrimp)	**rejer**	**righ**er

Soup

Have you any ... ?	**Har De ...?**	harr dee
Have you any chicken soup?	**Har De hønsekødssuppe?**	harr dee **hurnss**(g)ergurdssooper
vegetable soup	**grønsagssuppe**	**grurn**sar(gs)soaber
onion soup	**løgsuppe**	**lurg**soaber

Fish

I'd like some ...	**Jeg vil gerne have ...**	yay vil **gehr**ner **hai**(wer)
I'd like some fish.	**Jeg vil gerne have fisk.**	yay vil **gehr**ner **hai**(wer) fisg
sole	**søtunge**	**sur**doanger
trout	**ørred**	**ur**rerd
lobster	**hummer**	**hoa**merr
crayfish	**krebs**	krehbss
prawns	**store rejer**	**stoa**rer **righ**err
I'd like it ...	**Jeg vil gerne have den ...**	yay vil **gehr**ner **hai**(wer) dehn
I'd like it steamed.	**Jeg vil gerne have den dampkogt.**	yay vil **gehr**ner **hai**(wer) dehn **dahmp**kogd
grilled	**grilleret**	gri**lay**rerd
boiled	**kogt**	kogd
baked	**stegt i ovnen**	sdehgd ee **oaoo**nern
fried	**stegt**	sdehgd

Meat—Poultry—Game

I'd like some...	**Jeg vil gerne have...**	yay vil **gehr**ner **hai**(wer)
I'd like some beef.	**Jeg vil gerne have oksekød.**	yay vil **gehr**ner **hai**(wer) **og**serkurd
a beef steak	**en engelsk bøf**	ayn **ehng**erlsk burf
some roast beef	**roastbeef**	**rossd**bif
a veal cutlet	**en kalvekotelet**	ayn **kahl**verkoaterlehd
mutton	**fårekød**	**faw**rerkurdh
lamb	**lammekød**	**lah**morkurdh
a pork chop	**en svinekotelet**	ayn **svee**nerkoaterlehd
roast pork	**flæskesteg**	**flehss**gersdigh
hare	**hare**	**har**rer
chicken	**kylling**	**kew**ling
roast chicken	**stegt kylling**	sdehgd **kew**ling
duck	**and**	ahn
How do you like your meat?	**Hvordan vil De gerne have Deres kød tilberedt?**	vor**dahn** vil dee **gehr**ner **hai**(wer) **day**rerss kurdh **til**berrayd
rare	**rødt**	rurd
medium	**medium**	**may**deeom
well done	**gennemstegt**	**geh**nermsdehgd

Vegetables

What vegetables have you got?	**Hvilke grønsager har De?**	**vil**ger **grurn**sar(g)err harr dee
I'd like some...	**Jeg vil gerne have...**	yay vil **gehr**ner **hai**(wer)
I'd like some asparagus.	**Jeg vil gerne have asparges.**	yay vil **gehr**ner **hai**(wer) ahss**rah**rerss
green beans	**grønne bønner**	**gru**rner **bur**nerr
mushrooms	**champignoner**	**shahng**pinyongnerr
carrots	**gulerødder**	**goo**lerrurderr
onions	**løg**	lurg
red cabbage	**rødkål**	**rurdh**kawl
spinach	**spinat**	sbi**naid**
rice	**ris**	reess
peas	**ærter**	**air**terr
tomatoes	**tomater**	toa**mai**derr
green salad	**grøn salat**	grurn sah**laid**
potatoes	**kartofler**	kahr**tof**lerr

Desserts

Nothing more, thanks.	**Tak, ikke mere.**	tahk **i**gger **may**rer
Just a small portion, please.	**Kun en lille portion.**	koon ayn **li**ller por**syoan**
Have you any ice-cream?	**Har De is?**	harr dee eess
fruit salad	**frugtsalat**	**froagd**sahlaid
fresh fruit	**frisk frugt**	frisg froogd
cheese	**ost**	oossd

Drink

What would you like to drink?	**Hvad ønsker De at drikke?**	vahdh **urn**skerr dee ahd **dri**gger
I'll have a beer, please.	**Jeg vil gerne have en øl.**	yay vil **gehr**ner **hai**(wer) ayn url
I'll have a whisky, please.	**Jeg vil gerne have en whisky.**	yay vil **gehr**ner **hai**(wer) ayn **wiss**kee

Wine

I'd like a bottle of wine.	**Jeg vil gerne have en flaske vin.**	yay vil **gehr**ner **hai**(wer) ayn **flahss**ger veen
red wine	**rødvin**	**rurdh**veen
rosé wine	**rosé-vin**	roa**say**veen
white wine	**hvidvin**	**vidh**veen
Cheers!	**Skål!**	skawl

The bill (check)

May I have the bill (check) please?	**Jeg vil gerne have regningen.**	yay vil **gehr**ner **hai**(wer) **righ**ningern
Is service included?	**Er det med betjening?**	air day mehdh ber**tyay**ning
Everything's included.	**Alt er iberegnet.**	ahlt air **ee**berrighnert
Thank you, that was a very good meal.	**Mange tak, det smagte fortræffeligt.**	**mahng**er tahk day **smarg**der for**treh**ferligd

Travelling

Where's the railway station, please?	**Hvor er banegården?**	vor air **bai**nergawr(d)ern

DANISH

Where's the ticket office, please?	**Hvor er billet-kontoret?**	vor air bi**lehd**kontoarerd
I'd like a ticket to ...	**Jeg vil gerne have en billet til ...**	yay vil **gehr**ner **hai**(wer) ayn bi**lehd** til
First or second class?	**Første eller anden klasse?**	**furr**ster **eh**lerr **ahn**dern **klah**sser
First class, please.	**Første klasse.**	**furr**ster **klah**sser
Single or return (one way or round-trip)?	**Enkelt eller retur?**	**ehng**gerld **eh**lerr rer**toor**
Do I have to change trains?	**Skal jeg skifte tog?**	sgahl yigh **sgif**der taw(g)
What platform does the train leave from?	**Fra hvilken perron afgår toget?**	frar **vil**gern peh**rong ow**-gawr **taw**gerd
Where's the nearest underground (sub-way) station?	**Hvor er den nærmeste under-grundsstation?**	vor air dehn **nair**mersder **oa**nerrgroansssdahshoan
Where's the bus station, please?	**Hvor er rutebil-stationen?**	vor air **roo**derbeelsdah-shoanern
When's the first bus to ... ?	**Hvornår kører den første bus til ... ?**	vor**nawr kur**rerr dehn **fur**sder booss til
the last bus	**den sidste bus**	dehn **see(d)**sder booss
the next bus	**den næste bus**	dehn **neh**sder booss
Please let me off at the next stop.	**Jeg vil gerne af ved næste stoppested.**	yay vil **gehr**ner ahv vaydh **neh**sder **sdo**bbersdehdh

Relaxing

What's on at the cinema (movies)?	**Hvad går der i bio-grafen?**	vahdh gawr dair ee bioa-**grar**fern
What's on at the theatre?	**Hvad går der på teatret?**	vahdh gawr dair paw tay**ai**drerd
What time does the film begin? And the play?	**Hvornår begynder filmen? Og stykket?**	vor**nawr** ber**gew**nerr **fil**-mern? o **stew**gerd
Are there any tickets for tonight?	**Er der flere billetter til i aften?**	air dair **flay**rer bi**leh**derr til ee **ahf**dern
Where can we go dancing?	**Hvor kan vi gå ud og danse?**	vor kahn vee gaw oodh o **dahn**ser
Would you like to dance?	**Vil De danse?**	vil dee **dahn**ser

Introductions

How do you do?	**Goddag.**	goadh**dai**
How are you?	**Hvordan har De det?**	vor**dahn** harr dee day
Very well, thank you. And you?	**Godt, tak. Og De?**	god tahk. o dee
May I introduce Miss Philips?	**Må jeg præsentere Dem for frøken Philips?**	maw yigh praisern**tay**rer dehm for **frur**gern Philips
My name is . . .	**Mit navn er . . .**	mid nown air
I'm very pleased to meet you.	**Det glæder mig at træffe Dem.**	day **glai**dherr migh ahd **treh**fer dehm
How long have you been here?	**Hvor længe har De været her?**	vor **lahng**er harr dee **vai**rerd hair
It was nice meeting you.	**Det har glædet mig at træffe Dem.**	day harr **glai**dherd migh ahd **treh**fer dehm

Dating

Would you like a cigarette?	**Må jeg byde Dem en cigaret?**	maw yay **bew**dher dehm ayn sigah**rehd**
May I get you a drink?	**Må jeg byde Dem en drink?**	maw yay **bew**dher dehm ayn drink
Do you have a light, please?	**Undskyld, kan De give mig ild?**	**oon**sgewl kahn dee **gee**ver migh il
Are you waiting for someone?	**Venter De på nogen?**	**vehn**derr dee paw **noa**gern
Are you free this evening?	**Er De ledig i aften?**	air dee **lay**dhee ee **ahf**dern
Where shall we meet?	**Hvor skal vi mødes?**	vor sgahl vee **mur**dherss
What time shall I meet you?	**Hvornår skal vi mødes?**	vor**nawr** sgahl vee **mur**dherss
May I take you home?	**Må jeg følge Dem hjem?**	maw yay **furl**ger dehm yehm
Thank you, it's been a wonderful evening.	**Tusind tak, det har været en vidunderlig aften.**	**too**ssin tahg day harr **vai**rerd ayn vi**dhoa**nerrlee **ahf**dern
What's your telephone number?	**Hvad er Deres telefonnummer?**	vahdh air **day**rerss tayler**foan**noomerr
Do you live alone?	**Bor De alene?**	**boar** dee ah**lay**ner

What time is your last train?	**Hvornår går Deres sidste tog?**	vor**nawr** gawr **day**rerss **seess**der tawg
Good-night . . .	**Godnat . . .**	goadh**nahd**

Banks

Where's the nearest bank, please?	**Hvor er den nærmeste bank?**	vor air dehn **nair**mersder bahnk
Where can I cash some traveller's cheques?	**Hvor kan jeg indløse rejsechecks?**	vor kahn yay **in**lursser **righ**ssershehks
What time does the bank open/What time does it close?	**Hvornår åbner banken/Hvornår lukker den?**	vor**nawr** **awb**nerr **bahng**gern/vor**nawr** **loa**gerr dehn
I'm expecting some money from home. Has it arrived?	**Jeg venter nogle penge hjemmefra. Er de kommet?**	yay **vehn**derr **no(g)**ler **pehng**er **yeh**merfrar. air dee **ko**mmerd
Can you give me some small change, please?	**Vil De give mig nogle småpenge?**	vill dee **gee**(ver) migh **no(g)**ler **smaw**pehnger

Shops, stores and services

Where is the nearest chemist's (pharmacy)?	**Hvor er det nærmeste apotek?**	vor air day **nair**mersder ahpoa**tayg**
the nearest hairdresser's	**den nærmeste frisør**	dehn **nair**mersder fri**surr**
the photo shop	**fotoforretningen**	**foa**toaforehdningern
the jeweller's	**guldsmeden**	**gool**smaydhern
the department store	**stormagasinet**	**sdoar**mahgahsseenerd
the police station	**politistationen**	polee**tee**stahshoanern
the garage	**parkeringshuset**	pahr**kay**ringsshoosserd
How do I get there?	**Hvordan kommer jeg derhen?**	vor**dahn** **ko**mmerr yay **dehr**hehn
Is it within walking distance?	**Kan man nemt gå derhen?**	kahn mahn nehmd gaw **dehr**hehn

Service

Can you help me, please?	**Vil De hjælpe mig?**	vil dee **yehl**ber migh
Can you show me this? And that, too.	**Vil De vise mig den her? Og den der.**	vil dee **vee**ser migh dehn hair? o dehn dair
It's too expensive/too big/too small.	**Den er for dyr/for stor/for lille.**	dehn air for dewr/for stoar/for **li**ller

DANISH

Can you show me some more?	**Kan De vise mig nogle flere?**	kahn dee **vee**sser migh **no(g)**ler **flay**rer
something better	**noget bedre**	**noa**(g)erd **beh**dhrer
something cheaper	**noget billigere**	**noa**(g)erd **bi**lliggerrer
How much is this? And that?	**Hvor meget koster den her? Og den der?**	vor **migh**erd **koss**derr dehn hair? o dehn dair
It's not quite what I want.	**Det er ikke helt det, jeg gerne vil have.**	day air **i**gger hayld day yay **gehr**ner vil **hai**(wer)
I like it.	**Den kan jeg lide.**	dehn kahn yay **lee**(dher)

Chemist's (Pharmacy)

I'd like something for a cold/for a cough/for travel sickness.	**Jeg vil gerne have noget mod forkølelse/mod hoste/mod køresyge.**	yay vil **gehr**ner **hai**(wer) **noa**(g)erd moadh for**kur**lerlser/moadh **hoass**der/moadh **kur**rersew(g)er
Can you recommend something for hay-fever/for sunburn?	**Kan De anbefale noget mod høfeber/mod solforbrænding?**	kahn dee **ahn**berfailer **noa**(g)erd moadh **hur**fayberr/moadh **soal**forbrehning

DANISH

Toiletry

May I have some razor blades?	**Må jeg få nogle barberblade?**	maw yay faw **no(g)**ler bahr**bayr**blaidher
some shaving cream	**noget barbercreme**	**noa**gerd bahr**bay**kraym
some toothpaste	**noget tandpasta**	**noa**gerd **tahn**pahsdah
I'd like some soap.	**Jeg vil gerne have noget håndsæbe.**	yay vil **gehr**ner **hai**(wer) **noa**(g)erd **hon**saiber
some suntan oil	**noget sololie**	**noa**(g)erd **soal**oalyer

At the barber's

I'd like a haircut, please.	**Jeg vil gerne klippes.**	yay vil **gehr**ner **kli**bberss
Short/Leave it long.	**Kort/Lad det være langt.**	kord/lahdh day **vai**rer lahngd
A razor cut, please.	**Skåret med barberblad.**	**sgaw**rerd maydh bahr**bayr**blahdh

At the hairdresser's

I'd like a shampoo and set, please.	**Jeg vil gerne have en vask og vandondulation.**	yay vil **gehr**ner **hai**(wer) ayn vahsg o **vahn**ondoolahshoan
I'd like a bleach.	**Jeg vil gerne have en blegning.**	yay vil **gehr**ner **hai**(wer) ayn **bligh**ning
a permanent	**en permanent**	ayn pehr**mah**nehnd
a colour rinse	**en skylning**	ayn **sgewl**ning
a manicure	**en manicure**	ayn mahni**kewr**

Photography

I'd like a film for this camera.	**Jeg vil gerne have en film til dette apparat.**	yay vil **gehr**ner **hai**(wer) ayn film til **deh**der ahbah**rard**
This camera doesn't work.	**Dette apparat virker ikke.**	**deh**der ahbah**rard** **veer**ger **i**gger

At the post office

Where's the nearest post office, please?	**Hvor er det nærmeste posthus?**	vor air day **nair**mersder **possd**hooss
I'd like to send this by express (special delivery)/by air mail.	**Jeg vil gerne sende dette ekspres/som luftpost.**	yay vil **gehr**ner **seh**ner **deh**der ehks**brehss**/som **loofd**possd

Service stations

Where is the nearest service station, please?	**Hvor er den nærmeste service-station?**	vor air dehn **nair**mersder **surr**visssdahshoan
Fill her up, please.	**Vil De fylde den op?**	vil dee **few**ler dehn ob
Check the oil, please.	**Vil De kontrollere oliestanden?**	vil dee kontroa**lay**rer **oal**yersdahnern
Would you check the tyres?	**Vil De kontrollere dækkene?**	vil dee kontroa**lay**rer **deh**gerner

Street directions

Can you show me on the map where I am?	**Vil De vise mig på kortet, hvor jeg er?**	vil dee **vee**ser migh paw **kor**terd vor yay air
You're on the wrong road.	**De er ikke på den rigtige vej.**	dee air **i**gger paw dehn **rayg**di(g)er vigh

Go back to ...	**Kør tilbage til ...**	kurr til**bai**(g)er til
Go straight ahead.	**Kør ligeud.**	kurr **lee**(g)eroodh
It's on the left/on the right.	**Det er til venstre/til højre.**	day air til **vehn**strer/til **hol**rer

Accidents

May I use your telephone?	**Må jeg låne Deres telefon?**	maw yay **law**ner **day**rerss tayler**foan**
Call a doctor quickly.	**Tilkald straks en læge.**	**til**kahl sdrahgs ayn **lai**ger
Call an ambulance.	**Tilkald en ambulance.**	**til**kahl ayn ahmboo**lahng**ser
Please call the police.	**Tilkald politiet.**	**til**kahl polee**tee**erd

Numbers

zero	**nul**	nool
one	**en**	ayn
two	**to**	toa
three	**tre**	tray
four	**fire**	**fee**rer
five	**fem**	fehm
six	**seks**	sehgs
seven	**syv**	se**w**oo
eight	**otte**	**o**dder
nine	**ni**	nee
ten	**ti**	tee
eleven	**elleve**	**ehl**ver
twelve	**tolv**	tol
thirteen	**tretten**	**treh**tern
fourteen	**fjorten**	**fyor**tern
fifteen	**femten**	**fehm**tern
sixteen	**seksten**	**sehgs**tern
seventeen	**sytten**	**sew**tern
eighteen	**atten**	**ah**tern
nineteen	**nitten**	**ni**ttern
twenty	**tyve**	**tew**ver
twenty-one	**en og tyve**	ayn o **tew**ver
thirty	**tredive**	**trehd**ver
forty	**fyrre**	**few**rer
fifty	**halvtreds**	hahl**trayss**
sixty	**tres**	trayss
seventy	**halvfjerds**	hahl**fyehrss**
eighty	**firs**	feerss
ninety	**halvfems**	hahl**fehmss**

one hundred	**hundrede**	**hoon**rerdher
one thousand	**tusind**	**too**ssin
ten thousand	**ti tusind**	tee **too**ssin

Days

It's Sunday.	**Det er søndag.**	day air **surn**dai
Monday	**mandag**	**mahn**dai
Tuesday	**tirsdag**	**teerss**dai
Wednesday	**onsdag**	**oanss**dai
Thursday	**torsdag**	**torss**dai
Friday	**fredag**	**fray**dai
Saturday	**lørdag**	**lurr**dai
yesterday	**i går**	ee gawr
today	**i dag**	ee dai
tomorrow	**i morgen**	ee **mor**(g)ern
morning/afternoon	**formiddag/ eftermiddag**	**for**middai/**ehf**derrmiddai
evening/night	**aften/nat**	**ahf**dern/nahd

Months

January	**januar**	yahnoo**arr**
February	**februar**	faybroo**arr**
March	**marts**	mahrdss
April	**april**	ah**preel**
May	**maj**	migh
June	**juni**	**yoo**nee
July	**juli**	**yoo**lee
August	**august**	ow**goossd**
September	**september**	sehb**tehm**berr
October	**oktober**	og**toa**berr
November	**november**	noa**vehm**berr
December	**december**	day**sehm**berr
Merry Christmas! Happy New Year!	**Glædelig jul! Godt nytår!**	**glai**dherlee yool! goad **new**dawr

DANISH

DUTCH

Guide to Pronunciation

Letter	Approximate pronunciation	Symbol	Example	
Consonants				
c, f, h, k, l, m, n, p, q, t, v, x, y, z	as in English			
b	as in English, but when at the end of a word, like **p** in cu**p**	b p	**ben** **heb**	behn hehp
ch	1) generally like **ch** in Scottish lo**ch**	kh	**nacht**	nahkht
	2) in words of French origin like **sh** in **sh**ut	sh	**cheque**	shehk
chtj	like Dutch **ch** followed by Dutch **j**	khy	**nichtje**	**nikh**yer
d	as in English, but, when at the end of a word, like **t** in hi**t**	d t	**doe** **bed**	doo beht
g	1) generally like **ch** in Scottish lo**ch**, but often slightly softer and voiced	ğ	**goed**	ğoot
	2) in a few words of French origin, like **s** in plea**s**ure	zh	**genie**	zher**nee**
	3) like **ch** in Scottish lo**ch** when at the end of a word	kh	**deeg**	daykh

j	like **y** in **y**es	y	**ja**	yar
nj	like **ñ** in Spanish señor or like **ni** in on**i**on	ñ	**oranje**	oa**rah**ñer
r	always trilled, either in the front or the back of the mouth	r	**warm**	vahrm
s	always like **s** in **s**it	s/ss	**roos**	roass
sj, stj	like **sh** in **sh**ut	sh	**meisje**	**may**sher
sch	like **s** followed by a Dutch **ch**	skh	**schrijven**	**skhray**ver(n)
th	like **t**	t	**thee**	tay
tj	like **ty** in hi**t y**ou	ty	**katje**	**kah**tyer
w	something like **v**, but with the bottom lip raised a little higher	v	**water**	**var**terr

Vowels

In Dutch a vowel is *short* when followed by two consonants, or by one consonant at the end of a word. It is *long* when it is at the end of a word, or before a consonant followed by a vowel, or when written double.

a	1) when short, between **a** in c**a**t and **u** in c**u**t, or like **o** in American c**o**llege	ah	**kat**	kaht
	2) when long, like **a** in c**a**rt	ar*	**vader**	**var**derr
e	1) when short, like **e** in b**e**d	eh	**bed**	beht
	2) when long, like **a** in l**a**te, but a pure vowel	ay	**zee**	zay
	3) in unstressed syllables, like **a** in **a**bove	er*	**zitten**	**zit**tern
eu	(long) like **eu** in French f**eu**; approximately like **u** in f**u**r, said with rounded lips	ur*	**deur**	durr
i	1) when short, like **i** in b**i**t	i	**kind**	kint
	2) when long (also spelt *ie*), like **ee** in b**ee**	ee	**bier**	beer
	3) sometimes, in unstressed syllables, like **a** in **a**bove	er*	**monnik**	**mon**nerk
ij	sometimes, in unstressed syllables, like **a** in **a**bove	er*	**lelijk**	**lay**lerk
o	1) when short, like a very short version of **aw** in l**aw**n	o	**pot**	pot
	2) when long, something like **oa** in r**oa**d, but a pure vowel and with more rounded lips	oa	**boot**	boat

* The **r** should not be pronounced when reading this transcription.

DUTCH

oe	(long) like **oo** in m**oo**n and well rounded	oo	**hoe**	hoo
u	1) when short, something like **u** in h**u**rt, but with rounded lips	er*	**bus**	berss
	2) when long, like **u** in French s**u**r or **ü** in German f**ü**r; say **ee**, and without moving your tongue, round your lips.	ew	**nu**	new

Diphthongs

ai	like **igh** in s**igh**	igh	**ai**	igh
ei, ij	between **a** in late and **igh** in s**igh**	ay	**reis**	rayss
au, ou	Dutch short **o** followed by a weak, short **u**-sound; can sound very much like **ow** in n**ow**	ow	**koud**	kowt

The following diphthongs have a long vowel as their first element:

aai	like **a** in c**a**t followed by a short **ee** sound	aree*	**draai**	draree
eeuw	like **a** in l**a**te followed by a short **oo** sound	ayoo	**leeuw**	layoo
ieuw	like **ee** in fr**ee**, followed by a short **oo** sound	eeoo	**nieuw**	neeoo
ooi	like **o** in wr**o**te followed by a short **ee** sound	oaee	**nooit**	noaeet
oei	like **oo** in s**oo**n, followed by a short **ee** sound	ooee	**roeit**	rooeet
ui	like **u** in f**u**r, followed by a short Dutch **u** sound, as described in **u** number 2)	urew*	**huis**	hurewss
uw	like the sound described in **u** number 2), followed by a weak **oo** sound	ewoo	**duw**	dewoo

* The **r** should not be pronounced when reading this transcription.

N.B.

1) When two consonants are next to each other, one will often influence the other even if it is not in the same word, e.g., *ziens* is pronounced **zeenss**, but in the expression *tot ziens*, it is pronounced **seenss** under the influence of the **t** before it.
2) In the **-en** ending of verbs and plural nouns, the **n** is generally dropped in everyday speech.

Some basic expressions

Yes.	**Ja.**	yar
No.	**Nee.**	nay
Please.	**Alstublieft.**	ahlsstew**bleeft**
Thank you.	**Dank U.**	dahngk ew
Thank you very much.	**Hartelijk dank.**	**hahr**terlerk dahngk
That's all right.	**Niets te danken.**	neets ter **dahng**kern

Greetings

Good morning.	**Goedemorgen.**	ģooder**mor**ģern
Good afternoon.	**Goedemiddag.**	ģooder**mid**dahkh
Good evening.	**Goedenavond.**	ģooden**ar**vernt
Good night.	**Goedenacht.**	ģooder**nahkht**
Good-bye.	**Tot ziens.**	tot seenss
See you later.	**Tot straks.**	tot strahks
This is Mr. . . .	**Dit is Mijnheer . . .**	dit iss mer**nayr**
This is Mrs. . . .	**Dit is Mevrouw . . .**	dit iss mer**vrow**
This is Miss . . .	**Dit is Juffrouw . . .**	dit iss **yer**frow
I'm very pleased to meet you.	**Aangenaam kennis te maken.**	**arn**ģernarm **keh**nerss ter **mar**kern
How are you?	**Hoe gaat het?**	hoo **ģar**tert
Very well, thank you.	**Heel goed, dank U.**	hayl ģoot dahngk ew
And you?	**En U?**	ehn ew
Fine.	**Uitstekend.**	urewt**stay**kernt
Excuse me.	**Neemt U me niet kwalijk.**	naymt ew mer neet **kvar**lerk

Questions

Where?	**Waar?**	varr
Where is . . . ?	**Waar is . . . ?**	varr iss
Where are . . . ?	**Waar zijn . . . ?**	varr zayn
When?	**Wanneer?**	vahn**nayr**
What?	**Wat?**	vaht
How?	**Hoe?**	hoo
How much?	**Hoeveel?**	hoo**vayl**
How many?	**Hoeveel?**	hoo**vayl**

DUTCH

Who?	**Wie?**	vee
Why?	**Waarom?**	**var**rom
Which?	**Welk/Welke?**	vehlk/**vehl**ker
What do you call this?	**Hoe noemt U dit?**	hoo noomt ew dit
What do you call that?	**Hoe noemt U dat?**	hoo noomt ew daht
What does this mean?	**Wat betekent dit?**	vaht ber**tay**kernt dit
What does that mean?	**Wat betekent dat?**	vaht ber**tay**kernt daht

Do you speak . . . ?

Do you speak English?	**Spreekt U Engels?**	spraykt ew **ehng**erlss
Do you speak German?	**Spreekt U Duits?**	spraykt ew durewts
Do you speak French?	**Spreekt U Frans?**	spraykt ew frahnss
Do you speak Spanish?	**Spreekt U Spaans?**	spraykt ew sparnss
Do you speak Italian?	**Spreekt U Italiaans?**	spraykt ew itahli**arnss**
Could you speak more slowly, please?	**Kunt U wat langzamer spreken, alstublieft?**	kernt ew vaht **lahng**zarmerr **spray**kern ahlsstew**bleeft**
Please point to the phrase in the book.	**Wijs me de zin aan in het boek, alstublieft.**	vayss mer der zin arn in heht book ahlsstew**bleeft**
Just a minute. I'll see if I can find it in this book.	**Een ogenblik. Ik zal proberen het in dit boek op te zoeken.**	een **oa**ğernblik. ik zahl proa**bay**rern heht in dit book op te **zoo**kern
I understand.	**Ik begrijp het.**	ik ber**ğrayp**heht
I don't understand.	**Ik begrijp het niet.**	ik ber**ğrayp**heht neet

Can . . . ?

Can I have . . . ?	**Mag ik . . . hebben?**	mahkh ik . . . **heh**bern
Can we have . . . ?	**Mogen wij . . . hebben?**	**moa**ğern vay . . . **heh**bern

Can you show me . . . ?	**Kunt U me . . . tonen?**	kernt ew mer . . . **toa**nern
Can you tell me . . . ?	**Kunt U mij zeggen . . . ?**	kernt ew may **zeh**ğern
Can you help me, please?	**Kunt U mij helpen, alstublieft?**	kernt ew may **hehl**pern ahlsstew**bleeft**

Wanting

I'd like . . .	**Ik wil graag . . .**	ik vil ğrarkh
We'd like . . .	**Wij willen graag . . .**	vay **vil**lern ğrarkh
Please give me . . .	**Geeft U me . . . , alstublieft.**	ğayft ew mer . . . ahlsstee**bleeft**
Give it to me, please.	**Geeft U het me, alstublieft.**	ğayft ew heht mer ahlsstew**bleeft**
Please bring me . . .	**Brengt U me . . . , alstublieft.**	brehngt ew mer . . . ahlsstew**bleeft**
Bring it to me, please.	**Brengt U het me, alstublieft.**	brehngt ew heht mer ahlsstew**bleeft**
I'm hungry.	**Ik heb honger.**	ik hehp **hong**err
I'm thirsty.	**Ik heb dorst.**	ik hehp dorst
I'm tired.	**Ik ben moe.**	ik behn moo
I'm lost.	**Ik ben verdwaald.**	ik behn verr**dvarlt**
It's important.	**Het is belangrijk.**	heht iss ber**lahng**rayk
It's urgent.	**Het is dringend.**	heht iss **dring**ernt
Hurry up!	**Vlug!**	vlerkh

It is/There is . . .

It is/It's . . .	**Het is . . .**	heht iss
Is it . . . ?	**Is het . . . ?**	iss heht
It isn't . . .	**Het is niet . . .**	heht iss neet
There is/There are . . .	**Er is/Er zijn . . .**	ehr iss/ehr zayn
Is there/Are there . . . ?	**Is er/Zijn er . . . ?**	iss ehr/zayn ehr
There isn't/There aren't . . .	**Er is geen/Er zijn geen . . .**	ehr iss ğayn/ehr zayn ğayn
There isn't any/ There aren't any.	**Er is er geen/Er zijn er geen.**	ehr iss ehr ğayn/ehr zayn ehr ğayn

A few common words

big/small	**groot/klein**	ğroat/klayn
quick/slow	**snel/langzaam**	snehl/**lahng**zarm
early/late	**vroeg/laat**	vrookh/lart
cheap/expensive	**goedkoop/duur**	ğoot**koap**/dewr
near/far	**dichtbij/ver**	dikht**bay** vehr
hot/cold	**warm/koud**	vahrm/kowt
full/empty	**vol/leeg**	vol/laykh
easy/difficult	**gemakkelijk/moeilijk**	ğer**mah**kerlerk/**mooee**lerk
heavy/light	**zwaar/licht**	zvarr/likht
open/shut	**open/dicht**	**oa**pern/dikht
right/wrong	**juist/verkeerd**	yurewst/ver**kayrt**
old/new	**oud/nieuw**	owt/neeoo
old/young	**oud/jong**	owt/yong
beautiful/ugly	**mooi/lelijk**	moaee/**lay**lerk
good/bad	**goed/slecht**	ğoot/slehkht
better/worse	**beter/slechter**	**bay**ter/**slehkh**terr

Some prepositions and a few more useful words

at	**te**	ter
on	**op**	op
in	**in**	in
to	**naar**	narr
from	**van**	vahn
inside	**binnen**	**bin**nern
outside	**buiten**	**burew**tern
up	**op**	op
down	**neer**	nayr
before	**voor**	voar
after	**na**	nar
with	**met**	meht
without	**zonder**	**zon**derr
through	**door**	doar
towards	**naar**	narr
until	**tot**	tot
during	**tijdens**	**tay**dernss
and	**en**	ehn
or	**of**	off
not	**niet**	neet
nothing	**niets**	neets
none	**geen**	ğayn
very	**zeer**	zayr
also	**ook**	oak
soon	**spoedig**	**spoo**derkh
perhaps	**misschien**	miss**kheen**

here	**hier**	heer
there	**daar**	darr
now	**nu**	new
then	**dan**	dahn

Arrival

Your passport, please.	**Uw paspoort, alstublieft.**	ewoo **pahss**poart ahlsstew**bleeft**
Here it is.	**Alstublieft.**	ahlsstew**bleeft**
Have you anything to declare?	**Hebt U iets aan te geven?**	hehpt ew eets arn ter **g̊ay**vern
No, nothing at all.	**Nee, helemaal niets.**	nay **hay**lermarl neets
Porter!	**Kruier!**	**krurew**er
Can you help me with my luggage, please?	**Kunt U me met mijn bagage helpen, alstublieft?**	kernt ew mer meht mayn bah**g̊ar**zher **hehl**pern ahlsstew**bleeft**
That's my suitcase.	**Dat is mijn koffer.**	daht iss mayn **kof**ferr
Where's the bus to the centre of town, please?	**Waar is de bus naar het centrum, alstublieft?**	varr iss der berss narr heht **sehn**trerm ahlsstew**bleeft**
This way, please.	**Hierlangs, alstublieft.**	**heer**lahngss ahlsstew**bleeft**

Changing money

Can you change a traveller's cheque, please?	**Kunt U een reischeque wisselen, alstublieft?**	kernt ew ern **rays**shehk **vi**serlern ahlsstew**bleeft**
Where's the nearest bank, please?	**Waar is de dichtstbijzijnde bank, alstublieft?**	varr iss der **dikhtst**bayzaynder bahngk ahlsstew**bleeft**

Car rental

I'd like a car.	**Ik wil graag een auto huren.**	ik vil g̊rarkh ern **ow**toa **hew**rern
For how long?	**Voor hoe lang?**	voar hoo lahng
A day/Four days/ A week/Two weeks.	**Een dag/Vier dagen/Een week/ Twee weken.**	ayn dahkh/veer **dah**g̊er(n)/ayn vayk/tvay **vay**kern

Taxi

Where can I get a taxi?	**Waar kan ik een taxi krijgen?**	varr kahn ik ern **tak**see **kray**ğern
What's the fare to...?	**Wat kost het naar...?**	vaht kost heht narr
Take me to this address, please.	**Breng me naar dit adres, alstublieft.**	brehng mer narr dit ah**drehss** ahlsstew**bleeft**
I'm in a hurry.	**Ik heb haast.**	ik hehp harst
Could you drive more slowly, please?	**Wilt U wat langzamer rijden, alstublieft?**	vilt ew vaht **lahng**zarmerr **ray**dern ahlsstew**bleeft**

Hotel and other accommodation

My name is...	**Mijn naam is...**	mayn narm iss
Have you a reservation?	**Hebt U gereserveerd?**	hehpt ew ğerrayserr**vayrt**
Yes, here's the confirmation.	**Ja, hier is de bevestiging.**	yar heer iss der ber**vehss**tiğing
I'd like...	**Ik wil graag...**	ik vil ğrarkh
I'd like a single room/a double room.	**Ik wil graag een éénpersoonskamer/ een tweepersoonskamer.**	ik vil ğrarkh een **ayn**perrsoansskarmerr/ern **tvay**perrsoansskarmerr
a room with a bath/with a shower	**een kamer met bad/met douche**	ern **kar**merr meht baht/meht **doo**sher

How much?

What's the price per night/per week/per month?	**Hoeveel is het per nacht/per week/per maand?**	hoo**vayl** iss heht pehr nahkht/pehr vayk/pehr marnt
May I see the room?	**Mag ik de kamer zien?**	mahkh ik der **kar**merr zeen
I'm sorry, I don't like it.	**Het spijt me, hij bevalt me niet.**	heht spayt mer hay ber**vahlt** mer neet
Yes, that's fine. I'll take it.	**Ja, dat is goed. Die neem ik.**	yar daht iss ğoot. dee naym ik
What's my room number, please?	**Wat is mijn kamernummer, alstublieft?**	vaht iss mayn **kar**merrnermerr ahlsstew**bleeft**
Number 123.	**Nummer 123.**	**ner**merr 123.

DUTCH

Service, please

Who is it?	**Wie is daar?**	vee iss darr
Just a minute.	**Een ogenblikje.**	ern **oa**ğernblikyer
Come in! The door's open.	**Binnen! De deur is open.**	**bi**nern. der durr iss **oa**pern
May we have breakfast in our room?	**Kunnen we in onze kamer ontbijten?**	**ker**nern ver in **on**zer **kar**merr ont**bay**tern

Breakfast

I'll have ...	**Ik neem ...**	ik naym
I'll have some fruit juice.	**Ik neem vruchtensap.**	ik naym **vrerkh**ternsahp
a boiled egg	**een gekookt ei**	ern ğer**koakt** ay
a fried egg	**een gebakken ei**	ern ğer**bah**kern ay
some bacon/some ham	**spek/ham**	spehk/hahm
some toast	**toast**	toast
a pot of tea	**een kannetje thee**	ern **kah**nertyer tay
a cup of tea	**een kopje thee**	ern **kop**yer tay
some coffee	**koffie**	**ko**fee
some chocolate	**chocola**	shoakoa**lar**
more butter	**nog wat boter**	nokh vaht **boa**terr
some hot water	**wat warm water**	vaht vahrm **var**terr

Difficulties

The central heating doesn't work.	**De centrale verwarming werkt niet.**	der sehn**trar**ler verr**vahr**ming vehrkt neet
the light/the socket	**het licht/het stopcontact**	heht likht/heht **stop**kontahkt
the tap/the toilet	**de kraan/het toilet**	der krarn/heht tvah**leht**
There's no hot water.	**Er is geen warm water.**	ehr iss ğayn vahrm **var**terr
May I see the manager, please?	**Mag ik de direkteur spreken, alstublieft?**	mahkh ik der deererk**turr** **spray**kern ahlsstew**bleeft**

Telephone—Mail

There's a call for you.	**Er is telefoon voor U.**	ehr iss tayler**foan** voar ew
Hold the line, please.	**Blijft U aan het toestel, alstublieft.**	blayft ew arn heht **too**sterl ahlsstew**bleeft**

DUTCH

Operator, I've been cut off.	**Juffrouw, mijn gesprek is verbroken.**	yer**frow** mayn g̊er**sprehk** iss verr**broa**kern
Did anyone telephone me?	**Heeft er iemand voor mij opgebeld?**	hayft ehr **ee**mahnt voar may **op**g̊erbehlt
Is there any mail for me?	**Is er post voor mij?**	iss ehr post voar may
Are there any messages for me?	**Heeft iemand een boodschap voor mij achtergelaten?**	hayft **ee**mahnt ern **boat**skhahp voar may **ahkh**terrg̊er**lar**tern

Checking out

May I have my bill, please?	**Mag ik de rekening, alstublieft?**	mahkh ik der **ray**kerning ahlsstew**bleeft**
We're in a great hurry.	**Wij hebben erge haast.**	vay **heh**bern **ehr**g̊er harst
It's been a very enjoyable stay.	**Wij hebben het hier erg prettig gehad.**	vay **heh**bern het heer ehrkh **preh**terkh g̊er**haht**

Eating out

Good evening, sir/ Good evening, madam.	**Goedenavond, Mijnheer/Goedenavond Mevrouw.**	g̊oodern**ar**vernt mer**nayr** g̊oodern**ar**vernt mer**vrow**
Good evening. I'd like a table for two, please.	**Goedenavond. Ik wil graag een tafel voor twee personen.**	g̊oodern**ar**vernt. ik vil g̊rarkh ern **tar**ferl voar tvay perr**soa**nern
Do you have a fixed-price menu?	**Hebt U een menu à prix fixe?**	hehpt ew ern mer**new**ah pree feeks
May I see the à la carte menu?	**Mag ik het menu à la carte?**	mahkh ik heht mer**new** ah lah kahrt
May we have an ashtray, please?	**Kunt U ons een asbak brengen, alstublieft?**	kernt ew onss ern **ahss**bahk **brehng**ern ahlsstew**bleeft**
some bread	**wat brood**	vat broat
a fork	**een vork**	ern vork
a knife	**een mes**	ern mehss
a spoon	**een lepel**	ern **lay**perl
a plate	**een bord**	ern bort
a glass	**een glas**	ern g̊lahss
a napkin	**een servet**	ern sehr**veht**
another chair	**nog een stoel**	nokh ern stool

Where's the gentlemen's toilet (men's room)?	**Waar is het herentoilet?**	varr iss heht **hay**rerntvahleht
Where's the ladies' toilet (ladies' room)?	**Waar is het damestoilet?**	varr iss heht **dar**merss-tvahleht

Appetizers

I'd like some ...	**Ik wil graag ...**	ik vil ğrarkh
I'd like some assorted appetizers.	**Ik wil graag hors-d'oeuvre varié.**	ik vil ğrarkh or durvr vahree**ay**
orange juice	**sinaasappelsap**	**see**narsahperlsahp
ham	**ham**	hahm
melon	**meloen**	mer**loon**
pâté	**paté**	pah**tay**
smoked salmon	**gerookte zalm**	ğer**roak**ter zahlm
shrimps (shrimp)	**garnalen**	ğahr**nar**lern

Soup

Have you any ... ?	**Hebt U ... ?**	hehpt ew
Have you any chicken soup?	**Hebt U kippesoep?**	hehpt ew **ki**persoop
vegetable soup	**groentesoep**	**ğroon**tersoop
onion soup	**uiensoep**	**urew**ernsoop

Fish

I'd like some ...	**Ik wil graag ...**	ik vil ğrarkh
I'd like some fish.	**Ik wil graag vis.**	ik vil ğrarkh viss
sole	**zeetong**	**zay**tong
trout	**forel**	foa**rehl**
lobster	**kreeft**	krayft
crayfish	**rivierkreeft**	ree**veer**krayft
prawns	**steurgarnalen**	**sturr**ğahrnarlern
I'd like it ...	**Graag ...**	ğrarkh
I'd like it steamed.	**Graag gestoomd.**	ğrarkh ğer**stoamt**
grilled	**gegrilleerd**	ğerğri**layrt**
boiled	**gekookt**	ğer**koakt**
baked	**in de oven gebakken**	in der **oa**vern ğer**bah**kern
fried	**gebakken**	ğer**bah**kern

Meat—Poultry—Game

I'd like some...	**Ik wil graag...**	ik vil ĝrarkh
I'd like some beef.	**Ik wil graag rundvlees.**	ik vil ĝrarkh **rernt**vlayss
a beef steak	**een biefstuk**	ern **beef**sterk
some roast beef	**rosbief**	**ross**beef
a veal cutlet	**een kalfskotelet**	ern **kahlfs**koaterleht
mutton	**schapevlees**	**skhah**pervlayss
lamb	**lamsvlees**	**lahmss**vlayss
a pork chop	**een varkenskotelet**	ayn **vahr**kernsskoaterleht
roast pork	**varkensfricandeau**	**vahr**kernssfreekahndoa
hare	**haas**	harss
chicken	**kip**	kip
roast chicken	**gebraden kip**	ĝer**brar**dern kip
duck	**eend**	aynt
How do you like your meat?	**Hoe wenst U het vlees?**	hoo vehnst ew heht vlayss
rare	**rood**	roat
medium	**lichtgebakken**	**likht**ĝerbahkern
well done	**doorgebakken**	**doar**ĝerbahkern

DUTCH

Vegetables

What vegetables have you got?	**Wat voor groenten hebt U?**	vaht voar **ĝroon**tern hehpt ew
I'd like some...	**Ik wil graag...**	ik vil ĝrarkh
I'd like some asparagus.	**Il wil graag asperges.**	ik vil ĝrarkh ahss**pehr**zherss
green beans	**sperziebonen**	**spehr**zeeboanern
mushrooms	**champignons**	shahmpee**ñongss**
carrots	**worteltjes**	**vor**terltyehss
onions	**uien**	**urew**ern
red cabbage	**rode kool**	**roa**der koal
spinach	**spinazie**	spee**nar**zee
rice	**rijst**	rayst
peas	**doperwtjes**	**dop**ehrtyerss
tomatoes	**tomaten**	toa**mar**tern
green salad	**sla**	slar
potatoes	**aardappelen**	**arr**dahperlern

Desserts

Nothing more, thanks.	**Niets meer, dank U.**	neets mayr dangk ew

Just a small portion, please.	**Een kleine portie, alstublieft.**	ern **klay**ner **por**see ahlsstew**bleeft**
Have you any ice-cream?	**Hebt U ijs?**	hehpt ew ayss
fruit salad	**vruchtensla**	**vrerkh**ternslar
fresh fruit	**vers fruit**	vehrss frurewt
cheese	**kaas**	karss

Drink

What would you like to drink?	**Wat wilt U drinken?**	vaht vilt ew **dring**kern
I'll have a beer, please.	**Een pils, alstublieft.**	ern pilss ahlsstew**bleeft**
I'll have a whisky, please.	**Een whisky, alstublieft.**	ern **viss**kee ahlsstew**bleeft**

Wine

I'd like a bottle of wine.	**Ik wil graag een fles wijn.**	ik vil ğrarkh ern flehss vayn
red wine	**rode wijn**	**roa**der vayn
rosé wine	**rosé**	**roa**zay
white wine	**witte wijn**	**vi**ter vayn
Cheers!	**Proost!**	proast

The bill (check)

May I have the bill (check) please?	**Mag ik de rekening, alstublieft?**	mahkh ik der **ray**kerning ahlsstew**bleeft**
Is service included?	**Is de bediening inbegrepen?**	iss der ber**dee**ning **in**berğraypern
Everything's included.	**Alles inclusief.**	**ah**lerss inklew**zeef**
Thank you, that was a very good meal.	**Dank U, het was een uitstekende maaltijd.**	dangk ew heht vahss ern **urewt**staykernder **marl**tayt

Travelling

Where's the railway station, please?	**Waar is het station, alstublieft?**	varr iss heht stah**shon** ahlsstew**bleeft**
Where's the ticket office, please?	**Waar is het loket, alstublieft?**	varr iss heht loa**keht** ahlsstew**bleeft**

I'd like a ticket to...	**Ik wil graag een kaartje naar...**	ik vil ĝrarkh ern **karr**tyer narr
First or second class?	**Eerste of tweede klas?**	**ayr**ster off **tvay**der klahss
First class, please.	**Eerste klas, alstublieft.**	**ayr**ster klahss ahlsstew**bleeft**
Single or return (one way or round-trip)?	**Enkele reis of retour?**	**ehng**kerler rayss off rer**toor**
Do I have to change trains?	**Moet ik overstappen?**	moot ik **oa**verrstahpern
What platform does the train leave from?	**Van welk perron vertrekt de trein?**	vahn vehlk peh**ron** verr**trehkt** der trayn
Where's the nearest underground (subway) station?	**Waar is het dichtstbijzijnde metrostation?**	varr iss hert **dikhtst**bayzaynder **meh**troastah**shon**
Where's the bus station, please?	**Waar is het busstation, alstublieft?**	varr iss heht **berss**stahshon ahlsstew**bleeft**
When's the first bus to...?	**Om hoe laat vertrekt de eerste bus naar...?**	om hoo lart verr**trehkt** der **ayr**ster berss narr
the last bus	**de laatste bus**	der **lart**ster berss
the next bus	**de volgende bus**	der **vol**ĝernder berss
Please let me off at the next stop.	**Wilt U me bij de volgende halte laten uitstappen?**	vilt ew mer bay der **vol**ĝernder **hahl**ter **lar**tern **urewt**stahpern

Relaxing

What's on at the cinema (movies)?	**Wat wordt er in de bioscoop gegeven?**	vaht vort ehr in der beeo**skoap** ĝer**ĝay**vern
What's on at the theatre?	**Wat wordt er in de schouwburg gegeven?**	vahr vort ehr in der **skhow**berkh ĝer**ĝay**vern
What time does the film begin? And the play?	**Om hoe laat begint de film? En het toneelstuk?**	om hoo lart ber**ĝint** der film? ehn hert toa**nayl**sterk
Are there any tickets for tonight?	**Zijn er nog plaatsen vrij voor vanavond?**	zayn ehr nokh **plar**tsern vray voar vahn**ar**vont
Where can we go dancing?	**Waar kunnen we gaan dansen?**	varr **ker**nern ver ĝarn **dahn**sern
Would you like to dance?	**Wilt u dansen?**	vilt ew **dahn**sern

Introductions

How do you do?	**Hoe maakt U het?**	hoo markt ew heht
How are you?	**Hoe gaat het?**	hoo ğart heht
Very well, thank you. And you?	**Uitstekend, dank U. En U?**	urewt**stay**kernt dahngk ew. ehn ew
May I introduce Miss Philips?	**Mag ik U Juffrouw Philips voorstellen?**	mahkh ik ew **yer**frow Philips **voar**stehlern
My name is . . .	**Mijn naam is . . .**	mayn narm iss
I'm very pleased to meet you.	**Prettig kennis met U te maken.**	**preh**terkh **keh**nerss meht ew ter **mar**kern
How long have you been here?	**Hoelang bent U al hier?**	**hoo**lahng behnt ew ahl heer
It was nice meeting you.	**Het was mij een genoegen.**	heht vahss may ayn ğer**noo**ğern

Dating

Would you like a cigarette?	**Wilt u een sigaret?**	vilt ew ayn seeğar**reht**
May I get you a drink?	**Mag ik U iets te drinken aanbieden?**	mahkh ik ew eets ter **dring**kern **arn**beedern
Do you have a light, please?	**Hebt U een vuurtje, alstublieft?**	hehpt ew ern **vewrt**yer ahlsstew**bleeft**
Are you waiting for someone?	**Wacht U op iemand?**	vahkht ew op **ee**mahnt
Are you free this evening?	**Bent U vanavond vrij?**	behnt ew vahn**ar**vont vray
Where shall we meet?	**Waar spreken we af?**	varr **spray**kern ver ahf
What time shall I meet you?	**Hoe laat spreken we af?**	hoo lart **spray**kern ver ahf
May I take you home?	**Mag ik U naar huis brengen?**	mahkh ik ew narr hurewss **brehng**ern
Thank you, it's been a wonderful evening.	**Dank U, het was een heerlijke avond.**	dahngk ew heht vahss ern **hayr**lerker **ar**vernt
What's your telephone number?	**Wat is uw telefoonnummer?**	vaht iss ewoo taylER**foan**nermerr
Do you live alone?	**Woont U alleen?**	voant ew ah**leen**
What time is your last train?	**Om hoe laat gaat uw laatste trein?**	om hoo lart ğart ewoo **lart**ster trayn
Good-bye.	**Tot ziens.**	tot seenss

Banks

Where's the nearest bank, please?	**Waar is de dichtstbijzijnde bank, alstublieft?**	varr iss der **dikhtst**bayzaynder bahngk ahlsstew**bleeft**
Where can I cash some traveller's cheques?	**Waar kan ik reischeques inwisselen?**	varr kahn ik **rays**shehks **in**viserlern
What time does the bank open? What time does it close?	**Om hoe laat gaat de bank open? Om hoe laat gaat hij dicht?**	om hoo lart ĝart der bahngk **oa**pern? om hoo lart ĝart hay dikht
I'm expecting some money from home. Has it arrived?	**Ik verwacht geld van thuis. Is het aangekomen?**	ik verr**vahkht** ĝehlt vahn turewss. iss heht **arn**ĝer-koamern
Can you give me some small change, please?	**Kunt U me wat kleingeld geven, alstublieft?**	kernt ew mer vaht **klayn**ĝehlt **ĝay**vern ahlsstew**bleeft**

Shops, stores and services

Where is the nearest chemist's (pharmacy)?	**Waar is de dichtstbijzijnde apotheek?**	varr iss der **dikhtst**-bayzaynder arpoa**tayk**
the nearest hairdresser's	**de dichtstbijzijnde kapper**	der **dikhtst**bayzaynder **kah**perr
the photo shop	**de fotowinkel**	der **foa**toavingkerl
the jeweller's	**de juwelier**	der yewver**leer**
the department store	**het warenhuis**	heht **var**trrnhurewss
the police station	**het politiebureau**	heht po**lee**(t)seebewroa
the garage	**de garage**	der ĝah**rar**zher
How do I get there?	**Hoe kom ik daar?**	hoo kom ik darr
Is it within walking distance?	**Is het te lopen?**	iss heht ter **loa**pern

Service

Can you help me, please?	**Kunt U mij helpen, alstublieft?**	kernt ew may **hehl**pern ahlsstew**bleeft**
Can you show me this? And that, too.	**Kunt U me dit laten zien? En dat ook.**	kernt ew mer dit **lar**tern zeen ehn dat oak
It's too expensive/too big/too small.	**Het is te duur/te groot/te klein.**	heht iss ter dewr/ter ĝroat/ter klayn

Can you show me some more?	**Kunt U me er nog wat laten zien?**	kernt ew mer ehr mokh vaht **lar**tern zeen
something better	**iets beters**	eets **bay**terrss
something cheaper	**iets goedkopers**	eets ġoot**koa**perss
How much is this? And that?	**Hoeveel is dit? En dat?**	hoo**vayl** iss dit? ehn daht
It's not quite what I want.	**Het is niet precies wat ik zoek.**	heht iss neet prer**seess** vaht ik zook
I like it.	**Het bevalt me.**	heht ber**vahlt** mer

Chemist's (Pharmacy)

I'd like something for a cold/for a cough/for travel sickness.	**Ik wil graag iets tegen een verkoudheid/tegen hoesten/tegen wagenziekte.**	ik vil ġrarkh eets **tay**ġern ern ver**kow**thayt/**tay**ġern **hoo**stern/**tay**ġern **var**gernzeekter
Can you recommend something for hay-fever/for sunburn?	**Kunt U mij iets tegen hooikoorts aanbevelen/tegen zonnebrand?**	kernt ew may eets **tay**ġern **hoaee**koarts **arn**bervaylern/**tay**ġern **zo**nerbrahnt

Toiletry

May I have some razor blades?	**Mag ik scheer-mesjes?**	mahkh ik **skhayr**meh-sherss
some shaving cream	**scheercrème**	**skhayr**kraim
some toothpaste	**tandpasta**	**tahnt**pahstarr
I'd like some soap.	**Ik wil graag zeep.**	ik vil ġrarkh zayp
some suntan oil	**zonne-olie**	**zo**neroalee

At the barber's

I'd like a haircut, please.	**Knippen, alstublieft.**	**kni**pern ahlsstew**bleeft**
Short/Leave it long.	**Kort/Laat het lang.**	kort/lart heht lahng
A razor cut, please.	**Met het mes, alstublieft.**	meht heht mehss ahlsstew**bleeft**

At the hairdresser's

I'd like a shampoo and set, please.	**Wassen en water-golven, alstublieft.**	**vah**sern ehn **var**terrġol-vern ahlsstew**bleeft**

DUTCH

I'd like a bleach.	**Ik wil het laten bleken.**	ik vil heht **lar**tern **blay**kern
a permanent	**een permanent**	ern pehrmar**nehnt**
a colour rinse	**een kleurspoeling**	ern **klurr**spooling
a manicure	**een manicure**	ern marnee**kew**rer

Photography

I'd like a film for this camera.	**Ik wil graag een film voor dit toestel.**	ik vil ğrarkh ern film voar dit **too**sterl
This camera doesn't work.	**Deze camera doet het niet.**	**day**zer **kar**merrah doot heht neet

At the post office

Where's the nearest post office, please?	**Waar is het dichtstbijzijnde postkantoor, alstublieft?**	varr iss heht **dikhtst**-bayzaynder **post**kahn-toar ahlsstew**bleeft**
I'd like to send this by express (special delivery)/by air mail.	**Ik wil dit per express versturen/per luchtpost.**	ik vil pehr ehks**prehss** ver**stew**rern/pehr **lerkht**post

Service stations

Where is the nearest service station, please?	**Waar is het dichtstbijzijnde benzinestation, alstublieft?**	varr iss heht **dikhtst**-bayzaynder behn-**zee**nerstahshon ahlsstew**bleeft**
Fill her up, please.	**Vol, alstublieft.**	vol ahlsstew**bleeft**
Check the oil, please.	**Wilt U de olie controleren, alstublieft?**	vilt ew der **oa**lee kon-troa**lay**rern ahlsstew**bleeft**
Would you check the tyres?	**Wilt U de banden controleren?**	vilt ew der **bahn**dern kon-troa**lay**rern

Street directions

Can you show me on the map where I am?	**Kunt U mij op de kaart aanwijzen waar ik ben?**	kern ew may op der karrt **arn**vayzern varr ik behn
You're on the wrong road.	**U bent verkeerd gereden.**	ew behnt verr**kayrt** ğer-**ray**dern
Go back to ...	**Rijd terug naar ...**	rayt ter**rerkh** narr

DUTCH

Go straight ahead.	**Rijd rechtuit.**	rayt **rehkh**turewt
It's on the left/on the right.	**Het is aan de linkerkant/aan de rechterkant.**	heht iss arn der **ling**kerkahnt/arn der **rehkh**terkahnt

Accidents

May I use your telephone?	**Mag ik van uw telefoon gebruik maken?**	mahkh ik vahn ewoo taylerfoan ğer**brurewk** **mar**kern
Call a doctor quickly.	**Roep vlug een dokter.**	roop vlerkh ern **dok**terr
Call an ambulance.	**Roep een ambulance.**	roop ern ahmbew**lahn**ser
Please call the police.	**Roep de politie, alstublieft.**	roop de po**lee**(t)see ahlsstew**bleeft**

Numbers

zero	**nul**	nurl
one	**een**	ayn
two	**twee**	tvay
three	**drie**	dree
four	**vier**	veer
five	**vijf**	vayf
six	**zes**	zehss
seven	**zeven**	**zay**vern
eight	**acht**	ahkht
nine	**negen**	**nay**ğern
ten	**tien**	teen
eleven	**elf**	ehlf
twelve	**twaalf**	tvarlf
thirteen	**dertien**	**dehr**teen
fourteen	**veertien**	**vayr**teen
fifteen	**vijftien**	**vayf**teen
sixteen	**zestien**	**zehss**teen
seventeen	**zeventien**	**zay**vernteen
eighteen	**achttien**	**ahkh**teen
nineteen	**negentien**	**nay**ğernteen
twenty	**twintig**	**tvin**terkh
twenty-one	**eenentwintig**	**ayn**erntvinterkh
thirty	**dertig**	**dehr**terkh
forty	**veertig**	**vayr**terkh
fifty	**vijftig**	**vayf**terkh
sixty	**zestig**	**zehss**terkh
seventy	**zeventig**	**zay**vernterkh
eighty	**tachtig**	**tahkh**terkh
ninety	**negentig**	**nay**ğernterkh

one hundred	**honderd**	**hon**derrt
one thousand	**duizend**	**durew**zernt
ten thousand	**tienduizend**	**teen**durewzernt

Days

It's Sunday.	**Het is zondag.**	heht iss **zon**dahkh
Monday	**maandag**	**marn**dahkh
Tuesday	**dinsdag**	**dinss**dahkh
Wednesday	**woensdag**	**voonss**dahkh
Thursday	**donderdag**	**don**derrdahkh
Friday	**vrijdag**	**vray**dahkh
Saturday	**zaterdag**	**zar**terrdahkh
yesterday	**gisteren**	**g̊i**sterrern
today	**vandaag**	vahn**darkh**
tomorrow	**morgen**	**mor**g̊ern
morning/afternoon	**ochtend/namiddag**	**okh**ternt/nar**mi**dankh
evening/night	**avond/nacht**	**ar**vernt/nahkht

Months

January	**januari**	yahnew**ar**ree
February	**februari**	fehvrew**ar**ree
March	**maart**	marrt
April	**april**	ah**pril**
May	**mei**	may
June	**juni**	**yew**nee
July	**juli**	**yew**lee
August	**augustus**	ow**g̊erss**terss
September	**september**	sehp**tehm**berr
October	**oktober**	ok**toa**berr
November	**november**	noa**vehm**berr
December	**december**	day**sehm**berr
Merry Christmas!	**Prettig Kerstfeest!**	**preh**terkh **kehrst**fayst! er-
Happy New Year!	**Gelukkig Nieuwjaar!**	**ler**kerkh **neeoo**yarr

FINNISH

Guide to Pronunciation

Letter	Approximate pronunciation	Symbol	Example	
Consonants				
k, m, n, p, t, v	as in English			
d	as in rea**d**y, but sometimes very weak	d	**taide**	**tigh**day
g	only found after **n**; **ng** is pronounced as in si**ng**er	ng	**sangen**	**sahng**ayn
h	as in **h**ot, whatever its position in the word	h	**Lahti**	**lahh**ti
j	like **y** in **y**ou	y	**ja**	yah
l	as in **l**et	l	**talo**	**tah**loa
r	always rolled	r	**raha**	**rah**hah
s	always as in set	s/ss	**sillä** **kiitos**	**sill**æ **kee**toass

Vowels

a	like **a** in **car**, but shorter	ah	**matala**	**mah**tahlah
e	like **a** in **late**	ay	**kolme**	**koal**may
i	like **i** in **pin**	i	**takki**	**tahk**ki
o	like **aw** in **law**, but shorter	oa	**olla**	**oal**lah
u	like **u** in **pull**	oo	**hupsu**	**hoop**soo
y	like **u** in French **sur** or **ü** in German **über**; say **ee** as in **see** and round your lips while still trying to pronounce **ee**	ew	**yksi**	**ewk**si
ä	like **a** in **hat**	æ	**äkkiä**	**æk**kiæ
ö	like **ur** in **fur**, but with the lips rounded and without any r-sound	ur	**tyttö**	**tewt**tur

N.B. The letters **b, c, f, q, š, sh, w, x, z, ž** and **å** are only found in words borrowed from foreign languages, and they are pronounced as in the language of origin.

Diphthongs

In Finnish, diphthongs occur only in the first syllable of a word, except for those ending in **-i**, which can occur anywhere. They should be pronounced as a combination of the two vowel sounds represented by the spelling. The first vowel is pronounced louder in the following diphthongs: **ai**, **ei**, **oi**, **ui**, **yi**, **äi**, **öi**, **au**, **eu**, **ou**, **ey**, **äy**, **öy**, **iu**; the second vowel is louder in: **ie**, **uo**, **yö**.

Double letters

Remember that in Finnish *every* letter is pronounced, therefore a letter written double is pronounced long. Thus, the **kk** in ku**kk**a should be pronounced like the two k-sounds in the words thi**ck c**oat. Similarly, the **aa** in k**aa**tua should be pronounced long (like **a** in English c**a**r). These distinctions are important, not least because ku**k**a has a different meaning from ku**kk**a and k**a**tua a different meaning from k**aa**tua.

Stress

A strong stress always falls on the first syllable of a word.

FINNISH

Some basic expressions

Yes.	**Kyllä.**	**kewl**læ
No.	**Ei.**	ay
Please.	**Olkaa hyvä.**	**oal**kar **hew**væ
Thank you.	**Kiitos.**	**kee**toass
Thank you very much.	**Kiitoksia paljon.**	**kee**toaksiah **pahl**yoan
That's all right.	**Ei kestä.**	ay **kayss**tæ

Greetings

Good morning.	**Hyvää huomenta.**	**hew**vææ **hoooa**mayntah
Good afternoon.	**Hyvää päivää.**	**hew**vææ **pæi**vææ
Good evening.	**Hyvää iltaa.**	**hew**vææ **il**tar
Good night.	**Hyvää yötä.**	**hew**vææ **ewur**tæ
Good-bye.	**Näkemiin.**	**næ**kaymeen
See you later.	**Pikaisiin näkemiin.**	**pi**kighsseen **næ**kaymeen
This is Mr. . . .	**Tämä on herra . . .**	**tæ**mæ oan **hayr**rah
This is Mrs. . . .	**Tämä on rouva . . .**	**tæ**mæ oan **roa**vah
This is Miss . . .	**Tämä on neiti . . .**	**tæ**mæ oan **nay**ti
I'm very pleased to meet you.	**Hauska tutustua.**	**howss**kah **too**toosstooah
How are you?	**Mitä kuuluu?**	**mi**tæ **koo**loo
Very well, thank you.	**Erittäin hyvää, kiitos.**	**ay**rittæin **hew**vææ **kee**toass
And you?	**Entä teille?**	**ayn**tæ **tay**llay
Fine.	**Kiitos hyvää.**	**kee**toass **hew**vææ
Excuse me.	**Anteeksi.**	**ahn**tayksi

Questions

Where?	**Missä?**	**miss**sæ
Where is . . . ?	**Missä on . . . ?**	**miss**sæ oan
Where are . . . ?	**Missä ovat . . . ?**	**miss**sæ **oa**vaht
When?	**Milloin?**	**mil**loyn
What?	**Mikä?**	**mi**kæ
How?	**Kuinka?**	**kooing**kah
How much?	**Kuinka paljon?**	**kooing**kah **pahl**yoan

FINNISH

How many?	**Kuinka monta?**	**kooing**kah **moan**tah
Who?	**Kuka?**	**koo**kah
Why?	**Miksi?**	**mik**si
Which?	**Mikä?**	**mi**kæ
What do you call this?	**Miksi tätä kutsutaan?**	**mik**si **tæ**tæ **koot**sootarn
What do you call that?	**Miksi tuota kutsutaan?**	**mik**si **toooa**tah **koot**sootarn
What does this mean?	**Mitä tämä tarkoittaa?**	**mi**tæ **tæ**mæ **tahr**koyttar
What does that mean?	**Mitä tuo tarkoittaa?**	**mi**tæ toooa **tahr**koyttar

Do you speak ...?

Do you speak English?	**Puhutteko englantia?**	**poo**hoottaykoa **ayng**lahntiah
Do you speak German?	**Puhutteko saksaa?**	**poo**hoottaykoa **sahk**sah
Do you speak French?	**Puhutteko ranskaa?**	**poo**hoottaykoa **rahn**skar
Do you speak Spanish?	**Puhutteko espanjaa?**	**poo**hoottaykoa **ayss**pahnyar
Do you speak Italian?	**Puhutteko italiaa?**	**poo**hoottaykoa **i**taliar
Could you speak more slowly, please?	**Voisitteko puhua hitaammin?**	**voy**sittaykoa **poo**hooah **hi**tarmmin
Please point to the phrase in the book.	**Olkaa hyvä ja näyttäkää lause kirjasta.**	**oal**kar **hew**væ yah **næewt**tækææ **low**say **kir**yahsstah
Just a minute. I'll see if I can find it in this book.	**Hetkinen. Katson löydänkö sen tästä kirjasta.**	**hayt**kinayn. **kaht**soan **lurew**dængkur sayn **tæss**tæ **kir**yahsstah
I understand.	**Ymmärrän.**	**ewm**mærræn
I don't understand.	**En ymmärrä.**	ayn **ewm**mærræ

Can ...?

Can I have ...?	**Voinko saada ...?**	**voyng**koa **sar**dah
Can we have ...?	**Voimmeko saada ...?**	**voym**maykoa **sar**dah
Can you show me ...?	**Voitteko näyttää minulle ...?**	**voyt**taykoa **næewt**tææ **mi**noollay

Can you tell me ...?	**Voitteko sanoa minulle ...?**	**voyt**taykoa **sah**noaah **mi**noollay
Can you help me, please?	**Voitteko auttaa minua?**	**voyt**taykoa **owt**tar **mi**nooah

Wanting

I'd like ...	**Haluaisin ...**	**hah**looighssin
We'd like ...	**Haluaisimme ...**	**hah**looighssimmay
Please give me ...	**Olkaa hyvä ja antakaa minulle ...**	**oal**kar **hew**væ yah **ahn**tahkar **mi**noollay
Give it to me, please.	**Antakaa se minulle.**	**ahn**tahkar say **mi**noollay
Please bring me ...	**Tuokaa minulle ...**	**toooa**kar **mi**noollay
Bring it to me, please.	**Tuokaa se minulle.**	**toooa**kar say **mi**noollay
I'm hungry.	**Minun on nälkä.**	**mi**noon oan **næl**kæ
I'm thirsty.	**Minun on jano.**	**mi**noon oan **yah**noa
I'm tired.	**Olen väsynyt.**	**oa**layn **væ**sewnewt
I'm lost.	**Olen eksyksissä.**	**oa**layn **ayk**sewksisssæ
It's important.	**Se on tärkeää.**	say oan **tær**kayææ
It's urgent.	**Sillä on kiire.**	**sil**læ oan **kee**ray
Hurry up!	**Pitäkää kiirettä!**	**pi**tækææ **kee**rayttæ

It is/There is ...

It is/It's ...	**Se on ...**	say oan
Is it ...?	**Onko se ...?**	**oang**koa say
It isn't ...	**Se ei ole ...**	say ay **oa**lay
There is/There are ...	**Siellä on ...**	**siayl**læ oan
Is there/Are there ...?	**Onko siellä ...?**	**oang**koa **siayl**læ
There isn't/There aren't ...	**Siellä ei ole ...**	**siayl**læ ay **oa**lay
There isn't any/There aren't any.	**Ei ole yhtään.**	ay **oa**lay **ewh**tææn

A few common words

big/small	**suuri/pieni**	**soo**ri/**peeay**ni
quick/slow	**nopea/hidas**	**noa**payah/**hi**dahss
early/late	**aikaisin/myöhään**	**igh**kighssin/**mewur**hææn

cheap/expensive	**halpa/kallis**	**hahl**pah/**kahl**liss
near/far	**lähellä/kaukana**	**læ**hayllæ/**kow**kahnah
hot/cold	**kuuma/kylmä**	**koo**mah/**kewl**mæ
full/empty	**täysi/tyhjä**	**tæew**si/**tewh**yæ
easy/difficult	**helppo/vaikea**	**haylp**poa/**vigh**kayah
heavy/light	**painava/kevyt**	**pigh**nahvah/**kay**vewt
open/shut	**avoin/suljettu**	**ah**voyn/**sool**yayttoo
right/wrong	**oikea/väärä**	**oy**kayah/**vææ**ræ
old/new	**vanha/uusi**	**vahn**hah/**oo**si
old/young	**vanha/nuori**	**vahn**hah/**noooa**ri
beautiful/ugly	**kaunis/ruma**	**kow**niss/**roo**mah
good/bad	**hyvä/huono**	**hew**væ/**hoooa**noa
better/worse	**parempi/huonompi**	**pah**raympi/**hoooa**noampi

Some prepositions and a few more useful words

at	**-lla, -llä**	-llah, -llæ
on	**päällä**	**pææl**læ
in	**-ssa, -ssä**	-ssah, -ssæ
to	**-lle**	-llay
from	**-sta, -stä**	-stah, -stæ
inside	**sisäpuolella**	**si**sæpoooalayllah
outside	**ulkopuolella**	**ool**kaopoooalayllah
up	**ylös**	**ew**lurss
down	**alas**	**ah**lahss
before	**ennen**	**ayn**nayn
after	**jälkeen**	**yæl**kayn
with	**kanssa**	**kahns**sah
without	**ilman**	**il**mahn
through	**läpi**	**læ**pi
towards	**kohti**	**koah**ti
until	**asti**	**ahss**ti
during	**aikana**	**igh**kahnah
and	**ja**	yah
or	**tai**	tigh
not	**ei**	ay
nothing	**ei mitään**	ay **mi**tææn
none	**ei yhtään**	ay **ewh**tææn
very	**erittäin**	**ay**rittæin
also	**myös**	mewurss
soon	**pian**	piahn
perhaps	**ehkä**	**ayh**kæ
here	**tässä**	**tæss**sæ
there	**tuossa**	**toooass**sah
now	**nyt**	newt
then	**sitten**	**sit**tayn

FINNISH

Arrival

Your passport, please.	**Passinne, olkaa hyvä.**	**pahss**sinnay **oal**kar **hew**væ
Here it is.	**Tässä.**	**tæss**sæ
Have you anything to declare?	**Onko teillä mitään tullattavaa?**	**oang**koa **tayl**lä **mi**tææn **tool**lahttahvar
No, nothing at all.	**Ei, ei mitään.**	ay ay **mi**tææn
Porter!	**Kantaja!**	**kahn**tahyah
Can you help me with my luggage, please?	**Voitteko auttaa minua kantamaan matkatavarani?**	**voyt**taykoa **owt**tar **mi**nooah **kahn**tahmarn **maht**kahtahvahrahni
That's my suitcase.	**Tuo on minun matkalaukkuni.**	toooa oan **mi**noon **mat**kahlowkkooni
Where's the bus to the centre of town, please?	**Mistä lähtee bussi keskikaupungille?**	**miss**tæ **læh**tay **booss**si **kayss**kikowpoonggillay
This way, please.	**Tätä tietä, olkaa hyvä.**	**tæ**tæ **tiay**tæ **oal**kar **hew**væ

Changing money

Can you change a traveller's cheque, please?	**Voitteko vaihtaa matkašekin?**	**voyt**taykoa **vighh**tar **maht**kahshaykin
Where's the nearest bank, please?	**Missä on lähin pankki?**	**miss**sæ oan **læ**hin **pahnk**ki

Car rental

I'd like a car.	**Haluaisin auton.**	**hah**looighsin **ow**toan
For how long?	**Kuinka pitkäksi aikaa?**	**kooing**kah **pit**kæksi **igh**ka
A day/Four days/ A week/Two weeks.	**Päiväksi/Neljäksi päiväksi/Viikoksi/ Kahdeksi viikoksi.**	**pæi**væksi/**nayl**yæksi **pæi**væksi/**vee**koaksi/ **kahh**dayksi **vee**koaksi

Taxi

Where can I get a taxi?	**Mistä voin saada taksin?**	**miss**tæ voyn **sar**dah **tahk**sin
What's the fare to ... ?	**Paljonko se maksaa ... ?**	**pahl**yoangkoa say **mahk**sar

FINNISH

Take me to this address, please.	**Viekää minut tähän osoitteeseen.**	**viayk**ææ **mi**noot **tæ**hæn **oa**soyttayssayn
I'm in a hurry.	**Minulla on kiire.**	**mi**noollah oan **kee**ray
Could you drive more slowly, please?	**Voisitteko ajaa hitaammin?**	**voy**sittaykoa **ah**yar **hi**tarmmin

Hotel and other accommodation

My name is ...	**Nimeni on ...**	**ni**mayni oan
Have you a reservation?	**Onko teillä varaus?**	**oang**koa **tayl**læ **vah**rahooss
Yes, here's the confirmation.	**Kyllä, tässä on vahvistus.**	**kewl**læ **tæss**sæ oan **vahh**visstooss
I'd like ...	**Haluaisin ...**	**hah**looighsin
I'd like a single room/a double room.	**Haluaisin yhden hengen huoneen/ kahden hengen huoneen.**	**hah**looighssin **ewh**dayn **hayng**ayn **hoooa**nayn/ **kahh**dayn **hayng**ayn **hoooa**nayn
a room with a bath/with a shower	**huoneen jossa on kylpy/jossa on suihku**	**hoooa**nayn **yoass**sah oan **kewl**pew/**yoass**sah oan **sooih**koo

How much?

What's the price per night/per week/per month?	**Paljonko hinta on yöltä/viikolta/ kuukaudelta?**	**pahl**yoangkoa **hin**tah **oan** **ewurl**tæ/**vee**koaltah/ **koo**kowdayltah
May I see the room?	**Saanko nähdä huoneen?**	**sarng**koa **næh**dæ **hoooa**nayn
I'm sorry, I don't like it.	**Valitan, mutta en pidä siitä.**	**vah**litahn **moot**tah ayn **pi**dæ **see**tæ
Yes, that's fine. I'll take it.	**Kyllä, se sopii mainiosti. Otan sen.**	**kewl**læ say **soa**pee **migh**nioassti. **oa**tahn sayn
What's my room number, please?	**Mikä on huoneeni numero?**	**mi**kæ oan **hoooa**nayni **noo**mayroa
Number 123.	**Numero 123.**	**noo**mayroa 123

Service, please

Who is it?	**Kuka siellä?**	**koo**kah **siayl**læ
Just a minute.	**Hetkinen.**	**hayt**kinayn
Come in! The door's open.	**Sisään! Ovi on auki.**	**si**ssææn! **oa**vi oan owki
May we have breakfast in our room?	**Voimmeko saada varhaisaamiaisen huoneeseemme?**	**voym**maykoa **sar**dah **vahr**highssarmiighssayn **hooa**nayssaymmay

Breakfast

I'll have...	**Haluaisin...**	**hah**looighssin
I'll have some fruit juice.	**Haluaisin hedelmämehua.**	**hah**looighssin **hay**dayl-mæmayhooah
a boiled egg	**keitetyn munan**	**kay**taytewn **moo**nahn
a fried egg	**paistetun munan**	**pighss**taytoon **moo**nahn
some bacon/some ham	**pekonia/kinkkua**	**pay**koaniah/**kink**kooah
some toast	**paahtoleipää**	**parh**toalaypææ
a pot of tea	**annoksen teetä**	**ahn**noaksayn **tay**tæ
a cup of tea	**kupin teetä**	**koo**pin **tay**tæ
some coffee	**kahvia**	**kahh**viah
some chocolate	**kaakaota**	**kar**kahoatah
more butter	**lisää voita**	**li**sææ **voy**tah
some hot water	**kuumaa vettä**	**koo**mar **vayt**tæ

Difficulties

The central heating doesn't work.	**Keskuslämmitys ei toimi.**	**kayss**koosslæmmitewss ay **toy**mi
the light/the socket	**valo/pistorasia**	**vah**loa/**piss**toarahssiah
the tap/the toilet	**hana/wc**	**hah**nah/vay say
There's no hot water.	**Kuumaa vettä ei tule.**	**koo**mar **vayt**tæ ay **too**lay
May I see the manager, please?	**Haluaisin tavata johtajan.**	**hah**looighssin **tah**vahtah **yoah**tahyahn

Telephone—Mail

There's a call for you.	**Teille on puhelu.**	**tayl**lay oan **poo**hayloo
Hold the line, please.	**Hetkinen, olkaa hyvä.**	**hayt**kinayn **oal**kar **hew**væ
Operator, I've been cut off.	**Keskus, puhelu katkesi.**	**kayss**kooss **poo**hayloo **kaht**kayssi
Did anyone telephone me?	**Onko kukaan soittanut minulle?**	**oang**koa **koo**karn **soyt**-tahnoot **mi**noollay
Is there any mail for me?	**Onko minulle mitään postia?**	**oang**koa **mi**noollay **mi**tææn **poass**tiah
Are there any messages for me?	**Onko minulle mitään viestejä?**	**oang**koa **mi**noollay **mi**tææn **viayss**tayyæ

Checking out

May I have my bill, please?	**Saisinko laskuni?**	**sigh**singkoa **lahss**kooni
We're in a great hurry.	**Meillä on kova kiire.**	**mayl**læ oan **koa**vah **kee**ray
It's been a very enjoyable stay.	**Nautimme kovasti oleskelustamme.**	**now**timmay **koa**vahsti **oa**laysskayloosstahmmay

Eating out

Good evening, sir/ Good evening, madam.	**Hyvää iltaa.**	**hew**vææ **il**tar
Good evening. I'd like a table for two, please.	**Hyvää iltaa. Haluaisin pöydän kahdelle.**	**hew**vææ **il**tar. **hah**looighs-in **purew**dæn **kahh**-dayllay
Do you have a fixed-price menu?	**Onko teillä päivän ateriaa?**	**oang**koa **tayl**læ **pæi**væn **ah**tayriar
May I see the à la carte menu?	**Saanko à la carte -ruokalistan?**	**sarng**koa ah lah kahrt **roooa**kahlisstahn
May we have an ashtray, please?	**Saisimmeko tuhkakupin?**	**sigh**simmaykoa **tooh**kah-koopin
some bread	**leipää**	**lay**pææ
a fork	**haarukan**	**har**rookahn
a knife	**veitsen**	**vayt**sayn
a spoon	**lusikan**	**loo**sikahn
a plate	**lautasen**	**low**tahsayn
a glass	**lasin**	**lah**sin
a napkin	**lautasliinan**	**low**tahsleenahn
another chair	**vielä yhden tuolin**	**viay**lay **ewh**dayn **toooa**lin
Where's the gentlemen's toilet (men's room)?	**Missä on miestenhuone?**	**miss**sæ oan **miay**-staynhoooanay
Where's the ladies' toilet (ladies' room)?	**Missä on naistenhuone?**	**miss**sæ oan **nigh**-staynhoooanay

Appetizers

I'd like some ...	**Haluaisin ...**	**hah**looighssin
I'd like some assorted appetizers.	**Haluaisin alkupala-valikoiman.**	**hah**looighssin **ahl**koopah-lahvahlikoymahn
orange juice	**appelsiinimehua**	**ahp**paylseenimayhooah
ham	**kinkkua**	**kink**kooah

melon	**melonia**	**may**loaniah
pâté	**pasteijaa**	**pahs**stayar
smoked salmon	**savustettua lohta**	**sah**voosstayttooah **loah**tah
shrimps (shrimp)	**katkarapuja**	**kaht**kahrahpooyah

Soup

Have you any...?	**Onko teillä...?**	**oang**koa **tayl**læ
Have you any chicken soup?	**Onko teillä kanakeittoa?**	**oang**koa **tayl**læ **kah**nahkayttoaah
vegetable soup	**vihanneskeittoa**	**vi**hahnnaysskayttoaah
onion soup	**sipulikeittoa**	**si**poolikayttoaah

Fish

I'd like some...	**Haluaisin...**	**hah**looighssin
I'd like some fish.	**Haluaisin kalaa.**	**hah**looighssin **kah**lar
sole	**merianturaa**	**may**riahntoorah
trout	**taimenta**	**tigh**mayntah
lobster	**hummeria**	**hoom**mayiah
crayfish	**rapuja**	**rah**pooyah
prawns	**isoja katkarapuja**	**i**soayah **kaht**kahrahpooyah
I'd like it...	**Haluaisin sen...**	**hah**looighssin sayn
I'd like it steamed.	**Haluaisin sen höyrytettynä.**	**hah**looighssin sayn **hurew**rewtayttewnæ
grilled	**pariloituna**	**pah**riloytoonah
boiled	**keitettynä**	**kayt**tayttewnæ
baked	**uunissa paistettuna**	**oo**nisssah **pighs**stayttoonah
fried	**paistettuna**	**pighs**stayttoonah

Meat—Poultry—Game

I'd like some...	**Haluaisin...**	**hah**looighssin
I'd like some beef.	**Haluaisin naudanlihaa.**	**hah**looighssin **now**dahnlihar
a beef steak	**pihvin**	**pih**vin
some roast beef	**paahtopaistia**	**parh**toapighsstiah
a veal cutlet	**vasikanleikkeen**	**vah**sikahnlaykkayn
mutton	**lammasta**	**lahm**mahsstah
lamb	**karitsanlihaa**	**kah**ritsahnlihar
a pork chop	**porsaankyljyksen**	**por**sarngkewlyewksayn

roast pork	**porsaanpaistia**	**por**saanpighsstiah
hare	**jäniksenlihaa**	**yæ**niksaynlihar
chicken	**kanaa**	**kah**nar
roast chicken	**kanapaistia**	**kah**nahpighsstiah
duck	**ankkaa**	**ahnk**kar
How do you like your meat?	**Miten valmistettuna haluatte lihan?**	**mi**tayn **vahl**misstayttoonah **hah**looahttay **li**hahn
rare	**vähän paistettuna**	**væ**hæn **pighss**tayttoonah
medium	**puolikypsänä**	**pooo**likewpsænæ
well done	**hyvin paistettuna**	**hew**vin **pighss**tayttoonah

Vegetables

What vegetables have you got?	**Mitä vihanneksia teillä on?**	**mi**tæ **vi**hahnnayksiah **tayl**lah oan
I'd like some ...	**Haluaisin ...**	**hah**looighssin
I'd like some asparagus.	**Haluaisin parsaa.**	**hah**looighssin **pahr**sar
green beans	**vihreitä papuja**	**vih**raytæ **pah**pooyah
mushrooms	**sieniä**	**siay**niæ
carrots	**porkkanoita**	**pork**kahnoitah
onions	**sipulia**	**si**pooliah
red cabbage	**punakaalia**	**poo**nahkarliah
spinach	**pinaattia**	**pi**narttiah
rice	**riisiä**	**ree**siæ
peas	**herneitä**	**hayr**naytæ
tomatoes	**tomaatteja**	**toa**marttayyah
green salad	**vihreätä salaattia**	**vih**rayætæ sahlarttiah
potatoes	**perunoita**	**pay**roonoitah

Desserts

Nothing more, thanks.	**Ei muuta, kiitos.**	ay **moo**tah **kee**toass
Just a small portion, please.	**Vain pieni annos.**	**vighn piay**ni **ahn**noass
Have you any ice-cream?	**Onko teillä jäätelöä?**	**oang**koa **tayl**læ **yææ**tayluræ
fruit salad	**hedelmäsalaattia**	**hay**daylmæsahlarttiah
fresh fruit	**tuoreita hedelmiä**	**tooo**raytah **hay**daylmiæ
cheese	**juustoa**	**yooss**toa

Drink

What would you like to drink?	**Mitä haluaisitte juoda?**	**mi**tæ **hah**looighssittay **joooa**dah
I'll have a beer, please.	**Haluaisin oluen.**	**hah**looighssin **oa**looayn
I'll have a whisky, please.	**Haluaisin viskin.**	**hah**looighssin **viss**kin

Wine

I'd like a bottle of wine.	**Haluaisin pullon viiniä.**	**hah**looighssin **pool**loan **vee**niæ
red wine	**punaviiniä**	**poo**nahveeniæ
rosé wine	**rosé-viiniä**	**roa**sayveeniæ
white wine	**valkoviiniä**	**vahl**koaveeniæ
Cheers!	**Kippis!**	**kip**piss

The bill (check)

May I have the bill (check) please?	**Saisinko laskun?**	**sigh**singkoa **lahss**koon
Is service included?	**Sisältyykö siihen palvelu?**	**si**sæltewkur **see**hayn **pahl**vayloo
Everything's included.	**Kaikki on mukana.**	**kighk**ki oan **moo**kahnah
Thank you, that was a very good meal.	**Kiitoksia, se oli erittäin hyvä ateria.**	**kee**toaksiah say **oa**li **ay**rittæin **hew**væ **ah**tayriah

Travelling

Where's the railway station, please?	**Missä on rautatieasema?**	**miss**sæ oan **row**tahtiay-ahssaymah
Where's the ticket office, please?	**Missä on lippumyymälä?**	**miss**sæ oan **li**poo-mewmælæ
I'd like a ticket to ...	**Haluaisin lipun ...**	**hah**looighssin **li**poon
First or second class?	**Ensimmäinen vai toinen luokka?**	**ayn**simmæinayn vigh **toy**nayn **loooak**kah
First class, please.	**Ensimmäinen.**	**ayn**simmæinayn
Single or return (one way or roundtrip)?	**Yhdensuuntainen vai edestakainen?**	**ewh**daynsoontighnayn vigh **ay**daysstahkighnayn

Do I have to change trains?	**Täytyykö minun vaihtaa junaa?**	**tæew**tewkur **mi**noon **vighh**tar **yoo**nar
What platform does the train leave from?	**Miltä laiturilta juna lähtee?**	**mil**tæ **ligh**tooriltah **yoo**nah **læh**tay
Where's the nearest underground (subway) station?	**Missä on lähin maanalaisen asema?**	**miss**sæ oan **læ**hin **marn**hahlighssayn **ah**saymah
Where's the bus station, please?	**Missä on linja-autoasema?**	**miss**sæ oan **lin**yah **ow**toa-ahssaymah
When's the first bus to...?	**Milloin lähtee ensimmäinen bussi...?**	**mil**loyn **læh**tay **ayn**sim-mæinayn **booss**si
the last bus	**viimeinen bussi**	**vee**maynayn **booss**si
the next bus	**seuraava bussi**	**sayoo**rarvah **booss**si
Please let me off at the next stop.	**Päästäisittekö minut pois seuraavalla pysäkillä?**	**pææss**tæissittaykur **mi**noot poyss **sayoo**-rarvahllah **pew**sækillæ

Relaxing

What's on at the cinema (movies)?	**Mitä elokuvissa esitetään?**	**mi**tæ **ay**loakoovisssah **ay**sitaytææn
What's on at the theatre?	**Mitä teatterissa esitetään?**	**mi**tæ **tay**ahttayrisssah **ay**sitaytææn
What time does the film begin? And the play?	**Mihin aikaan elokuva alkaa? Entä näytelmä?**	**mi**hin **igh**karn **ay**loakoovah **ahl**karr? **ayn**tæ **næew**taylmæ
Are there any tickets for tonight?	**Onko täksi illaksi vielä lippuja?**	**oang**koa **tæ**ksi **il**laksi **vi**aylæ **lip**pooyah
Where can we go dancing?	**Mihin voimme mennä tanssimaan?**	**mi**hin **voym**may **mayn**næ **tahnss**simarn
Would you like to dance?	**Haluaisitteko tanssia?**	**hah**looighssittaykoa **tahnss**siah

Introductions

How do you do?	**Hyvää päivää.**	**hew**vææ **pæi**vææ
How are you?	**Mitä kuuluu?**	**mi**tæ **koo**loo
Very well, thank you. And you?	**Kiitos, erittäin hyvää. Entä teille?**	**kee**toass **ayr**rittæin **hew**vææ. **ayn**tæ **tayl**lay
May I introduce Miss Philips?	**Saanko esitellä neiti Philipsin?**	**sarng**koa **ay**sitayllæ **nay**ti **fi**lipsin

My name is...	**Minun nimeni on...**	**mi**noon **ni**mayni oan
I'm very pleased to meet you.	**Hauska tavata.**	**howss**kah **tah**vahtah
How long have you been here?	**Kauanko olette ollut täällä?**	**kow**ahngkoa **oa**layttay **oal**loot **tææl**læ
It was nice meeting you.	**Oli hauska tavata.**	**oa**li **howss**kah **tah**vahtah

Dating

Would you like a cigarette?	**Haluaisitteko savukkeen?**	**hah**looighssittaykoa **sa**vookkayn
May I get you a drink?	**Saanko tarjota teille lasillisen?**	**sarng**koa **tahr**yoatah **tayl**lay **lah**sillissayn
Do you have a light, please?	**Onko teillä tulta?**	**oang**koa **tayl**læ **tool**tah
Are you waiting for someone?	**Odotatteko jotakuta?**	**oa**doatahttaykoa **yoa**tahkootah
Are you free this evening?	**Oletteko vapaa tänä iltana?**	**oa**layttaykoa **vah**par **tæ**næ **il**tahnah
Where shall we meet?	**Missä tapaamme?**	**miss**sæ **tah**parmmay
What time shall I meet you?	**Mihin aikaan tapaan teidät?**	**mi**hin **igh**karn **tah**parn **tay**dæt
May I take you home?	**Saanko saattaa teidät kotiin?**	**sarng**koa **sart**tar **tay**dæt **koa**teen
Thank you, it's been a wonderful evening.	**Kiitos, oli ihana ilta.**	**kee**toass **oa**li **i**hahnah **il**tah
What's your telephone number?	**Mikä on puhelinnumeronne?**	**mi**kæ oan **poo**haylinnoomayroannay
Do you live alone?	**Asutteko yksin?**	**ah**soottaykoa **ewk**sin
What time is your last train?	**Mihin aikaan viimeinen junanne lähtee?**	**mi**hin **igh**karn **vee**maynayn **yoo**nahnnay **læh**tay
Good-night...	**Hyvää yötä...**	**hew**vææ **ewur**tæ

Banks

Where's the nearest bank, please?	**Missä on lähin pankki?**	**miss**sæ oan **læ**hin **pahnk**ki
Where can I cash some traveller's cheques?	**Missä voin vaihtaa matkašekkejä?**	**miss**sæ voyn **vighh**tar **maht**kahshaykkayyæ

FINNISH

What time does the bank open? What time does it close?	**Mihin aikaan pankki avataan? Mihin aikaan se suljetaan?**	**mi**hin **igh**karn **pahnk**ki **ah**vahtarn? **mi**hin **igh**karn say **sool**yaytarn
I'm expecting some money from home. Has it arrived?	**Odotan rahaa kotoa. Onkohan se jo tullut?**	**oa**doatahn **rah**har **koa**toaah. **oang**koahahn say yoa **tool**loot
Can you give me some small change, please?	**Voitteko antaa minulle hiukan vaihtorahaa?**	**voyt**taykoa **ahn**tar **mi**noollay **hioo**kahn **vighh**toarahhar

Shops, stores and services

Where is the nearest chemist's (pharmacy)?	**Missä on lähin apteekki?**	**miss**sæ oan **læ**hin **ahp**taykki
the nearest hairdresser's	**lähin kampaamo**	**læ**hin **kahm**parmoa
the photo shop	**valokuvausliike**	**vah**loakoovahoossleekay
the jeweller's	**kultaseppä**	**kool**tassayppæ
the department store	**tavaratalo**	**tah**vahrahtahloa
the police station	**poliisiasema**	**poa**leessiahssaymah
the garage	**pysäköintitalo**	**pews**ækurintitahloa
How do I get there?	**Miten sinne pääsee?**	**mi**tayn **sin**nay **pææ**say
Is it within walking distance?	**Onko se kävelymatkan päässä?**	**oang**koa say **kæ**vaylewmahtkahn **pææss**sæ

Service

Can you help me, please?	**Voitteko auttaa minua?**	**voyt**taykoa **owt**taa **mi**nooah
Can you show me this? And that, too.	**Voitteko näyttää minulle tätä? Ja myös tuota.**	**voyt**taykoa **næewt**tææ **mi**noollay **tæ**tæ? yah mewurss **toooa**tah
It's too expensive/ too big/too small.	**Se on liian kallis/ liian suuri/liian pieni.**	say oan **lee**ahn **kahl**lis/ **lee**ahn **soo**ri/**lee**ahn **piay**ni
Can you show me some more?	**Voitteko näyttää minulle vielä joitakin muita?**	**voyt**taykoa **næewt**iææ **mi**noollay **viay**læ **yoy**tahkin **mooi**tah
something better	**jotakin parempaa**	**yoa**tahkin **pah**raympar
something cheaper	**jotakin halvempaa**	**yoa**tahkin **hahl**vaympar

How much is this? And that?	**Paljonko tämä maksaa? Entä tuo?**	**pahl**yoangkoa **tæ**mæ **mahk**sar? **ayn**tæ toooa
It's not quite what I want.	**Se ei ole aivan sitä mitä haluan.**	say ay **oa**lay **igh**vahn **si**tæ **mi**tæ **hah**looahn
I like it.	**Pidän siitä.**	**pi**dæn **see**tæ

Chemist's (Pharmacy)

I'd like something for a cold/for a cough/for travel sickness.	**Haluaisin jotakin vilustumiseen/yskään/matkapahoinvointiin.**	**hah**looighssin **yoa**tahkin **vi**loosstoomissayn/**ewss**kææn/**maht**kahpahhoynvoynteen
Can you recommend something for hay-fever/for sunburn?	**Voitteko suositella jotakin heinänuhaan/auringonpolttamaan?**	**voyt**taykoa **soooa**sitayllah **yoa**tahkin **hay**nænooharn/**ow**ringoanpoalttahmarn

Toiletry

May I have some razor blades?	**Saisinko parranajokoneenteriä?**	**sigh**singkoa **pahr**rahnahyoakoanayntayriæ
some shaving cream	**partavaahdoketta**	**pahr**tahvarhdoakayttah
some toothpaste	**hammastahnaa**	**hahm**mahsstahhnar
I'd like some soap.	**Haluaisin saippuaa.**	**hah**looighssin **sighp**pooar
some suntan oil	**aurinkoöljyä**	**ow**ringkoaurlyewæ

At the barber's

I'd like a haircut, please.	**Haluaisin hiustenleikkuun.**	**hah**looighssin **hioos**staynlaykkoon
Short/Leave it long.	**Lyhyiksi/Jättäkää ne pitkiksi.**	**lew**hewiksi/**yæt**tækææ nay **pit**kiksi
A razor cut, please.	**Veitsileikkuu, olkaa hyvä.**	**vayt**silaykkoo **oal**kar **hew**væ

At the hairdresser's

I'd like a shampoo and set, please.	**Haluaisin pesun ja kampauksen.**	**hah**looighssin **pay**soon yah **kahm**pahooksayn
I'd like a bleach.	**Haluaisin vaalennuksen.**	**hah**looighssin **var**laynnooksayn
a permanent	**permanentin**	**payr**mahnayntin
a colour rinse	**värihuuhtelun**	**væ**rihoohtayloon
a manicure	**käsienhoidon**	**kæ**siaynhoydoan

Photography

I'd like a film for this camera.	**Haluaisin filmin tähän kameraan.**	**hah**looighssin **fil**min **tæ**hæn **kah**mayrarn
This camera doesn't work.	**Tämä kamera ei toimi.**	**tæ**mæ **kah**mayrah ay **toy**mi

At the post office

Where's the nearest post office, please?	**Missä on lähin postitoimisto?**	**miss**sæ oan **læ**hin **poass**titoymisstoa
I'd like to send this by express (special delivery)/by air mail.	**Haluaisin lähettää tämän pikakirjeenä/lentopostitse.**	**hah**looighssin **læ**hayttææ **tæ**mæn **pi**kahkiryaynæ/ **layn**toapoasstitsay

Service stations

Where is the nearest service station, please?	**Missä on lähin huoltoasema?**	**miss**sæ oan **læ**hin **hoooal**toaahssaymah
Fill her up, please.	**Tankki täyteen, olkaa hyvä.**	**tahnk**ki **tæew**tayn **oal**kar **hew**væ
Check the oil, please.	**Tarkistakaa öljy.**	**tahr**kisstahkar **url**yew
Would you check the tyres?	**Tarkistaisitteko renkaat?**	**tahr**kisstighssittaykoa **rayng**kart

Street directions

Can you show me on the map where I am?	**Voitteko näyttää minulle kartalta missä olen?**	**voyt**taykoa **næewt**tææ **mi**noollay **kahr**tahltah **miss**sæ **oa**layn
You're on the wrong road.	**Olette väärällä tiellä.**	**oa**layttay **væær**ællæ **teeayl**læ
Go back to ...	**Menkää takaisin ...**	**mayng**kææ **tah**kighssin
Go straight ahead.	**Ajakaa suoraan eteenpäin.**	**ah**yahkar **soooa**raan **ay**taynpæin
It's on the left/on the right.	**Se on vasemmalla/ oikealla.**	say oan **vah**saymmahllah/ **oy**kayahllah

Accidents

May I use your telephone?	**Saanko käyttää puhelintanne?**	**sarng**koa **kæewt**tææ **poo**haylintahnnay
Call a doctor quickly.	**Kutsukaa nopeasti lääkäri.**	**koot**sookar **noa**payahssti **lææ**kæri

Call an ambulance.	**Kutsukaa ambulanssi.**	**koot**sookar **ahm**boolahnsssi
Please call the police.	**Olkaa hyvä ja kutsukaa poliisi.**	**oal**kar **hew**væ yah **koot**sookar **poa**leessi

Numbers

zero	**nolla**	**noal**lah
one	**yksi**	**ewk**si
two	**kaksi**	**kahk**si
three	**kolme**	**koal**may
four	**neljä**	**nayl**yæ
five	**viisi**	**vee**si
six	**kuusi**	**koo**si
seven	**seitsemän**	**sayt**saymæn
eight	**kahdeksan**	**kahh**dayksahn
nine	**yhdeksän**	**ewh**dayksæn
ten	**kymmenen**	**kewm**maynayn
eleven	**yksitoista**	**ewk**sitoysstah
twelve	**kaksitoista**	**kahk**sitoysstah
thirteen	**kolmetoista**	**koal**maytoysstah
fourteen	**neljätoista**	**nayl**yætoysstah
fifteen	**viisitoista**	**vee**sitoysstah
sixteen	**kuusitoista**	**koo**sitoysstah
seventeen	**seitsemäntoista**	**sayt**saymæntoysstah
eighteen	**kahdeksantoista**	**kahh**dayksahntoysstah
nineteen	**yhdeksäntoista**	**ewh**dayksæntoysstah
twenty	**kaksikymmentä**	**kahk**sikewmmayntæ
twenty-one	**kaksikymmentäyksi**	**kahk**sikewmmayntæewksi
thirty	**kolmekymmentä**	**koal**maykewmmayntæ
forty	**neljäkymmentä**	**nayl**yækewmmayntæ
fifty	**viisikymmentä**	**vee**sikewmmayntæ
sixty	**kuusikymmentä**	**koo**sikewmmayntæ
seventy	**seitsemänkymmentä**	**sayt**saymængkewmmayntæ
eighty	**kahdeksankymmentä**	**kahh**dayksahngkewmmayntæ
ninety	**yhdeksänkymmentä**	**ewh**dayksængkewmmayntæ
one hundred	**sata**	**sah**tah
one thousand	**tuhat**	**too**hat
ten thousand	**kymmenentuhatta**	**kewm**maynayntoohahttah

Days

It's Sunday.	**On sunnuntai.**	oan **soon**noontigh
Monday	**maanantai**	**mar**nahntigh
Tuesday	**tiistai**	**teess**tigh
Wednesday	**keskiviikko**	**kayss**kiveekkoa

FINNISH

Thursday	**torstai**	**toarss**tigh
Friday	**perjantai**	**payr**yayntigh
Saturday	**lauantai**	**low**ahntigh
yesterday	**eilen**	**ay**layn
today	**tänään**	**tæ**nææn
tomorrow	**huomenna**	**hoooa**maynnah
morning/afternoon	**aamupäivä/iltapäivä**	**ar**moopæivæ/**il**tahpæivæ
evening/night	**ilta/yö**	**il**tah/ewur

Months

January	**tammikuu**	**tahm**mikoo
February	**helmikuu**	**hayl**mikoo
March	**maaliskuu**	**mar**lisskoo
April	**huhtikuu**	**hooh**tikoo
May	**toukokuu**	**toaoo**koakoo
June	**kesäkuu**	**kay**sækoo
July	**heinäkuu**	**hay**nækoo
August	**elokuu**	**ay**loakoo
September	**syyskuu**	**sewss**koo
October	**lokakuu**	**loa**kahkoo
November	**marraskuu**	**mahr**rahsskoo
December	**joulukuu**	**yoaoo**lookoo
Merry Christmas!	**Hyvää joulua!**	**hew**vææ **yoaoo**looah!
Happy New Year!	**Onnellista uutta vuotta!**	**oan**nayllisstah **oot**tah **vooat**tah

FRENCH

Guide to Pronunciation

Letter	Approximate pronunciation	Symbol	Example	
Consonants				
b, c, d, f, k, l, m, n, p, s, t, v, x, z	as in English			
ch	like **sh** in **sh**ut	sh	**chercher**	shehrshay
ç	like **s** in **s**it	s	**ça**	sah
g	1) before **e**, **i**, **y**, like **s** in plea**s**ure	zh	**manger**	mahngzhay
	2) before **a**, **o**, **u**, like **g** in **g**o	g	**garçon**	gahrsawng
gn	like **ni** in o**ni**on	ñ	**ligne**	leeñ
h	always silent		**homme**	om
j	like **s** in plea**s**ure	zh	**jamais**	zhahmeh
qu	like **k** in **k**ill	k	**qui**	kee
r	rolled in the back of the mouth, rather like gargling	r	**rouge**	roozh
w	usually like **v** in **v**oice	v	**wagon**	vahgawng

Vowels

a, à or **â**	between the **a** in h**a**t and the **a** in f**a**ther	ah	**mari**	mahree
é, er, et, e	like **a** in l**a**te	ay	**enchanté**	ahngshahngtay
è, ê, e + most consonants	like **e** in g**e**t	eh	**même**	mehm
e	sometimes (when at the end of a syllable or of a one-syllable word), like **er** in oth**er** (quite short)	er*	**me**	mer
i	like **ee** in m**ee**t	ee	**il**	eel
o	generally like **o** in h**o**t but sometimes like **o** in wr**o**te	o	**donner**	donay
ô	like **o** in wr**o**te	oa	**Rhône**	roan
u	no equivalent in English. Round your lips and try to say **ee**; this should sound more or less correct	ew	**cru**	krew

Sounds spelt with two or more letters

ai, ay	can be pronounced as **a** in l**a**te	ay	**j'ai**	zhay
aient, ais, ait, aî	like **e** in g**e**t	eh	**chaîne**	shehn
(e)au	similar to **o** in wr**o**te	oa	**chaud**	shoa
ei	like **e** in g**e**t	eh	**peine**	pehn
eu	like **ur** in f**ur**, but with lips rounded, not spread	ur*	**peu**	pur
oi	like **w** followed by the **a** in h**a**t	wah	**moi**	mwah
ou	like **oo** in l**oo**k	oo	**nouveau**	noovoa
ui	approximately like **wee** in betw**ee**n	wee	**traduire**	trahdweer

Nasal sounds

The following sounds are pronounced through the mouth and the nose at the same time, very much like the twang found in speech in some parts of America or Britain.

an	something like **arn** in t**arn**ish	ahng	**tante**	tahngt
en	generally like the previous sound	ahng	**enchanté**	ahngshahngtay

---

* The **r** should not be pronounced when reading this transcription.

ien	sounds like **yan** in **yan**k	yang	**bien**	byang
(a)in	approximately like **ang** in r**ang**	ang	**instant**	angstahng
on	approximately like **orn** in c**orn**	awng	**maison**	mayzawng
un	approximately like **ang** in r**ang**	ang	**brun**	brang

Liaison

Normally, the final consonants are not pronounced in French. However, when a word ending in a consonant is followed by one beginning with a vowel, they are often run together, and the consonant is pronounced as if it began the following word. For instance, **nous** (*we*) is pronounced **noo**, but, in the sentence **"Nous avons un enfant"** (*We have a child*), the **s** of **nous** is pronounced, and the sentence sounds something like: **noozahvawngzangnahngfahng**. Another example: "**comment**" is pronounced **komahng**, but the **t** is pronounced in "**Comment allez-vous?**" (*How are you*), which sounds something like: **komahngtahlay voo**.

Some basic expressions

Yes.	**Oui.**	wee
No.	**Non.**	nawng
Please.	**S'il vous plaît.**	seel voo play
Thank you.	**Merci.**	mehrsee
Thank you very much.	**Merci beaucoup.**	mehrsee boakoo
That's all right.	**Il n'y a pas de quoi.**	eel nee ah pah der kwah

Greetings

Good morning.	**Bonjour.**	bawngzhoor
Good afternoon.	**Bonjour.**	bawngzhoor
Good evening.	**Bonsoir.**	bawngswahr
Good night.	**Bonne nuit.**	bon nwee
Good-bye.	**Au revoir.**	oa rervwahr
See you later.	**A bientôt.**	ah byangtoa
This is Mr. . . .	**Voici Monsieur . . .**	vwahssee merssyur
This is Mrs. . . .	**Voici Madame . . .**	vwahssee mahdahm
This is Miss . . .	**Voici Mademoiselle . . .**	vwahssee mahdmwahzehl
I'm very pleased to meet you.	**Enchanté.**	ahngshahngtay
How are you?	**Comment allez-vous?**	komahngtahlayvoo
Very well, thank you.	**Très bien, merci.**	treh byang mehrsee.
And you?	**Et vous?**	ay voo
Fine.	**Bien.**	byang
Excuse me.	**Excusez-moi.**	ehkskewzaymwah

Questions

Where?	**Où?**	oo
Where is . . . ?	**Où se trouve . . .?**	oo ser troov
Where are . . . ?	**Où se trouvent . . .?**	oo ser troov
When?	**Quand?**	kahng

What?	**Quoi?**	kwah
How?	**Comment?**	komahng
How much?	**Combien?**	kawngbyang
How many?	**Combien?**	kawngbyang
Who?	**Qui?**	kee
Why?	**Pourquoi?**	poorkwah
Which?	**Lequel/Laquelle?**	lerkehl/lahkehl
What do you call this?	**Comment appelez-vous ceci?**	komahng ahperlayvoo serssee
What do you call that?	**Comment appelez-vous cela?**	komahng ahperlayvoo serlah
What does this mean?	**Que veut dire ceci?**	ker vur deer serssee
What does that mean?	**Que veut dire cela?**	ker vur deer serlah

Do you speak . . . ?

Do you speak English?	**Parlez-vous anglais?**	pahrlayvoo ahngglay
Do you speak German?	**Parlez-vous allemand?**	pahrlayvoo ahlmahng
Do you speak French?	**Parlez-vous français?**	pahrlayvoo frahngsay
Do you speak Spanish?	**Parlez-vous espagnol?**	pahrlayvoo ehspahñol
Do you speak Italian?	**Parlez-vous italien?**	pahrlayvoo eetahlyang
Could you speak more slowly, please?	**Pourriez-vous parler plus lentement, s'il vous plaît?**	pooreeayvoo pahrlay plew lahngtermahng seelvooplay
Please point to the phrase in the book.	**Montrez-moi la phrase dans le livre, s'il vous plaît.**	mawngtraymwah lah frahz dahng ler leevr seelvooplay
Just a minute. I'll see if I can find it in this book.	**Un instant. Je vais voir si je la trouve dans ce livre.**	angnangstahng. zher vay vwahr see zher lah troov dahng ser leevr
I understand.	**Je comprends.**	zher kawngprahng
I don't understand.	**Je ne comprends pas.**	zher ner kawngprahng pah

Can . . . ?

Can I have . . . ?	**Puis-je avoir . . .?**	pweezh ahvwahr
Can we have . . . ?	**Pouvons-nous avoir . . .?**	poovawngnoo ahvwahr
Can you show me . . . ?	**Pouvez-vous m'indiquer . . .?**	poovayvoo mangdeekay
Can you tell me . . . ?	**Pouvez-vous me dire . . .?**	poovayvoo mer deer
Can you help me, please?	**Pouvez-vous m'aider, s'il vous plaît?**	poovayvoo mayday seelvooplay

Wanting

I'd like . . .	**Je voudrais . . .**	zher voodray
We'd like . . .	**Nous voudrions . . .**	noo voodreeawng
Please give me . . .	**S'il vous plaît, donnez-moi . . .**	seelvooplay donaymwah
Give it to me, please.	**Donnez-le moi, s'il vous plaît.**	donaylermwah seelvoo-play
Please bring me . . .	**S'il vous plaît, apportez-moi . . .**	seelvooplay ahpor-taymwah
Bring it to me, please.	**Apportez-le moi, s'il vous plaît.**	ahportayler mwah seelvooplay
I'm hungry.	**J'ai faim.**	zhay fang
I'm thirsty.	**J'ai soif.**	zhay swahf
I'm tired.	**Je suis fatigué.**	zher swee fahteegay
I'm lost.	**Je me suis perdu.**	zher mer swee pehrdew
It's important.	**C'est important.**	saytangportahng
It's urgent.	**C'est urgent.**	saytewrzhahng
Hurry up!	**Dépêchez-vous!**	daypayshayvoo

It is/There is . . .

It is/It's . . .	**C'est . . .**	say
Is it . . . ?	**Est-ce . . .?**	ehss
It isn't . . .	**Ce n'est pas . . .**	ser nay pah

FRENCH

There is/There are . . .	**Il y a . . .**	eel ee ah
Is there/Are there . . . ?	**Y a-t-il . . . ?**	ee ahteel
There isn't/There aren't . . .	**Il n'y a pas . . .**	eel nee ah pah
There isn't any/ There aren't any.	**Il n'y en a pas.**	eel nee ahngnah pah

A few common words

big/small	**grand/petit**	grahng/pertee
quick/slow	**rapide/lent**	rahpeed/lahng
early/late	**tôt/tard**	toa/tahr
cheap/expensive	**bon marché/cher**	bawng mahrshay/shehr . . .
near/far	**près/loin**	pray/lwang
hot/cold	**chaud/froid**	shoa/frwah
full/empty	**plein/vide**	plang/veed
easy/difficult	**facile/difficile**	fahsseel/deefeesseel
heavy/light	**lourd/léger**	loor/layzhay
open/shut	**ouvert/fermé**	oovair/fehrmay
right/wrong	**juste/faux**	zhewst/foa
old/new	**ancien/nouveau**	ahngsyang/noovoa
old/young	**vieux/jeune**	vyur/zhurn
beautiful/ugly	**beau/laid**	boa/lay
good/bad	**bon/mauvais**	bawng/movay
better/worse	**meilleur/pire**	mayyurr/peer

Some prepositions and a few more useful words

at	**à**	ah
on	**sur**	sewr
in	**dans**	dahng
to	**à**	ah
from	**de**	der
inside	**dedans**	derdahng
outside	**dehors**	derawr
up	**en haut**	ahng oa
down	**en bas**	ahng bah
before	**avant**	ahvahng
after	**après**	ahpray
with	**avec**	ahvehk
without	**sans**	sahng
through	**à travers**	ah trahvehr
towards	**vers**	vehr
until	**jusqu'à**	zhewskah
during	**pendant**	pahngdahng
and	**et**	ay

or	**ou**	oo
not	**ne . . . pas**	ner . . . pah
nothing	**rien**	ryang
none	**aucun**	oakang
very	**très**	tray
also	**aussi**	oasee
soon	**bientôt**	byangtoa
perhaps	**peut-être**	purtehtr
here	**ici**	eesee
there	**là**	lah
now	**maintenant**	mangternahng
then	**alors**	ahlawr

Arrival

Your passport, please.	**Votre passeport, s'il vous plaît.**	votr pahsspawr seel-vooplay
Here it is.	**Le voici.**	lervwahsee
Have you anything to declare?	**Avez-vous quelque chose à déclarer?**	ahvayvoo kehlkershoaz ah dayklahray
No, nothing at all.	**Non, rien du tout.**	nawng ryang dew too
Porter!	**Porteur!**	porturr
Can you help me with my luggage, please?	**Pouvez-vous prendre mes bagages, s'il vous plaît?**	poovayvoo prahngdr may bahgahzh seelvooplay
That's my suitcase.	**C'est ma valise.**	say mah vahleez
Where's the bus to the centre of town, please?	**Où est le bus qui va en ville, s'il vous plaît?**	oo ay ler bewss kee vah ahng veel seelvooplay
This way, please.	**Par ici, s'il vous plaît.**	pahr eessee seelvooplay

Changing money

Can you change a traveller's cheque, please?	**Pouvez-vous changer un chèque de voyage, s'il vous plaît?**	poovayvoo shanhngzhay ang shekh der vwahyahzh seelvooplay
Where's the nearest bank, please?	**Où est la banque la plus proche, s'il vous plaît?**	oo ay lah bahngk lah plew prosh seelvooplay

Car rental

I'd like a car.	**Je voudrais une voiture.**	zher voodray ewn vwahtewr
For how long?	**Pour combien de temps?**	poor kawngbyang der tahng
A day/Four days/ A week/Two weeks.	**Un jour/Quatre jours/ Une semaine/Deux semaines.**	ang zhoor/kahtr zhoor/ewn sermehn/dur sermehn

Taxi

Where can I get a taxi?	**Où puis-je avoir un taxi?**	oo pweezh ahvwahr ang tahksee
What's the fare to . . . ?	**Quel est le tarif pour . . . ?**	kehl ay ler tahreef poor
Take me to this address, please.	**Conduisez-moi à cette adresse, s'il vous plaît.**	kawngdweezaymwah ah seht ahdrehss seelvooplay
I'm in a hurry.	**Je suis pressé.**	zher swee prehssay
Could you drive more slowly, please?	**Pourriez-vous conduire plus lentement, s'il vous plaît?**	pooreeayvoo kawngdweer plew lahngtermahng seelvooplay

Hotel and other accommodation

My name is . . .	**Je m'appelle . . .**	zher mahpehl
Have you a reservation?	**Avez-vous fait réserver?**	ahvayvoo fay rayzehrvay
Yes, here's the confirmation.	**Oui, voici la confirmation.**	wee, vwahsee lah kawngfeermahsyawng
I'd like . . .	**J'aimerais . . .**	zhehmerray
I'd like a single room/a double room.	**J'aimerais une chambre pour une personne/pour deux personnes.**	zhehmerray ewn shahngbr poor ewn pehrson/poor dur pehrson
a room with a bath/with a shower	**une chambre avec bain/avec douche**	ewn shahngbr ahvehk bang/ahvehk doosh

How much?

What's the price per night/per week/per month?	**Quel est le prix pour une nuit/pour une semaine/pour un mois?**	kehl ay ler pree poor ewn nwee/poor ewn sermehn/poor ang mwah
May I see the room?	**Puis-je voir la chambre?**	pweezh vwahr lah shahngbr
I'm sorry, I don't like it.	**Je regrette, elle ne me plaît pas.**	zher rergreht ehl ner mer play pah
Yes, that's fine. I'll take it.	**Oui, c'est bien. Je la prends.**	wee say byang. zher lah prahng
What's my room number, please?	**Quel est le numéro de ma chambre, s'il vous plaît?**	kehl ay ler newmayroa der mah shahngbr seel-vooplay
Number 123.	**Numéro 123.**	newmayroa 123.

Service, please

Who is it?	**Qui est-ce?**	kee ehss
Just a minute.	**Un instant, s'il vous plaît.**	angnangstahng seel-vooplay
Come in! The door's open.	**Entrez! La porte est ouverte.**	ahngtray! lah port aytoovairt
May we have breakfast in our room?	**Pouvons-nous prendre le petit déjeuner dans notre chambre?**	poovawngnoo prahngdr le pertee dayzhurnay dahng notr shahngbr

Breakfast

I'll have ...	**Je voudrais ...**	zher voodray
I'll have some fruit juice.	**Je voudrais un jus de fruit.**	zher voodray ang zhew der frwee
a boiled egg	**un œuf à la coque**	angnurf ah lah kok
a fried egg	**un œuf sur le plat**	angnurf sewr ler plah
some bacon/some ham	**du bacon/du jambon**	dew baykern/dew zhahngbawng
some toast	**des toasts**	day toast
a pot of tea	**du thé**	dew tay
a cup of tea	**une tasse de thé**	ewn tahss der tay
some coffee	**du café**	dew kahfay
some chocolate	**du chocolat**	dew shokolah
more butter	**davantage de beurre**	dahvahngtahzh der burr
some hot water	**de l'eau chaude**	der loa shoad

Difficulties

The central heating doesn't work.	**Le chauffage central ne marche pas.**	ler shoafahzh sahngtrahl ner mahrsh pah
the light/the socket the tap/the toilet	**la lumière/la prise le robinet/les toilettes**	lah lewmyair/lah preez ler robeenay/lay twahleht
There's no hot water.	**Il n'y a pas d'eau chaude.**	eel nee ah pah doa shoad
May I see the manager, please?	**Puis-je voir le directeur, s'il vous plaît?**	pweezh vwahr ler deerehkturr seelvooplay

Telephone—Mail

There's a call for you.	**Il y a un appel pour vous.**	eel ee ah angnahpehl poor voo
Hold the line, please.	**Ne quittez pas, s'il vous plaît.**	ner keetay pah seelvoo-play
Operator, I've been cut off.	**Mademoiselle, la communication a été coupée.**	mahdmwahzehl lah komewneekahsyawng ah aytay koopay
Did anyone telephone me?	**Est-ce qu'on m'a appelé?**	ehss kawng mah ahperlay
Is there any mail for me?	**Y a-t-il du courrier pour moi?**	ee ahteel dew kooreeay poor mwah
Are there any messages for me?	**Y a-t-il un message pour moi?**	ee ahteel ang mehssahzh poor mwah

Checking out

May I have my bill, please?	**Puis-je avoir ma note, s'il vous plaît?**	pweezh ahvwahr mah not seelvooplay
We're in a great hurry.	**Nous sommes très pressés.**	noo som tray prehssay
It's been a very enjoyable stay.	**Le séjour a été très agréable.**	ler sayzhoor ah aytay trayzahgrayahbl

Eating out

Good evening, sir/ Good evening, madam.	**Bonsoir, Monsieur/ Bonsoir, Madame.**	bawngswahr mersyur/ bawngswahr mahdahm

Good evening, I'd like a table for two, please.	**Bonsoir. Je voudrais une table pour deux personnes, s'il vous plaît.**	bawngswahr. zher voodray ewn tahbl poor dur pehrson seelvooplay
Do you have a fixed-price menu?	**Avez-vous un menu?**	ahvayvoo ang mernew
May I see the à la carte menu?	**Puis-je voir la carte?**	pweezh vwahr lah kahrt
May we have an ashtray, please?	**Pouvons-nous avoir un cendrier, s'il vous plaît?**	poov**aw**ngnoo ahvwahr ang sahngdreeay seelvooplay
some bread	**du pain**	dew pang
a fork	**une fourchette**	ewn foorsheht
a knife	**un couteau**	ang kootoa
a spoon	**une cuillère**	ewn kweeyair
a plate	**une assiette**	ewn ahssyeht
a glass	**un verre**	ang vair
a napkin	**une serviette**	ewn sehrvyeht
another chair	**une autre chaise**	ewn oatr shaiz
Where's the gentlemen's toilet (men's room)?	**Où sont les toilettes pour messieurs?**	oo sawng lay twahleht poor maysyur
Where's the ladies' toilet (ladies' room)?	**Où sont les toilettes pour dames?**	oo sawng lay twahleht poor dahm

FRENCH

Appetizers

I'd like some ...	**Je voudrais ...**	zher voodray
I'd like some assorted appetizers.	**Je voudrais des hors-d'œuvre variés.**	zher voodray day ordurvr vahreeay
orange juice	**un jus d'orange**	ang zhew dorahngzh
ham	**du jambon**	dew zhahngbawng
melon	**du melon**	der merlawng
pâté	**du pâté**	dew pahtay
smoked salmon	**du saumon fumé**	dew soamawng fewmay
shrimps (shrimp)	**des crevettes**	day krerveht

Soup

Have you any ... ?	**Avez-vous ...?**	ahvayvoo
Have you any chicken soup?	**Avez-vous du potage au poulet?**	ahvayvoo dew potahzh oa poolay
vegetable soup	**une soupe de légumes**	ewn soop der laygewm
onion soup	**de la soupe à l'oignon**	der lah soop ah loñawng

Fish

I'd like some...	**J'aimerais...**	zhehmerray
I'd like some fish.	**J'aimerais du poisson.**	zhehmerray dew pwahssawng
sole	**de la sole**	der lah sol
trout	**de la truite**	der lah trweet
lobster	**du homard**	dew omahr
crayfish	**des écrevisses**	day aykrerveess
prawns	**des langoustines**	day lahnggoosteen
I'd like it...	**Je l'aimerais...**	zher lehmerray
I'd like it steamed.	**Je l'aimerais cuit à la vapeur.**	zher lehmerray kwee ah lah vahpurr
grilled	**grillé**	greeyay
boiled	**au court-bouillon**	oa koor booyawng
baked	**cuit au four**	kwee oa foor
fried	**frit**	free

Meat—Poultry—Game

I'd like some...	**Je voudrais...**	zher voodray
I'd like some beef.	**Je voudrais du bœuf.**	zher voodray dew burf
a beef steak	**un bifteck**	ang beeftehk
some roast beef	**du rosbif**	dew roazbeef
a veal cutlet	**une côtelette de veau**	ewn koatleht de voa
mutton	**du mouton**	dew mootawng
lamb	**de l'agneau**	der lahñoa
a pork chop	**une côtelette de porc**	ewn koatleht der pawr
roast pork	**du rôti de porc**	dew roatee der pawr
hare	**du lièvre**	dew lyehvr
chicken	**du poulet**	dew poolay
roast chicken	**du poulet rôti**	dew poolay roatee
duck	**du canard**	dew kahnahr
How do you like your meat?	**Comment désirez-vous la viande?**	komahng dayzeerayvoo lah vyahngd
rare	**saignante**	sehñahngt
medium	**à point**	ah pwang
well done	**bien cuite**	byang kweet

Vegetables

What vegetables have you got?	**Quels légumes servez-vous?**	kehl laygewm sehrvayvoo
I'd like some . . .	**Je voudrais . . .**	zher voodray
I'd like some asparagus.	**Je voudrais des asperges.**	zher voodray dayzahspehrzh
green beans	**des haricots verts**	day ahreekoa vair
mushrooms	**des champignons**	day shahngpeeñawng
carrots	**des carottes**	day kahrot
onions	**des oignons**	dayzoñawng
red cabbage	**du chou rouge**	dew shoo roozh
spinach	**des épinards**	dayzaypeenahr
rice	**du riz**	dew ree
peas	**des petits pois**	day pertee pwah
tomatoes	**des tomates**	day tomaht
green salad	**de la salade verte**	der lah sahlahd vairt
potatoes	**des pommes de terre**	day pom der tair

Desserts

Nothing more, thanks.	**Je ne veux plus rien, merci.**	zher ner vur plew ryang mehrsee
Just a small portion, please.	**Juste une petite portion, s'il vous plaît.**	zhewst ewn perteet porsyawng seelvooplay
Have you any ice-cream?	**Avez-vous des glaces?**	ahvayvoo day glahss
fruit salad	**une salade de fruits**	ewn sahlahd der frwee
fresh fruit	**des fruits frais**	day frwee fray
cheese	**du fromage**	dew fromahzh

Drink

What would you like to drink?	**Qu'aimeriez-vous boire?**	kehmerreeayvoo bwahr
I'll have a beer, please.	**J'aimerais une bière, s'il vous plaît.**	zhehmerray ewn byair seelvooplay
I'll have a whisky, please.	**Je voudrais un whisky, s'il vous plaît.**	zher voodray ang weeskee seelvooplay

Wine

I'd like a bottle of wine.	**Je voudrais une bouteille de vin.**	zher voodray ewn bootay der vang
red wine	**vin rouge**	vang roozh
rosé wine	**vin rosé**	vang roazay
white wine	**vin blanc**	vang blahng
Cheers!	**A votre santé!**	ah votr sahngtay

The bill (check)

May I have the bill (check) please?	**Puis-je avoir l'addition, s'il vous plaît?**	pweezh ahvwahr lahdeessyawng seelvooplay
Is service included?	**Le service est-il compris?**	ler sehrveess ayteel kawngpree
Everything's included.	**Tout est compris.**	tootay kawngpree
Thank you, that was a very good meal.	**Merci, c'était très bon.**	mehrsee saytay tray bawng

Travelling

Where's the railway station, please?	**Où se trouve la gare, s'il vous plaît?**	oo ser troov lah gahr seelvooplay
Where's the ticket office, please?	**Où est le guichet, s'il vous plaît?**	oo ay ler geeshay seelvooplay
I'd like a ticket to ...	**J'aimerais un billet pour ...**	zhehmerray ang beeyay poor
First or second class?	**Première ou deuxième classe?**	prermyair oo durzyehm klahss
First class, please.	**Première classe, s'il vous plaît.**	prermyair klahss seelvooplay
Single or return (one way or roundtrip)?	**Aller simple ou aller et retour?**	ahlay sangpl oo ahlay ay rertoor
Do I have to change trains?	**Est-ce que je dois changer de train?**	ehss ker zher dwah shahngzhay der trang
What platform does the train leave from?	**De quel quai le train part-il?**	der kehl kay ler trang pahrteel
Where's the nearest underground (subway) station?	**Où est la station de métro la plus proche?**	oo ay lah stahsyawng der maytroa la plew prosh
Where's the bus station, please?	**Où est la gare routière, s'il vous plaît?**	oo ay lah gahr rootyair seelvooplay

When's the first bus to . . . ?	**A quelle heure est le premier autobus pour . . . ?**	ah kehl urr ay ler prer-myayroatoabewss poor
the last bus	**le dernier autobus**	ler dehrnyayroatoabewss
the next bus	**le prochain autobus**	ler proshehnoatoabewss
Please let me off at the next stop.	**S'il vous plaît, déposez-moi au prochain arrêt.**	seelvooplay daypoazay-mwah oa proshehnahray

Relaxing

What's on at the cinema (movies)?	**Que donne-t-on au cinéma?**	ker dontawng oa see-naymah
What's on at the theatre?	**Que joue-t-on au théâtre?**	ker zhootawng oa tayahtr
What time does the film begin?	**A quelle heure commence le film?**	ah kehl urr komahngss ler feelm
And the play?	**Et la pièce?**	ay lah pyehss
Are there any tickets for tonight?	**Reste-t-il encore des places pour ce soir?**	rehstteel ahngkawr day plahss poor ser swahr
Where can we go dancing?	**Où pouvons-nous aller danser?**	oo poovawngnoo ahlay dahngsay
Would you like to dance?	**Voulez-vous danser?**	voolayvoo dahngsay

Introductions

How do you do?	**Bonjour.**	bawngzhoor
How are you?	**Comment allez-vous?**	komahngtahlayvoo
Very well, thank you. And you?	**Très bien, merci. Et vous?**	tray byang mehrsee. ay voo
May I introduce Miss Philips?	**Puis-je vous présenter Mademoiselle Philips?**	pweezh voo prayzahngtay mahdmwahzehl feeleeps
My name is . . .	**Je m'appelle . . .**	zher mahpehl
I'm very pleased to meet you.	**Je suis ravi de vous connaître.**	zher swee rahvee der voo konaitr

FRENCH

How long have you been here?	**Depuis combien de temps êtes-vous ici?**	derpwee kawngbyang der tahng ehtvoo eesee
It was nice meeting you.	**Enchanté d'avoir fait votre connaissance.**	ahngshahngtay dahvwahr fay votr konaysahngss

Dating

Would you like a cigarette?	**Voulez-vous une cigarette?**	voolayvoo ewn seegahreht
May I get you a drink?	**Puis-je vous offrir un verre?**	pweezh vooz offreer ang vair
Do you have a light, please?	**Avez-vous du feu, s'il vous plaît?**	ahvayvoo dew fur seelvooplay
Are you waiting for someone?	**Attendez-vous quelqu'un?**	ahtahngdayvoo kehlkang
Are you free this evening?	**Etes-vous libre ce soir?**	ehtvoo leebr ser swahr
Where shall we meet?	**Où nous retrouverons-nous?**	oo noo rertrooverrawngnoo
What time shall I meet you?	**A quelle heure vous verrai-je?**	ah kehl urr voo vairayzh
May I take you home?	**Puis-je vous ramener chez vous?**	pweezh voo rahmnay shay voo
Thank you, it's been a wonderful evening.	**Merci pour cette merveilleuse soirée.**	mehrsee poor seht mehrvayyurz swahray
What's your telephone number?	**Quel est votre numéro de téléphone?**	kehl ay votr newmayroa der taylayfon
Do you live alone?	**Habitez-vous seule?**	ahbeetayvoo surl
What time is your last train?	**A quelle heure est votre dernier train?**	ah kehl urr ay votr dairnyay trang
Good-night...	**Bonne nuit...**	bon nwee

Banks

Where's the nearest bank, please?	**Où se trouve la banque la plus proche, s'il vous plaît?**	oo ser troov lah bahngk lah plew prosh seelvooplay
Where can I cash some traveller's cheques?	**Où puis-je toucher des chèques de voyage?**	oo pweezh tooshay day shehk der vwahyahzh

What time does the bank open?	**A quelle heure la banque ouvre-t-elle?**	ah kehl urr lah bahngk oovrertehl
What time does it close?	**A quelle heure ferme-t-elle?**	ah kehl urr fairmtehl
I'm expecting some money from home. Has it arrived?	**J'attends de l'argent de la maison. Est-il arrivé?**	zhahtahng der lahrzhahng der lah mayzawng ayteel ahreevay
Can you give me some small change, please?	**Pouvez-vous me donner de la monnaie, s'il vous plaît?**	poovayvoo mer donay der lah monay seelvooplay

Shops, stores and services

Where is the nearest chemist's (pharmacy)?	**Où est la pharmacie la plus proche?**	oo ay lah fahrmahssee lah plew prosh
the nearest hairdresser's	**le coiffeur le plus proche**	le kwahfurr ler plew prosh
the photo shop	**le magasin de photographie**	le mahgahzang der foatoagrahfee
the jeweller's	**la bijouterie**	lah beezhooterree
the department store	**le grand magasin**	ler grahng mahgahzang
the police station	**le poste de police**	ler post der poleess
the garage	**le garage**	ler gahrahzh
How do I get there?	**Comment puis-je m'y rendre?**	komahng pweezh mee rahngdr
Is it within walking distance?	**Est-il possible d'y aller à pied?**	ayteel posseebl dee ahlay ah pyay

Service

Can you help me, please?	**Pouvez-vous m'aider, s'il vous plaît?**	poovayvoo mayday seelvooplay
Can you show me this? And that, too.	**Pouvez-vous me montrer ceci? Et cela aussi.**	poovayvoo mer mawngtray serssee? ay serlah oasee
It's too expensive/too big/too small.	**C'est trop cher/trop grand/trop petit.**	say troa shair/troa grahng/troa pertee
Can you show me some more?	**Pouvez-vous me montrer un plus grand choix?**	poovayvoo mer mawngtray ang plew grahng shwah
something better	**quelque chose de mieux**	kehlker shoaz der myur
something cheaper	**quelque chose de meilleur marché**	kehlker shoaz der mayyurr mahrshay

FRENCH

How much is this? And that?	**Combien coûte ceci? Et cela?**	kawngbyang koot sersee ay serlah
It's not quite what I want.	**Ce n'est pas exactement ce que je désire.**	ser nay pah ehgzahktermahng ser ker zher dayzeer
I like it.	**Cela me plaît.**	serlah mer play

Chemist's (Pharmacy)

I'd like something for a cold/for a cough/for travel sickness.	**J'aimerais quelque chose contre le rhume/contre la toux/contre le mal au cœur.**	zhehmerray kehlkershoaz kawngtr ler rewm/kawngtr lah too/kawngtr ler mahl oa kurr
Can you recommend something for hay-fever/for sunburn?	**Pouvez-vous m'indiquer quelque chose contre le rhume des foins/contre un coup de soleil?**	poovayvoo mangdeekay kehlker shoaz kawngtr ler rewm day fwang/kawngtr ang koo der solay

Toiletry

May I have some razor blades?	**Puis-je avoir des lames de rasoir?**	pweezh ahvwahr day lahm de rahzwahr
some shaving cream	**de la crème à raser**	der lah krehm ah rahzay
some toothpaste	**du dentifrice**	dew dahngteefreess
I'd like some soap.	**Je voudrais du savon.**	zher voodray dew sahvawng
some suntan oil	**de l'huile solaire**	der lweel solair

At the barber's

I'd like a haircut, please.	**Je voudrais me faire couper les cheveux, s'il vous plaît.**	zher voodray mer fair koopay lay shervur seelvooplay
Short/Leave it long.	**Courts/Laissez-les longs.**	koor/layssaylay lawng
A razor cut, please.	**Une coupe au rasoir, s'il vous plaît.**	ewn koop oa rahzwahr seelvooplay

At the hairdresser's

I'd like a shampoo and set, please.	**J'aimerais un shampooing-mise en plis, s'il vous plaît.**	zhehmerray ang shahngpwangmeezahng plee seelvooplay

I'd like a bleach.	**Je voudrais une décoloration.**	zher voodray ewn daykolorahsyawng
a permanent a colour rinse a manicure	**une permanente un rinçage une manucure**	ewn pehrmahnahngt ang rangsahzh ewn mahnewkewr

Photography

I'd like a film for this camera.	**J'aimerais un film pour cet appareil.**	zhehmerray ang feelm poor seht ahpahray
This camera doesn't work.	**Cet appareil ne marche pas.**	seht ahpahray ner mahrsh pah

At the post office

Where's the nearest post office, please?	**Où est le bureau de poste le plus proche, s'il vous plaît?**	oo ay ler bewroa der post ler plew prosh seelvooplay
I'd like to send this by express (special delivery)/by air mail.	**J'aimerais envoyer ceci par express/par avion.**	zhehmerray ahngvwahyay serssee pahr ehksprehss/pahr ahvyawng

Service stations

Where is the nearest service station, please?	**Où est la station-service la plus proche, s'il vous plaît?**	oo ay lah stahs-syawngsehrveess lah plew prosh seelvooplay
Fill her up, please.	**Le plein, s'il vous plaît.**	ler plang seelvooplay
Check the oil, please.	**Contrôlez l'huile, s'il vous plaît.**	kawngtroalay lweel seelvooplay
Would you check the tyres?	**Voudriez-vous vérifier les pneus?**	voodreeayvoo vayreefeeay lay pnur

Street directions

Can you show me on the map where I am?	**Pouvez-vous me montrer sur la carte où je me trouve?**	poovayvoo mer mawngtray sewr lah kahrt oo zher mer troov
You're on the wrong road.	**Vous n'êtes pas sur la bonne route.**	voo neht pah sewr lah bon root
Go back to ...	**Retournez à ...**	rertoornay ah

FRENCH

Go straight ahead.	**Continuez tout droit.**	kawngteeneway too drwah
It's on the left/on the right.	**C'est à gauche/à droite.**	saytah goash/ah drwaht

Accidents

May I use your telephone?	**Puis-je utiliser votre téléphone?**	pweezh ewteeleezay votr taylayfon
Call a doctor quickly.	**Appelez vite un docteur.**	ahperlay veet ang dokturr
Call an ambulance.	**Appelez une ambulance.**	ahperlay ewn ahngbewlahngss
Please call the police.	**Appelez la police, s'il vous plaît.**	ahperlay lah poleess seelvooplay

Numbers

zero	**zéro**	zayroa
one	**un**	ang
two	**deux**	dur
three	**trois**	trwah
four	**quatre**	kahtr
five	**cinq**	sangk
six	**six**	seess
seven	**sept**	seht
eight	**huit**	weet
nine	**neuf**	nurf
ten	**dix**	deess
eleven	**onze**	awngz
twelve	**douze**	dooz
thirteen	**treize**	traiz
fourteen	**quatorze**	kahtorz
fifteen	**quinze**	kangz
sixteen	**seize**	saiz
seventeen	**dix-sept**	deess-seht
eighteen	**dix-huit**	deez-weet
nineteen	**dix-neuf**	deez-nurf
twenty	**vingt**	vangt
twenty-one	**vingt et un**	vang-tay-ang
thirty	**trente**	trahngt
forty	**quarante**	kahrahngt
fifty	**cinquante**	sangkahngt
sixty	**soixante**	swahsahngt
seventy	**soixante-dix**	swahsahngtdeess
eighty	**quatre-vingts**	kahtrervang
ninety	**quatre-vingt-dix**	kahtrervangdeess
one hundred	**cent**	sahng
one thousand	**mille**	meel
ten thousand	**dix mille**	dee meel

Days

It's Sunday.	**C'est dimanche.**	say deemahngsh
Monday	**lundi**	langdee
Tuesday	**mardi**	mahrdee
Wednesday	**mercredi**	mehrkrerdee
Thursday	**jeudi**	zhurdee
Friday	**vendredi**	vahngdrerdee
Saturday	**samedi**	sahmdee
yesterday	**hier**	eeair
today	**aujourd'hui**	oazhoordwee
tomorrow	**demain**	dermang
morning/afternoon	**matin/après-midi**	mahtang/ahpraymeedee
evening/night	**soir/nuit**	swahr/nwee

Months

January	**janvier**	zhahngveeay
February	**février**	fayvreeay
March	**mars**	mahrss
April	**avril**	ahvreel
May	**mai**	may
June	**juin**	zhwang
July	**juillet**	zhweeyay
August	**août**	oot
September	**septembre**	sehptahngbr
October	**octobre**	oktobr
November	**novembre**	novahngbr
December	**décembre**	daysahngbr
Merry Christmas! Happy New Year!	**Joyeux Noël! Bonne Année!**	zhwahyur noaehl! bon ahnay

GERMAN

Guide to Pronunciation

Letter	Approximate pronunciation	Symbol	Example	
Consonants				
f, h, k, l, m n, p, t, x	normally pronounced as in English			
b	1) at the end of a word, or between a vowel and a consonant, like **p** in up	p	**ab**	ahp
	2) elsewhere as in English	b	**bis**	biss
c	1) before **e**, **i**, **ö**, and **ä**, like **ts** in hi**ts**	ts	**Celsius**	**tsehl**zeeuss
	2) elsewhere like **c** in **c**at	k	**Café**	kah**fay**
ch	like **ch** in Scottish lo**ch**	kh	**ich**	ikh
d	1) at the end of a word, or between a vowel and a consonant, like **t** in eat	t	**bald**	bahlt
	2) elsewhere, like **d** in **d**o	d	**durstig**	**dur**stikh
g	1) always hard as in **g**o, but, at the end of a word, often more like **ck** in ta**ck**	g k	**gehen** **weg**	**gay**ern vehk
	2) when preceded by **i** at the end of a word, like Scottish lo**ch**	kh	**billig**	**bi**likh
j	like **y** in **y**es	y	**Juni**	**yoo**nee
qu	like **k** followed by **v** in **v**at	kv	**Quark**	kvahrk
r	generally rolled in the back of the mouth	r	**warum**	vah**rum**

s	1) before or between vowels like **z** in **z**oo	z	**sie**	zee
	2) before **p** and **t**, at the beginning of a syllable like **sh** in **sh**ut	sh	**spät**	shpait
	3) elsewhere, like **s** in **s**it	s/ss	**es ist**	ehss ist
ß	always like **s** in **s**it	ss	**heiß**	highss
sch	like **sh** in **sh**ut	sh	**schnell**	shnehl
tsch	like **ch** in **ch**ip	ch	**deutsch**	doych
tz	like **ts** in hi**ts**	ts	**Platz**	plahts
v	like **f** in **f**or	f	**vier**	feer
w	like **v** in **v**ice	v	**wie**	vee
z	like **ts** in hi**ts**	ts	**zeigen**	**tsigh**gern

Vowels

N.B. In German, vowels are generally long when followed by **h** or by one consonant and short when followed by two or more consonants.

a	1) short, like **u** in c**u**t	ah	**hat**	haht
	2) long, like **a** in c**a**r	ar*	**Abend**	**ar**bernt
ä	1) short, like **e** in l**e**t	eh	**nächst**	nehkhst
	2) long, like **ai** in h**ai**r	ai	**spät**	sphait
e	1) short, like **e** in l**e**t	eh	**sprechen**	**shpreh**khern
	2) long, like **a** in l**a**te	ay	**gehen**	**gay**ern
	3) in unstressed syllables, like **a** in **a**bout	er*	**bitte**	**bi**ter
			geben	**gay**bern
i	1) short, like **i** in h**i**t	i	**bis**	biss
	2) long, like **ee** in m**ee**t	ee	**ihm**	eem
ie	like **ee** in b**ee**	ee	**hier**	heer
o	1) short, like **o** in g**o**t	o	**voll**	fol
	2) long, like **o** in n**o**te	oa	**ohne**	**oa**ner
ö	like **ur** in f**ur** (long or short)	ur*	**können**	**kur**nern
u	1) short, like **oo** in f**oo**t	u	**Nuß**	nuss
	2) long, like **oo** in m**oo**n	oo	**gut**	goot
ü	like French **u** in **u**ne; no English equivalent. Round your lips and try to say **ea** as in m**ea**n	ew	**über**	**ew**berr
y	like German **ü**	ew	**Symphonie**	zewmfoa**nee**

Diphthongs

ai, ay, ei, ey	like **igh** in h**igh**	igh	**mein**	mighn
au	like **ow** in n**ow**	ow	**auf**	owf
äu, eu	like **oy** in b**oy**	oy	**neu**	noy

* The **r** should not be pronounced when reading this transcription.

Some basic expressions

Yes.	**Ja.**	yar
No.	**Nein.**	nighn
Please.	**Bitte.**	**bi**ter
Thank you.	**Danke.**	**dahng**ker
Thank you very much.	**Vielen Dank.**	**fee**lern dahngk
That's all right.	**Gern geschehen.**	gairn ger**shay**ern

Greetings

Good morning.	**Guten Morgen.**	**goo**tern **mor**gern
Good afternoon.	**Guten Tag.**	**goo**tern targ
Good evening.	**Guten Abend.**	**goo**tern **ar**bernt
Good night.	**Gute Nacht.**	**goo**ter nahkht
Good-bye.	**Auf Wiedersehen.**	owf **vee**derrzayern
See you later.	**Auf bald.**	owf bahlt
This is Mr. . . .	**Das ist Herr . . .**	dahss ist hair
This is Mrs. . . .	**Das ist Frau . . .**	dahss ist frow
This is Miss . . .	**Das ist Fräulein . . .**	dahss ist **froy**lighn
I'm very pleased to meet you.	**Sehr erfreut.**	zair ehr**froyt**
How are you?	**Wie geht es Ihnen?**	vee gayt ehss **ee**nern
Very well, thank you. And you?	**Sehr gut, danke. Und Ihnen?**	zair goot **dahng**ker. unt **ee**nern
Fine.	**Gut.**	goot
Excuse me.	**Verzeihung.**	fehr**tsigh**ung

Questions

Where?	**Wo?**	voa
Where is . . . ?	**Wo ist . . . ?**	voa ist
Where are . . . ?	**Wo sind . . . ?**	voa zint
When?	**Wann?**	vahn
What?	**Was?**	vahss
How?	**Wie?**	vee
How much?	**Wieviel?**	vee**feel**
How many?	**Wie viele?**	vee**fee**ler

Who?	**Wer?**	vair
Why?	**Warum?**	vah**rum**
Which?	**Welcher/Welche/ Welches?**	**vehl**kherr/**vehl**kher/ **vehl**kherss
What do you call this?	**Wie heißt dies?**	vee highst deess
What do you call that?	**Wie heißt das?**	vee highst dahss
What does this mean?	**Was bedeutet dies?**	vahss ber**doy**tert deess
What does that mean?	**Was bedeutet das?**	vahss ber**doy**tert dahss

Do you speak . . . ?

Do you speak English?	**Sprechen Sie Englisch?**	**shpreh**khern zee **ehng**lish
Do you speak German?	**Sprechen Sie Deutsch?**	**shpreh**khern zee doych
Do you speak French?	**Sprechen Sie Französisch?**	**shpreh**khern zee frahn**tsur**zish
Do you speak Spanish?	**Sprechen Sie Spanisch?**	**shpreh**khern zee **shpar**nish
Do you speak Italian?	**Sprechen Sie Italienisch?**	**shpreh**khern zee itahl**yay**nish
Could you speak more slowly, please?	**Könnten Sie bitte langsamer sprechen?**	**kurn**tern zee **bi**ter **lahng**zarmerr **shpreh**khern
Please point to the phrase in the book.	**Bitte zeigen Sie mir den Satz im Buch.**	**bi**ter **tsigh**gern zee meer dayn zahts im bookh
Just a minute. I'll see if I can find it in this book.	**Einen Augenblick, ich sehe mal nach, ob ich es in diesem Buch finde.**	**igh**nern **ow**gernblik ikh **zay**er mahl nahkh op ikh ehss in **dee**zerm bookh **fin**der
I understand.	**Ich verstehe.**	ikh fehr**shtay**er
I don't understand.	**Ich verstehe nicht.**	ikh fehr**shtay**er nikht

Can . . . ?

Can I have . . . ?	**Kann ich . . . haben?**	kahn ikh . . . **har**bern
Can we have . . . ?	**Können wir . . . haben?**	**kur**nern veer . . . **har**bern

GERMAN

Can you show me . . . ?	**Können Sie mir . . . zeigen?**	**kur**nern zee meer . . . **tsigh**gern
Can you tell me . . . ?	**Können Sie mir sagen . . . ?**	**kur**nern zee meer **zar**gern
Can you help me, please?	**Können Sie mir bitte helfen?**	**kur**nern zee meer **bi**ter **hehl**fern

Wanting

I'd like . . .	**Ich hätte gern . . .**	ikh **heh**ter gairn
We'd like . . .	**Wir hätten gern . . .**	veer **heh**tern gairn
Please give me . . .	**Geben Sie mir bitte . . .**	**gay**bern zee meer **bi**ter
Give it to me, please.	**Bitte geben Sie es mir.**	**bi**ter **gay**bern zee ehss meer
Please bring me . . .	**Bringen Sie mir bitte . . .**	**bring**ern zee meer **bi**ter
Bring it to me, please.	**Bitte bringen Sie es mir.**	**bi**ter **bring**ern zee ehss meer
I'm hungry.	**Ich habe Hunger.**	ikh **har**ber **hung**er
I'm thirsty.	**Ich habe Durst.**	ikh **har**ber durst
I'm tired.	**Ich bin müde.**	ikh bin **mew**der
I'm lost.	**Ich habe mich verirrt.**	ikh **har**ber mikh fehr**irt**
It's important.	**Es ist wichtig.**	ehss ist **vikh**tikh
It's urgent.	**Es ist dringend.**	ehss ist **dring**ernt
Hurry up!	**Beeilen Sie sich!**	ber**igh**lern zee zikh

It is/There is . . .

It is/It's . . .	**Es ist . . .**	ehss ist
Is it . . . ?	**Ist es . . . ?**	ist ehss
It isn't . . .	**Es ist nicht . . .**	ehss ist nikht
There is/There are . . .	**Es gibt . . .**	ehss gibt
Is there/Are there . . . ?	**Gibt es . . . ?**	gibt ehss
There isn't/There aren't . . .	**Es gibt keinen/Es gibt keine/Es gibt kein . . .**	ehss gibt **kigh**nern/ehss gibt **kigh**ner/ehss gibt kighn

There isn't any/ There aren't any.	**Es gibt keinen/Es gibt keine/Es gibt keins.**	ehss gibt **kigh**nern/ehss gibt **kigh**ner/ehss gibt kighnss

A few common words

big/small	**groß/klein**	groass/klighn
quick/slow	**schnell/langsam**	shnehl/**lahng**zarm
early/late	**früh/spät**	frew/shpait
cheap/expensive	**billig/teuer**	**bi**likh/**toy**err
near/far	**nah/weit**	nar/vight
hot/cold	**heiß/kalt**	highss/kahlt
full/empty	**voll/leer**	fol/layr
easy/difficult	**leicht/schwierig**	lighkht/**shvee**rikh
heavy/light	**schwer/leicht**	shvair/lighkht
open/shut	**offen/geschlossen**	**o**fern/ger**shloss**ern
right/wrong	**richtig/falsch**	**rikh**tikh/fahlsh
old/new	**alt/neu**	ahlt/noy
old/young	**alt/jung**	ahlt/yung
beautiful/ugly	**schön/häßlich**	shurn/**hehss**likh
good/bad	**gut/schlecht**	goot/shlehkht
better/worse	**besser/schlechter**	**behss**err/**shlekh**terr

Some prepositions and a few more useful words

at	**an**	ahn
on	**auf**	owf
in	**in**	in
to	**zu**	tsoo
from	**von**	fon
inside	**drinnen**	**drin**ern
outside	**draußen**	**drow**ssern
up	**hinauf**	hin**owf**
down	**hinunter**	hin**un**ter
before	**vor**	fawr
after	**nach**	nahkh
with	**mit**	mit
without	**ohne**	**oa**ner
through	**durch**	doorkh
towards	**gegen**	**gay**gern
until	**bis**	biss
during	**während**	**vai**rernt
and	**und**	unt
or	**oder**	**oa**derr
not	**nicht**	nikht
nothing	**nichts**	nikhts
none	**kein**	kighn

very	**sehr**	zair
also	**auch**	owkh
soon	**bald**	bahlt
perhaps	**vielleicht**	fee**lighkht**
here	**hier**	heer
there	**dort**	dort
now	**jetzt**	yehtst
then	**dann**	dahn

Arrival

Your passport, please.	**Ihren Paß, bitte.**	**ee**rern pahss **bi**ter
Here it is.	**Hier, bitte.**	heer **bi**ter
Have you anything to declare?	**Haben Sie etwas zu vorzollen?**	**har**bern zee **eht**vahss tsoo fehr**tsol**ern
No, nothing at all.	**Nein, gar nichts.**	nighn garr nikhts
Porter!	**Gepäckträger!**	ger**pehk**traigerr
Can you help me with my luggage, please?	**Können Sie mir mit meinem Gepäck helfen, bitte?**	**kur**nern zee meer mit **migh**nerm ger**pehk** **hehl**fern **bi**ter
That's my suitcase.	**Das ist mein Koffer.**	dahss ist mighn **kof**err
Where's the bus to the centre of town, please?	**Wo ist der Bus zum Stadtzentrum, bitte?**	voa ist dehr buss tsum **shtaht**tsehntrum **bi**ter
This way, please.	**Hier durch, bitte.**	heer doorkh **bi**ter

Changing money

Can you change a traveller's cheque, please?	**Können Sie einen Reisescheck einlösen, bitte?**	**kur**nern zee **igh**nern **righ**zershehk **ighn**lurzern **bi**ter
Where's the nearest bank, please?	**Wo ist die nächste Bank, bitte?**	voa ist dee **nehkh**ster bahngk **bi**ter

Car rental

I'd like a car.	**Ich möchte einen Wagen.**	ikh **murkh**ter **igh**nern **var**gern
For how long?	**Für wie lange?**	fewr vee **lahng**er
A day/Four days/ A week/Two weeks.	**Einen Tag/Vier Tage/Eine Woche/ Zwei Wochen.**	**igh**nern targ/feer **tar**ger/**igh**ner **vo**kher/ tsvigh **vo**khern

GERMAN

Taxi

Where can I get a taxi?	**Wo finde ich ein Taxi?**	voa **fin**der ikh ighn **tahk**see
What's the fare to...?	**Was kostet es bis...?**	vahss **koss**tert ehss biss
Take me to this address, please.	**Fahren Sie mich bitte zu dieser Adresse.**	**far**rern zee mikh **bi**ter tsoo **dee**zerr ah**dreh**sser
I'm in a hurry.	**Ich habe es eilig.**	ikh **har**ber ehss **igh**likh
Could you drive more slowly, please?	**Könnten Sie bitte langsamer fahren?**	**kurn**tern zee **bi**ter **lahng**zarmerr **far**rern

Hotel and other accommodation

My name is...	**Mein Name ist...**	mighn **nar**mer ist
Have you a reservation?	**Haben Sie vorbestellt?**	**har**bern zee **for**bershtehlt
Yes, here's the confirmation.	**Ja, hier ist die Bestätigung.**	yar heer ist dee ber**shtai**tigung
I'd like...	**Ich hätte gern...**	ikh **heh**ter gairn
I'd like a single room/a double room.	**Ich hätte gern ein Einzelzimmer/ein Doppelzimmer.**	ikh **heh**ter gairn ighn **ighn**tserltsimerr/ighn **dop**erltsimerr
a room with a bath/with a shower	**ein Zimmer mit Bad/mit Dusche**	ighn **tsim**err mit bart/mit **du**sher

How much?

What's the price per night/per week/per month?	**Wieviel kostet es pro Nacht/pro Woche/pro Monat?**	vee**feel koss**tert ehss proa nahkht/proa **vo**kher/proa **moa**nart
May I see the room?	**Kann ich das Zimmer sehen?**	kahn ikh dahss **tsi**merr **zay**ern
I'm sorry, I don't like it.	**Bedaure, es gefällt mir nicht.**	ber**dow**rer ehss ger**fehlt** meer nikht
Yes, that's fine. I'll take it.	**Ja, sehr gut. Ich nehme es.**	yar zair goot. ikh **nay**mer ehss
What's my room number, please?	**Welche Zimmernummer habe ich, bitte?**	**vehl**kher **tsi**merrnumerr **har**ber ikh **bi**ter
Number 123.	**Nummer 123.**	**nu**merr 123

GERMAN

Service, please

Who is it?	**Wer ist da?**	vair ist dar
Just a minute.	**Einen Augenblick, bitte.**	**igh**nern **ow**gernblik **bi**ter
Come in! The door's open.	**Herein! Die Tür ist offen.**	hair**ighn**! dee tewr ist **o**fern
May we have breakfast in our room?	**Können wir in unserem Zimmer frühstücken?**	**kur**nern veer in **un**zerrerm **tsi**merr **frew**shtewkern

Breakfast

I'll have ...	**Ich möchte ...**	ikh **murkh**ter
I'll have some fruit juice.	**Ich möchte einen Fruchtsaft.**	ikh **murkh**ter **igh**nern **frookht**zahft
a boiled egg	**ein gekochtes Ei**	ighn ger**kokh**terss igh
a fried egg	**ein Spiegelei**	ighn **shpee**gerligh
some bacon/some ham	**Speck/Schinken**	shpehk/**shing**kern
some toast	**Toast**	toast
a pot of tea	**ein Kännchen Tee**	ighn **kehn**khern tay
a cup of tea	**eine Tasse Tee**	**igh**ner **tah**sser tay
some coffee	**Kaffee**	**kah**fay
some chocolate	**Schokolade**	shoakoa**lar**der
more butter	**noch etwas Butter**	nokh **eht**vahss **bu**terr
some hot water	**etwas heißes Wasser**	**eht**vahss **high**sserss **vah**sserr

Difficulties

The central heating doesn't work.	**Die Zentralheizung funktioniert nicht.**	dee tsehn**trarl**hightsung fungktseeoa**neert** nikht
the light/the socket	**das Licht/die Steckdose**	dahss likht/dee **shtehk**doazer
the tap/the toilet	**der Wasserhahn/die Toilette**	dair **vah**sserrharn/dee toy**leh**ter
There's no hot water.	**Es kommt kein warmes Wasser.**	ehss komt kighn **vahr**merss **vah**sserr
May I see the manager, please?	**Kann ich bitte den Direktor sprechen?**	kahn ikh **bi**ter dayn dee**rehk**tawr **shpreh**khern

Telephone—Mail

There's a call for you.	**Hier ist ein Anruf für Sie.**	heer ist ighn **ahn**roof fewr zee

Hold the line, please.	**Bitte bleiben Sie am Apparat.**	**bi**ter **bligh**bern zee ahm ahpah**rart**
Operator, I've been cut off.	**Fräulein, ich bin unterbrochen worden.**	**froy**lighn ikh bin unterr**bro**khern **vor**dern
Did anyone telephone me?	**Hat mich jemand angerufen?**	haht mikh **yay**mahnt **ahn**gerroofern
Is there any mail for me?	**Ist Post für mich da?**	ist post fewr mikh dar
Are there any messages for me?	**Hat jemand eine Nachricht für mich hinterlassen?**	haht **yay**mahnt **igh**ner **nahkh**rikht fewr mikh hinter**lah**ssern

Checking out

May I have my bill, please?	**Kann ich bitte meine Rechnung haben?**	kahn ikh **bi**ter **migh**ner **rehkh**nung **har**bern
We're in a great hurry.	**Wir haben es sehr eilig.**	veer **har**bern ehss zair **igh**likh
It's been a very enjoyable stay.	**Der Aufenthalt war sehr angenehm.**	dair **owf**ehnthahlt varr zair **ahn**gernaym

Eating out

Good evening, sir/ Good evening, madam.	**Guten Abend, mein Herr/Guten Abend, gnädige Frau.**	**goo**tern **ar**bernt mighn hair/**goo**tern **ar**bernt **gnai**diger frow
Good evening. I'd like a table for two, please.	**Guten Abend. Ich hätte gern einen Tisch für zwei Personen, bitte.**	**goo**tern **ar**bernt. ikh **heh**ter gairn **igh**nern tish fewr tsvigh pehr**zoa**nern **bi**ter
Do you have a fixed-price menu?	**Haben Sie ein Menü?**	**har**bern zee ighn meh**new**
May I see the à la carte menu?	**Kann ich die Speisekarte sehen?**	kahn ikh dee **shpigh**zerkahrter **zay**ern
May we have an ashtray, please?	**Können wir bitte einen Aschenbecher haben?**	**kur**nern veer **bi**ter **igh**nern **ah**shernbehkher **har**bern
some bread	**etwas Brot**	**eht**vahss broat
a fork	**eine Gabel**	**igh**ner **gar**berl
a knife	**ein Messer**	ighn **meh**sserr
a spoon	**einen Löffel**	**igh**nern **lur**ferl
a plate	**einen Teller**	**igh**nern **teh**lerr

a glass	**ein Glas**	ighn glahss
a napkin	**eine Serviette**	**igh**ner zairvee**eh**ter
another chair	**noch einen Stuhl**	nokh **igh**nern shtool
Where's the gentlemen's toilet (men's room)?	**Wo ist die Herren-toilette?**	voa ist dee **heh**rern-twahlehter
Where's the ladies' toilet (ladies' room)?	**Wo ist die Damen-toilette?**	voa ist dee **dar**mern-twahlehter

Appetizers

I'd like some ...	**Ich hätte gern ...**	ikh **heh**ter gairn
I'd like some assorted appetizers.	**Ich hätte gern gemischte Vorspeisen.**	ikh **heh**ter gairn ger**mish**ter **fawr**shpighzern
orange juice	**Orangensaft**	oa**rahng**zhernzahft
ham	**Schinken**	**shing**kern
melon	**Melone**	may**loa**ner
pâté	**Pastete**	pahss**tay**ter
smoked salmon	**geräucherten Lachs**	ger**roy**kherrtern lahks
shrimps (shrimp)	**Krevetten**	krer**veh**tern

Soup

Have you any ... ?	**Haben Sie ... ?**	**har**bern zee
Have you any chicken soup?	**Haben Sie Hühnersuppe?**	**har**bern zee **hew**nerrzuper
vegetable soup	**Gemüsesuppe**	ger**mew**zerzuper
onion soup	**Zwiebelsuppe**	**tsvee**berlzuper

Fish

I'd like some ...	**Ich hätte gern ...**	ikh **heh**ter gairn
I'd like some fish.	**Ich hätte gern Fisch.**	ikh **heh**ter gairn fish
sole	**Seezunge**	**zay**tsunger
trout	**Forelle**	fo**reh**ler
lobster	**Hummer**	**hu**merr
crayfish	**Krebs**	krayps
prawns	**Garnelen**	gahr**nay**lern
I'd like it ...	**Ich hätte es gern ...**	ikh **heh**ter ehss gairn
I'd like it steamed.	**Ich hätte es gern gedämpft.**	ikh **heh**ter ehss gairn ger**dehmpft**
grilled	**gegrillt**	ger**grillt**
boiled	**gekocht**	ger**kokht**

GERMAN

baked	**gebacken**	ger**bah**kern
fried	**in der Pfanne gebraten**	in dair **pfah**ner ger**brar**-tern

Meat—Poultry—Game

I'd like some ...	**Ich hätte gern ...**	ikh **heh**ter gairn
I'd like some beef.	**Ich hätte gern Rindfleisch.**	ikh **heh**ter gairn **rint**flighsh
a beef steak	**ein Beefsteak**	ighn **beef**stayk
some roast beef	**Roastbeef**	**rost**beef
a veal cutlet	**ein Kalbskotelett**	ighn **kahlps**kaoterleht
mutton	**Hammelfleisch**	**hah**merlflighsh
lamb	**Lammfleisch**	**lahm**flighsh
a pork chop	**ein Schweins-kotelett**	ighn **shvighns**koaterleht
roast pork	**Schweinebraten**	**shvigh**nerbrartern
hare	**Hase**	**har**zer
chicken	**Huhn**	hoon
roast chicken	**Brathühnchen**	**brar**thewnkhern
duck	**Ente**	**ehn**ter
How do you like your meat?	**Wie möchten Sie Ihr Fleisch?**	vee **murkh**tern zee eer flighsh
rare	**halbroh**	**hahl**proa
medium	**mittel**	**mi**terl
well done	**durchgebraten**	**doorkh**gerbrartern

Vegetables

What vegetables have you got?	**Was für Gemüse haben Sie?**	vahss fewr ger**mew**zer **har**bern zee
I'd like some ...	**Ich hätte gern ...**	ikh **heh**ter gairn
I'd like some asparagus.	**Ich hätte gern Spargel.**	ikh **heh**ter gairn **shparr**-gerl
green beans	**grüne Bohnen**	**grew**ner **boa**nern
mushrooms	**Pilze**	**pil**tser
carrots	**Karotten**	kah**ro**tern
onions	**Zwiebeln**	**tsvee**berln
red cabbage	**Rotkohl**	**roat**koal
spinach	**Spinat**	shpi**nart**
rice	**Reis**	righss
peas	**Erbsen**	**airp**sern
tomatoes	**Tomaten**	toa**mar**tern
green salad	**grünen Salat**	**grew**nern zah**lart**
potatoes	**Kartoffeln**	kahr**tof**ferln

Desserts

Nothing more, thanks.	**Nein danke, nichts mehr.**	nighn **dahng**ker nikhts mair
Just a small portion, please.	**Nur eine kleine Portion, bitte.**	noor **igh**ner **kligh**ner portsee**oan bi**ter
Have you any ice-cream?	**Haben Sie Eis?**	**har**bern zee ighss
fruit salad	**Obstsalat**	**oapst**zahlart
fresh fruit	**frisches Obst**	**frish**erss oapst
cheese	**Käse**	**kai**zer

Drink

What would you like to drink?	**Was möchten Sie gern trinken?**	vahss **murkh**tern zee gairn **tring**kern
I'll have a beer, please.	**Ich nehme ein Bier, bitte.**	ikh **nay**mer ighn beer **bi**ter
I'll have a whisky, please.	**Ich möchte einen Whisky, bitte.**	ikh **murkh**te **igh**nern **viss**kee **bi**ter

Wine

I'd like a bottle of wine.	**Ich möchte eine Flasche Wein.**	ikh **murkh**ter **igh**ner **flah**sher vighn
red wine	**Rotwein**	**roat**vighn
rosé wine	**Roséwein**	roa**zay**vighn
white wine	**Weißwein**	**vighss**vighn
Cheers!	**Zum Wohl!**	tsum voal

The bill (check)

May I have the bill (check) please?	**Die Rechnung, bitte.**	dee **rehkh**nung **bi**ter
Is service included?	**Ist Bedienung inbegriffen?**	ist ber**dee**nung **in**bergrifern
Everything's included.	**Alles ist inbegriffen.**	**ah**lerss ist **in**bergrifern
Thank you, that was a very good meal.	**Danke, das Essen war sehr gut.**	**dang**ker dahss **eh**ssern varr zair goot

GERMAN

Travelling

Where's the railway station, please?	**Wo ist der Bahnhof, bitte?**	voa ist dair **barn**hoaf **bi**ter
Where's the ticket office, please?	**Wo ist der Fahrkartenschalter, bitte?**	voa ist dair **farr**kahrternshahlterr **bi**ter
I'd like a ticket to...	**Ich möchte eine Fahrkarte nach...**	ikh **murkh**ter **igh**ner **farr**kahrter nahkh
First or second class?	**Erste oder zweite Klasse?**	**air**ster **oa**derr **tsvigh**ter **klah**sser
First class, please.	**Erste Klasse, bitte.**	**air**ster **klah**sser **bi**ter
Single or return (one way or round-trip)?	**Einfach oder hin und zurück?**	**ighn**fahkh **oa**derr hin unt tsu**rewk**
Do I have to change trains?	**Muß ich umsteigen?**	muss ikh **um**shtighgern
What platform does the train leave from?	**Auf welchem Bahnsteig fährt der Zug ab?**	owf **vehl**kherm **barn**shtighg fairt dair tsoog ahp
Where's the nearest underground (subway) station?	**Wo ist die nächste U-Bahnstation?**	voa ist dee **nehkh**ster **oo**barnshtahtsioan
Where's the bus station, please?	**Wo ist der Busbahnhof, bitte?**	voa ist dair **buss**barnhoaf **bi**ter
When's the first bus to...?	**Wann fährt der erste Bus nach...?**	vahn fairt dair **ehr**ster buss nahkh
the last bus	**der letzte Bus**	dair **leht**ster buss
the next bus	**der nächste Bus**	der **nehkh**ster buss
Please let me off at the next stop.	**Bitte lassen Sie mich an der nächsten Haltestelle aussteigen.**	**bi**ter **lah**ssern zee mikh ahn dair **nehkh**stern **hahl**tershtehler **owss**shtighgern

Relaxing

What's on at the cinema (movies)?	**Was gibt es im Kino zu sehen?**	vahss gibt ehss im **kee**noa tsoo **zay**ern
What's on at the theatre?	**Was gibt es im Theater?**	vahss gibt ehss im tay**ar**terr
What time does the film begin? And the play?	**Wann beginnt der Film? Und das Stück?**	vahn ber**gint** dair film? unt dahss shtewk

Are there any tickets for tonight?	**Gibt es noch Karten für heute abend?**	gibt ehss nokh **kahr**tern fewr **hoy**ter **ar**bernt
Where can we go dancing?	**Wohin können wir tanzen gehen?**	voa**hin kur**nern veer **tahn**tsern **gay**ern
Would you like to dance?	**Darf ich bitten?**	dahrf ikh **bi**tern

Introductions

How do you do?	**Guten Tag.**	**goo**tern targ
How are you?	**Wie geht es Ihnen?**	vee gayt ehss **ee**nern
Very well, thank you. And you?	**Sehr gut, danke. Und Ihnen?**	zair goot **dahng**ker. unt **ee**nern
May I introduce Miss Philips?	**Darf ich Fräulein Philips vorstellen?**	dahrf ikh **froy**lighn **fi**lips **for**shtehlern
My name is . . .	**Ich heiße . . .**	ikh **high**sser
I'm very pleased to meet you.	**Sehr erfreut.**	zair ehr**froyt**
How long have you been here?	**Wie lange sind Sie schon hier?**	vee **lahng**er zint zee shoan heer
It was nice meeting you.	**Es war mir ein Vergnügen.**	ehss varr meer ighn fehr**gnew**gern

Dating

Would you like a cigarette?	**Möchten Sie eine Zigarette?**	**murkh**tern zee **igh**ner tsigah**reh**ter
May I get you a drink?	**Darf ich Ihnen etwas zu trinken bestellen?**	dahrf ikh **ee**nern **eht**vahss tsoo **tring**kern ber**shteh**lern
Do you have a light, please?	**Haben Sie Feuer, bitte?**	**har**bern zee **foy**err **bi**ter
Are you waiting for someone?	**Warten Sie auf jemanden?**	**vahr**tern zee owf **yay**mahndern
Are you free this evening?	**Sind Sie heute abend frei?**	zint zee **hoy**ter **ar**bernt frigh
Where shall we meet?	**Wo treffen wir uns?**	voa **treh**fern veer unss
What time shall I meet you?	**Wann treffe ich Sie?**	vahn **treh**fer ikh zee
May I take you home?	**Darf ich Sie nach Hause bringen?**	dahrf ikh zee nahkh **how**zer **bring**ern

GERMAN

Thank you, it's been a wonderful evening.	**Danke, es war ein wunderbarer Abend.**	**dahng**ker ehss varr ighn **vun**derrbarrerr **ar**bernt
What's your telephone number?	**Wie ist Ihre Telephonnummer?**	vee ist **ee**rer tailai**foan**-numerr
Do you live alone?	**Wohnen Sie allein?**	**voa**nern zee ah**lighn**
What time is your last train?	**Wann fährt Ihr letzter Zug?**	vahn fairt eer **lehts**terr tsoog
Good-night...	**Gute Nacht...**	**goo**ter nahkht

Banks

Where's the nearest bank, please?	**Wo ist die nächste Bank, bitte?**	voa ist dee **nehkh**ster bahngk **bi**ter
Where can I cash some traveller's cheques?	**Wo kann ich Reiseschecks einlösen?**	voa kahn ikh **righ**zer-shehks **ighn**lurzern
What time does the bank open? What time does it close?	**Wann öffnet die Bank? Wann schließt sie?**	vahn **urf**nert dee bahngk? vahn shleest zee
I'm expecting some money from home. Has it arrived?	**Ich erwarte Geld von zu Hause. Ist es eingetroffen?**	ikh air**vahr**ter gehlt fon tsoo **how**zer. ist ehss **ighn**gertrofern
Can you give me some small change, please?	**Können Sie mir bitte Kleingeld geben?**	**kur**nern zee meer **bi**ter **klighn**gehlt **gay**bern

Shops, stores and services

Where is the nearest chemist's (pharmacy)?	**Wo ist die nächste Apotheke?**	voa ist dee **nehkh**ster ahpoa**tay**ker
the nearest hair-dresser's	**der nächste Friseur**	dair **nehkh**ster fri**zurr**
the photo shop	**das Photogeschäft**	dahss **foa**toagershehft
the jeweller's	**der Juwelier**	dair yoover**leer**
the department store	**das Warenhaus**	dahss **var**rernhowss
the police station	**die Polizeiwache**	dee poali**tsigh**vahkher
the garage	**die Garage**	dee gah**rar**zher
How do I get there?	**Wie komme ich dorthin?**	vee **ko**mer ikh dort**hin**
Is it within walking distance?	**Kann man zu Fuß gehen?**	kahn mahn tsoo fooss **gay**ern

Service

Can you help me, please?	**Können Sie mir helfen, bitte?**	**kur**nern zee meer **hehl**fern **bi**ter
Can you show me this? And that, too.	**Können Sie mir dies zeigen? Und das ebenfalls.**	**kur**nern zee meer deess **tsigh**gern? unt dahss **ay**bernfahlss
It's too expensive/too big/too small.	**Es ist zu teuer/zu groß/zu klein.**	ehss ist tsoo **toy**err/tsoo groass/tsoo klighn
Can you show me some more?	**Können Sie mir noch mehr zeigen?**	**kur**nern zee meer nokh mair **tsigh**gern
something better	**etwas Besseres**	**eht**vahss **beh**sserrerss
something cheaper	**etwas Billigeres**	**eht**vahss **bi**ligerrerss
How much is this? And that?	**Wieviel kostet dies? Und das?**	vee**feel koss**tert deess? unt dahss
It's not quite what I want.	**Es ist nicht ganz das, was ich möchte.**	ehss ist nikht gahnts dahss vahss ikh **murkh**ter
I like it.	**Es gefällt mir.**	ehss ger**fehlt** meer

Chemist's (Pharmacy)

I'd like something for a cold/for a cough/for travel sickness.	**Ich möchte etwas gegen eine Erkältung/gegen Husten/gegen Reisekrankheit.**	ikh **murkh**ter **eht**vahss **gay**gern **igh**ner ehr**kehl**tung/**gay**gern **hooss**tern/**gay**gern **righ**zerkrahngkhight
Can you recommend something for hay-fever/for sunburn?	**Können Sie mir etwas gegen Heufieber/gegen Sonnenbrand empfehlen?**	**kur**nern zee meer **eht**vahss **gay**gern **hoy**feeberr/**gay**gern **zon**ernbrahnt ehmpf**ay**lern

Toiletry

May I have some razor blades?	**Kann ich Rasierklingen haben?**	kahn ikh rah**zeer**klingern **har**bern
some shaving cream	**Rasiercreme**	ra**zeer**kraym
some toothpaste	**Zahnpasta**	**tsarn**pahstah
I'd like some soap.	**Ich hätte gern Seife.**	ikh **heh**ter gairn **zigh**fer
some suntan oil	**Sonnenöl**	**zon**ernurl

At the barber's

I'd like a haircut, please.	**Ich möchte mir das Haar schneiden lassen, bitte.**	ikh **murkh**ter meer dahss harr **shnigh**dern **lah**ssern

Short/Leave it long.	**Kurz/Lassen Sie es lang.**	koorts/**lah**ssern zee ehss lahng
A razor cut, please.	**Einen Messerschnitt, bitte.**	**igh**nern **meh**sserrshnit **bi**ter

At the hairdresser's

I'd like a shampoo and set, please.	**Waschen und legen, bitte.**	**vah**shern unt **lay**gern **bi**ter
I'd like a bleach.	**Ich möchte eine Aufhellung.**	ikh **murkh**ter **igh**ner **owf**hehlung
a permanent	**eine Dauerwelle**	**igh**ner **dow**errvehler
a colour rinse	**eine Farbspülung**	**igh**ner **fahrp**shpewlung
a manicure	**eine Maniküre**	**igh**ner mahni**kew**rer

Photography

I'd like a film for this camera.	**Ich möchte einen Film für diese Kamera.**	ikh **murkh**ter **igh**nern film fewr **dee**zer **kah**merrah
This camera doesn't work.	**Diese Kamera ist defekt.**	**dee**zer **kah**merrah ist dai**fehkt**

At the post office

Where's the nearest post office, please?	**Wo ist das nächste Postamt, bitte?**	voa ist dahss **nehkh**ster **post**ahmt **bi**ter
I'd like to send this by express (special delivery)/by air mail.	**Ich möchte dies durch Eilboten/ mit Luftpost schicken.**	ikh **murkh**ter deess doorkh **ighl**boatern/ mit **luft**post **shik**ern

Service stations

Where is the nearest service station, please?	**Wo ist die nächste Tankstelle, bitte?**	voa ist dee **nehkh**ster **tahngk**shtehler **bi**ter
Fill her up, please.	**Voll, bitte.**	fol **bi**ter
Check the oil, please.	**Kontrollieren Sie bitte den Ölstand.**	kontro**lee**rern zee **bi**ter dayn **url**shtahnt
Would you check the tyres?	**Würden Sie bitte die Reifen prüfen?**	**vewr**dern zee **bi**ter dee **righ**fern **prew**fern

Street directions

Can you show me on the map where I am?	**Können Sie mir auf der Karte zeigen, wo ich bin?**	**kur**nern zee meer owf dair **kahr**ter **tsigh**gern voa ikh bin
You're on the wrong road.	**Sie sind auf der falschen Straße.**	zee zint owf dair **fahl**shern **shtrar**sser
Go back to ...	**Fahren Sie zurück nach ...**	**far**rern zee tsoo**rewk** nahkh
Go straight ahead.	**Fahren Sie geradeaus.**	**far**rern zee gerrarder**owss**
It's on the left/on the right.	**Es ist linker Hand/rechter Hand.**	ehss ist **ling**kerr hahnt/**rehkh**terr hahnt

Accidents

May I use your telephone?	**Darf ich Ihr Telephon benutzen?**	dahrf ikh eer tailai**foan** ber**new**tsern
Call a doctor quickly.	**Rufen Sie schnell einen Arzt.**	**roo**fern zee shnehl **igh**nern ahrtst
Call an ambulance.	**Rufen Sie einen Krankenwagen.**	**roo**fern zee **igh**nern **krahng**kernvargern
Please call the police.	**Rufen Sie bitte die Polizei.**	**roo**fern zee **bi**ter dee poali**tsigh**

Numbers

zero	**null**	nool
one	**eins**	ighnss
two	**zwei**	tsvigh
three	**drei**	drigh
four	**vier**	feer
five	**fünf**	fewnf
six	**sechs**	zehks
seven	**sieben**	**zee**bern
eight	**acht**	ahkht
nine	**neun**	noyn
ten	**zehn**	tsayn
eleven	**elf**	ehlf
twelve	**zwölf**	tsvurlf
thirteen	**dreizehn**	**drigh**tsayn
fourteen	**vierzehn**	**feer**tsayn
fifteen	**fünfzehn**	**fewnf**tsayn
sixteen	**sechzehn**	**zehkh**tsayn
seventeen	**siebzehn**	**zeep**tsayn
eighteen	**achtzehn**	**ahkh**tsayn
nineteen	**neunzehn**	**noyn**tsayn

twenty	**zwanzig**	**tsvahn**tsikh
twenty-one	**einundzwanzig**	**ighn**unttsvahntsikh
thirty	**dreißig**	**drigh**ssikh
forty	**vierzig**	**feer**tsikh
fifty	**fünfzig**	**fewnf**tsikh
sixty	**sechzig**	**zehkh**tsikh
seventy	**siebzig**	**zeep**tsikh
eighty	**achtzig**	**ahkh**tsikh
ninety	**neunzig**	**noyn**tsikh
one hundred	**hundert**	**hun**derrt
one thousand	**tausend**	**tow**zernt
ten thousand	**zehntausend**	**tsayn**towzernt

Days

It's Sunday.	**Es ist Sonntag.**	ehss ist **zon**tark
Monday	**Montag**	**moan**tark
Tuesday	**Dienstag**	**deenss**tark
Wednesday	**Mittwoch**	**mit**vokh
Thursday	**Donnerstag**	**do**nerrsstark
Friday	**Freitag**	**frigh**tark
Saturday	**Sonnabend**	**zon**arbernt
yesterday	**gestern**	**gehss**terrn
today	**heute**	**hoy**ter
tomorrow	**morgen**	**mor**gern
morning/afternoon	**Vormittag/Nachmittag**	**for**mitark/**nahkh**mitark
evening/night	**Abend/Nacht**	**ar**bernt/nahkht

Months

January	**Januar**	**yah**nooarr
February	**Februar**	**fay**brooarr
March	**März**	mairts
April	**April**	ah**pril**
May	**Mai**	migh
June	**Juni**	**yoo**nee
July	**Juli**	**yoo**lee
August	**August**	ow**gust**
September	**September**	zehp**tehm**berr
October	**Oktober**	ok**toa**berr
November	**November**	noa**vehm**berr
December	**Dezember**	day**tsehm**berr
Merry Christmas! Happy New Year!	**Fröhliche Weihnachten! Glückliches Neues Jahr!**	**frur**likher **vigh**nahkhtern! **glewk**likherss **noy**erss yarr

GERMAN

GREEK

Guide to Pronunciation

Letter	Approximate pronunciation	Symbol	Example	
Vowels				
α	like the vowel in car, but pronounced further forward in the mouth	ah	άρωμα	**ah**romah
ε	like **e** in s**e**ll	eh	μέρα	**meh**rah
η, ι, υ	like **ee** in m**ee**t	ee	κύριος	**kee**reeoss
ο, ω	like **o** in g**o**t	o	παρακαλῶ	pahrahkah**lo**
Consonants				
β	like **v** in **v**ine	v	βιβλίο	vee**vlee**o
γ	1) before α, ο, ω, ου, and consonants, a voiced version of the **ch** sound in Scottish lo**ch**	ģ	μεγάλος	meh**ģah**loss
	2) before ε, αι, η, ι, υ, ει, οι, like **y** in **y**et	y	γεμᾶτος	yeh**mah**toss
δ	like **th** in **th**is	dh	δέν	dhehn
ζ	like **z** in **z**oo	z	ζεστός	ze**stoss**
θ	like **th** in **th**ing	th	θά	thah
κ	like **k** in **k**it	k	καλός	kah**loss**
λ	like **l** in **l**emon	l	λάθος	**lah**thoss
μ	like **m** in **m**an	m	μέσα	**meh**ssah

ν	like **n** in **n**ew	n	νέος	**neh**oss
ξ	like **x** in si**x**	ks	ἔξω	**eh**kso
π	like **p** in **p**ot	p	πρός	pross
ρ	like **r** in **r**ed	r	πρίν	preen
σ, ς	1) before β, γ, δ, ζ, μ, ν, ρ, like **z** in **z**oo	z	κόσμος	**koz**moss
	2) elsewhere, like **s** in **s**ee	s/ss	στό	sto
τ	like **t** in **t**ea	t	τότε	**to**teh
φ	like **f** in **f**ive	f	φέρτε	**fehr**teh
χ	like **ch** in Scottish lo**ch**	kh	ἄσχημος	**ahss**kheemoss
ψ	like **ps** in dro**psy**	ps	διψῶ	dhee**pso**

Groups of letters

αι	like **e** in g**e**t	eh	εἶναι	**ee**neh
ει, οι	like **ee** in s**ee**	ee	πεῖτε	**pee**teh
ου	like **oo** in r**oo**t	oo	μοῦ	moo
αυ	similar to **ave** in h**ave**	ahv	αὐτό	ahv**to**
ευ	like **ev** in l**ev**el	ehv	Εὐρώπη	ehv**ro**pee
γγ	like **ng** in li**ng**er	ngg	'Αγγλία	ahng**glee**ah
γκ	1) at the beginning of a word like **g** in **g**o	g	γκαμήλα	gah**mee**lah
	2) in the middle of a word, like **ng** in li**ng**er	ngg	ἄγκυρα	**ahng**geerah
γξ	like **nks** in li**nks**	ngks	φάλαγξ	**fah**lahngks
γχ	like **ng** followed by the **ch** of Scottish lo**ch**	ngkh	μελαγχολία	mehlahngkho**lee**ah
μπ	1) at the beginning of a word like **b** in **b**eer	b	μπορεῖτε	bo**ree**teh
	2) in the middle of a word like **mb** in lu**mb**er	mb	Ὄλυμπος	**o**leemboss
ντ	1) at the beginning of a word, like **d** in **d**ear	d	ντομάτα	do**mah**tah
	2) in the middle of a word, like **nd** in u**nd**er	nd	κέντρο	**kehn**dro
τζ	like **ds** in see**ds**	dz	τζάκι	**dzah**kee

Accent marks

These are written in various ways, e.g., ὰ, ά, or ᾶ, but all of them indicate the stressed syllable. The signs for the "breathing" of initial vowels (α, ἀ) can be ignored. A diaeresis (two dots) written over a letter means that the letter is pronounced separately from the previous one, e.g., καιρός is pronounced keh**ross**, but in Κάϊρο, the α and ι are pronounced separately, **kah**eero.

GREEK

The alphabet

Here are the characters which comprise the Greek alphabet. The column at left shows the printed capital and small letters, while written letters are shown in the center column. The column at right gives you the name of these letters as pronounced by Greeks.

Α α	Α α	**ahl**fah
Β β	Β β	**vee**tah
Γ γ	Γ γ	**ghah**mah
Δ δ	Δ δ	**dhehl**tah
Ε ε	Ε ε	**eh**pseelon
Ζ ζ	Ζ ζ	**zee**tah
Η η	Η η	**ee**tah
Θ θ	Θ θ	**thee**tah
Ι ι	Ι ι	yee**o**tah
Κ κ	Κ κ	**kah**pah
Λ λ	Λ λ	**lahm**dhah
Μ μ	Μ μ	mee
Ν ν	Ν ν	nee
Ξ ξ	Ξ ξ	ksee
Ο ο	Ο ο	**o**meekron
Π π	Π π	pee
Ρ ρ	Ρ ρ	ro
Σ σ ς	Σ σ ς	**seegh**mah
Τ τ	Τ τ	tahf
Υ υ	Υ υ	**ee**pseelon
Φ φ	Φ φ	fee
Χ χ	Χ χ	khee
Ψ ψ	Ψ ψ	psee
Ω ω	Ω ω	o**meh**ghah

Some basic expressions

Yes.	Ναί.	neh
No.	Ὄχι.	**o**khee
Please.	Παρακαλῶ.	pahrahkah**lo**
Thank you.	Εὐχαριστῶ.	ehvkhahree**sto**
Thank you very much.	Ευχαριστῶ πολύ.	ehvkhahree**sto** po**lee**
That's all right.	Τίποτα.	**tee**potah

Greetings

Good morning.	Καλημέρα.	kahlee**meh**rah
Good afternoon.	Καλησπέρα.	kahlee**speh**rah
Good evening.	Καλησπέρα.	kahlee**speh**rah
Good night.	Καληνύκτα.	kahlee**neek**tah
Good-bye.	Ἀντίο.	ahn**dee**o
See you later.	Εἰς τό ἐπανιδεῖν.	eess to ehpahnee**dheen**
This is Mr....	Ὁ κύριος ...	o **kee**reeoss
This is Mrs....	Ἡ κυρία ...	ee kee**ree**ah
This is Miss ...	Ἡ δεσποινίς ...	ee dhehspee**neess**
I'm very pleased to meet you.	Χαίρομαι πού σᾶς γνωρίζω.	**kheh**romeh poo sahss gno**ree**zo
How are you?	Τί κάνετε;	tee **kah**nehteh
Very well, thank you.	Πολύ καλά, εὐχαριστῶ.	po**lee** kah**lah** ehvkhahree**sto**
And you?	Καί ἐσεῖς;	keh eh**sseess**
Fine.	Πολύ καλά.	po**lee** kah**lah**
Excuse me.	Μέ συγχωρεῖτε.	meh seengkho**ree**teh

Questions

Where?	Ποῦ;	poo
Where is ... ?	Ποῦ εἶναι ... ;	poo **ee**neh
Where are ... ?	Ποῦ εἶναι ... ;	poo **ee**neh
When?	Πότε;	**po**teh
What?	Τί;	tee

How?	**Πῶς;**	poss
How much?	**Πόσο;**	**po**sso
How many?	**Πόσα;**	**po**ssah
Who?	**Ποιός;**	pee**oss**
Why?	**Γιατί;**	yeeah**tee**
Which?	**Ποιός/Ποιά/Ποιό;**	pee**oss**/pee**ah**/pee**o**
What do you call this?	**Πῶς λέγεται αὐτό;**	poss **leh**yehteh ahv**to**
What do you call that?	**Πῶς λέγεται ἐκεῖνο;**	poss **leh**yehteh eh**kee**no
What does this mean?	**Τί σημαίνει αὐτό;**	tee see**meh**nee ahv**to**
What does that mean?	**Τί σημαίνει ἐκεῖνο;**	tee see**meh**nee eh**kee**no

Do you speak ...?

Do you speak English?	**Μιλᾶτε 'Αγγλικά;**	mee**lah**teh ahnggglee**kah**
Do you speak German?	**Μιλᾶτε Γερμανικά;**	mee**lah**teh yehrmahnee**kah**
Do you speak French?	**Μιλᾶτε Γαλλικά;**	mee**lah**teh ĝahlee**kah**
Do you speak Spanish?	**Μιλᾶτε 'Ισπανικά;**	mee**lah**teh eespahnee**kah**
Do you speak Italian?	**Μιλᾶτε 'Ιταλικά;**	mee**lah**teh eetahlee**kah**
Could you speak more slowly, please?	**Μπορεῖτε νά μιλᾶτε πιό ἀργά, παρακαλῶ;**	bo**ree**teh nah mee**lah**teh pe**eo** ahr**ĝah** pahrahkah**lo**
Please point to the phrase in the book.	**Παρακαλῶ δεῖξτε τή φράση στό βιβλίο.**	pahrahkah**lo** **dheek**steh tee **frah**ssee sto vee**vlee**o
Just a minute. I'll see if I can find it in this book.	**Ἕνα λεπτό. Θά δῶ ἄν μπορῶ, νά τό βρῶ σ'αὐτό τό βιβλίο.**	**eh**nah lehp**to**. thah dho ahn bo**ro** nah to vro s ahv**to** to vee**vlee**o
I understand.	**Καταλαβαίνω.**	kahtahlah**veh**no
I don't understand.	**Δέν καταλαβαίνω.**	dhehn kahtahlah**veh**no

Can . . . ?

Can I have . . . ?	Μπορῶ νά ἔχω . . . ;	boro nah ehkho
Can we have . . . ?	Μποροῦμε νά ἔχουμε . . . ;	boroomeh nah eh-khoomeh
Can you show me . . . ?	Μπορεῖτε νά μοῦ δείξετε . . . ;	boreeteh nah moo dheek-steh
Can you tell me . . . ?	Μπορεῖτε νά μοῦ πῆτε . . . ;	boreeteh nah moo peeteh
Can you help me, please?	Μπορεῖτε νά μέ βοηθήσετε, παρακαλῶ;	boreeteh nah meh voee-theesehteh, pahrahkahlo

Wanting

I'd like . . .	Θά ἤθελα . . .	thah eethehlah
We'd like . . .	Θά θέλαμε . . .	thah thehlahmeh
Please give me . . .	Παρακαλῶ δῶστε μου . . .	pahrahkahlo dhossteh moo
Give it to me, please.	Δῶστε μοῦ το, παρακαλῶ.	dhossteh moo to pahrahkahlo
Please bring me . . .	Παρακαλῶ, φέρτε μου . . .	pahrahkahlo fehrteh moo
Bring it to me, please.	Φέρτε μοῦ το, παρακαλῶ.	fehrteh moo to pahrahkahlo
I'm hungry.	Πεινῶ.	peeno
I'm thirsty.	Διψῶ.	dheepso
I'm tired.	Εἶμαι κουρασμένος.	eemeh koorahsmehnoss
I'm lost.	Χάθηκα.	kahtheekah
It's important.	Εἶναι σοβαρό.	eeneh sovahro
It's urgent.	Εἶναι ἐπεῖγον.	eeneh ehpeeg̊on
Hurry up!	Γρήγορα!	g̊reeg̊orah

It is/There is . . .

It is/It's . . .	Εἶναι . . .	eeneh
Is it . . . ?	Εἶναι . . . ;	eeneh
It isn't . . .	Δέν εἶναι . . .	dhehn eeneh
There is/There are . . .	Ὑπάρχει/ Ὑπάρχουν . . .	eepahrkhee/eepahrkhoon

GREEK

Is there/Are there . . . ?	Ὑπάρχει/ Ὑπάρχουν . . . ;	ee**pahr**khee/ee**pahr**khoon
There isn't/There aren't . . .	Δέν ὑπάρχει/Δέν ὑπάρχουν . . .	dhehn ee**pahr**khee/ dhehn ee**pahr**khoon
There isn't any/ There aren't any.	Δέν ὑπάρχει καθόλου/Δέν ὑπάρχουν καθόλου.	dhehn ee**pahr**khee kah**tho**loo/dhehn ee**pahr**khoon kah**tho**loo

A few common words

big/small	μεγάλος/μικρός	meh**g̊ah**loss/mee**kross**
quick/slow	γρήγορος/ἀργός	**g̊ree**goross/ahr**g̊oss**
early/late	νωρίς/ἀργά	no**reess**/ahr**g̊ah**
cheap/expensive	φτηνός/ἀκριβός	ftee**noss**/ahkree**voss**
near/far	κοντά/μακρυά	kon**dah**/mahkree**ah**
hot/cold	ζεστός/κρῦος	zeh**stoss**/**kree**oss
full/empty	γεμᾶτος/ἄδειος	yeh**mah**toss/**ah**dheeoss
easy/difficult	εὔκολος/δύσκολος	**ehv**koloss/**dhee**skoloss
heavy/light	βαρύς/ἐλαφρός	vah**reess**/ehlah**fross**
open/shut	ἀνοικτός/κλειστός	ahneek**toss**/klee**stoss**
right/wrong	σωστός/λάθος	so**stos**/**lah**thoss
old/new	παληός/καινούργιος	pahlee**oss**/keh**noor**yeeoss
old/young	γέρος/νέος	**yeh**ros/**neh**oss
beautiful/ugly	ὡραῖος/ἄσχημος	or**eh**oss/**ahss**kheemoss
good/bad	καλός/κακός	kah**loss**/kah**koss**
better/worse	καλύτερος/χειρότερος	kah**lee**tehross/khee**ro**tehross

Some prepositions and a few more useful words

at	στό	sto
on	ἐπάνω	eh**pah**no
in	μέσα	**meh**ssah
to	πρός	pross
from	ἀπό	ah**po**
inside	μέσα	**meh**ssah
outside	ἔξω	**eh**kso
up	ἐπάνω	eh**pah**no
down	κάτω	**kah**to
before	πρίν	preen
after	μετά	meh**tah**
with	μέ	meh
without	χωρίς	kho**reess**
through	ἀνάμεσα	ah**nah**mehssah
towards	πρός	pross
until	μέχρι	**meh**khree
during	κατά τή διάρκεια	ka**tah** tee dheeah**hr**keeah
and	καί	keh

or	ἤ	ee
not	δέν	dhehn
nothing	τίποτε	**tee**poteh
none	κανένα	kah**neh**nah
very	πολύ	po**lee**
also	ἐπίσης	eh**pee**sseess
soon	σύντομα	**seen**domah
perhaps	ἴσως	**ee**ssoss
here	ἐδῶ	eh**dho**
there	ἐκεῖ	eh**kee**
now	τώρα	**to**rah
then	τότε	**to**teh

Arrival

Your passport, please.	Τό διαβατήριό σας, παρακαλῶ.	to dheeahvah**tee**reeo sahss pahrahkah**lo**
Here it is.	'Ορίστε.	o**ree**steh
Have you anything to declare?	"Εχετε κάτι νά δηλώσετε;	**eh**khehteh **kah**tee nah dhee**lo**sehteh
No, nothing at all.	"Οχι, τίποτε.	**o**khee **tee**poteh
Porter!	'Αχθοφόρε!	ahkhtho**fo**reh
Can you help me with my luggage, please?	Μπορεῖτε νά μέ βοηθήσετε μέ τίς ἀποσκευές μου, παρακαλῶ;	bo**ree**teh nah meh vo-ee**thee**ssehteh meh teess ahposkeh**vehss** moo pahrahkah**lo**
That's my suitcase.	Αὐτή εἶναι ἡ βαλίτσα μου.	ah**ftee** eeneh ee vah**leet**-sah moo
Where's the bus to the centre of town, please?	Ποῦ εἶναι τό λεωφορεῖο γιά τό κέντρο τῆς πόλεως, παρακαλῶ;	poo **ee**neh to lehofo**ree**o yee**ah** to **keh**ndro teess **po**lehoss pahrahkah**lo**
This way, please.	'Από ἐδῶ, παρακαλῶ.	ah**po** eh**dho** pahrahkah**lo**

Changing money

Can you change a traveller's cheque, please?	Μπορεῖτε νά ἀλλάξετε ἕνα τράβελερ τσέκ, παρακαλῶ;	bo**ree**teh nah ah**lah**kseh-teh **eh**nah **trah**vehlehr tsehk pahrahkah**lo**
Where's the nearest bank, please?	Ποῦ εἶναι ἡ πλησιέστερη τράπεζα, παρακαλῶ;	poo **ee**neh ee pleessee**eh**stehree **trah**pehzah pahrahkah**lo**

GREEK

Car rental

I'd like a car.	**Θά ἤθελα ἕνα αὐτοκίνητο.**	thah **ee**thehlah **eh**nah ahfto**kee**neeto
For how long?	**Γιά πόσο καιρό;**	yee**ah** **po**sso keh**ro**
A day/Four days/ A week/Two weeks.	**Μία ἡμέρα/ Τέσσερεις ἡμέρες/ Μία ἑβδομάδα/ Δύο ἑβδομάδες.**	**mee**ah ee**meh**rah/ **teh**ssehreess ee**meh**rehss/ **mee**ah ehvdho**mah**dhah/ **dhee**o ehvdho**mah**dhehss

Taxi

Where can I get a taxi?	**Ποῦ μπορῶ νά βρῶ ἕνα ταξί;**	poo bo**ro** nah vro **eh**nah tah**ksee**
What's the fare to . . . ?	**Ποιά εἶναι ἡ τιμή γιά . . . ;**	pee**ah** **ee**neh ee tee**mee** yeeah
Take me to this address, please.	**Πηγαίνετέ με σ'αὐτή τή διεύθυνσι, παρακαλῶ.**	pee**yeh**neh**teh** meh sahf**tee** tee dhee**ehf**theensee pahrahkah**lo**
I'm in a hurry.	**Εἶμαι βιαστικός.**	**ee**meh veeahstee**koss**
Could you drive more slowly, please?	**Μπορεῖτε νά ὁδηγῆτε πιό ἀργά, παρακαλῶ;**	bo**ree**teh nah odhee**yee**teh peeoo ahr**gah** pahrahkah**lo**

Hotel and other accommodation

My name is . . .	**Τό ὄνομά μου εἶναι . . .**	to **o**no**mah** moo **ee**neh
Have you a reservation?	**Ἔχετε κρατήσει δωμάτιο;**	**eh**khehteh krah**tee**ssee dho**mah**teeo
Yes, here's the confirmation.	**Μάλιστα, ἰδού ἡ διαβεβαίωση.**	**mah**leestah ee**dhoo** ee dheeahveh**veh**ossee
I'd like . . .	**Θά ἤθελα . . .**	thah **ee**thehlah
I'd like a single room/a double room.	**Θά ἤθελα ἕνα μονό δωμάτιο/ἕνα διπλό δωμάτιο.**	thah **ee**thehlah **eh**nah mo**no** dho**mah**teeo/**eh**nah dhee**plo** dho**mah**teeo
a room with a bath/ with a shower	**ἕνα δωμάτιο μέ μπάνιο/μέ ντούς**	**eh**nah dho**mah**teeo meh **bah**neeo/meh dooss

How much?

What's the price per night/per week/per month?	**Ποιά εἶναι ἡ τιμή γιά μία νύχτα/μία ἑβδομάδα/ἕνα μῆνα;**	pee**ah** **ee**neh ee tee**mee** yee**ah** **mee**ah **nee**khtah/ **mee**ah ehvdho**mah**dhah/ **eh**nah **mee**nah
May I see the room?	**Μπορῶ νά δῶ τό δωμάτιο;**	bo**ro** nah dho to dho**mah**teeo

GREEK

I'm sorry, I don't like it.	**Μέ συγχωρεῖτε, δέν μοῦ ἀρέσει.**	meh seenkho**ree**teh dhehn moo ah**reh**ssee
Yes, that's fine. I'll take it.	**Ναί, εἶναι καλό. Θά τό πάρω.**	neh **ee**neh kah**lo**. thah to **pah**ro
What's my room number, please?	**Ποιός εἶναι ὁ ἀριθμός τοῦ δωματίου μου, παρακαλῶ;**	pee**oss ee**neh o ahreeth**moss** too dhomah**tee**oo moo pahrahkah**lo**
Number 123.	**Νούμερο 123.**	**noo**mehro 123

Service, please

Who is it?	**Ποιός εἶναι;**	pee**oss ee**neh
Just a minute.	**Ἕνα λεπτό.**	**eh**nah leh**pto**
Come in! The door's open.	**Ὁρίστε. Ἡ πόρτα εἶναι ἀνοικτή.**	o**ree**steh. ee **por**tah **ee**neh ahnee**ktee**
May we have breakfast in our room?	**Μποροῦμε νά πάρουμε τό πρόγευμα στό δωμάτιό μας;**	bo**roo**meh nah **pah**roomeh to **pro**yehvmah sto dho**mah**teeo mahss

Breakfast

I'll have ...	**Θά πάρω ...**	thah **pah**ro
I'll have some fruit juice.	**Θά πάρω ἕνα χυμό φρούτων.**	thah **pah**ro **eh**nah khee**mo froo**ton
a boiled egg	**ἕνα βραστό αὐγό**	**eh**nah vrah**sto** ahv**go**
a fried egg	**ἕνα τηγανιτό αὐγό**	**eh**nah teeyahnee**to** ahv**go**
some bacon/some ham	**χοιρομέρι/ζαμπόν**	kheero**meh**ree zahm**bon**
some toast	**μερικά τόστ**	mehree**kah** tost
a pot of tea	**τσάϊ**	**tsah**ee
a cup of tea	**ἕνα φλυτζάνι τσάϊ**	**eh**nah fleen**tzah**nee **tsah**ee
some coffee	**καφέ**	kah**feh**
some chocolate	**κακάο**	kah**kah**o
more butter	**περισσότερο βούτυρο**	pehree**sso**tehro **voo**teero
some hot water	**ζεστό νερό**	zeh**sto** neh**ro**

Difficulties

The central heating doesn't work.	**Ἡ κεντρική θέρμανση δέν δουλεύει.**	ee kehndhree**kee thehr**mahnsee dhehn dhoo**leh**vee
the light/the socket	**τό φῶς/ἡ πρίζα**	to foss/ee **pree**zah
the tap/the toilet	**τό ρομπινέ/ἡ τουαλέττα**	to rombee**neh**/ee tooah**leh**tah

There's no hot water.	**Δέν ἔχει ζεστό νερό.**	dhehn **eh**khee zeh**sto** neh**ro**
May I see the manager, please?	**Μπορῶ νά δῶ τόν διευθυντή, παρακαλῶ;**	bo**ro** nah dho ton dheeehftheen**dee** pahrahkah**lo**

Telephone—Mail

There's a call for you.	**Σας ζητοῦν στό τηλέφωνο.**	sahss zee**toon** sto tee**leh**fono
Hold the line, please.	**Περιμένετε στό ἀκουστικό σας, παρακαλῶ.**	pehree**meh**nehteh sto ahkoostee**ko** sahss pahrahkah**lo**
Operator, I've been cut off.	**Δεσποινίς μέ διέκοψαν.**	dhehspee**neess** meh dheee**eh**kopsahn
Did anyone telephone me?	**Μοῦ τηλεφώνησε κανείς;**	moo teeleh**fo**neesseh kah**neess**
Is there any mail for me?	**Ὑπάρχουν γράμματα γιά μένα;**	ee**pahr**khoon **g̊rah**mahtah yee**ah** **meh**nah
Are there any messages for me?	**Ὑπάρχουν παραγγελίες γιά μένα;**	ee**pahr**khoon pahrzhnggeh**lee**ehss yee**ah** **meh**nah

Checking out

May I have my bill, please?	**Μπορῶ νά ἔχω τόν λογαριασμό, παρακαλῶ;**	bo**ro** nah **eh**kho ton log̊ahreeahz**mo** pahrahkah**lo**
We're in a great hurry.	**Εἴμαστε πολύ βιαστικοί.**	**ee**mahsteh po**lee** veeah-stee**kee**
It's been a very enjoyable stay.	**Ἡ διαμονή ἦταν πολύ εὐχάριστη.**	eedheeahmo**nee** **ee**tahn po**lee** ehf**khah**reestee

Eating out

Good evening, sir/Good evening, madam.	**Καλησπέρα, κύριε/Καλησπέρα, κυρία.**	kahlee**speh**rah **kee**reeeh/kahlee**speh**rah kee**ree**ah
Good evening. I'd like a table for two, please.	**Καλησπέρα. Θά ἤθελα ἕνα τραπέζι γιά δύο, παρακαλῶ.**	kahlee**speh**rah. thah **ee**thehlah **eh**nah trah**peh**zee yee**ah** **dhee**o pahrahkah**lo**
Do you have a fixed-price menu?	**Ἔχετε φαγητό μέ καθωρισμένη τιμή;**	**eh**khehteh fahyee**to** meh kahthoreez**meh**nee tee**mee**

May I see the à la carte menu?	Μπορῶ νά δῶ τό μενοῦ ά-λά-κάρτ;	bo**ro** nah dho to meh**noo** ahlahkahrt
May we have an ashtray, please?	Μποροῦμε νά ἔχουμε ἕνα σταχτοδοχεῖο, παρακαλῶ;	bo**roo**meh nah **eh**khoomeh **eh**nah stahktodho**khee**o pahrahkah**lo**
some bread	ψωμί	pso**mee**
a fork	ἕνα πειρούνι	**eh**nah pee**roo**nee
a knife	ἕνα μαχαίρι	**eh**nah mah**kheh**ree
a spoon	ἕνα κουτάλι	**eh**nan koo**tah**lee
a plate	ἕνα πιάτο	**eh**nah pee**ah**to
a glass	ἕνα ποτήρι	**eh**nah po**tee**ree
a napkin	ἕνα τραπεζομάντηλο	**eh**nah trahpehzo**mahn**deelo
another chair	μία καρέκλα ἀκόμη	**mee**ah kah**reh**klah ah**ko**mee
Where's the gentlemen's toilet (men's room)?	Ποῦ εἶναι οἱ τουαλέττες τῶν ἀνδρῶν;	poo **ee**neh ee tooah**leh**tehss ton ahn**dhron**
Where's the ladies' toilet (ladies' room)?	Ποῦ εἶναι οἱ τουαλέττες τῶν γυναικῶν;	poo **ee**neh ee tooah**leh**tehss ton yeeneh**kon**

GREEK

Appetizers

I'd like some ...	Θά ἤθελα ...	thah **ee**thehlah
I'd like some assorted appetizers.	Θά ἤθελα μία ποικιλία ὀρεκτικῶν.	thah **ee**thehlah **mee**ah peekee**lee**ah orehktee**kon**
orange juice	ἕνα χυμό πορτοκαλιοῦ	**eh**nah khee**mo** portokahlee**oo**
ham	ζαμπόν	zahm**bon**
melon	πεπόνι	peh**po**nee
pâté	πατέ	pah**teh**
smoked salmon	καπνιστό σολωμό	kahpnee**sto** solo**mo**
shrimps (shrimp)	γαρίδες	ğah**ree**dhehss

Soup

Have you any ... ?	Ἔχετε ... ;	**eh**khehteh
Have you any chicken soup?	Ἔχετε κοτόσουπα;	**eh**khehteh ko**to**ssoopah
vegetable soup	χορτόσουπα	khor**to**ssoopah
onion soup	κρεμμυδόσουπα	krehmee**dho**ssoopah

Fish

I'd like some...	Θά ἤθελα...	thah **ee**thehlah
I'd like some fish.	Θά ἤθελα ψάρι.	thah **ee**thehlah **psah**ree
sole	γλῶσσα	**ĝlo**sah
trout	πέστροφα	**peh**strofah
lobster	ἀστακό	ahstah**ko**
crayfish	καραβίδες	kahrah**vee**dhehss
prawns	καβούρια	kah**voo**reeah
I'd like it...	Θά τό ἤθελα...	thah to **ee**thehlah
I'd like it steamed.	Θά τό ἤθελα στόν ἀτμό.	thah to **ee**thehlah ston aht**mo**
grilled	ψητό	psee**to**
boiled	βραστό	vrah**sto**
baked	μαγειρευμένο	mahyeerehv**meh**no
fried	τηγανιτό	teeĝahnee**to**

Meat—Poultry—Game

I'd like some...	Θά ἤθελα...	thah **ee**thehlah
I'd like some beef.	Θά ἤθελα μοσχάρι.	thah **ee**thehlah moss**khah**ree
a beef steak	μία μπριζόλα	**mee**ah bree**zo**lah
some roast beef	ροζ-μπήφ	roz**beef**
a veal cutlet	μία μοσχαρίσια μπριζόλα	**mee**ah mosskhah**ree**-sseeah bree**zo**lah
mutton	ἀρνί	ahr**nee**
lamb	ἀρνάκι γάλακτος	ahr**nah**kee **ĝah**lahktoss
a pork chop	μία χοιρινή μπριζόλα	**mee**ah kheeree**nee** bree**zo**lah
roast pork	ψητό χοιρινό	psee**to** kheeree**no**
hare	λαγό	lah**ĝo**
chicken	κοτόπουλο	ko**to**poolo
roast chicken	κοτόπουλο ψητό	ko**to**poolo psee**to**
duck	πάπια	**pah**peeah
How do you like your meat?	Πῶς θέλετε τό κρέας σας;	poss **theh**lehteh to **kreh**ahss sahss
rare	λίγο ψημένο	**lee**ĝo psee**meh**no
medium	μέτριο	**meh**treeo
well done	καλοψημένο	kahlopsee**meh**no

Vegetables

What vegetables have you got?	Τί λαχανικά ἔχετε;	tee lahkhahneek**ah** **eh**khehteh
I'd like some...	Θά ἤθελα...	thah **ee**thehlah

GREEK

I'd like some asparagus.	Θά ἤθελα σπαράγγια.	thah **ee**thehlah spah**rahng**geeah
green beans	φασόλια φρέσκα	fah**sso**leeah **freh**skah
mushrooms	μανιτάρια	mahnee**tah**reeah
carrots	καρόττα	kah**ro**tah
onions	κρεμμύδια	kreh**mee**dheeah
red cabbage	κόκκινο λάχανο	**ko**keeno **lah**khahno
spinach	σπανάκι	spah**nah**kee
rice	ρύζι	**ree**zee
peas	μπιζέλια	bee**zeh**leeah
tomatoes	τομάτες	to**mah**tehss
green salad	πράσινη σαλάτα	**prah**sseenee sah**lah**tah
potatoes	πατάτες	pah**tah**tehss

Desserts

Nothing more, thanks.	Τίποτε ἄλλο, εὐχαριστῶ.	**tee**poteh **ah**lo ehfkhahree**sto**
Just a small portion, please.	Μία μικρή μερίδα, παρακαλῶ.	**mee**ah mee**kree** meh**ree**dhah pahrahkah**lo**
Have you any ice-cream?	Ἔχετε παγωτά;	**eh**khehteh pahg̊o**tah**
fruit salad	φρουτοσαλάτα	frootossah**lah**tah
fresh fruit	φρέσκα φροῦτα	**freh**skah **froo**tah
cheese	τυρί	tee**ree**

Drink

What would you like to drink?	Τί θά θέλατε νά πιῆτε;	tee thah **theh**lahteh nah pee**ee**teh
I'll have a beer, please.	Θά πάρω μία μπύρα, παρακαλῶ.	thah **pah**ro **mee**ah **bee**rah pahrahkah**lo**
I'll have a whisky, please.	Θά πάρω ἕνα οὐΐσκυ, παρακαλῶ.	thah **pah**ro **eh**nah oo**ees**kee pahrahkah**lo**

Wine

I'd like a bottle of wine.	Θά ἤθελα ἕνα μπουκάλι κρασί.	thah **ee**thehlah **eh**nah boo**kah**lee krah**ssee**
red wine	κόκκινο κρασί	**ko**keeno krah**ssee**
rosé wine	ρόζέ κρασί	ro**zeh** krah**ssee**
white wine	ἄσπρο κρασί	**ah**spro krah**ssee**
Cheers!	Στήν ὑγειά σας.	steen eeyee**ah** sahss

GREEK

The bill (check)

May I have the bill (check) please?	Μπορῶ νά ἔχω τό λογαριασμό, παρακαλῶ;	bo**ro** nah **eh**kho to loğahreeahz**mo** pahrahkah**lo**
Is service included?	Τό φιλοδώρημα περιλαμβάνεται;	to feelo**dho**reemah pehreelahm**vah**nehteh
Everything's included.	Ὅλα περιλαμβάνονται.	**o**lah pehreelahm**vah**nondheh
Thank you, that was a very good meal.	Εὐχαριστῶ, τό γεῦμα ἦταν πολύ καλό.	ehfkhahree**sto** to **yehv**mah **ee**tahn po**lee** kah**lo**

Travelling

Where's the railway station, please?	Ποῦ εἶναι ὁ σιδηροδρομικός σταθμός, παρακαλῶ;	poo **ee**neh o seedheerodhromee**koss** stahth**moss** pahrahkah**lo**
Where's the ticket office, please?	Ποῦ εἶναι τό γραφεῖο ἐκδόσεως εἰσιτηρίων, παρακαλῶ;	poo **ee**neh to ğrah**fee**o ehk**dho**ssehoss eesseetee**ree**on pahrahkah**lo**
I'd like a ticket to...	Θά ἤθελα ενα εἰσιτήριο γιά...	thah **ee**thehlah **eh**nah eessee**tee**reeo yee**ah**
First or second class?	Πρώτη ἤ δευτέρα θέση;	**pro**tee ee dhehf**teh**rah **theh**ssee
First class, please.	Πρώτη θέση, παρακαλῶ.	**pro**tee **theh**ssee pahrahkah**lo**
Single or return (one way or round-trip)?	Ἁπλῆ διαδρομή ἤ μετ'ἐπιστροφῆς;	ah**plee** dheeahdhro**mee** ee mehtehpeestro**feess**
Do I have to change trains?	Πρέπει νά ἀλλάξω τραῖνο;	**preh**pee nah ah**lah**kso **treh**no
What platform does the train leave from?	Ἀπό ποιά ἀποβάθρα φεύγει τό τραῖνο;	ah**po** pee**ah** ahpo**vah**thrah **fehv**yee to **treh**no
Where's the nearest underground (subway) station?	Ποῦ εἶναι ὁ πλησιέστερος σταθμός τοῦ Ἠλεκτρικοῦ;	poo **ee**neh o pleessee**eh**stehross stath**moss** too eelehktree**koo**
Where's the bus station, please?	Ποῦ εἶναι ο σταθμός τῶν λεωφορείων παρακαλῶ;	poo **ee**neh o stath**moss** ton lehofo**ree**on pahrahkah**lo**

When's the first bus to . . . ?	Πότε εἶναι τό πρῶτο λεωφορεῖο γιά . . . ;	**po**teh **ee**neh to **pro**to lehofo**ree**o yee**ah**
the last bus	τό τελευταῖο λεωφορεῖο	to tehlehf**teh**o lehofo**ree**o
the next bus	τό ἑπόμενο λεωφορεῖο	to eh**po**mehno lehofo**ree**o
Please let me off at the next stop.	Παρακαλῶ, θέλω νά κατεβῶ στήν ἑπομένη στάση.	pahrahkah**lo** **theh**lo nah kahteh**vo** steen ehpo**meh**nee **stah**ssee

Relaxing

What's on at the cinema (movies)?	Τί παίζουν στόν κινηματογράφο;	tee **peh**zoon ston keeneemahto**grah**fo
What's on at the theatre?	Τί παίζουν στό θέατρο;	tee **peh**zoon sto **theh**ahtro
What time does the film begin? And the play?	Τί ὥρα ἀρχίζει τό φίλμ; Καί τό ἔργο;	tee **o**rah ahr**khee**zee to feelm? keh to **ehr**go
Are there any tickets for tonight?	Ὑπάρχουν εἰσητήρια γι'ἀπόψε;	ee**pahr**khoon eessee**tee**reeah yeeah**po**pseh
Where can we go dancing?	Ποῦ μποροῦμε νά πᾶμε νά χορέψουμε;	poo bo**roo**meh nah **pah**meh nah kho**reh**psoomeh
Would you like to dance?	Θά θέλατε νά χορέψετε;	thah **theh**lahteh nah kho**reh**psehteh

Introductions

How do you do?	Πῶς εἶσθε;	poss **ee**stheh
How are you?	Τί κάνετε;	tee **kah**nehteh
Very well, thank you. And you?	Πολύ καλά, εὐχαριστῶ. Καί ἐσεῖς;	po**lee** kah**lah** ehfkhahree**sto**. keh eh**sseess**
May I introduce Miss Philips?	Μπορῶ νά σᾶς συστήσω τή δεσποινίδα Φίλιπς;	bo**ro** nah sahss see**stee**sso tee dhehspee**nee**dhah Philips
My name is . . .	Ὀνομάζομαι . . .	ono**mah**zomeh
I'm very pleased to meet you.	Χαίρω πολύ πού σᾶς γνωρίζω.	**kheh**ro po**lee** poo sahss gno**ree**zo
How long have you been here?	Πόσο καιρό εἶσθε ἐδῶ;	**po**so keh**ro** **ee**stheh eh**dho**
It was nice meeting you.	Χάρηκα πού σᾶς γνώρισα.	**khah**reekah poo sahss **gno**reessah

Dating

Would you like a cigarette?	**Θά θέλατε ἕνα τσιγάρο;**	thah **theh**lahteh **eh**nah tseeğ**ah**ro
May I get you a drink?	**Μπορῶ νά σᾶς φέρω ἕνα ποτό;**	bo**ro** nah sahss **feh**ro **eh**nah po**to**
Do you have a light, please?	**Ἔχετε φωτιά, παρακαλῶ;**	**eh**khehteh foteeah pahrahkah**lo**
Are you waiting for someone?	**Περιμένετε κάποιον;**	pehree**meh**nehteh **kah**peeon
Are you free this evening?	**Εἶσθε ἐλεύθερη ἀπόψε;**	**ee**stheh eh**lehf**thehree ah**po**pseh
Where shall we meet?	**Ποῦ θά συναντηθοῦμε;**	poo thah seenahndee**thoo**meh
What time shall I meet you?	**Τί ὥρα θά σᾶς συναντήσω;**	tee **o**rah thah sahss seenahn**dee**sso
May I take you home?	**Μπορῶ νά σᾶς πάω στό σπίτι σας;**	bo**ro** nah sahss **pah**o sto **spee**tee sahss
Thank you, it's been a wonderful evening.	**Εὐχαριστῶ, ἦταν μία ὑπέροχη βραδυά.**	ehfkhahree**sto** **ee**tahn **mee**ah ee**peh**rokhee vrahdhee**ah**
What's your telephone number?	**Ποιός εἶναι ὁ ἀριθμός τοῦ τηλεφώνου σας;**	pee**oss** **ee**neh o ahreeth**moss** too teeleh**fo**noo sahss
Do you live alone?	**Μένετε μόνη σας;**	**meh**nehteh **mo**nee sahss
What time is your last train?	**Τί ὥρα εἶναι τό τελευταῖο τραῖνο σας;**	tee **o**rah **ee**neh to tehlehf**teh**o **treh**no sahss
Good-night . . .	**Καληνύκτα . . .**	kahlee**neek**tah

Banks

Where's the nearest bank, please?	**Ποῦ εἶναι ἡ πλησιέστερη τράπεζα, παρακαλῶ;**	poo **ee**neh ee pleesseeeh**eh**stehree **trah**pehzah pahrahkah**lo**
Where can I cash some traveller's cheques?	**Ποῦ μπορῶ νά ἐξαργυρώσω μερικά τράβελερς τσέκ;**	poo bo**ro** nah ehksahryee**ro**sso mehree**kah** **trah**vehlehrs tsehk
What time does the bank open? What time does it close?	**Τί ὥρα ἀνοίγει ἡ τράπεζα; Τί ὥρα κλείνει;**	tee **o**rah ah**nee**yee ee **trah**pehzah? tee **o**rah **klee**nee

I'm expecting some money from home. Has it arrived?	**Περιμένω χρήματα ἀπό τό σπίτι. Μήπως ἦλθαν;**	pehree**meh**no **khree**mahtah ah**po** to **spee**tee. **mee**poss **eel**thahn
Can you give me some small change, please?	**Μπορεῖτε νά μοῦ δώσετε μερικά κέρματα, παρακαλῶ;**	bo**ree**teh nah moo **dho**ssehteh mehree**kah** **kehr**mahtah pahrahkah**lo**

Shops, stores and services

Where is the nearest chemist's (pharmacy)?	**Ποῦ εἶναι τό πλησιέστερο φαρμακεῖο;**	poo **ee**neh to pleessee**eh**stehro fahrmah**kee**o
the nearest hairdresser's	**τό πλησιέστερο κουρεῖο**	to pleessee**eeh**stehro koo**ree**o
the photo shop	**τό φωτογραφεῖο**	to fotograh**fee**o
the jeweller's	**τό κοσμηματοπωλεῖο**	to kozmeemahtopol**ee**o
the department store	**τό ἐμπορικό κατάστημα**	to ehmboree**ko** kah**tah**steemah
the police station	**τό ἀστυνομικό τμῆμα**	to ahsteenomee**ko** **tmee**mah
the garage	**τό γκαράζ**	to gah**rahz**
How do I get there?	**Πῶς νά πάω ἐκεῖ;**	poss nah **pah**o eh**kee**
Is it within walking distance?	**Μπορῶ νά πάω μέ τά πόδια;**	bo**ro** nah **pa**ho meh tah **po**dheeah

Service

Can you help me, please?	**Μπορεῖτε νά μέ βοηθήσετε, παρακαλῶ;**	bo**ree**teh nah meh voee**thee**ssehteh pahrahkah**lo**
Can you show me this? And that, too.	**Μπορεῖτε νά μοῦ δείξετε αὐτό; Καί ἐκεῖνο ἐπίσης.**	bo**ree**teh nah moo **dhee**ksehteh ahf**to**? keh eh**kee**no eh**pee**sseess
It's too expensive/ too big/too small.	**Εἶναι πολύ ἀκριβό/ πολύ μεγάλο/ πολύ μικρό.**	**ee**neh po**lee** ahkree**vo**/po**lee** meh**gah**lo/ po**lee** mee**kro**
Can you show me some more?	**Μπορεῖτε νά μοῦ δείξετε περισσότερα;**	bo**ree**teh nah moo **dhee**ksehteh pehree**sso**tehrah
something better	**κάτι καλύτερο**	**kah**tee kah**lee**tehro
something cheaper	**κάτι φθηνότερο**	**kah**tee fthee**no**tehro

How much is this? And that?	Πόσο κοστίζει αὐτό; Καί ἐκεῖνο;	**po**sso ko**stee**zee ahf**to**? keh eh**kee**no
It's not quite what I want.	Δέν εἶναι ἀκριβῶς αὐτό πού θέλω.	dhehn **ee**neh ahkree**voss** ahf**to** poo **theh**lo
I like it.	Μοῦ ἀρέσει.	moo ah**reh**see

Chemist's (Pharmacy)

I'd like something for a cold/for a cough/for travel sickness.	Θά ἤθελα κάτι γιά τό κρύωμα/γιά τό βῆχα/γιά τή ναυτία.	thah **ee**thehlah **kah**tee ye**eah** to **kree**omah/yee**ah** to **vee**khah/yee**ah** tee nahf**tee**ah
Can you recommend something for hay-fever/for sunburn?	Μπορεῖτε νά μοῦ συστήσετε κάτι γιά τόν υψηλό πυρετό/ γιά τά ἐγκαύματα τοῦ ἡλίου;	bo**ree**teh nah moo sees**tee**ssehteh **kah**tee yee**ah** ton eepsee**lo** peereh**to**/ yee**ah** tah ehng**gahv**mahtah too ee**lee**oo

Toiletry

May I have some razor blades?	Μπορῶ νά ἔχω μερικά ξυραφάκια ξυρίσματος;	bo**ro** nah **eh**kho mehree**kah** kseerah**fah**keeah ksee**reez**mahtoss
some shaving cream	κρέμα ξυρίσματος	**kreh**mah ksee**reez**mahtoss
some toothpaste	ὀδοντόπαστα	odhon**do**pahstah
I'd like some soap.	Θά ἤθελα ἕνα σαπούνι.	thah **ee**thehlah **eh**nah sah**poo**nee
some suntan oil	λάδι ἡλίου	**lah**dhee ee**lee**oo

At the barber's

I'd like a haircut, please.	Θά ἤθελα νά μοῦ κόψετε τά μαλλιά παρακαλῶ.	thah **ee**thehlah nah moo **ko**psehteh tah mahlee**ah** pahrahkah**lo**
Short/Leave it long.	Κοντά/'Αφῆστε τα μακρυά.	kon**dah**/ah**fee**steh tah mahkree**ah**
A razor cut, please.	Κόψιμο μέ ξυράφι, παρακαλῶ.	**ko**pseemo meh ksee**rah**fee pahrahkah**lo**

At the hairdresser's

I'd like a shampoo and set, please.	Θά ἤθελα λούσιμο καί μίζ-αν-πλί, παρακαλῶ.	thaht **ee**thehlah **loo**seemo keh meezahn**plee** pahrahkah**lo**

I'd like a bleach.	Θά ἤθελα μία ντεκολορασιόν.	thah **ee**thehlah **mee**ah dehkolorahsee**on**
a permanent	μία περμανάντ	**mee**ah pehrmah**nahnd**
a colour rinse	ἕνα ντεκαπάζ	**eh**nah dehkah**pahz**
a manicure	μανικιούρ	mahneekee**oor**

Photography

I'd like a film for this camera.	Θά ἤθελα ἕνα φίλμ γι'αὐτή τή μηχανή.	thah **ee**thehlah **eh**nah feelm yeeah**ftee** tee meekhah**nee**
This camera doesn't work.	Αὐτή ἡ μηχανή δέν δουλεύει.	ah**ftee** ee meekhah**nee** dhehn dhoo**lehv**ee

At the post office

Where's the nearest post office, please?	Ποῦ εἶναι τό πλησιέστερο ταχυδρομεῖο, παρακαλῶ;	poo **ee**neh to pleessee**eh**stehro tahkhee-dhro**mee**o pahrahkah**lo**
I'd like to send this by express (special delivery)/by air mail.	Θά ἤθελα νά στείλω αὐτό ἐξπρές/ἀεροπορικῶς.	thah **ee**thehlah nah **stee**lo ah**fto** ehks**prehss**/ ahehroporee**koss**

Service stations

Where is the nearest service station, please?	Ποῦ εἶναι τό πλησιέστερο πρατήριο βενζίνης, παρακαλῶ;	poo **ee**neh to pleessee**eh**stehro prah**tee**-reeo vehn**zee**neess pahrahkah**lo**
Fill her up, please.	Νά τό γεμίσετε, παρακαλῶ.	nah to yeh**mee**ssehteh pahrahkah**lo**
Check the oil, please.	'Ελέγξατε τό λάδι, παρακαλῶ.	eh**lehn**ksahteh to **lah**dhee pahrahkah**lo**
Would you check the tyres?	Θά μπορούσατε νά ἐλέγξετε τά λάστιχα;	thah bo**roo**ssahteh nah eh**lehn**ksehteh tah **lah**steekhah

Street directions

Can you show me on the map where I am?	Μπορεῖτε νά μοῦ δείξετε στό χάρτη ποῦ εἶμαι;	bo**ree**teh nah moo **dhee**ksehteh sto **khahr**tee poo **ee**meh
You're on the wrong road.	Ἔχετε πάρει λάθος δρόμο.	**eh**khehteh **pah**ree **lah**thoss **dhro**mo

GREEK

Go back to...	**Γυρῖστε πίσω στό...**	yee**ree**steh **pee**sso sto
Go straight ahead.	**Νά πᾶτε εὐθεία.**	nah **pah**teh ehf**thee**ah
It's on the left/on the right.	**Εἶναι ἀριστερά/δεξιά.**	**ee**neh ahreesteh**rah**/dhehksee**ah**

Accidents

May I use your telephone?	**Μπορῶ νά χρησιμοποιήσω τό τηλέφωνό σας;**	bo**ro** nah khreesseemopee**ee**sso to tee**leh**fo**no** sahss
Call a doctor quickly.	**Καλέστε ἕνα γιατρό γρήγορα.**	kah**leh**steh **eh**nah yeeah**tro** **gree**ǥorah
Call an ambulance.	**Καλέστε ἕνα ἀσθενοφόρο.**	kah**leh**steh **eh**nah ahsthehno**fo**ro
Please call the police.	**Παρακαλῶ καλέστε τήν ἀστυνομία.**	pahrahkah**lo** kah**leh**steh teen ahsteeno**mee**ah

Numbers

zero	**μηδέν**	mee**dhehn**
one	**ἕνα**	**eh**nah
two	**δύο**	**dhee**o
three	**τρία**	**tree**ah
four	**τέσσερα**	**teh**sehrah
five	**πέντε**	**pehn**deh
six	**ἕξη**	**eh**ksee
seven	**ἑπτά**	eh**ptah**
eight	**ὀκτώ**	o**kto**
nine	**ἐννέα**	eh**neh**ah
ten	**δέκα**	**dheh**kah
eleven	**ἕντεκα**	**ehn**dehkah
twelve	**δώδεκα**	**dho**dhehkah
thirteen	**δεκατρία**	dhehkah**tree**ah
fourteen	**δεκατέσσερα**	dhehkah**teh**sehrah
fifteen	**δεκαπέντε**	dhehkah**pehn**deh
sixteen	**δεκαέξη**	dhehkah**eh**ksee
seventeen	**δεκαεπτά**	dhehkahehp**tah**
eighteen	**δεκαοκτώ**	dhehkaho**kto**
nineteen	**δεκαεννέα**	dhehkaheh**neh**ah
twenty	**εἴκοσι**	**ee**kossee
twenty-one	**εἴκοσι ἕνα**	**ee**kossee **eh**nah
thirty	**τριάντα**	tree**ahn**dah
forty	**σαράντα**	sha**rahn**dah
fifty	**πενῆντα**	peh**neen**dah
sixty	**ἑξῆντα**	ee**kseen**dah
seventy	**ἑβδομῆντα**	ehvdho**meen**dah

GREEK

eighty	ὀγδόντα	oğ**dhon**dah
ninety	ἐνενῆντα	ehneh**neen**dah
one hundred	ἑκατό	ehkah**to**
one thousand	χίλια	**khee**leeah
ten thousand	δέκα χιλιάδες	**dheh**kah kheelee**ah**dhehss

Days

It's Sunday.	Εἶναι Κυριακή.	**ee**neh keereeah**kee**
Monday	Δευτέρα	dhehf**teh**rah
Tuesday	Τρίτη	**tree**tee
Wednesday	Τετάρτη	ter**tahr**tee
Thursday	Πέμπτη	**pehm**ptee
Friday	Παρασκευή	pahrahskehv**ee**
Saturday	Σάββατο	**sha**vahto
yesterday	χθές	khthehss
today	σήμερα	**see**mehrah
tomorrow	αὔριο	**ahv**reeo
morning/afternoon	πρωΐ/ἀπόγευμα	pro**ee**/ah**po**yehvmah
evening/night	βράδυ/νύκτα	**vrah**dhee/**neek**tah

Months

January	Ἰανουάριος	eeahnoo**ah**reeoss
February	Φεβρουάριος	fehvroo**ah**reeoss
March	Μάρτιος	**mahr**teeoss
April	Ἀπρίλιος	ah**pree**leeoss
May	Μάϊος	**mah**eeoss
June	Ἰούνιος	ee**oo**neeoss
July	Ἰούλιος	ee**oo**leeoss
August	Αὔγουστος	**ahv**goostoss
September	Σεπτέμβριος	seh**ptehm**vreeoss
October	Ὀκτώβριος	o**kto**vreeoss
November	Νοέμβριος	no**ehm**vreeoss
December	Δεκέμβριος	dheh**kehm**vreeoss
Merry Christmas!	Καλά Χριστούγεννα.	kah**lah** khree**stoo**yehnah
Happy New Year!	Εὐτυχισμένος ὁ καινούργιος χρόνος.	ehfteekheez**meh**noss o keh**noor**yeeoss **khro**noss

ITALIAN

Guide to Pronunciation

Letter	Approximate pronunciation	Symbol	Example	
Consonants				
b, d, f, k, l, m, n, p, q, t, v	are pronounced as in English			
c	1) before **e** and **i**, like **ch** in **ch**ip	ch	**cerco**	**chayr**koa
	2) elsewhere, like **c** in **c**at	k	**conto**	**koan**toa
ch	like **c** in **c**at	k	**che**	kay
g	1) before **e** and **i**, like **j** in **j**et	j	**leggero**	layd**jair**oa
	2) elsewhere, like **g** in **g**o	g	**grande**	**grahn**day
gh	like **g** in **g**o	g	**ghiaccio**	gee**aht**choa
gl	like **lli** in mi**lli**on	ly	**gli**	lyee
gn	like **ni** in o**ni**on	ñ	**bagno**	**bah**ñoa
h	always silent		**ha**	ah

r	trilled like a Scottish **r**	r	**caro**	**kar**roa
s	1) generally like **s** in **s**it	s/ss	**casa** **questo**	**kar**ssah kooa**ys**toa
	2) sometimes like **z** in **z**oo	z	**viso**	**vee**zoa
sc	1) before **e**, **i**, like **sh** in **sh**ut	sh	**uscita**	oo**shee**tah
	2) elsewhere, like **sk** in **sk**in	sk	**scarpa**	**skahr**pah
z or zz	1) generally like **ts** in hi**ts**	ts	**grazie**	**grah**tseeay
	2) sometimes like **ds** in roa**ds**	dz	**romanzo**	roa**mahn**dzoa

Vowels

a	1) short, like **a** in **car**, but shorter	ah	**gatto**	**gaht**toa
	2) long, like **a** in **car** (but without any **r**-sound)	ar	**casa**	**kar**ssah
e	1) can always be pronounced like **ay** in g**ay**	ay	**sera**	**say**rah
	2) in correct speech, it is sometimes pronounced like **e** in g**e**t	eh	**bello**	**behl**loa
	or, when long, more like **ai** in h**air**	ai	**bene**	**bai**nay
i	like the **ee** in m**ee**t	ee	**vini**	**vee**nee
o	1) can always be pronounced like **oa** in g**oa**t	oa	**sole**	**soa**lay
	2) in correct speech, it is sometimes pronounced like **o** in g**o**t,	o	**notte**	**not**tay
	or when long, more like **aw** in l**aw**	aw	**rosa**	**raw**zah
u	like the **oo** in f**oo**t	oo	**fumo**	**foo**moa

Two or more vowels

In groups of vowels, **a**, **e**, and **o** are strong vowels, and **i** and **u** are weak vowels. When two strong vowels are next to each other, they are pronounced as two separate syllables, e.g., *beato* = bay**ah**toa. When a strong and weak vowel are next to each other, the weak one is pronounced more quickly and with less stress (less loudly) than the strong one, e.g., *piede* = pee**ay**day; such sounds are diphthongs and constitute only one syllable. If the weak vowel is stressed, then it is pronounced as a separate syllable, e.g., *due* = **doo**ay. Two weak vowels together are pronounced as a diphthong, and it is generally the second one that is more strongly stressed, e.g., *guida* = goo**ee**dah.

Stressing of words

Generally, the vowel of the next to the last syllable is stressed. When a final vowel is stressed, it has an accent written over it *(più)*. Normally an accent is used only when the stress falls on a final vowel, and not when it falls on syllables before the next to the last one.

ITALIAN

Some basic expressions

Yes.	**Sì.**	see
No.	**No.**	no
Please.	**Per favore.**	pair fah**voa**ray
Thank you.	**Grazie.**	**grah**tseeay
Thank you very much.	**Mille grazie.**	**meel**lay **grah**tseeay
That's all right.	**Prego.**	**pray**goa

Greetings

Good morning.	**Buon giorno.**	bwon **joar**noa
Good afternoon.	**Buon giorno.**	bwon **joar**noa
Good evening.	**Buona sera.**	**bwo**nah **say**rah
Good night.	**Buona notte.**	**bwo**nah **not**tay
Good-bye.	**Arrivederci.**	ahreevay**dair**chee
See you later.	**A più tardi.**	a pyoo **tahr**dee
This is Mr. ...	**Questo è il signor ...**	koo**ayss**toa ay eel see**ñor**
This is Mrs. ...	**Questa è la signora ...**	koo**ayss**tah ay lah seeñ**oa**rah
This is Miss ...	**Questa è la signorina ...**	koo**ayss**tah ay lah seeñoa**ree**nah
I'm very pleased to meet you.	**Piacere.**	peeah**chay**ray
How are you?	**Come sta?**	**koa**may stah
Very well, thank you.	**Molto bene. Grazie.**	**moal**toa **bai**nay. **grah**tseeay
And you?	**E lei?**	ay **lai**ee
Fine.	**Bene.**	**bai**nay
Excuse me.	**Mi scusi.**	mee **skoo**zee

Questions

Where?	**Dove?**	**doa**vay
Where is ... ?	**Dov'è ... ?**	doa**vai**
Where are ... ?	**Dove sono ... ?**	**doa**vay **soa**noa

ITALIAN

When?	**Quando?**	**kwahn**doa
What?	**Cosa?**	**kaw**ssah
How?	**Come?**	**koa**may
How much?	**Quanto?**	**kwahn**toa
How many?	**Quanti?**	**kwahn**tee
Who?	**Chi?**	kee
Why?	**Perchè?**	pehr**kay**
Which?	**Quale?**	**kwar**lay
What do you call this?	**Come si chiama questo?**	**koa**may see kee**ar**mah koo**ayss**toa
What do you call that?	**Come si chiama quello?**	**koa**may see kee**ar**mah koo**ayl**loa
What does this mean?	**Cosa significa questo?**	**kaw**ssah see**ñee**feekah koo**ay**stoa
What does that mean?	**Cosa significa quello?**	**kaw**ssah see**ñee**feekah koo**ayl**loa

Do you speak . . . ?

Do you speak English?	**Parla inglese?**	**pahr**lah eeng**glay**ssay
Do you speak German?	**Parla tedesco?**	**pahr**lah tay**day**skoa
Do you speak French?	**Parla francese?**	**pahr**lah frahn**chay**zay
Do you speak Spanish?	**Parla spagnolo?**	**pahr**lah spah**ñoa**loa
Do you speak Italian?	**Parla italiano?**	**pahr**lah **ee**tah**lyar**noa
Could you speak more slowly, please?	**Può parlare più adagio, per piacere?**	pwo pahr**lar**ray pee**oo** ah**dar**joa pair peeah**chay**ray
Please point to the phrase in the book.	**Per favore, mi indichi la frase nel libro.**	pair fah**voa**ray mee **een**deekee lah **frar**zay nehl **lee**broa
Just a minute. I'll see if I can find it in this book.	**Un momento. Vedo se posso trovarla nel libro.**	oon moa**mayn**toa. **vay**doa say **poss**soa troa**varr**lah nayl **lee**broa
I understand.	**Capisco.**	kah**peess**koa
I don't understand.	**Non capisco.**	noan kah**peess**kao

Can . . . ?

Can I have . . . ?	**Posso avere . . . ?**	**poss**soa ah**vay**ray
Can we have . . . ?	**Possiamo avere . . . ?**	possseea**r**moa ah**vay**ray
Can you show me . . . ?	**Può indicarmi . . . ?**	pwo eendee**karr**mee
Can you tell me . . . ?	**Può dirmi . . . ?**	pwo **deer**mee
Can you help me, please?	**Può aiutarmi, per piacere?**	pwo ighoo**tarr**mee pair peeah**chay**ray

Wanting

I'd like . . .	**Vorrei . . .**	vorr**aiee**
We'd like . . .	**Vorremmo . . .**	vor**rehm**moa
Please give me . . .	**Per favore, mi dia . . .**	pair fah**voa**ray mee **dee**ah
Give it to me, please.	**Me lo dia, per favore.**	may loa **dee**ah pair fah**voa**ray
Please bring me . . .	**Per favore, mi porti . . .**	pair fah**voa**ray mee **por**tee
Bring it to me, please.	**Me lo porti, per favore.**	may loa **por**tee pair fah**voa**ray
I'm hungry.	**Ho fame.**	oa **far**may
I'm thirsty.	**Ho sete.**	oa **say**tay
I'm tired.	**Sono stanco.**	**soa**noa **stahng**koa
I'm lost.	**Mi sono perso.**	mee **soa**noa **pehr**soa
It's important.	**È importante.**	ay eempor**tahn**tay
It's urgent.	**È urgente.**	ay oor**jehn**tay
Hurry up!	**Si affretti!**	see ahf**frayt**tee

It is/There is . . .

It is/It's . . .	**È . . .**	ai
Is it . . . ?	**È . . . ?**	ai
It isn't . . .	**Non è . . .**	noan ai
There is/There are . . .	**C'è/Ci sono . . .**	chai/chee **soa**noa
Is there/Are there . . . ?	**C'è/Ci sono . . . ?**	chai/chee **soa**noa

ITALIAN

There isn't/There aren't ...	**Non c'è/Non ci sono ...**	noan chai/noan chee **soa**noa
There isn't any/ There aren't any.	**Non ce n'è/Non ce ne sono.**	noan chay nai/noan chay nay **soa**noa

A few common words

big/small	**grande/piccolo**	**grahn**day/**peek**koaloa
quick/slow	**rapido/lento**	**rar**peedoa/**lehn**toa
early/late	**presto/tardi**	**prehss**toa/**tahr**dee
cheap/expensive	**economico/costoso**	aykoa**naw**meekoa/koss**toa**soa
near/far	**vicino/lontano**	vee**chee**noa/lon**tar**noa
hot/cold	**caldo/freddo**	**kahl**doa/**frayd**doa
full/empty	**pieno/vuoto**	pee**ay**noa/voo**aw**toa
easy/difficult	**facile/difficile**	**far**cheelay/dee**fee**cheelay
heavy/light	**pesante/leggero**	pay**sahn**tay/layd**jai**roa
open/shut	**aperto/chiuso**	ah**pehr**toa/kee**oo**ssoa
right/wrong	**giusto/sbagliato**	**jooss**toa/zbah**lyar**toa
old/new	**vecchio/nuovo**	**vehk**keeoa/noo**aw**voa
old/young	**vecchio/giovane**	**vehk**keeoa/**joa**vahnay
beautiful/ugly	**bello/brutto**	**behl**loa/**broot**toa
good/bad	**buono/cattivo**	boo**aw**noa/kaht**tee**voa
better/worse	**migliore/peggiore**	mee**lyoa**ray/payd**joa**ray

Some prepositions and a few more useful words

at	**a**	ah
on	**sopra**	**soa**prah
in	**in**	een
to	**a**	ah
from	**da**	dah
inside	**dentro**	**dayn**troa
outside	**fuori**	foo**aw**ree
up	**sù**	soo
down	**giù**	joo
before	**prima di**	**pree**mah dee
after	**dopo di**	**daw**poa dee
with	**con**	kon
without	**senza**	**sayn**tsah
through	**attraverso**	ahttrah**vehr**soa
towards	**verso**	**vehr**soa
until	**fino a**	**fee**noa ah
during	**durante**	doo**rahn**tay
and	**e**	ay
or	**o**	oa
not	**non**	noan
nothing	**niente**	nee**ehn**tay
none	**nessuno**	nayss**soo**noa

very	**molto**	**moal**toa
also	**anche**	**ahng**kay
soon	**presto**	**prehss**toa
perhaps	**forse**	**for**say
here	**qui**	koo**ee**
there	**là**	lah
now	**ora**	**oa**rah
then	**poi**	poy

Arrival

Your passport, please.	**Il passaporto, per favore.**	eel pahsssah**por**toa pair fah**voa**ray
Here it is.	**Eccolo.**	**ehk**koaloa
Have you anything to declare?	**Ha qualcosa da dichiarare?**	ah kwahl**kaw**ssah dah deekeeah**rar**ray
No, nothing at all.	**No. Non ho nulla.**	noa noan oa **nool**lah
Porter!	**Facchino!**	fahk**kee**noa
Can you help me with my luggage, please?	**Può prendere le mie valige, per favore?**	pwo **prehn**dayray lay **mee**ay vah**lee**jay pair fah**voa**ray
That's my suitcase.	**Quella è la mia valigia.**	koo**ayl**lah ai lah **mee**ah vah**lee**jah
Where's the bus to the centre of town, please?	**Dov'è l'autobus per il centro della città, per favore?**	doa**vai** lowtoa**booss** pair eel **chehn**troa **dayl**lah cheet**tah** pair fah**voa**ray
This way, please.	**Da questa parte, per piacere.**	dah koo**ayss**tah **pahr**tay pair peeah**chay**ray

Changing money

Can you change a traveller's cheque, please?	**Può cambiarmi un traveller's cheque, per favore?**	pwo kahmbee**arr**mee oon "traveller's cheque" pair fah**voa**ray
Where's the nearest bank, please?	**Dov'è la banca più vicina, per favore?**	doa**vai** lah **bahng**kah pee**oo** vee**chee**nah pair fah**voa**ray

Car rental

I'd like a car.	**Vorrei un'automobile.**	vor**rai**ee oon owtoa**maw**beelay
For how long?	**Per quanto tempo?**	pair koo**ahn**toa **tehm**poa
A day/Four days/ A week/Two weeks.	**Un giorno/Quattro giorni/Una settimana/Due settimane.**	oon **joar**noa/koo**aht**troa **joar**nee/**oo**nah saytee**mar**nah/**doo**ay saytte**mar**nay

Taxi

Where can I get a taxi?	**Dove posso trovare un tassì?**	**doa**vay **poss**soa troa**var**-ray oon tahss**see**
What's the fare to . . . ?	**Quanto costa la corsa per . . . ?**	**kwahn**toa **koss**tah lah **kor**sah pair
Take me to this address, please.	**Mi porti a questo indirizzo, per favore.**	mee **por**tee ah koo**ayss**-toa eendee**reet**tsoa pair fah**voa**ray
I'm in a hurry.	**Ho fretta.**	oa **frayt**tah
Could you drive more slowly, please?	**Può guidare più adagio, per favore?**	pwo gooee**dar**ray pee**oo** ah**dar**joa pair fah**voa**ray

Hotel and other accommodation

My name is . . .	**Mi chiamo . . .**	mee kee**ar**moa
Have you a reservation?	**Ha fatto la prenotazione?**	ah **faht**toa lah praynoatahtsee**oa**nay
Yes, here's the confirmation.	**Sì; ecco la conferma.**	see **ehk**koa lah kon**fehr**mah
I'd like . . .	**Vorrei . . .**	vor**rai**ee
I'd like a single room/a double room.	**Vorrei una camera singola/per due persone.**	vor**rai**ee **oo**nah **kar**mayrah **seeng**goalah/pair **doo**ay payr**soa**nay
a room with a bath/ with a shower	**una camera con bagno/con doccia**	**oo**nah **kar**mayrah kon **bah**ñoa/kon **dot**chah

How much?

What's the price per night/per week/per month?	**Qual è il prezzo per una notte/per una settimana/per un mese?**	kwah**lai** eel **preht**tsoa pàir **oo**nah **not**tay/pair **oo**nah saytteemarnah/pair oon **may**ssay
May I see the room?	**Posso vedere la camera?**	**poss**soa vay**day**ray lah **kar**mayrah
I'm sorry, I don't like it.	**Mi dispiace: non è di mio gradimento.**	mee despee**ar**chay noan ai dee **mee**oa grahdee**mayn**toa
Yes, that's fine. I'll take it.	**Sì, va bene. La prendo.**	see vah **bai**nay lah **prayn**doa
What's my room number, please?	**Qual è il numero della mia camera?**	kwah**lai** eel **noo**mayroa **day**llah **mee**ah **kar**mayrah
Number 123.	**Numero 123.**	**noo**mayroa 123

Service, please

Who is it?	**Chi è?**	kee ai
Just a minute.	**Un momento, per favore.**	oon moa**mayn**toa pair fah**voa**ray
Come in! The door's open.	**Avanti! La porta è aperta.**	ah**vahn**tee lah **por**tah ai ah**pehr**tah
May we have breakfast in our room?	**Possiamo fare la prima colazione in camera?**	possseea**ar**moa **far**ray lah **pree**mah koalahtsee**oa**nay een **kar**mayran

Breakfast

I'll have ...	**Vorrei ...**	vor**rai**ee
I'll have some fruit juice.	**Vorrei un succo di frutta.**	vor**rai**ee oon **sook**koa dee **froot**tah
a boiled egg	**un uovo alla "coque"**	oon oo**aw**voa **ahl**lah kok
a fried egg	**un uovo al tegame**	oon oo**aw**voa ahl tay**gar**may
some bacon/some ham	**della pancetta affumicata/del prosciutto**	**dayl**lah pahn**cheht**tah ahffoomee**kar**tah/dayl proa**shoot**toa
some toast	**del pane tostato**	dayl **par**nay toas**star**toa
a pot of tea	**del tè**	dayl tay
a cup of tea	**una tazza di tè**	**oo**nah **taht**tsah dee tay
some coffee	**del caffè**	dayl kah**ffay**
some chocolate	**della cioccolata**	**dayl**lah choakkoa**lar**tah
more butter	**un altro po'di burro**	oon **ahl**troa po dee **boor**roa
some hot water	**dell'acqua calda**	dayl**ahk**kooah **kahl**dah

Difficulties

The central heating doesn't work.	**Il riscaldamento centrale non funziona.**	eel reesskahldah**mayn**toa chayn**trar**lay noan foontsee**oa**nah
the light/the socket	**la luce/la presa**	lah **loo**chay/lah **pray**sah
the tap/the toilet	**il rubinetto/il gabinetto**	eel roobee**nayt**toa/eel gahbee**nayt**toa
There's no hot water.	**Non c'è acqua calda.**	noan chai **ahk**kooah **kahl**dah
May I see the manager, please?	**Posso vedere il direttore, per piacere?**	**poss**soa vay**day**ray eel deerayt**toa**ray pair peeah**chay**ray

Telephone—Mail

There's a call for you.	**C'è una telefonata per lei.**	chai **oo**nah taylayfoa**nar**tah pair **lai**ee
Hold the line, please.	**Resti in linea, per piacere.**	**rehss**tee een **lee**nayah pair peeah**chay**ray
Operator, I've been cut off.	**Signorina, mi hanno interrotto.**	seeñoa**ree**nah mee **ahn**noa eentehr**rot**toa
Did anyone telephone me?	**Mi ha telefonato qualcuno?**	mee ah taylayfoa**nar**toa kwahl**koo**noa
Is there any mail for me?	**C'è posta per me?**	chai **poss**tah pair may
Are there any messages for me?	**Ci sono comunicazioni per me?**	chee **soa**noa komooneekahtsee**oa**nee pair may

Checking out

May I have my bill, please?	**Posso avere il mio conto, per favore?**	**poss**soa ah**vay**ray eel **mee**oa **koan**toa pair fah**voa**ray
We're in a great hurry.	**Abbiamo molta fretta.**	ahbbee**ar**moa **moal**tah **frayt**tah
It's been a very enjoyable stay.	**È stato un soggiorno molto piacevole.**	ai **star**toa oon soad**joar**noa **moal**toa peeah**chay**voalay

Eating out

Good evening, sir/ Good evening, madam.	**Buona sera, signore/Buona sera, signora.**	**bwo**nah **say**rah seeñoaray/**bwo**nah **say**rah seeñ**oa**rrah
Good evening. I'd like a table for two, please.	**Buona sera. Vorrei una tavola per due, per favore.**	**bwo**nah **say**rah. vor**rai**ee **oo**nah **tar**voalah pair **doo**ay pair fah**voa**ray
Do you have a fixed-price menu?	**Avete un menu a prezzo fisso?**	ah**vay**tay oon may**noo** ah **preht**tsoa **feess**soa
May I see the à la carte menu?	**Posso vedere il menu a scelta?**	**poss**soa vay**day**ray eel may**noo** ah **shayl**tah
May we have an ashtray, please?	**Posso avere un portacenere, per favore?**	**poss**soa ah**vay**ray oon portah**chay**nayray pair fah**voa**ray
some bread	**un po'di pane**	oon po dee **par**nay
a fork	**una forchetta**	**oo**nah for**keht**tah
a knife	**un coltello**	oon koal**tehl**loa

ITALIAN

a spoon	**un cucchiaio**	oon kookkee**igh**oa
a plate	**un piatto**	oon pee**aht**toa
a glass	**un bicchiere**	oon beekkee**ai**ray
a napkin	**un tovagliolo**	oon toavah**lyaw**loa
another chair	**un'altra sedia**	oon**ahl**trah **sai**deeah
Where's the gentlemen's toilet (men's room)?	**Dove sono i gabinetti per uomini?**	**doa**vay **soa**noa ee gahbee**nayt**tee pair oo**o**meenee
Where's the ladies' toilet (ladies' room)?	**Dove sono i gabinetti per signore?**	**doa**vay **soa**noa ee gahbee**nayt**tee pair see**ñoa**ray

Appetizers

I'd like some...	**Vorrei...**	vor**rai**ee
I'd like some assorted appetizers.	**Vorrei degli antipasti assortiti.**	vor**rai**ee **day**lyee ahntee**pahs**stee ahssor**tee**tee
orange juice	**un succo d'arancia**	oon **sook**koa dah**rahn**chah
ham	**del prosciutto**	day proa**shoot**toa
melon	**del melone**	dayl may**loa**nay
pâté	**del pâté**	dayl pah**tay**
smoked salmon	**del salmone affumicato**	dayl sahl**moa**nay ahffoomee**kar**toa
shrimps (shrimp)	**dei gamberetti**	**dai**ee gahmbay**rayt**tee

Soup

Have you any...?	**Ha...?**	ah
Have you any chicken soup?	**Ha un brodo di pollo?**	ah oon **braw**doa dee **poal**loa
vegetable soup	**una minestra di verdure**	**oo**nah mee**nehss**trah dee vehr**doo**ray
onion soup	**una minestra di cipolle**	**oo**nah mee**nehss**trah dee chee**poal**lay

Fish

I'd like some...	**Vorrei...**	vor**rai**ee
I'd like some fish.	**Vorrei del pesce.**	vor**rai**ee dayl **pay**shay
sole	**della sogliola**	**dayl**lah **saw**lyoalah
trout	**delle trote**	**dayl**lay **traw**tay
lobster	**un'aragosta**	oon ahrah**goass**tah
crayfish	**dei gamberi d'acqua dolce**	**dai**ee **gahm**bayree **dahk**kooah **dol**chay
prawns	**dei gamberi**	**dai**ee **gahm**bayree

ITALIAN

I'd like it...	**Li vorrei...**	lee vor**raiee**
I'd like it steamed.	**Li vorrei al vapore.**	lee vor**raiee** ahl vah**poa**ray
grilled	**alla griglia**	**ahl**lah **gree**lyah
boiled	**bolliti**	bol**lee**tee
baked	**al forno**	ahl **for**noa
fried	**fritti**	**freet**tee

Meat—Poultry—Game

I'd like some...	**Vorrei...**	vor**raiee**
I'd like some beef.	**Vorrei del manzo.**	vor**raiee** dayl **mahn**dzoa
a beef steak	**una bistecca di manzo**	**oo**nah bee**stayk**kah dee **mahn**dzoa
some roast beef	**un arrosto di manzo**	oon ahr**roass**toa dee **mahn**dzoa
a veal cutlet	**una cotoletta di vitello**	**oo**nah koatoa**layt**tah dee vee**tehl**loa
mutton	**del montone**	dayl moan**toa**nay
lamb	**dell'agnello**	dayl ah**ñehl**loa
a pork chop	**una braciola di maiale**	**oo**nah brah**choa**lah dee migh**ar**lay
roast pork	**un arrosto di maiale**	oon ahr**ross**toa dee migh**ar**lay
hare	**della lepre**	**dayl**lah **lai**pray
chicken	**del pollo**	dayl **poal**loa
roast chicken	**del pollo arrosto**	dayl **poal**loa ahr**roass**toa
duck	**dell'anatra**	dayl **ar**nahtrah
How do you like your meat?	**Come vuole la carne?**	**koa**may vooa**w**lay lah **kahr**nay
rare	**al sangue**	ahl **sahn**gooay
medium	**non troppo cotta**	noan **trop**poa **kot**tah
well done	**ben cotta**	bain **kot**tah

Vegetables

What vegetables have you got?	**Quali legumi ha?**	koo**ar**lee lay**goo**mee ah
I'd like some...	**Vorrei...**	vor**raiee**
I'd like some asparagus.	**Vorrei degli asparagi.**	vor**raiee day**lyee ah**spar**rahjee
green beans	**dei fagiolini**	**dai**ee fahjoa**lee**nee
mushrooms	**dei funghi**	**dai**ee **foong**gee
carrots	**delle carote**	**day**llay kah**raw**tay
onions	**delle cipolle**	**day**llay chee**poal**lay
red cabbage	**dei cavoli rossi**	**dai**ee **kah**voalee **ross**see

spinach	**degli spinaci**	**day**lyee spee**nar**chee
rice	**del riso**	dayl **ree**soa
peas	**dei piselli**	**dai**ee pee**sehl**lee
tomatoes	**dei pomodori**	**dai**ee poamoa**daw**ree
green salad	**dell'insalata**	dayl eensah**lar**tah
potatoes	**delle patate**	**dayl**lay pah**tar**tay

Desserts

Nothing more, thanks.	**Nient'altro. Grazie.**	nee**ehn**tahltroa **grah**tseeay
Just a small portion, please.	**Solo una piccola porzione, per favore.**	**soa**loa **oo**nah **peek**koalah portsee**oa**nay pair fah**voa**ray
Have you any ice-cream?	**Ha un gelato?**	ah oon jay**lar**toa
fruit salad	**una macedonia**	**oo**nah mahchay**daw**neeah
fresh fruit	**della frutta fresca**	**dayl**lah **froot**tah **frays**skah
cheese	**del formaggio**	dayl for**mahd**joa

Drink

What would you like to drink?	**Cosa desidera da bere?**	**kaw**ssah day**zee**dayrah dah **bay**ray
I'll have a beer, please.	**Mi dia una birra, per piacere.**	mee **dee**ah **oo**nah **beer**rah pair peeah**chay**ray
I'll have a whisky, please.	**Mi dia un whisky, per favore.**	mee **dee**ah oon whisky (**wiss**kee) pair fah**voa**ray

Wine

I'd like a bottle of wine.	**Vorrei una bottiglia di vino.**	vor**rai**ee **oo**nah bot**tee**lyah dee **vee**noa
red wine	**di vino rosso**	dee **vee**noa **roass**soa
rosé wine	**di rosé**	dee roa**zay**
white wine	**di vino bianco**	dee **vee**noa bee**ahng**koa
Cheers!	**Salute!**	sah**loo**tay

The bill (check)

May I have the bill (check) please?	**Posso avere il mio conto, per piacere?**	**poss**soa ah**vay**ray eel **mee**oa **koan**toa pair peeah**chay**ray
Is service included?	**È compreso il servizio?**	ai koam**pray**zoa eel sayr**vee**tseeoa

ITALIAN

Everything's included.	**Tutto compreso.**	**toot**toa koam**pray**zoa
Thank you, that was a very good meal.	**Grazie. Abbiamo mangiato molto bene.**	**grah**tseeay ahbbee**ar**moa mahn**jar**toa **moal**toa **bai**nay

Travelling

Where's the railway station, please?	**Dove si trova la stazione, per favore?**	**doa**vay see **traw**vah lah stahtsee**oa**nay pair fah**voa**ray
Where's the ticket office, please?	**Dove si trova lo sportello dei biglietti, per favore?**	**doa**vay see **traw**vah loa spor**tehl**loa **dai**ee bee**lyayt**tee pair fah**voa**ray
I'd like a ticket to...	**Vorrei un biglietto per...**	vor**rai**ee oon bee**lyayt**toa pair
First or second class?	**Di prima o di seconda classe?**	dee **pree**mah oa dee say**koan**dah **klahss**say
First class, please.	**Di prima classe, per piacere.**	dee **pree**mah **klahss**say pair peeah**chay**ray
Single or return (one way or round-trip)?	**Andata o andata e ritorno?**	ahn**dar**tah oa ahn**dar**tah ay ree**tor**noa
Do I have to change trains?	**Devo cambiare treno?**	**day**voa kahmbee**ar**ray **tray**noa
What platform does the train leave from?	**Da che binario parte il treno?**	dah kay bee**nar**reeoa **pahr**tay eel **tray**noa
Where's the nearest underground (subway) station?	**Dov'è la più vicina stazione della metropolitana?**	doa**vai** lah pee**oo** vee**chee**nah stahtsee**oa**nay **day**llah may-troapoalee**tar**nah
Where's the bus station, please?	**Dov'è la stazione degli autobus, per piacere?**	doa**vai** lah stahtsee**oa**nay **day**lyee **ow**toabooss pair peeah**chay**ray
When's the first bus to...?	**Quando passa il primo autobus per...?**	**kwahn**doa **pahss**sah eel **pree**moa **ow**toabooss pair
the last bus/the next bus	**l'ultimo autobus/il prossimo autobus**	**lool**teemoa **ow**toabooss/ eel **pross**seemoa **ow**toabooss
Please let me off at the next stop.	**Mi faccia scendere alla prossima fermata, per piacere.**	mee **faht**chah **shayn**dayray **ahl**lah **pross**seemah fehr**mar**tah pair peeah**chay**ray

Relaxing

What's on at the cinema (movies)?	**Cosa danno al cinema?**	**kaw**ssah **dahn**noa ahl **chee**naymah
What's on at the theatre?	**Cosa danno al teatro?**	**kaw**ssah **dahn**noa ahl tay**ar**troa
What time does the film begin? And the play?	**A che ora incomincia il film? E la rappresentazione?**	ah kay **oa**rah eengkoa**meen**cheeah eel feelm? ay lah rahpprayssayntahtsee**oa**nay
Are there any tickets for tonight?	**Ci sono ancora posti liberi per questa sera?**	chee **soa**noa ahng**koa**rah **poas**tee **lee**bayree pair koo**ayss**tah **say**rah
Where can we go dancing?	**Dove possiamo andare a ballare?**	**doa**vay possee**ar**moa ahn**dar**ray ah bahl**lar**ray
Would you like to dance?	**Vuole ballare?**	voo**aw**lay bahl**lar**ray

Introductions

How do you do?	**Buon giorno.**	bwon **joar**noa
How are you?	**Come sta?**	**koa**may stah
Very well, thank you. And you?	**Molto bene, grazie. E lei?**	**moal**toa **bai**nay **grah**tseeay. ay **lai**ee
May I introduce Miss Philips?	**Posso presentarle la signorina Philips?**	**poss**soa prayzayn**tarr**lay lah seeñoa**ree**nah Philips
My name is ...	**Mi chiamo ...**	mee kee**ar**moa
I'm very pleased to meet you.	**Sono molto lieto di fare la sua conoscenza.**	**soa**noa **moal**toa lee**ay**toa dee **far**ray lah **soo**ah koanoa**shehn**tsah
How long have you been here?	**Da quanto tempo è qui?**	dah **kwahn**toa **tehm**poa ai koo**ee**
It was nice meeting you.	**Sono lieto di aver fatto la sua conoscenza.**	**soa**noa lee**ay**toa dee ah**vayr faht**toa lah **soo**ah koanoa**shehn**tsah

Dating

Would you like a cigarette?	**Accetta una sigaretta?**	aht**chayt**tah **oo**nah seegah**rayt**tah
May I get you a drink?	**Posso offrirle da bere?**	**poss**soa off**freer**lay dah **bay**ray

Do you have a light, please?	**Mi fa accendere, per piacere?**	mee fah aht**chehn**dayray pair peeah**chay**ray
Are you waiting for someone?	**Attende qualcuno?**	aht**tehn**day kooahl**koo**noa
Are you free this evening?	**È libera, stasera?**	ai **lee**bayrah stah**say**rah
Where shall we meet?	**Dove possiamo incontrarci?**	**doa**vay possseearmoa eengkon**trarr**chee
What time shall I meet you?	**A che ora la vedrò?**	ah kay **oa**rah lah vay**droa**
May I take you home?	**Posso accompagnarla a casa?**	**poss**soa ahkkoampah**ñarr**lah ah **kar**ssah
Thank you, it's been a wonderful evening.	**Grazie! È stata una magnifica serata.**	**grah**tseeay! ai **star**tah **oo**nah mañ**ee**feekah say**rar**tah
What's your telephone number?	**Qual è il suo numero di telefono?**	kwah**lai** eel **soo**oa **noo**mayroa dee tay**lai**foanoa
Do you live alone?	**Vive sola?**	**vee**vay **soa**lah
What time is your last train?	**A che ora parte il suo ultimo treno?**	ah kay **oa**rah **pahr**tay eel **soo**oa **ool**teemoa **tray**noa
Good-night...	**Buona notte...**	**bwo**nah **not**tay

Banks

Where's the nearest bank, please?	**Dov'è la banca più vicina, per favore?**	doa**vai** lah **bahng**kah pee**oo** vee**chee**nah pair fah**voa**ray
Where can I cash some traveller's cheques?	**Dove posso cambiare un traveller's cheque?**	**doa**vay **poss**soa kahm**beearr**ay oon "traveller's cheque"
What time does the bank open/What time does it close?	**A che ora apre la banca/A che ora chiude?**	ah kay **oa**rah **ah**pray la **bahng**kah/ah kay **oa**rah kee**oo**day
I'm expecting some money from home. Has it arrived?	**Aspetto del denaro da casa. È arrivato?**	ah**spayt**toa dayl day**nar**roa dah **kars**sah. ai ahr**ree**var**toa**
Can you give me some small change, please?	**Potrebbe darmi della moneta spicciola, per favore?**	poa**trayb**bay **darr**mee **dayl**lah moa**nay**tah **speet**choalah pair fah**voa**ray

ITALIAN

Shops, stores and services

Where is the nearest chemist's (pharmacy)?	**Dov'è la più vicina farmacia?**	doa**vai** lah pe**eoo** vee**chee**nah fahrmah**chee**ah
the nearest hairdresser's	**il parrucchiere più vicino**	eel pahrrookkee**ai**ray pee**oo** vee**chee**noa
the photo shop	**il fotografo**	eel foa**taw**grahfoa
the jeweller's	**la gioielleria**	lah joyayllay**ree**ah
the department store	**il grande magazzino**	eel **grahn**day mahgahd**dzee**noa
the police station	**la questura (il posto di polizia)**	lah kooayss**too**rah (eel **poass**toa dee poalee**tsee**ah)
the garage	**l'autorimessa**	lowtoaree**mayss**sah
How do I get there?	**Come ci si può arrivare?**	**koa**may chee see pwo ahrree**var**ray
Is it within walking distance?	**Ci si può andare anche a piedi?**	chee see pwo ahn**dar**ray **ahng**kay ah pee**ay**dee

Service

Can you help me, please?	**Può aiutarmi, per piacere?**	pwo ighoo**tarr**mee pair peeah**chay**ray
Can you show me this? And that, too.	**Può mostrarmi questo? E anche quello.**	pwo moass**trarr**mee koo**ayss**toa? ay **ahng**kay koo**ayl**loa
It's too expensive/ too big/too small.	**È troppo caro/ troppo grande/ troppo piccolo.**	ay **trop**poa **kar**roa/**trop**poa **grahn**day/**trop**poa **peek**koaloa
Can you show me some more?	**Mi può mostrare una scelta più ampia?**	mee pwo moass**trar**ray **oo**nah **shayl**tah pee**oo** **ahm**peeah
something better	**qualcosa migliore**	kwahl**kaw**ssah mee**lyoa**ray
something cheaper	**qualcosa di più economico**	kwahl**kaw**ssah dee pee**oo** aykoa**naw**meekoa
How much is this? And that?	**Quanto costa questo? E quello?**	**kwahn**toa **koss**tah koo**ayss**toa? ay koo**ayl**loa
It's not quite what I want.	**Non è proprio quello che volevo.**	noan ay **praw**preeoa koo**ayl**loah kay voa**lay**voa
I like it.	**Questo mi piace.**	koo**ayss**toa mee pee**ar**chay

Chemist's (Pharmacy)

I'd like something for a cold/for a cough/for travel sickness.	**Vorrei qualcosa per il raffreddore/per la tosse/per il mal di moto.**	vor**rai**ee kwahl**kaw**ssah pair eel rahffrayd**doa**ray/ pair lah **toass**say/pair eel mahl dee **maw**toa
Can you recommend something for hay-fever/for sunburn?	**Puo consigliarmi qualcosa per la febbre del fieno/per una scottatura di sole?**	pwo koansee**lyarr**mee kwahl**kaw**ssah pair lah **fayb**bray dayl fee**eh**noa/ pair **oo**nah skottah**too**rah dee **soa**lay

Toiletry

May I have some razor blades?	**Potrei avere delle lamette da barba?**	poa**trai**ee ah**vay**ray **dayl**lay lah**mayt**tay dah **bahr**bah
some shaving cream	**una crema da barba**	**oo**nah **krai**mah dah **bahr**bah
some toothpaste	**un dentifricio**	oon daynteefree**choa**
I'd like some soap.	**Vorrei una saponetta.**	vor**rai**ee **oo**nah sahpoa**nayt**tah
some suntan oil	**dell'olio per la tintarella**	dayl **aw**lyoa pair lah teen-tah**rehl**lah

At the barber's

I'd like a haircut, please.	**Vorrei farmi tagliare i capelli, per favore.**	vor**rai**ee **farr**mee tah**lyar**-ray ee kah**payl**lee pair fah**voa**ray
Short/Leave it long.	**Corti/Li lasci lunghi.**	**koar**tee/lee **lah**shee **loong**gee
A razor cut, please.	**Un taglio col rasoio, per piacere.**	oon **tar**lyoa koal rah**saw**-eeoa pair peeah**chay**ray

At the hairdresser's

I'd like a shampoo and set, please.	**Vorrei uno shampoo e una messa in piega, per piacere.**	vor**rai**ee **oo**noa "shampoo" ay **oo**nah **mayss**sah een pee**ai**gah pair peeah-**chay**ray
I'd like a bleach.	**Vorrei una decolorazione.**	vor**rai**ee **oo**na day-koaloarahtsee**oa**nay
a permanent	**una permanente**	**oo**nah payrmah**nehn**tay
a colour rinse	**un "cachet"**	oon kah**shay**
a manicure	**una manicure**	**oo**nah mahnee**koo**ray

Photography

I'd like a film for this camera.	**Vorrei un rullino per questa macchina fotografica.**	vor**rai**ee oon rool**lee**noa pair koo**ayss**tah **mahk**keenah foatoa**grar**feekah
This camera doesn't work.	**Questa macchina fotografica non funziona.**	koo**ayss**tah **mahk**keenah foatoa**grar**feekah noan foontsee**oa**nah

At the post office

Where's the nearest post office, please?	**Dove si trova l'ufficio postale più vicino, per favore?**	**doa**vay see **traw**vah looff**ee**choa poass**tar**lay pee**oo** vee**chee**noa pair fah**voa**ray
I'd like to send this by express (special delivery)/by air mail.	**Vorrei spedire questo per espresso/per via aerea.**	vor**rai**ee spay**dee**ray koo**ayss**toa pair ayss**prehss**soa/pair **vee**ah ah**ai**rayah

Service stations

Where is the nearest service station, please?	**Dove si trova la più vicina stazione di rifornimento, per favore?**	**doa**vay see **traw**vah lah pee**oo** vee**chee**nah stahtsee**oa**nay dee reefornee**mayn**toa pair fah**voa**ray
Fill her up, please.	**Faccia il pieno, per favore.**	**faht**chah eel pee**ai**noa pair fah**voa**ray
Check the oil, please.	**Controlli l'olio, per favore.**	koan**troal**lee **law**lyoa pair fah**voa**ray
Would you check the tyres?	**Vorrebbe controllare le gomme?**	vor**rayb**bay koantroal**lar**ray lay **gom**may

Street directions

Can you show me on the map where I am?	**Può indicarmi sulla carta dove mi trovo?**	pwo eendee**karr**mee **sool**lah **kahr**tah **doa**vay mee **traw**voa
You're on the wrong road.	**È sulla strada sbagliata.**	ay **sool**lah **strar**dah zbah**lyar**tah
Go back to ...	**Ritorni a ...**	ree**toar**nee ah
Go straight ahead.	**Continui diritto.**	koan**tee**nooee dee**reet**toa
It's on the left/on the right.	**È a sinistra/a destra.**	ai ah see**neess**trah/ah **dehs**trah

Accidents

May I use your telephone?	**Potrei usare il suo telefono?**	poa**trai**ee oo**zar**ray eel **soo**oa tay**lai**foanoa
Call a doctor quickly.	**Chiami subito un medico.**	kee**ar**mee **soo**beetoa oon **mai**deekoa
Call an ambulance.	**Chiami un'autoambulanza.**	kee**ar**mee oon owtoaahmboo**lahn**tsah
Please call the police.	**Per piacere, chiami la polizia.**	pair peeah**chay**ray kee**ar**mee lah poalee**tsee**ah

Numbers

zero	**zero**	**dzay**roa
one	**uno**	**oo**noa
two	**due**	**doo**ay
three	**tre**	tray
four	**quattro**	koo**aht**troa
five	**cinque**	**cheeng**kooay
six	**sei**	**seh**ee
seven	**sette**	**seh**ttay
eight	**otto**	**ot**toa
nine	**nove**	**naw**vay
ten	**dieci**	dee**ai**chee
eleven	**undici**	**oon**deechee
twelve	**dodici**	**doa**deechee
thirteen	**tredici**	**tray**deechee
fourteen	**quattordici**	kooaht**tor**deechee
fifteen	**quindici**	koo**een**deechee
sixteen	**sedici**	**say**deechee
seventeen	**diciassette**	deechahss**seht**tay
eighteen	**diciotto**	dee**chot**toa
nineteen	**diciannove**	deechah**naw**vay
twenty	**venti**	**vayn**tee
twenty-one	**ventuno**	vayn**too**noa
thirty	**trenta**	**trayn**tah
forty	**quaranta**	kooah**rahn**tah
fifty	**cinquanta**	cheengkoo**ahn**tah
sixty	**sessanta**	sayss**sahn**tah
seventy	**settanta**	sayt**tahn**tah
eighty	**ottanta**	oat**tahn**tah
ninety	**novanta**	noa**vahn**tah
one hundred	**cento**	**cheh**ntoa
one thousand	**mille**	**meel**lay
ten thousand	**diecimila**	deeehchee**mee**lah

Days

It's Sunday.	**È domenica.**	ai doa**may**neekah
Monday	**lunedì**	loonay**dee**
Tuesday	**martedì**	mahrtay**dee**
Wednesday	**mercoledì**	mehrkoalay**dee**
Thursday	**giovedì**	joavay**dee**
Friday	**venerdì**	vaynayr**dee**
Saturday	**sabato**	**sar**bahtoa
yesterday	**ieri**	ee**ai**ree
today	**oggi**	**od**jee
tomorrow	**domani**	doa**mar**nee
morning/afternoon	**mattino/pomeriggio**	maht**tee**noa/poamay-**reed**joa
evening/night	**sera/notte**	**say**rah/**not**tay

Months

January	**gennaio**	jay**nigh**oa
February	**febbraio**	fehb**brigh**oa
March	**marzo**	**mahr**tsoa
April	**aprile**	ah**pree**lay
May	**maggio**	**mahd**joa
June	**giugno**	**joo**ñoa
July	**luglio**	**loo**lyoa
August	**agosto**	ah**goass**toa
September	**settembre**	sayt**tehm**bray
October	**ottobre**	oat**toa**bray
November	**novembre**	noa**vehm**bray
December	**dicembre**	dee**chehm**bray
Merry Christmas!	**Buon Natale!**	bwon nah**tar**lay!
Happy New Year!	**Buon Anno!**	bwon **ahn**noa

ITALIAN

NORWEGIAN

Guide to Pronunciation

Letter	Approximate pronunciation	Symbol	Example	
Consonants				
b, d, f, h, m, n, p, t, v	as in English			
g	1) before **i**, **y** or **ei**, like **y** in **y**et	y	**gi**	yee
	2) otherwise, like **g** in **g**o	g	**gate**	**gar**ter
j, gj, hj, lj	like **y** in **y**et	y	**ja**	yar
			hjem	yehm
k	1) before **i**, **y** or **j**, like **ch** in German i**ch**, or something like **ch** in Scottish lo**ch**; it is similar to the first sound of **h**uge	kh	**kirke**	**kheer**ker
			kyst	khewst
	2) otherwise like **k** in **k**it	k	**kaffe**	**kahf**fer
l	always as in **l**ee, never as in bell	l	**tale**	**tar**ler

r	in southwestern Norway, it is pronounced in the back of the mouth (as in French), elsewhere it is slightly rolled in the front of the mouth	r	**rask**	rahsk

N.B. In the groups **rd**, **rl**, **rn** and **rt**, the **r** tends not to be pronounced but influences the pronunciation of the following consonant, which is then pronounced with the tongue behind the upper teeth ridge (turned upwards at the front). We don't use a special symbol for this retroflex pronunciation of **d**, **l**, **n** or **t**.

rs	is generally pronounced like **sh** in **sh**ut in eastern Norway	sh	**norsk**	noshk
s	always as in **s**o	s/ss	**rose**	**roo**sser
sj, skj, sk	when followed by **i**, **y**, **ø** or **øy**, like **sh** in **sh**ut	sh	**sjø** **ski**	shur shee

N.B. The letters **c**, **q**, **w**, **z** are only found in foreign words, and tend to be pronounced as in the language of origin.

NORWEGIAN

Vowels

In Norwegian, vowels in stressed syllables are long when followed by, at most, one pronounced consonant. They are generally short when followed by two or more consonants.

a	1) when long, like **a** in c**ar**	ar*	**dag**	darg
	2) when short, fairly like **u** in c**u**t or **o** in American c**o**llege	ah	**vaske**	**vahs**ker
e	1) when long, like **ay**, in s**ay**, but a pure sound, *not* a diphthong	ay	**se**	say
	2) when short, like **e** in g**e**t	eh	**penn**	pehn
	3) when followed by **r**, like **a** in b**a**d; long or short	ææ æ	**her** **sterk**	hæær stærk
	4) when unstressed, like **er** in oth**er**	er*	**nese**	**nay**sser
i	1) when long, like **ee** in s**ee**, but with the tongue more raised, and the lips more drawn back at the sides	ee	**ti**	tee
	2) when short, like **ee** in m**ee**t	i	**drikke**	**drik**ker
o	1) when long, like **oo** in s**oo**n, but with the lips more rounded (when followed by **-rt**, **-st**, **-m** and **-nd**, it can be short)	oo	**god**	goo

* The **r** should not be pronounced when reading this transcription.

	2) when short, generally like **o** in h**o**t	o	**tolv**	tol
u	1) something like the **ew** in f**ew**, or Scottish **oo** in g**oo**d; you will find it very hard to distinguish from Norwegian **y**, so we use the same symbol for both	ew	**mur**	mewr
	2) in some words, like **oo** in f**oo**t	oo	**nummer**	**noom**merr
y	put your tongue in the position for the **ee** in b**ee**, and then round your lips as for the **oo** in p**oo**l: the vowel you pronounce like this should be more or less correct	ew	**by** **tynn**	bew tewn
æ	1) before **r** like **a** in b**a**d; usually long but sometimes short	ææ æ	**lære** **lærd**	**ææ**rer læd
	2) otherwise, like **ay** in s**ay**	ay	**hæl**	hayl
ø	like **u** in f**u**r; either long or short	ur*	**dør** **søtt**	durr surt
å	1) when long, like **aw** in s**aw**	aw	**på**	paw
	2) when short (rare), more like **o** in h**o**t	o	**gått**	got

Diphthongs

au	this sounds like **ow** in n**ow**, but, in fact, the first part is a Norwegian **ø**-sound	ow	**sau**	sow
ei	like **ay** in **say** but often reminiscent of **igh** in s**igh**	ay	**vei**	vay
øy	fairly like **oy** in b**oy**	oy	**høy**	hoy

Silent letters

1) The letter **g** is generally silent in the endings **-lig** and **-ig**.
2) The letter **d** is generally silent after **l** or **n** or after **r** at the end of a word (with lengthening of the vowel) or often after a long vowel, e.g. ho**ld**e, la**nd**, gå**rd**.
3) The letter **t** is silent in the definite form ("the") of neuter nouns (e.g., ep**let**) and in the pronoun **det**.
4) The letter **v** is silent in a few words, e.g., sel**v**, tol**v**, hal**v**, søl**v**.

* The **r** should not be pronounced when reading this transcription.

Some basic expressions

Yes.	**Ja.**	yar
No.	**Nei.**	nay
Please.	**Vennligst.**	**vehn**ligst
Thank you.	**Takk.**	tahk
Thank you very much.	**Mange takk.**	**mahng**er tahk
That's all right.	**Ingen årsak.**	**ing**ern **aw**shahk

Greetings

Good morning.	**God morgen.**	goo **maw**ern
Good afternoon.	**God dag.**	goo darg
Good evening.	**God kveld./ God aften.**	goo kvehl/goo **ahf**tern
Good night.	**God natt.**	goo naht
Good-bye.	**Adjø.**	ah**dyur**
See you later.	**På gjensyn.**	paw **yehn**sewn
This is Mr....	**Dette er herr ...**	**deht**ter ær hær
This is Mrs....	**Dette er fru ...**	**deht**ter ær frew
This is Miss ...	**Dette er frøken ...**	**deht**ter ær **frur**kern
I'm very pleased to meet you.	**Det gleder meg å treffe Dem.**	day **glay**derr may aw **trehf**fer dehm
How are you?	**Hvordan står det til?**	**voor**dahn stawr day til
Very well, thank you. And you?	**Bare bra, takk. Og med Dem?**	**bar**rer brar tahk. awg may(d) dehm
Fine.	**Fint.**	fint
Excuse me.	**Unnskyld.**	**ewn**shewl

Questions

Where?	**Hvor?**	voor
Where is ... ?	**Hvor er ... ?**	voor ær
Where are ... ?	**Hvor er ... ?**	voor ær
When?	**Når?**	nawr

NORWEGIAN

What?	**Hva?**	var
How?	**Hvordan?**	**voor**dahn
How much?	**Hvor mye?**	voor **mew**er
How many?	**Hvor mange?**	voor **mahng**er
Who?	**Hvem?**	vehm
Why?	**Hvorfor?**	**voor**for
Which?	**Hvilken?**	**vil**kern
What do you call this?	**Hva heter dette?**	var **hay**terr **deht**ter
What do you call that?	**Hva heter det?**	var **hay**terr day
What does this mean?	**Hva betyr dette?**	var ber**tewr** **deht**ter
What does that mean?	**Hva betyr det?**	var ber**tewr** day

Do you speak . . . ?

Do you speak English?	**Snakker De engelsk?**	**snahk**kerr dee **ehng**erlsk
Do you speak German?	**Snakker De tysk?**	**snahk**kerr dee tewsk
Do you speak French?	**Snakker De fransk?**	**snahk**kerr dee frahnsk
Do you speak Spanish?	**Snakker De spansk?**	**snahk**kerr dee spahnsk
Do you speak Italian?	**Snakker De italiensk?**	**snahk**kerr de itahlee**ehnsk**
Could you speak more slowly, please?	**Kunne De snakke litt saktere?**	**kewn**ner dee **snahk**ker lit **sahk**terrer
Please point to the phrase in the book.	**Kunne De peke på setningen i boken.**	**kewn**ner dee **pay**ker paw **seht**ningern ee **boo**kern
Just a minute. I'll see if I can find it in this book.	**Et øyeblikk. Jeg skal se om jeg kan finne det i denne boken.**	eht **oy**erblik. yay skal say om yay karn **fin**ner day ee **dehn**ner **boo**kern
I understand.	**Jeg forstår.**	yay for**shtawr**
I don't understand.	**Jeg forstår ikke.**	yay for**shtawr** **ik**ker

Can . . . ?

Can I have . . . ?	**Kan jeg få . . . ?**	kahn yay faw
Can we have . . . ?	**Kan vi få . . . ?**	kahn vee faw
Can you show me . . . ?	**Kan De vise meg . . . ?**	kahn dee **vee**sser may
Can you tell me . . . ?	**Kan De si meg . . . ?**	kahn dee see may
Can you help me, please?	**Kan De være så vennlig å hjelpe meg?**	kahn dee **vææ**rer saw **vehn**lee aw **yehl**per may

Wanting

I'd like . . .	**Jeg vil gjerne ha . . .**	yay vil **yææ**ner har
We'd like . . .	**Vi ville gjerne ha . . .**	vee **vi**ler **yææ**ner har
Please give me . . .	**Vennligst, gi meg . . .**	**vehn**ligst yee may
Give it to me, please.	**Vennligst, gi det til meg.**	**vehn**ligst yee day til may
Please bring me . . .	**Vennligst, hent . . . til meg.**	**vehn**ligst hehnt . . . til may
Bring it to me, please.	**Vennligst, hent det til meg.**	**vehn**ligst hehnt day til may
I'm hungry.	**Jeg er sulten.**	yay ær **sewl**tern
I'm thirsty.	**Jeg er tørst.**	yay ær tursht
I'm tired.	**Jeg er trett.**	yay ær treht
I'm lost.	**Jeg har gått meg vill.**	yay har got may vil
It's important.	**Det er viktig.**	day ær **vik**tee
It's urgent.	**Det haster.**	day **hahss**terr
Hurry up!	**Skynd Dem!**	shewn dehm

It is/There is . . .

It is/It's . . .	**Det er . . .**	day ær
Is it . . . ?	**Er det . . . ?**	ær day
It isn't . . .	**Det er ikke . . .**	day ær **ik**ker
There is/There are . . .	**Det finnes . . .**	day **fin**nerss
Is there/Are there . . . ?	**Finnes det . . . ?**	**fin**nerss day

There isn't/There aren't . . .	**Det finnes ikke . . .**	day **fin**nerss **ik**ker
There isn't any/ There aren't any.	**Det finnes ingen.**	day **fin**nerss **ing**ern

A few common words

big/small	**stor/liten**	stoor/**lee**tern
quick/slow	**hurtig/langsom**	**hew**tee/**lahng**som
early/late	**tidlig/sen**	**tee**lee/sayn
cheap/expensive	**billig/dyr**	**bil**lee/dewr
near/far	**nær/langt borte**	næær/lahngt **boor**ter
hot/cold	**varm/kald**	vahrm/kahl
full/empty	**full/tom**	fewl/tom
easy/difficult	**lett/vanskelig**	leht/**vahn**skerlee
heavy/light	**tung/lett**	tewng/leht
open/shut	**åpen/lukket**	**aw**pern/**look**kert
right/wrong	**riktig/gal**	**rik**tee/garl
old/new	**gammel/ny**	**gahm**merl/new
old/young	**gammel/ung**	**gahm**merl/oong
beautiful/ugly	**pen/stygg**	payn/stewg
good/bad	**god/dårlig**	goo/**dawr**lee
better/worse	**bedre/verre**	**bayd**rer/**vær**rer

Some prepositions and a few more useful words

at	**ved**	vay(d)
on	**på**	paw
in	**i**	ee
to	**til**	til
from	**fra**	frar
inside	**innenfor**	**in**nernfor
outside	**utenfor**	**ew**ternfor
up	**opp**	op
down	**ned**	nay(d)
before	**før**	furr
after	**etter**	**eht**terr
with	**med**	may(d)
without	**uten**	**ew**tern
through	**gjennom**	**yehn**nom
towards	**mot**	moot
until	**til**	til
during	**i løpet av**	ee **lur**pert ahv
and	**og**	aw(g)
or	**eller**	**ehl**lerr
not	**ikke**	**ik**ker
nothing	**ingenting**	**ing**ernting

none	**ingen**	**ing**ern
very	**veldig**	**vehl**dee
also	**også**	**aw**ssaw
soon	**snart**	snahrt
perhaps	**kanskje**	**kahn**sher
here	**her**	hæær
there	**der**	dæær
now	**nå**	naw
then	**da**	dar

Arrival

Your passport, please.	**Passet Deres, takk.**	**pahs**sser **day**rerss tahk
Here it is.	**Vær så god.**	væær saw goo
Have you anything to declare?	**Har De noe å fortolle?**	harr dee **noo**er aw for**tol**ler
No, nothing at all.	**Nei, ingen ting.**	nay **ing**ernting
Porter!	**Bærer!**	**bææ**rerr
Can you help me with my luggage, please?	**Kan De hjelpe meg med bagasjen?**	kahn dee **yehl**per may may(d) bah**gar**shern
That's my suitcase.	**Det er min koffert.**	day ær meen **koof**ferrt
Where's the bus to the centre of town, please?	**Hvor tar man bussen inn til sentrum?**	voor tarr mahn **bews**ssern in til **sehn**trewm
This way, please.	**Denne vei.**	**dehn**ner vay

Changing money

Where's the nearest bank, please?	**Hvor ligger nærmeste bank?**	voor **lig**gerr **nær**merster bahnk
Can you change a traveller's cheque, please?	**Kan De innløse en reisesjekk?**	kahn dee **in**lursser ayn **righ**ssershehk

Car rental

I'd like a car.	**Jeg vil gjerne leie en bil.**	yay vil **yææ**ner **lay**er ayn beel
For how long?	**Hvor lenge?**	voor **lehng**er
A day/Four days/ A week/Two weeks.	**En dag/Fire dager/ En uke/To uker.**	ayn darg/**fee**rer **dar**gerr/ ayn **ew**ker/too **ew**kerr

NORWEGIAN

Taxi

Where can I get a taxi?	**Hvor kan jeg få tak i en drosje?**	voor kahn yay faw tark ee ayn **drosh**er
What's the fare to ... ?	**Hva koster det til ... ?**	var **koss**terr day til
Take me to this address, please.	**Vennligst, kjør meg til denne adressen.**	**vehn**ligst khurr may til **dehn**ner ah**drehss**sern
I'm in a hurry.	**Jeg har det travelt.**	yay harr day **trar**verlt
Could you drive more slowly, please?	**Kunne De kjøre litt saktere?**	**kewn**ner dee **khur**rer lit **sahk**terrer

Hotel and other accommodation

My name is ...	**Mitt navn er ...**	mit nahvn ær
Have you a reservation?	**Har De reservert?**	harr dee raysehr**vayrt**
Yes, here's the confirmation.	**Ja, her er bekreftelsen.**	yar hæær ær ber**krehf**terlssern
I'd like ...	**Jeg vil gjerne ha ...**	yay vil **yææ**ner har
I'd like a single room/a double room.	**Jeg vil gjerne ha et enkeltrom/et dobbeltrom.**	yay vil **yææ**ner har eht **ehng**kerltroom/eht **dob**berltroom
a room with a bath/ with a shower	**et rom med bad/ med dusj**	eht room may(d) bard/ may(d) dewsh

How much?

What's the price per night/per week/per month?	**Hva koster det for en natt/for en uke/for en måned?**	var **koss**terr day for ayn naht/for ayn **ew**ker/for ayn **maw**nerd
May I see the room?	**Kan jeg få se rommet?**	kahn yay faw say **room**mert
I'm sorry, I don't like it.	**Jeg beklager, men jeg liker det ikke.**	yay ber**klar**gerr mayn yay **lee**kerr day **ik**ker
Yes, that's fine. I'll take it.	**Ja, det er bra. Jeg tar det.**	yar day ær brar. yay tarr day
What's my room number, please?	**Hvilket værelsenummer har jeg?**	**vil**kert **vææ**rerlssernoommerr harr yay
Number 123.	**Nummer 123.**	**noom**merr 123

Service, please

Who is it?	**Hvem er det?**	vehm ær day
Just a minute.	**Et øyeblikk.**	eht **oy**erblik
Come in! The door's open.	**Kom inn! Døren er åpen.**	kom in. **dur**rern ær **aw**pern
May we have breakfast in our room?	**Kan vi få frokost på rommet?**	kahn vee faw **froo**koost paw **room**mer

Breakfast

I'll have ...	**Jeg vil gjerne ha ...**	yay vil **yææ**ner har
I'll have some fruit juice.	**Jeg vil gjerne ha litt fruktsaft.**	yay vil **yææ**ner har lit **frewkt**sahft
a boiled egg	**et kokt egg**	eht kookt ehg
a fried egg	**et speilegg**	eht **spay**lehg
some bacon/some ham	**litt bacon/litt skinke**	lit **bay**kern/lit **shing**ker
some toast	**litt ristet loff**	litt **riss**tert loof
a pot of tea	**en kanne te**	ayn **kahn**ner tay
a cup of tea	**en kopp te**	ayn kop tay
some coffee	**kaffe**	**kah**ffer
some chocolate	**sjokolade**	shookoo**lar**der
more butter	**mer smør**	mair smurr
some hot water	**litt varmt vann**	lit vahrmt vahn

Difficulties

The central heating doesn't work.	**Sentralvarmen virker ikke.**	sehn**trarl**vahrmern **veer**ker **ik**ker
the light/the socket	**lyset/støpslet**	**lew**sser/**sturp**sler
the tap/the toilet	**vannkranen/toalettet**	**vahn**krarnern/twah**leht**ter
There's no hot water.	**Det er ikke noe varmt vann.**	day ær **ik**ker **noo**er vahrmt vahn
May I see the manager, please?	**Kan jeg få snakke med direktøren?**	kahn yay faw **snahk**ker may(d) deerehk**tur**rern

Telephone—Mail

There's a call for you.	**Det er telefon til Dem.**	day ær tayler**foon** til dehm
Hold the line, please.	**Ikke legg på røret.**	**ik**ker lehg paw **rur**rer

Operator, I've been cut off.	**Frøken, jeg er blitt avbrutt.**	**frur**kern yay ær blit **ahv**brewt
Did anyone telephone me?	**Har noen ringt til meg?**	harr **noo**ern ringt til may
Is there any mail for me?	**Er det noe post til meg?**	ær day **noo**er post til may
Are there any messages for me?	**Er det noen beskjed til meg?**	ær day **noo**ern ber**shay(d)** til may

Checking out

May I have my bill, please?	**Kan jeg få regningen, takk.**	kahn yay faw **ray**ningern tahk
We're in a great hurry.	**Vi har det svært travelt.**	vee harr day svæt **trar**verlt
It's been a very enjoyable stay.	**Det har vært et meget hyggelig opphold.**	day harr væt eht **may**gert **hewg**gerlee **op**hol

Eating out

Good evening, sir/ Good evening, madam.	**God aften.**	goo **ahf**tern
Good evening. I'd like a table for two, please.	**God aften. Jeg vil gjerne ha et bord for to, takk.**	goo **ahf**tern. yay vil **yææ**ner har eht boor for too tahk
Do you have a fixed-price menu?	**Har De en fastsatt meny?**	harr dee ayn **fahst**saht meh**new**
May I see the à la carte menu?	**Kan jeg få se spisekartet?**	kahn yay faw say **spee**sserkahrter
May we have an ashtray, please?	**Kan vi få et askebeger.**	kahn vee faw eht **ah**skerbaygerr
some bread	**litt brød**	lit brur(d)
a fork	**en gaffel**	ayn **gahf**ferl
a knife	**en kniv**	ayn kneev
a spoon	**en skje**	ayn shay
a plate	**en tallerken**	ayn tahl**lær**kern
a glass	**et glass**	eht glahss
a napkin	**en serviett**	ayn særvi**eht**
another chair	**en stol til**	ayn stool til

Where's the gentlemen's toilet (men's room)?	**Hvor er herre-toalettet?**	voor ær **hæ**rerr-twahlehtter
Where's the ladies' toilet (ladies' room)?	**Hvor er dametoalettet?**	voor ær **dar**mer-twahlehtter

Appetizers

I'd like some ...	**Jeg vil gjerne ha ...**	yay vil **yææ**ner har
I'd like some assorted appetizers.	**Jeg vil gjerne ha noen assorterte hors-d'œuvres.**	yay vil **yææ**ner har **noo**ern ahssor**tair**ter or**durvr**
orange juice	**appelsinsaft**	**ahp**perlsseenssahft
ham	**skinke**	**shing**ker
melon	**melon**	meh**loon**
pâté	**postei**	pooss**tay**
smoked salmon	**røkelaks**	**rur**kerlahks
shrimps (shrimp)	**reker**	**ray**kerr

Soup

Have you any ... ?	**Har De ...?**	harr dee
Have you any chicken soup?	**Har De hønse-suppe?**	harr dee **hurn**sserssewpper
vegetable soup	**grønnsaksuppe**	**grurn**ssahksewpper
onion soup	**løksuppe**	**lurk**sewpper

Fish

I'd like some ...	**Jeg vil gjerne ha ...**	yay vil **yææ**ner har
I'd like some fish.	**Jeg vil gjerne ha fisk.**	yay vil **yææ**ner har fisk
sole	**sjøtunge**	**shur**toonger
trout	**ørret**	**urr**rert
lobster	**hummer**	**hoom**merr
crayfish	**kreps**	krehps
prawns	**store reker**	**stoo**rer **ray**kerr
I'd like it ...	**Jeg vil gjerne ha det ...**	yay vil **yææ**ner har day
I'd like it steamed.	**Jeg vil gjerne ha det dampet.**	yay vil **yææ**ner har day **dahm**pert
grilled	**grillstekt**	**gril**staykt
boiled	**kokt**	kookt
baked	**ovnstekt**	**ovn**staykt
fried	**stekt**	staykt

Meat—Poultry—Game

I'd like some ...	**Jeg vil gjerne ha ...**	yay vil **yææ**ner har
I'd like some beef.	**Jeg vil gjerne ha oksekjøtt.**	yay vil **yææ**ner har **ook**serkhurt
a beef steak	**en biff**	ayn bif
some roast beef	**roastbiff**	**roast**bif
a veal cutlet	**en kalvekotelett**	ayn **kahl**verkotterleht
mutton	**fårekjøtt**	**faw**rerkhurt
lamb	**lammekjøtt**	**lahm**merkhurt
a pork chop	**en svinekotelett**	ayn **svee**nerkotterleht
roast pork	**svinestek**	**svee**nerstayk
hare	**hare**	**har**rer
chicken	**kylling**	**khewl**ling
roast chicken	**stekt kylling**	staykt **khewl**ling
duck	**and**	ahn
How do you like your meat?	**Hvordan vil De ha kjøttet tilberedt?**	**voor**dahn vil dee har **khurt**tert **til**berreht
rare	**blodig**	**bloo**dee
medium	**medium**	**may**diewm
well done	**godt stekt**	got staykt

Vegetables

What vegetables have you got?	**Hvilke grønnsaker har De?**	**vil**ker **grurn**ssakerr harr dee
I'd like some ...	**Jeg vil gjerne ha ...**	yay vil **yææ**ner har
I'd like some asparagus.	**Jeg vil gjerne ha asparges.**	yay vil **yææ**ner har ah**spar**gerss
green beans	**grønne bønner**	**grurn**ner **burn**nerr
mushrooms	**sopp**	sop
carrots	**gulrøtter**	**gewl**rurtterr
onions	**løk**	lurk
red cabbage	**rødkål**	**rurd**kawl
spinach	**spinat**	spi**nart**
rice	**ris**	rees
peas	**erter**	æterr
tomatoes	**tomater**	too**mar**terr
green salad	**grønn salat**	grurn sah**lart**
potatoes	**poteter**	poo**tay**terr

Desserts

Nothing more, thanks.	**Takk, jeg er forsynt.**	tahk yay ær fo**shewnt**

Just a small portion, please.	**Bare en liten porsjon.**	**bar**rer ayn **lee**tern poo**shoon**
Have you any ice-cream?	**Har De iskrem?**	harr dee **ees**krehm
fruit salad	**fruktsalat**	**frewkt**sahlart
fresh fruit	**frisk frukt**	frisk frewkt
cheese	**ost**	oost

Drink

What would you like to drink?	**Hva vil De ha å drikke?**	var vil dee har aw **drik**ker
I'll have a beer, please.	**Jeg vil gjerne ha en øl.**	yay vil **yææ**ner har ayn url
I'll have a whisky, please.	**Jeg vil gjerne ha en whisky.**	yay vil **yææ**ner har ayn **wiss**kee

Wine

I'd like a bottle of wine.	**Jeg vil gjerne ha en flaske vin.**	yay vil **yææ**ner har ayn **flah**sker veen
red wine	**rødvin**	**rur(d)**vin
rosé wine	**rosévin**	roa**say**vin
white wine	**hvitvin**	**veet**vin
Cheers!	**Skål!**	skawl

The bill (check)

May I have the bill (check) please?	**Kan jeg få regningen, takk!**	karn yay faw **ray**ningern tahk
Is service included?	**Er service inkludert?**	ær **sehr**viss ingklew**dai(r)t**
Everything's included.	**Alt er inkludert.**	ahlt ær ingklew**dai(r)t**
Thank you, that was a very good meal.	**Takk, det var et utmerket måltid.**	tahk day varr eht **ewt**mærkert **mawl**tid

Travelling

Where's the railway station, please?	**Hvor ligger jernbanestasjonen?**	voor **lig**gerr **yææn**barner-stahshoonern
Where's the ticket office, please?	**Hvor er billettkontoret?**	voor ær bil**leht**koontoorer
I'd like a ticket to ...	**Jeg vil gjerne ha en billett til ...**	yay vil **yææ**ner har ayn bil**leht** til

First or second class?	**Første eller annen klasse?**	**fursh**ter **ehl**lerr **ahn**nern **klahss**ser
First class, please.	**Første, takk.**	**fursh**ter tahk
Single or return (one way or round-trip)?	**Enveis eller tur-retur?**	**ayn**vayss **ehl**ler tewr-rer**tewr**
Do I have to change trains?	**Må jeg bytte tog?**	maw yay **bewt**ter tawg
What platform does the train leave from?	**Fra hvilken plattform går toget?**	frar **vil**kern **plaht**form gawr **taw**ger
Where's the nearest underground (subway) station?	**Hvor ligger nærmeste undergrunnsstasjon?**	voor **lig**gerr **nær**mersster **ewn**nergrennwnsstahshoon
Where's the bus station, please?	**Hvor er buss-stasjonen?**	voor ær **bewss**-stahshoonern
When's the first bus to . . . ?	**Når går den første bussen til . . . ?**	nawr gawr dayn **fursh**ter **bewss**sern til
the last bus	**den siste bussen**	dayn **siss**ter **bewss**sern
the next bus	**den neste bussen**	dayn **nehss**ter **bewss**sern
Please let me off at the next stop.	**Vil De slippe meg av på neste stop-pested?**	vil dee **slip**per may ahv paw **nehss**ter **stop**per-stehd

Relaxing

What's on at the cinema (movies)?	**Hva går på kino?**	var gawr paw **khee**noo
What's on at the theatre?	**Hva går på teatret?**	var gawr paw tay**ar**trer
What time does the film begin? And the play?	**Når begynner filmen? Og stykket?**	nawr ber**yewn**nerr **fil**mern? awg **stewk**ker
Are there any tickets for tonight?	**Er det noen billetter igjen til i kveld?**	ær day **noo**ern bil**leht**terr **ee**yern til ee kvehl
Where can we go dancing?	**Hvor kan vi gå for å danse?**	voor kahn vee gaw for aw **dahn**ser
Would you like to dance?	**Vil De danse?**	vil dee **dahn**ser

Introductions

How do you do?	**God dag.**	goo darg
How are you?	**Hvordan står det til?**	**voor**dahn stawr day til

NORWEGIAN

Very well, thank you. And you?	**Bare bra, takk. Og med Dem?**	**bar**rer brar tahk. awg may(d) dehm
May I introduce Miss Philips?	**Kan jeg få presentere frøken Philips?**	kahn yay faw praysahng**tay**rert **frur**kern Philips
My name is ...	**Mitt navn er ...**	mit nahvn ær
I'm very pleased to meet you.	**Det gleder meg å trefle Dem.**	day **glay**derr may aw **trehf**fer dehm
How long have you been here?	**Hvor lenge har De vært her?**	voor **lehng**er harr dee vært hær
It was nice meeting you.	**Det var hyggelig å trefle Dem.**	day varr **hewg**gerlee aw **trehf**fer dehm

Dating

Would you like a cigarette?	**Vil De ha en sigarett?**	vil dee har ayn sigah**reht**
May I get you a drink?	**Kan jeg by Dem på en drink?**	kahn yay bew dehm paw ayn drink
Do you have a light, please?	**Unnskyld, har De en fyrstikk?**	**ewn**shewl harr dee ayn **few**shtik
Are you waiting for someone?	**Venter De på noen?**	**vehn**terr dee paw **noo**ern
Are you free this evening?	**Er De ledig i kveld?**	ær dee **lay**dee ee kvehl
Where shall we meet?	**Hvor skal vi møtes?**	voor skahl ve **mur**terss
What time shall I meet you?	**Når skal jeg møte Dem?**	nawr skahl yay **mur**ter dehm
May I take you home?	**Kan jeg få følge Dem hjem?**	kahn yay faw **fur**ler dehm yehm
Thank you, it's been a wonderful evening.	**Mange takk, det har vært en hyggelig kveld.**	**mahng**er tahk day harr vært ayn **hewg**gerlee kvehl
What's your telephone number?	**Hva er telefonnummeret Deres?**	var ær taylerfoon-noommerrer **day**rerss
Do you live alone?	**Bor De alene?**	boor dee ah**lay**ner
What time is your last train?	**Når går det siste toget Deres?**	nawr gawr day **sis**ster **taw**ger **day**rerss
Good-night ...	**God natt ...**	goo naht

Banks

Where's the nearest bank, please?	**Unnskyld, hvor ligger nærmeste bank?**	**ewn**shewl voor **lig**gerr **nær**merster bahnk
Where can I cash some traveller's cheques?	**Hvor kan jeg innløse noen reisesjekker?**	voor kahn yay **in**lursser **noo**ern **righ**ssershehkkerr
What time does the bank open/What time does it close?	**Når åpner banken/ Når stenger den?**	nawr **awp**nerr **bahng**kern/nawr **stehng**err dehn
I'm expecting some money from home. Has it arrived?	**Jeg venter penger hjemmefra. Har de kommet?**	yay **vehn**terr **pehng**err **yehm**merfrar. harr dee **kom**mert
Can you give me some small change, please?	**Kan De gi meg litt vekslepenger?**	kahn dee yee may lit **vehk**slerpehngerr

Shops, stores and services

Where is the nearest chemist's (pharmacy)?	**Hvor er nærmeste apotek?**	voor ær **nær**merster ahpo**tayk**
the nearest hairdresser's	**den nærmeste frisør**	dehn **nær**merster fri**ssurr**
the photo shop	**fotoforretningen**	**foo**tooforrehtningern
the jeweller's	**gullsmeden**	**gewl**ssmaydern
the department store	**varemagasinet**	**var**rermahgahsseener
the police station	**politistasjonen**	pooli**tee**stahshoonern
the garage	**parkeringshuset**	pahr**kay**ringsshewsser
How do I get there?	**Hvordan kommer jeg dit?**	**voor**dahn **kom**merr yay deet
Is it within walking distance?	**Er det for langt å gå dit?**	ær day for lahngt aw gaw deet

Service

Can you help me, please?	**Kan De være så vennlig å hjelpe meg?**	kahn dee **væ**ærer saw **vehn**lee aw **yehl**per may
Can you show me this? And that, too.	**Kan De vise meg den? Og den også.**	kahn dee **vee**ser may dehn. awg dehn **aw**ssaw
It's too expensive/ too big/too small.	**Det er for dyrt/for stort/for lite.**	day ær for dewrt/for stoort/for **lee**ter

NORWEGIAN

Can you show me some more?	**Kan De vise meg flere?**	kahn dee **vee**sser may **flay**rer
something better	**noe bedre**	**noo**er **bayd**rer
something cheaper	**noe billigere**	**noo**er **bil**ligerrer
How much is this? And that?	**Hvor mye koster dette? Og det?**	voor **mew**er **koss**terr **deht**ter? awg day
It's not quite what I want.	**Det er ikke akkurat hva jeg vil ha.**	day ær **ik**ker **ahk**hewrart var yay vil har
I like it.	**Jeg liker det.**	yay **lee**kerr day

Chemist's (Pharmacy)

I'd like something for a cold/for a cough/for travel sickness.	**Jeg vil gjerne ha noe for en forkjølelse/mot hoste/mot reisesyke.**	yay vil **yææ**ner har **noo**er for ayn for**khur**lerlser/moot **hooss**ter/moot **righ**sserssewker
Can you recommend something for hay-fever/for sunburn?	**Kan De anbefale noe mot høysnue/mot solbrenthet?**	kahn dee ahnber**far**ler **noo**er moot **hoy**ssnewer/moot **sool**brehnthayt

Toiletry

May I have some razor blades?	**Kan jeg få noen barberblader?**	kahn yay faw **noo**ern bahr**bayr**blarderr
some shaving cream	**en barberkrem**	ayn bahr**bayr**krehm
some toothpaste	**en tannpasta**	ayn **tahn**pahsstah
I'd like some soap.	**Jeg vil gjerne ha en såpe.**	yay vil **yææ**ner har ayn **saw**per
some suntan oil	**en solbadolje**	ayn **sool**bardolyer

At the barber's

I'd like a haircut, please.	**Jeg vil gjerne ha håret klippet.**	yay vil **yææ**ner har **haw**rer **klip**pert
Short/Leave it long.	**Kort/La det være langt.**	kort/lar day **vææ**rer lahngt
A razor cut, please.	**Skåret med barberkniv.**	**skaw**rert may(d) bahr**bayr**kneev

At the hairdresser's

I'd like a shampoo and set, please.	**Jeg vil gjerne ha vask og legg.**	yay vil **yææ**ner har vahsk awg lehg

I'd like a bleach.	**Jeg vil gjerne ha det bleket.**	yay vil **yææ**ner har day **blay**kert
a permanent	**en permanent**	ayn pehrmah**nehnt**
a colour rinse	**en fargeskylling**	ayn **fahr**gershewlling
a manicure	**en manikyr**	ayn mahnee**kewr**

Photography

I'd like a film for this camera.	**Jeg ville gjerne ha en film til dette apparatet.**	yay vil **yææ**ner har ayn film til **deht**ter ahppah**rar**ter
This camera doesn't work.	**Dette apparatet virker ikke.**	**deht**ter ahppah**rar**ter **veer**ker **ik**ker

At the post office

Where's the nearest post office, please?	**Hvor ligger det nærmeste post-kontoret?**	voor **lig**gerr day **nær**-merster **post**koontoorer
I'd like to send this by express (special delivery)/by air mail.	**Jeg vil gjerne sende dette som ilpost/med luftpost.**	yay vil **yææ**ner **sehn**ner **deht**ter som **eel**post/may(d) **lewft**post

Service stations

Where is the nearest service station, please?	**Kan De si meg hvor den nærmeste ben-sinstasjonen ligger?**	kahn dee see may voor dehn **nær**merster behn-**seen**stahshoonern **lig**gerr
Fill her up, please.	**Full tank, takk.**	fewl tahnk tahk
Check the oil, please.	**Vil de kontrollere oljen?**	vil dee koontrool**lay**rer **ol**yern
Would you check the tyres?	**Vil De kontrollere dekkene?**	vil dee koontrool**lay**rer **dehk**kerner

Street directions

Can you show me on the map where I am?	**Kan De vise meg på kartet hvor jeg er?**	kahn dee **vee**sser may paw **kah**ter voor yay ær
You're on the wrong road.	**De er på feil vei.**	dee ær paw fayl vay
Go back to ...	**Kjør tilbake til ...**	khurr til**bar**ker til
Go straight ahead.	**Kjør rett frem.**	khurr reht frehm
It's on the left/on the right.	**Det er på venstre side/på høyre side.**	day ær paw **vehn**strer **see**der/paw **hoy**rer **see**der

Accidents

May I use your telephone?	**Kan jeg få låne telefonen Deres?**	kahn yay faw **law**ner taylerf**oo**nern **day**rerss
Call a doctor quickly.	**Tilkall en lege øyeblikkelig.**	**til**kahl ayn **lay**ger **oyer**-blikkerlee
Call an ambulance.	**Ring etter en sykebil.**	ring **eht**terr ayn **sew**ker-beel
Please call the police.	**Vennligst ring til politiet.**	**vehn**ligst ring til pooli**tee**er

Numbers

zero	**null**	newl
one	**en**	ayn
two	**to**	too
three	**tre**	tray
four	**fire**	**fee**rer
five	**fem**	fehm
six	**seks**	sehks
seven	**sju**	shew
eight	**åtte**	**ot**ter
nine	**ni**	nee
ten	**ti**	tee
eleven	**elleve**	**ehl**ver
twelve	**tolv**	tol
thirteen	**tretten**	**treht**tern
fourteen	**fjorten**	**fyoor**tern
fifteen	**femten**	**fehm**tern
sixteen	**seksten**	**sigh**stern
seventeen	**sytten**	**sewt**tern
eighteen	**atten**	**aht**tern
nineteen	**nitten**	**nit**tern
twenty	**tjue**	**khew**er
twenty-one	**tjueen**	khewer**ayn**
thirty	**tretti**	**treht**tee
forty	**førti**	**fur**tee
fifty	**femti**	**fehm**tee
sixty	**seksti**	**sehks**tee
seventy	**sytti**	**sewt**tee
eighty	**åtti**	**ot**tee
ninety	**nitti**	**nit**tee
one hundred	**hundre**	**hewn**drer
one thousand	**tusen**	**tew**ssern
ten thousand	**ti tusen**	tee **tew**ssern

Days

It's Sunday.	**Det er søndag.**	day ær **surn**darg
Monday	**mandag**	**mahn**darg
Tuesday	**tirsdag**	**teerss**darg
Wednesday	**onsdag**	**oonss**darg
Thursday	**torsdag**	**torsh**darg
Friday	**fredag**	**fray**darg
Saturday	**lørdag**	**lur**darg
yesterday	**i går**	ee gawr
today	**i dag**	ee darg
tomorrow	**i morgen**	ee **maw**ern
morning/afternoon	**morgen/ettermiddag**	**maw**ern/**eht**terrmiddarg
evening/night	**aften/natt**	**ahf**tern/naht

Months

January	**januar**	yahnew**arr**
February	**februar**	faybrew**arr**
March	**mars**	mahsh
April	**april**	ah**preel**
May	**mai**	**migh**
June	**juni**	**yew**nee
July	**juli**	**yew**lee
August	**august**	**ow**gewst
September	**september**	sehp**tehm**berr
October	**oktober**	ok**taw**berr
November	**november**	no**vehm**berr
December	**desember**	days**sehm**berr
Merry Christmas! Happy New Year!	**God Jul! Godt Nytt År!**	goo yewl! got newtt awr

POLISH

Guide to Pronunciation

Note that Polish has some diacritical letters—letters with accent marks—which we do not know in English.

Letter	Approximate pronunciation	Symbol	Example	
Consonants				
b, f, k, l, m, p, z	are pronounced as in English			
cz	like **ch** in **ch**urch	ch	**czy**	chi
dż	like **j** in **j**am	j	**dżem**	jehm
g	as in **g**irl	g	**guma**	**gu**mah
j	like **y** in **y**et	y	**jak**	yahk
ł	like **w** in **w**in	w	**ładny**	**wahd**ni
n	as in English but put your tongue against the front teeth and not the teeth ridge	n	**na**	nah
s	as in **s**it	s/ss	**sam**	sahm
sz	like **sh** in **sh**ine	sh	**szal**	shahl
t, d	as in English but put your tongue against the front teeth and not against the teeth ridge	t d	**tak** **dom**	tahk dom
w	like **v** in **v**an	v	**woda**	**vo**dah
ż or **rz**	like **s** in plea**s**ure	zh	**żelazo** rzeka	zheh**lah**zo **zhehk**ah

Sounds distinctly different

An often recurring phenomenon in the Slavic languages is "softening", or the "softened" pronunciation of consonants. Examples of this in Polish are **ć**, **dź**, **ń**, **ś** and **ź**. A similar effect can be produced by pronouncing **y** as in **y**et— but very, very short—after the consonant.

c	like the English sequence **ts** in **tsets**e pronounced quickly	ts	**co**	tso
ć	pronounced like the Polish **c** but softer	tsh	**ciało**	**tshah**wo
dz	like the English sequence **ds** in be**ds** pronounced quickly	dz	**dzwonek**	**dzvo**nehk
dź or **dzi**	pronounced like the Polish **dz** but softer	dzh	**dział**	dzhahw
h or **ch**	similar to English **h** but with much more friction	h	**herbata** **chudy**	hehr**bah**tah **hoo**di
ń or **ni**	pronounced like the English **n** but softer	ñ	**nie**	ñeh
r	like the Scottish **r** (vibration of the tip of the tongue); note that it is also pronounced at the end of words	r	**rak**	rahk
ś or **si**	pronounced like the English **s** but softer	s'	**się** **ktoś**	s'eh ktos'
ź or **zi**	pronounced like the English **z** but softer	z'	**zielony**	z'eh**lo**ni

Notice that voiced sounds become completely devoiced at the end of a word or in the context of other voiceless sounds, i.e., they are pronounced like their voiceless counterparts (e.g., **b** of chle**b** is pronounced like **p**; **w** of ró**w** is pronounced like **f**; **rz** and **z** in p**rz**e**z** like **sz** and **s**, etc.).

POLISH

Vowels

a	like English **u** in c**u**lt or American **o** in c**o**llege	ah	**tak**	tahk
e	like **e** in t**e**n	eh	**lek**	lehk
i	like **ee** in f**ee**t	ee	**ile**	**ee**leh
y	like **i** in f**i**t	i	**ty**	ti
o	like **o** in c**o**t	o	**kot**	kot
u or **ó**	a sound between the English **u** in p**u**t and **oo** in b**oo**ts	oo	**drut**	droot
ą	is pronounced **on** before a consonant; when it's the final letter, it is pronounced like French **an** in fi**an**cé	on awng	**prąd** **są**	pront sawng
ę	is pronounced **en** before a consonant or like **e** in b**e**d when it is the final letter	ehn eh	**pęd** **tę**	pehnt teh

Some diphthongs

ej	like **a** in t**a**ke	ay	**dobrej**	**dob**ray
aj	like **i** in l**i**ke	igh	**daj**	digh

The stress falls in Polish on the next to the last syllable, e.g., **głodny** (**gwod**ni), **drogeria** (dro**geh**ryah).

Some basic expressions

Yes.	**Tak.**	tahk
No.	**Nie.**	ñeh
Please.	**Proszę.**	**pro**sheh
Thank you.	**Dziękuję.**	dzhehn**koo**yeh
Thank you very much.	**Dziękuję bardzo.**	dzhehn**koo**yeh **bahr**dzo
That's all right.	**Proszę bardzo.**	**pro**sheh **bahr**dzo

Greetings

Good morning.	**Dzień dobry.**	dzhehñ **do**bri
Good afternoon.	**Dzień dobry.**	dzhehñ **do**bri
Good evening.	**Dobry wieczór.**	**do**bri **vyeh**choor
Good night.	**Dobranoc.**	do**brah**nots
Good-bye.	**Do widzenia.**	do vee**dzeh**ñah
See you later.	**Do zobaczenia.**	do zobah**cheh**ñah
This is Mr. . . .	**To jest pan . . .**	to yehst pahn
This is Mrs. . . .	**To jest pani . . .**	to yehst **pah**ñee
This is Miss . . .	**To jest pani . . .**	to yehst **pah**ñee
I'm very pleased to meet you.	**Miło mi pana/panią poznać.**	**mee**wo mee **pah**na/ **pah**ñawng **po**znahtsh
How are you?	**Jak się pan/pani miewa?**	yahk s'eh pahn/**pah**ñee **myeh**vah
Very well, thank you.	**Bardzo dobrze, dziękuję.**	**bahr**dzo **do**bzheh dzhehn**koo**yeh
And you?	**A pan/pani?**	ah pahn/**pah**ñee
Fine.	**Dobrze.**	**do**bzheh
Excuse me.	**Przepraszam.**	psheh**prah**shahm

Questions

Where?	**Gdzie?**	gdzheh
Where is . . . ?	**Gdzie jest . . . ?**	gdzheh yehst
Where are . . . ?	**Gdzie są . . . ?**	gdzheh sawng
When?	**Kiedy?**	**kyeh**di

POLISH

What?	**Co?**	tso
How?	**Jak?**	yahk
How much?	**Ile?**	**ee**leh
How many?	**Ile?**	**ee**leh
Who?	**Kto?**	kto
Why?	**Dlaczego?**	dlah**cheh**go
Which?	**Który?**	**ktoo**ri
What do you call this?	**Jak się to nazywa?**	yahk s'eh to nah**zi**vah
What do you call that?	**Jak się tamto nazywa?**	yahk s'eh **tahm**to nah**zi**vah
What does this mean?	**Co to znaczy?**	tso to **znah**chi
What does that mean?	**Co tamto znaczy?**	tso **tahm**to **znah**chi

Do you speak . . . ?

Do you speak English?	**Czy pan/pani mówi po angielsku?**	chi pahn/**pah**ñee **moo**vee po ahn**gyehl**skoo
Do you speak German?	**Czy pan/pani mówi po niemiecku?**	chi pahn/**pah**ñee **moo**vee po nyeh**myeh**tskoo
Do you speak French?	**Czy pan/pani mówi po francusku?**	chi pahn/**pah**ñee **moo**vee po frahn**tsoo**skoo
Do you speak Spanish?	**Czy pan/pani mówi po hiszpańsku?**	chi pahn/**pah**ñee **moo**vee po heesh**pahñ**skoo
Do you speak Italian?	**Czy pan/pani mówi po włosku?**	chi pahn/**pah**ñee **moo**vee po **vwo**skoo
Could you speak more slowly, please?	**Proszę mówić trochę wolniej.**	**pro**sheh **moo**veetsh **tro**heh **vol**ñay
Please point to the phrase in the book.	**Proszę wskazać odpowiednie zdanie w moich rozmówkach.**	**pro**sheh **fskah**zahtsh odpo**vyeh**dñeh **zdah**ñeh f**mo**eeh roz**moof**kahh
Just a minute. I'll see if I can find it in this book.	**Chwileczkę. Zobaczę czy to jest w moich rozmówkach.**	hfee**leh**chkeh. zo**bah**cheh chi to yehst f**mo**eeh roz**moof**kahh
I understand.	**Rozumiem.**	ro**zoo**myehm
I don't understand.	**Nie rozumiem.**	ñeh ro**zoo**myehm

Can . . . ?

Can I have . . . ?	**Czy mogę dostać . . . ?**	chi **mo**geh **doss**tahtsh
Can we have . . . ?	**Czy możemy dostać . . . ?**	chi mo**zheh**my **doss**tahtsh
Can you show me . . . ?	**Czy może mi pan/pani pokazać . . . ?**	chi **mo**zheh mee pahn/**pah**ñee po**kah**zahtsh
Can you tell me . . . ?	**Czy może mi pan/pani powiedzieć . . . ?**	chi **mo**zheh mee pahn/**pah**ñee po**vyeh**dzhehtsh
Can you help me, please?	**Czy może mi pan/pani pomóc?**	chi **mo**zheh mee pahn/**pah**ñee **po**moots

Wanting

I'd like . . .	**Chciałbym . . .**	**htshahw**bim
We'd like . . .	**Chcielibyśmy . . .**	**htsheh**leebis'mi
Please give me . . .	**Proszę mi dać . . .**	**pro**sheh mee dahsh
Give it to me, please.	**Proszę mi to dać.**	**pro**sheh mee to dahtsh
Please bring me . . .	**Proszę przynieść mi . . .**	**pro**sheh **pshi**ñehs'tsh mee
Bring it to me, please.	**Proszę mi to przynieść.**	**pro**sheh mee to **pshi**ñehs'tsh
I'm hungry.	**Chce mi się jeść.**	htseh mee s'eh yes'tsh
I'm thirsty.	**Chce mi się pić.**	htseh mee s'eh peetsh
I'm tired.	**Jestem zmęczony.**	**yehss**tehm zmehn**cho**ni
I'm lost.	**Zgubiłem się.**	zgoo**bee**wehm s'eh
It's important.	**To ważne.**	to **vahzh**neh
It's urgent.	**To pilne.**	to **peel**neh
Hurry up!	**Niech się pan/pani pospieszy!**	ñehh s'eh pahn/**pah**ñee pos**pyeh**shi

It is/There is . . .

It is/It's . . .	**To jest . . .**	to yehst
Is it . . . ?	**Czy to jest . . . ?**	chi to yehst
It isn't . . .	**To nie jest . . .**	to ñeh yehst

There is/There are...	**Jest/Są...**	yehst/sawng
Is there/Are there...?	**Czy jest/Czy są...?**	chi yehst/chi sawng
There isn't/There aren't...	**Nie ma...**	ñeh mah
There isn't any/ There aren't any.	**Nie ma.**	ñeh mah

A few common words

big/small	**duży/mały**	**doo**zhi/**mah**wi
quick/slow	**szybki/wolny**	**ship**kee/**vol**ni
early/late	**wczesny/późny**	**fchehss**ni/**pooz**'ni
cheap/expensive	**tani/drogi**	**tah**ñee/**dro**gee
near/far	**bliski/daleki**	**bleess**kee/dah**leh**kee
hot/cold	**gorący/zimny**	go**ront**si/**z'eem**ni
full/empty	**pełny/pusty**	**pehw**ni/**pooss**ti
easy/difficult	**łatwy/trudny**	**waht**fi/**trood**ni
heavy/light	**ciężki/lekki**	**tshehn**shkee/**lehk**kee
open/shut	**otwarty/zamknięty**	ot**fahr**ti/zahmk**ñehn**ti
right/wrong	**słuszny/niesłuszny**	**swoosh**ni/ñeh**swoosh**ni
old/new	**stary/nowy**	**stah**ri/**no**vi
old/young	**stary/młody**	**stah**ri/**mwo**di
beautiful/ugly	**piękny/brzydki**	**pyehnk**ni/**bzhit**kee
good/bad	**dobry/zły**	**dob**ri/zwi
better/worse	**lepszy/gorszy**	**lehp**si/**gor**shi

A few prepositions and some more useful words

at	**w**	v
on	**na**	nah
in	**w**	v
to	**do**	do
from	**z, od**	z od
inside	**wewnątrz**	**vehv**nontsh
outside	**na zewnątrz**	nah **zehv**nontsh
up	**do góry**	do **goo**ri
down	**na dół**	nah doow
before	**przed**	psheht
after	**po**	po
with	**z**	z
without	**bez**	behss
through	**przez**	pshehss
towards	**w kierunku**	fkyeh**roon**koo
until	**aż do**	ahzh do

POLISH

during	**podczas**	**pot**chahss
and	**i**	ee
or	**lub**	loop
not	**nie**	ñeh
nothing	**nic**	ñeets
none	**żaden**	**zhah**dehn
very	**bardzo**	**bahr**dzo
also	**także**	**tahg**zheh
soon	**wkrótce**	**fkroot**tseh
perhaps	**może**	**mo**zheh
here	**tutaj**	**too**tigh
there	**tam**	tahm
now	**teraz**	**teh**rahss
then	**potem**	**po**tehm

Arrival

Your passport, please.	**Paszport proszę.**	**pahsh**port **pro**sheh
Here it is.	**Proszę.**	**pro**sheh
Have you anything to declare?	**Czy ma pan/pani coś do zadeklarowania?**	chi mah pahn/**pah**ñee tsos' do zahdehklahro**vah**ñah
No, nothing at all.	**Nie, nic.**	ñeh ñeets
Porter!	**Bagażowy!**	bahgah**zho**vi
Can you help me with my luggage, please?	**Proszę pomóc mi nieść te walizki.**	**pro**sheh **po**moots mee ñehs'tsh teh vah**lee**skee
That's my suitcase.	**To moja walizka.**	to **mo**yah vah**lee**skah
Where's the bus for the centre of town, please?	**Gdzie jest autobus do centrum?**	gdzheh yehst ahw**to**booss do **tsehn**troom
This way, please.	**Proszę tędy.**	**pro**sheh **tehn**di

Changing money

Can you change a traveller's cheque, please?	**Czy może pan/pani wymienić mi czek podróżny?**	chi **mo**zheh pahn/**pah**ñee vi**myeh**ñeetsh mee chehk po**droozh**ni
Where's the nearest bank, please?	**Gdzie jest najbliższy bank?**	gdzheh yehst nigh**bleesh**shi bahnk

POLISH

Car rental

I'd like a car.	**Chcę wynająć samochód.**	htseh vi**nam**yontsh sah**mo**hoot
For how long?	**Na jak długo?**	nah yahk **dwoo**go
A day/Four days/ A week/Two weeks.	**Jeden dzień/Cztery dni/Tydzień/Dwa tygodnie.**	**yeh**dehn dzhehñ/**chteh**ri dñee/**ti**dzhehñ/dvah ti**go**dñeh

Taxi

Where can I get a taxi?	**Gdzie są taksówki?**	gdzheh sawng tahk**soof**kee
What's the fare to ... ?	**Ile kosztuje przejazd do ... ?**	**ee**leh kosh**too**yeh **psheh**yahst do
Take me to this address, please.	**Proszę mnie zawieźć na ten adres.**	**pro**sheh mñeh **zah**vyehs'tsh nah tehn **ah**drehss
I'm in a hurry.	**Spieszy mi się.**	**spyeh**shi mee s'eh
Could you drive more slowly, please?	**Proszę jechać wolniej.**	**pro**sheh **veh**hahtsh **vol**ñay

Hotel and other accommodation

My name is ...	**Nazywam się ...**	nah**zi**vahm s'eh
Have you a reservation?	**Czy ma pan/pani rezerwację?**	chi mah pahn/**pah**ñee rehzehr**vah**tsyeh
Yes, here's the confirmation.	**Tak, oto kwit.**	tahk **o**to kfeet
I'd like ...	**Proszę ...**	**pro**sheh
I'd like a single room/a double room.	**Proszę jednoosobowy pokój/dwuosobowy pokój.**	**pro**sheh yehdnooso**bo**vi **po**kooy/dvooso**bo**vi **po**kooy
a room with a bath/ with a shower	**pokój z łazienką/ z prysznicem**	**po**kooy zwah**z'ehn**kawng/ sprish**ñee**tsehm

How much?

What's the price per night/per week/per month?	**Ile kosztuje doba/ tydzień/miesiąc?**	**ee**leh kosh**too**yeh **do**bah/ **ti**dzhehñ/**myeh**s'onts
May I see the room?	**Czy mogę zobaczyć pokój?**	chi **mo**geh zo**bah**chitsh **po**kooy

I'm sorry, I don't like it.	**Niestety nie podoba mi się.**	ñehss**teh**ti ñeh po**do**bah mee s'eh
Yes, that's fine. I'll take it.	**Dobrze. Biorę go.**	**dob**zheh. **byo**reh go
What's my room number, please?	**Jaki jest numer mojego pokoju?**	**yah**kee yehst **noo**mehr mo**yeh**go po**ko**yoo
Number 123.	**Numer 123.**	**noo**mehr 123

Service, please

Who is it?	**Kto tam?**	kto tahm
Just a minute.	**Chwileczkę.**	hfee**lehch**keh
Come in! The door's open.	**Proszę! Drzwi otwarte.**	**pro**sheh! jvee ot**fahr**teh
May we have breakfast in our room?	**Czy możemy zjeść śniadanie w pokoju?**	chi mo**zheh**mi zyehs'tsh s'ñah**dah**ñeh fpo**ko**yoo

Breakfast

I'll have ...	**Proszę ...**	**pro**sheh
I'll have some fruit juice.	**Proszę sok.**	**pro**sheh sok
a boiled egg	**jajko gotowane**	**yigh**ko goto**vah**neh
a fried egg	**jajko sadzone**	**yigh**ko sah**dzo**neh
some bacon/some ham	**bekon/szynkę**	**beh**kon/**shin**keh
some toast	**grzanki**	**gzhahn**kee
a pot of tea	**dzbanek herbaty**	**dzbah**nehk hehr**bah**ti
a cup of tea	**filiżankę herbaty**	feelee**zhahn**keh hehr**bah**ti
some coffee	**kawę**	**kah**veh
some chocolate	**gorącą czekoladę**	go**ron**tsawng chehko**lah**deh
more butter	**więcej masła**	**vyehn**tsay **mahss**wah
some hot water	**trochę gorącej wody**	**tro**heh go**ron**tsay **vo**di

Difficulties

The central heating doesn't work.	**Centralne ogrzewanie nie działa.**	tsehn**trahl**neh ogzheh**vah**ñeh ñeh **dzhah**wah
the light/the socket	**światło/gniazdko**	**s'fyah**two/**gñahss**tko
the tap/the toilet	**kurek/ubikacja**	**koo**rehk/oobee**kah**tsyah

There's no hot water.	**Nie ma ciepłej wody.**	ñeh mah **tsheh**pway **vo**di
May I see the manager, please?	**Chcę rozmawiać z kierownikiem.**	htseh roz**mah**vyahtsh skehrov**nee**kehm

Telephone—Mail

There's a call for you.	**Telefon do pana/pani.**	teh**leh**fon do **pah**nah/**pah**ñee
Hold the line, please.	**Proszę się nie rozłączać.**	**pro**sheh s'eh ñeh roz**won**chahtsh
Operator, I've been cut off.	**Proszę pana, przerwano mi.**	**pro**sheh **pah**nah pshehr**vah**no mee
Did anyone telephone me?	**Czy ktoś do mnie dzwonił?**	chi ktos' do mñeh **dzvo**ñeew
Is there any mail for me?	**Czy jest dla mnie poczta?**	chi yehst dlah mñeh **poch**tah
Are there any messages for me?	**Czy jest jakaś wiadomość dla mnie?**	chi yehst **yah**kahs' vyah**do**mos'tsh dlah mñeh

Checking out

May I have my bill, please?	**Proszę rachunek.**	**pro**sheh rah**hoo**nehk
We're in a great hurry.	**Bardzo się spieszymy.**	**bahr**dzo s'eh spyeh**shi**mi
It's been a very enjoyable stay.	**Bardzo miło spędziliśmy tutaj czas.**	**bahr**dzo **mee**wo spehndzhee**lees'**mi **too**tigh chahss

Eating out

Good evening, sir/ Good evening, madam.	**Dobry wieczór panu/Dobry wieczór pani.**	**dob**ri **vyeh**choor pahnoo/**dob**ri **vyeh**choor **pah**ñee
Good evening. I'd like a table for two, please.	**Dobry wieczór. Proszę o stolik dla dwóch osób.**	**dob**ri **vyeh**choor. **pro**sheh o **sto**leek dlah dyooh **o**soop
Do you have a fixed-price menu?	**Czy są obiady firmowe?**	chi sawng o**byah**di feer**mo**veh
May I see the à la carte menu?	**Proszę kartę.**	**pro**sheh **kahr**teh

POLISH

May we have an ashtray, please?	**Proszę popielniczkę.**	**pro**sheh popyehl**ñeech**keh
some bread	**pieczywo**	pyeh**chi**vo
a fork	**widelec**	vee**deh**lehts
a knife	**nóż**	noosh
a spoon	**łyżkę**	**wish**keh
a plate	**talerz**	**tah**lehsh
a glass	**szklankę**	**shklahn**keh
a napkin	**serwetkę**	sehr**veht**keh
another chair	**jeszcze jedno krzesło**	**yehsh**cheh **yehd**no **kshehss**wo
Where's the gentlemen's toilet (men's room)?	**Gdzie jest toaleta dla panów?**	gdzheh yehst twah**leh**tah dlah **pah**noof
Where's the ladies' toilet (ladies' room)?	**Gdzie jest toaleta dla pań?**	gdzheh yehst twah**leh**tah dlah pahñ

Appetizers

I'd like some . . .	**Proszę . . .**	**pro**sheh
I'd like some assorted appetizers.	**Proszę zestaw zakąsek.**	**pro**sheh **zehss**tahf zah**kon**sehk
orange juice	**sok pomarańczowy**	sok pomahrahñ**cho**vi
ham	**szynkę**	**shin**keh
melon	**melona**	meh**lo**nah
pâté	**pasztet**	**pah**shteht
smoked salmon	**wędzonego łososia**	vehndzo**neh**go wo**sso**s'ah
shrimps (shrimp)	**krewetki**	kreh**veht**kee

Soup

Have you any . . . ?	**Czy jest . . . ?**	chi yehst
Have you any chicken soup?	**Czy jest rosół z kury?**	chi yehst **ro**ssoow **skoo**ri
vegetable soup	**zupa jarzynowa**	**zoo**pah yahzhi**no**vah
onion soup	**zupa cebulowa**	**zoo**pah tsehboo**lo**vah

Fish

I'd like some . . .	**Proszę . . .**	**pro**sheh
I'd like some fish.	**Proszę rybę.**	**pro**sheh **ri**beh
sole	**solę**	**so**leh
trout	**pstrąga**	**pstron**gah
lobster	**homara**	ho**mah**rah
crayfish	**langustę**	lahn**gooss**teh
prawns	**krewetki**	kreh**veht**kee

POLISH

I'd like it . . .	**Proszę rybę . . .**	**pro**sheh **ri**beh
I'd like it steamed.	**Proszę rybę duszoną.**	**pro**sheh **ri**beh doo**sho**nawng
grilled	**z rusztu**	**zroosh**too
boiled	**gotowaną**	goto**vah**nawng
baked	**zapiekaną**	zahpyeh**kah**nawng
fried	**smażoną**	smah**zho**nawng

Meat—Poultry—Game

I'd like some . . .	**Proszę . . .**	**pro**sheh
I'd like some beef.	**Proszę wołowinę.**	**pro**sheh vowo**vee**neh
a beef steak	**befsztyk**	**behf**shtik
some roast beef	**pieczeń wołową**	**pyeh**chehñ vo**wo**vawng
a veal cutlet	**sznycel cielęcy**	**shni**tsehl tsheh**lehn**tsi
mutton	**baraninę**	bahrah**ñee**neh
lamb	**jagnię**	**yah**gñeh
a pork chop	**kotlet schabowy**	**kot**leht shah**bo**vi
roast pork	**pieczeń wieprzową**	**pyeh**chehñ vyehp**sho**vawng
hare	**danie z zająca**	**dah**ñeh z zah**yon**tsah
chicken	**kurczę**	**koor**cheh
roast chicken	**kurczę pieczone**	**koor**cheh pyeh**cho**neh
duck	**kaczkę**	**kah**chkeh
How do you like your meat?	**Jak ma być podane?**	yahk mah bitsh po**dah**neh
rare	**po angielsku**	po ahn**gehl**skoo
medium	**średnio wysmażone**	**s'rehd**ño vissmah**zho**neh
well done	**mocno wysmażone**	**mots**no vissmah**zho**neh

Vegetables

What vegetables have you got?	**Jakie są jarzyny?**	**yah**keh sawng yah**zhi**ni
I'd like some . . .	**Proszę . . .**	**pro**sheh
I'd like some asparagus.	**Proszę szparagi.**	**pro**sheh shpah**rah**gee
green beans	**zieloną fasolkę**	z'eh**lo**nawng fah**ssol**keh
mushrooms	**pieczarki**	pyeh**chahr**kee
carrots	**marchewkę**	mahr**hehf**keh
onions	**cebulę**	tseh**boo**leh
red cabbage	**czerwoną kapustę**	chehr**vo**nawng kah**pooss**teh
spinach	**szpinak**	**shpee**nahk
rice	**ryż**	rish

POLISH

peas	**groszek**	**gro**shehk
tomatoes	**pomidory**	pomee**do**ri
green salad	**sałatę**	sah**wah**teh
potatoes	**ziemniaki**	z'ehm**ñah**kee

Desserts

Nothing more, thanks.	**To wszystko, dziękuję.**	to **fshiss**tko dzhehn**koo**yeh
Just a small portion, please.	**Małą porcję proszę.**	**mah**wawng **por**tsyeh **pro**sheh
Have you any ice-cream?	**Czy są lody?**	chi sawng **lo**di
fruit salad	**sałatka owocowa**	sah**waht**kah ovo**tso**vah
fresh fruit	**świeże owoce**	**s'fyeh**zheh o**vo**tseh
cheese	**ser**	sehr

Drink

What would you like to drink?	**Co podać do picia?**	tso **po**dahtsh do **pee**tshah
I'll have a beer, please.	**Proszę piwo.**	**pro**sheh **pee**vo
I'll have a whisky, please.	**Proszę whisky.**	**pro**sheh **wiss**kee

Wine

I'd like a bottle of wine.	**Proszę butelkę wina.**	**pro**sheh boo**tehl**keh **vee**nah
red wine	**czerwonego wina**	chehrvo**neh**go **vee**nah
rosé wine	**rosé**	„rosé"
white wine	**białego wina**	byah**weh**go **vee**nah
Cheers!	**Na zdrowie!**	nah **zdro**vyeh

The bill (check)

May I have the bill (check) please?	**Proszę o rachunek.**	**pro**sheh o rah**hoo**nehk
Is service included?	**Czy obejmuje obsługę?**	chi obay**moo**yeh ops**woo**geh
Everything's included.	**Rachunek obejmuje wszystko.**	rah**hoo**nehk obay**moo**yeh **fshiss**tko
Thank you, that was a very good meal.	**Dziękuję, jedzenie było bardzo dobre.**	dzhehn**koo**yeh yeh**dzeh**ñeh **bi**wo **bahr**dzo **do**breh

Travelling

Where's the railway station, please?	**Przepraszam, gdzie jest stacja kolejowa?**	psheh**prah**shahm gdzheh yehst **stah**tsyah koleh**yo**vah
Where's the ticket office, please?	**Przepraszam, gdzie jest kasa biletowa?**	psheh**prah**shahm gdzheh yehst **kąh**ssah beeleh**to**vah
I'd like a ticket to ...	**Proszę bilet do ...**	**pro**sheh **bee**leht do
First or second class?	**Pierwsza czy druga klasa?**	**pyehr**shah chi **droo**gah **klah**ssah
First class, please.	**Proszę pierwszą klasę.**	**pro**sheh **pyehr**shawng **klah**sseh
Single or return (one way or roundtrip)?	**W jedną stronę czy powrotny?**	v **yehd**nawng **stro**neh chi po**vrot**ni
Do I have to change trains?	**Czy muszę się przesiadać?**	chi **moo**sheh s'eh psheh**s'ay**dahtsh
What platform does the train leave from?	**Z którego peronu odchodzi pociąg?**	sktoo**reh**go peh**ro**noo ot**ho**dzhee **po**tshonk
Where's the nearest underground station?	**Gdzie jest najbliższa stacja metro?**	gdzheh yehst nigh**bleesh**shah **stah**tsyah **meht**ro
Where's the bus station, please?	**Gdzie jest dworzec autobusowy?**	gdżheh yehst **dvo**zhehts ahwtoboo**sso**vi
When's the first bus to ... ?	**Kiedy odjeżdża pierwszy autobus do...?**	**keh**di od**yehzh**jah **pyehr**shi ahw**to**booss do
the last bus	**ostatni autobus**	oss**taht**ñee ahw**to**booss
the next bus	**następny autobus**	nahss**tehm**pni ahw**to**booss
Please let me off at the next stop.	**Proszę się zatrzymać na następnym przystanku.**	**pro**sheh s'eh zah**tshi**mahtsh nah nahss**tehm**pnim pshiss**tahn**koo

Relaxing

What's on at the cinema (movies)?	**Co grają w kinie?**	tso **grah**yawng **fkee**ñeh
What's on at the theatre?	**Co grają w teatrze?**	tso **grah**yawng fteh**ah**chsheh
What time does the film begin? And the play?	**O której zaczyna się film? A sztuka?**	o **ktoo**ray zah**chi**nah s'eh feelm? ah **shtoo**kah
Are there any tickets for tonight?	**Czy są bilety na dzisiaj wieczór?**	chi sawng bee**leh**ti nah **dzhee**ss'igh **vyeh**chóor

Where can we go dancing?	**Gdzie można pójść potańczyć?**	gdzheh **mo**zhnah pooys'tsh po**tahñ**chitsh
Would you like to dance?	**Czy mogę prosić?**	chi **mo**geh **pross**'eetsh

Introductions

How do you do?	**Dzień dobry.**	dzhehñ **dob**ri
How are you?	**Jak się pan/pani miewa?**	yahk s'eh pahn/**pah**ñee **myeh**vah
Very well, thank you. And you?	**Dobrze, dziękuję. A pan/pani?**	**dob**zheh dzhehn**koo**yeh. ah pahn/**pah**ñee
May I introduce Miss Philips?	**To jest pani Philips.**	to yehst **pah**ñee Philips
My name is...	**Nazywam się...**	nah**zi**vahm s'eh
I'm very pleased to meet you.	**Bardzo mi miło.**	**bahr**dzo mee **mee**wo
How long have you been here?	**Od jak dawna pan/pani jest tutaj?**	od yahk **dahv**nah pahn/**pah**ñee yehst **too**tigh
It was nice meeting you.	**Miło mi było pana/panią poznać.**	**mee**wo mee **bi**wo **pah**nah/**pah**ñawng **poz**nahtsh

Dating

Would you like a cigarette?	**Czy zapali pani?**	chi zah**pah**lee **pah**ñee
May I get you a drink?	**Czy napije się pani czegoś?**	chi nah**pee**yeh s'eh **pah**ñee **cheh**gos'
Do you have a light, please?	**Czy mogę prosić o ogień?**	chi **mo**geh **pross**'eetsh o **o**gehñ
Are you waiting for someone?	**Czy pan/pani na kogoś czeka?**	chi pahn/**pah**ñee nah **ko**gos' **cheh**kah
Are you free this evening?	**Czy pan/pani ma dzisiaj wolny wieczór?**	chi pahn/**pah**ñee mah **dzhee**ss'igh **vol**ni **vyeh**choor
Where shall we meet?	**Gdzie się spotkamy?**	gdzheh s'eh spot**kah**mi
What time shall I meet you?	**O której się spotkamy?**	o **ktoo**ray s'eh spot**kah**mi
May I take you home?	**Czy mogę panią odwieźć do domu?**	chi **mo**geh **pah**ñawng **od**vyehs'tsh do **do**moo

Thank you, it's been a wonderful evening.	**Dziękuję za cudowny wieczór.**	dzhehn**koo**yeh zah tsoo**dov**ni **vyeh**choor
What's your telephone number?	**Jaki jest pana/pani numer telefonu?**	**yah**kee yehst **pah**nah/**pah**ñee **noo**mehr tehlehf**fo**noo
Do you live alone?	**Czy pani mieszka sama?**	chi **pah**ñee **myehsh**kah **sah**mah
What time is your last train?	**O której ma pan/pani ostatni pociąg?**	o **ktot**ray mah pahn/**pah**ñee os**taht**nee **po**tshonk
Good-night...	**Dobranoc...**	do**brah**nots

Banks

Where's the nearest bank, please?	**Przepraszam, gdzie jest najbliższy bank?**	psheh**prah**shahm gdzheh yehst nigh**bleesh**shi bahnk
Where can I cash some traveller's cheques?	**Gdzie mogę wymienić czeki podróżne?**	gdzheh **mo**geh vi**myeh**ñeetsh **cheh**kee po**droozh**neh
What time does the bank open? What time does it close?	**O której otwiera się bank? O której się zamyka?**	o **ktoo**ray ot**fyeh**rah s'eh bahnk o **ktoo**ray s'eh zah**mi**kah
I'm expecting some money from home. Has it arrived?	**Oczekuję na przekaz pieniężny z domu. Czy już nadszedł?**	ocheh**koo**yeh nah **psheh**kahss pyeh**ñehn**zhni **zdo**moo. chi yoosh **naht**sheht
Can you give me some small change, please?	**Proszę mi dać trochę drobnych.**	**pro**sheh mee dahtsh **tro**heh **drob**nih

Shops, stores and services

Where is the nearest chemist's (pharmacy)?	**Gdzie jest najbliższa apteka?**	gdzheh yehst nigh**bleesh**shah ahp**teh**kah
the nearest hairdresser's	**zakład fryzjerski**	**zah**kwaht friz **yehr**skee
the photo shop	**sklep fotograficzny**	sklehp fotograh**feech**ni
the jeweller's	**jubiler**	yoo**bee**lehr
the department store	**dom towarowy**	dom tovah**ro**vi
the police station	**posterunek milicji**	posteh**roo**nehk mee**lee**tsyee
the garage	**warsztat samochodowy**	**vahr**shtaht sahmoho**do**vi

POLISH

How do I get there?	**Jak się tam dostać?**	yahk s'eh tahm **doss**tahtsh
Is it within walking distance?	**Czy dojdę tam pieszo?**	chi **doy**deh tahm **pyeh**sho

Service

Can you help me, please?	**Proszę pana/panią!**	**pro**sheh **pah**nah/**pah**ñawng
Can you show me this? And that, too.	**Proszę mi to pokazać! I tamto też.**	**pro**sheh mee to po**kah**-zahtsh. ee **tahm**to tehsh
It's too expensive/ too big/too small.	**Jest za drogi/za duży/za mały.**	yehst zah **dro**gee/zah **doo**zhi/zah **mah**wi
Can you show me some more?	**Czy może mi pan/ pani pokazać inne?**	chi **mo**zheh mee pahn/ **pah**ñee po**kah**zahtsh **een**neh
something better	**coś lepszego**	tsos'lehp**sheh**go
something cheaper	**coś tańszego**	tsos' tahñ**sheh**go
How much is this? And that?	**Ile to kosztuje? A tamto?**	**ee**leh to kosh**too**yeh? ah **tahm**to
It's not quite what I want.	**Nie to chciałem.**	ñeh to **htshah**wehm
I like it.	**Podoba mi się to.**	po**do**bah mee s'eh to

Chemist's (Pharmacy)

I'd like something for a cold/for a cough/for travel sickness.	**Proszę coś na przeziębienie/na kaszel/na mdłości.**	**pro**sheh tsos' nah pshehz'ehm**byeh**ñeh/nah **kah**shehl/nah **mdwos**'tshee
Can you recommend something for hay-fever/for sunburn?	**Czy może mi pan/pani polecić coś na katar sienny/na oparzenie słoneczne?**	chi **mo**zheh mee pahn/ **pah**ñee po**leh**tsheetsh tsos' nah kahtahr **s'ehn**ni/ nah opah**zheh**ñeh swo**nehch**neh

Toiletry

May I have some razor blades?	**Poproszę żyletki.**	po**pro**sheh zhi**leht**kee
some shaving cream	**krem do golenia**	krehm do go**leh**ñah
some toothpaste	**pastę do zębów**	**pahss**teh do **zehm**boof
I'd like some soap.	**Proszę mydło.**	**pro**sheh **mid**wo
some suntan oil	**olejek do opalania**	o**leh**yehk do opah**lah**ñah

POLISH

At the barber's

I'd like a haircut, please.	**Proszę mnie ostrzyc.**	**pro**sheh mñeh **oss**tshits
Short/Leave it long.	**Krótko/Proszę zostawić długie.**	**kroot**ko/**pro**sheh zos**tah**veetsh **dwoo**gyeh
A razor cut, please.	**Strzyżenie brzytwą, proszę.**	stshi**zheh**ñeh **bzhit**fawng **pro**sheh

At the hairdresser's

I'd like a shampoo and set, please.	**Proszę mycie i ułożenie.**	**pro**sheh **mi**tsheh ee oowo**zheh**ñeh
I'd like a bleach.	**Proszę rozjaśnić.**	**pro**sheh roz**yahs**'ñeetsh
a permanent	**trwałą**	**trfah**wawng
a colour rinse	**płukankę koloryzującą**	pwoo**kahn**keh kolorizoo**yon**tsawng
a manicure	**manicure**	mahñee**kyoor**

Photography

I'd like a film for this camera.	**Proszę film do tego aparatu.**	**pro**sheh feelm do **teh**go ahpah**rah**too
This camera doesn't work.	**Popsuł mi się aparat.**	**pop**soow mee s'eh ah**pah**raht

At the post office

Where's the nearest post office, please?	**Przepraszam, gdzie jest najbliższa poczta?**	psheh**prah**shahm gdzheh yehst nigh**bleesh**shah **poch**tah
I'd like to send this by express (special delivery)/by air mail.	**Chcę to nadać ekspresem/pocztą lotniczą.**	htseh to **nah**dahtsh ehk**spreh**ssehm/**poch**tawng lot**ñee**chawng

Service stations

Where is the nearest service station, please?	**Przepraszam, gdzie jest najbliższa stacja benzynowa?**	psheh**prah**shahm gdzheh yehst nigh**bleesh**shah **stah**tsyah behnzi**no**vah
Fill her up, please.	**Proszę napełnić zbiornik.**	**pro**sheh nah**pehw**ñeetsh **zbyor**ñeek
Check the oil, please.	**Proszę sprawdzić olej.**	**pro**sheh **sprahv**dzheetsh **o**lay
Would you check the tyres?	**Proszę sprawdzić opony.**	**pro**sheh **sprahv**dzheetsh o**po**ni

Street directions

Can you show me on the map where I am?	**Czy może pan/pani pokazać mi na mapie gdzie teraz jestem?**	chi **mo**zheh pahn/**pah**ñee po**kah**zahtsh mee nah **mah**pyeh gdzheh **teh**rahss **yehss**tehm
You're on the wrong road.	**Pan/pani jedzie nie tą szosą.**	pahn/**pah**ñee **yeh**dzheh ñeh tawng **sho**ssawng
Go back to...	**Proszę zawrócić do...**	**pro**sheh zahv**roo**tsheetsh do
Go straight ahead.	**Proszę jechać prosto.**	**pro**sheh **yeh**hahtsh **pross**to
It's on the left/on the right.	**To jest na lewo/na prawo.**	to yehst nah **leh**vo/nah **prah**vo

Accidents

May I use your telephone?	**Czy mogę skorzystać z telefonu?**	chi **mo**geh sko**zhiss**tahtsh stehleh**fo**noo
Call a doctor quickly.	**Proszę wezwać lekarza, szybko.**	**pro**sheh **vehz**vahtsh leh**kah**zhah **ship**ko
Call an ambulance.	**Proszę wezwać pogotowie.**	**pro**sheh **vehz**vahtsh pogo**to**vyeh
Please call the police.	**Proszę wezwać milicję.**	**pro**sheh **vehz**vahtsh mee**lee**tsyeh

Numbers

one	**jeden**	**yeh**dehn
two	**dwa**	dvah
three	**trzy**	chshi
four	**cztery**	**chteh**ri
five	**pięć**	pyehñtsh
six	**sześć**	shehs'tsh
seven	**siedem**	**s'eh**dehm
eight	**osiem**	**o**s'ehm
nine	**dziewięć**	**dzheh**vyehñtsh
ten	**dziesięć**	**dzheh**s'ehñtsh
eleven	**jedenaście**	yehdeh**nahs'**tsheh
twelve	**dwanaście**	dvah**nahs'**tsheh
thirteen	**trzynaście**	chshi**nahs'**tsheh
fourteen	**czternaście**	chtehr**nahs'**tsheh
fifteen	**piętnaście**	pyeht**nahs'**tsheh
sixteen	**szesnaście**	shehss**nahs'**tsheh
seventeen	**siedemnaście**	s'ehdehm**nahs'**tsheh
eighteen	**osiemnaście**	os'ehm**nahs'**tsheh
nineteen	**dziewiętnaście**	dzhehvyeht**nahs'**tsheh

twenty	**dwadzieścia**	dvah**dzhehs**'tshah
twenty-one	**dwadzieścia jeden**	dvah**dzhehs**'tshah **yeh**dehn
thirty	**trzydzieści**	chshi**dzhehs**'tshee
forty	**czterdzieści**	chtehr**dzhehs**'tshee
fifty	**pięćdziesiąt**	pyehñ**dzheh**s'ont
sixty	**sześćdziesiąt**	shehs'**dzheh**s'ont
seventy	**siedemdziesiąt**	s'ehdehm**dzheh**s'ont
eighty	**osiemdziesiąt**	os'ehm**dzheh**s'ont
ninety	**dziewięćdziesiąt**	dzhehvyehñ**dzheh**s'ont
one hundred	**sto**	sto
one thousand	**tysiąc**	**ti**s'onts
ten thousand	**dziesięć tysięcy**	**dzheh**s'ehñtsh. ti**s'ehn**tsi

Days

It's Sunday.	**Dzisiaj jest niedziela.**	**dzhee**ss'igh yehst ñeh**dzeh**lah
Monday	**poniedziałek**	poñeh**dzhah**wehk
Tuesday	**wtorek**	**fto**rehk
Wednesday	**środa**	**s'ro**dah
Thursday	**czwartek**	**chfahr**tehk
Friday	**piątek**	**pyon**tehk
Saturday	**sobota**	so**bo**tah
yesterday	**wczoraj**	**fcho**righ
today	**dzisiaj**	**dzhee**ss'igh
tomorrow	**jutro**	**yoo**tro
morning/afternoon	**rano/popołudnie**	**rah**no/popo**woo**dñeh
evening/night	**wieczór/noc**	**vyeh**choor/nots

Months

January	**styczeń**	**sti**chehñ
February	**luty**	**loo**ti
March	**marzec**	**mah**zhehts
April	**kwiecień**	**kfyeh**tshehñ
May	**maj**	migh
June	**czerwiec**	**chehr**vyehts
July	**lipiec**	**lee**pyehts
August	**sierpień**	**s'ehr**pyehñ
September	**wrzesień**	**vzheh**ss'ehñ
October	**październik**	pahz'**dzhehr**ñeek
November	**listopad**	leess**to**paht
December	**grudzień**	**groo**dzhehñ
Merry Christmas!	**Wesołych Świąt!**	veh**so**wih s'fyont!
Happy New Year!	**Szczęśliwego Nowego Roku!**	schehehns'lee**veh**go no**veh**go **ro**koo

PORTUGUESE

Guide to Pronunciation

Consonants

Letter	Approximate pronunciation	Symbol	Example	
f, k, l, p, t, v	as in English			
b	as in English, but often less decisive (more like **v**)	b bh	**boca** **abrir**	**boa**ker erbh**reer**
c	1) before **e** and **i**, like **s** in **s**it 2) elsewhere, like **k** in **k**ill	s k	**cedo** **casa**	**say**dhoo **kah**zer
ç	like **s** in **s**it	s	**começar**	koomer**sahr**
ch	like **sh** in **sh**ut	sh	**chamar**	sher**mahr**
d	as in English, but often less decisive (more like **th** in **th**is)	d dh	**dia** **nada**	**dee**er **nah**dher
g	1) before **a**, **o** and **u** or a consonant, or after **l**, **n** and **r**, like **g** in **g**o 2) between vowels, like a soft version of the **ch** in Scottish lo**ch** 3) before **e** and **i**, like **s** in plea**s**ure	g g̊ zh	**garfo** **rogar** **gelo**	**gahr**foo roo**g̊ahr** **zhay**loo

h	always silent		**homem**	**o**mahng^{y}
j	like **s** in plea**s**ure	zh	**já**	zhah
lh	like **lli** in mi**lli**on	ly	**olho**	**o**lyoo
m	1) between a vowel and a consonant, or at the end of a word ("finally"), it indicates that the vowel is nasalized (see "Nasal vowels")		**embalar** **bom**	ahng^{y}bah**lahr** bawng
	2) elsewhere like **m** in **m**et	m	**mais**	mighsh
n	1) when initial or between vowels, like **n** in **n**o	n	**novo**	**noa**voo
	2) in a consonant group and in plural endings it nasalizes the preceding vowel, but is generally silent		**branco** **homens**	**brahng**koo **o**mahng^{y}sh
nh	like **ni** in o**ni**on	ny	**vinho**	**vee**nyoo
q	like **k** in **k**ill	k	**quadro**	**kwahdh**roo
r	strongly trilled as in Scottish speech	r	**rua**	**roo**er
s	1) when initial, after a consonant or written **ss**, like **s** in **s**it	s	**saber**	ser**bhayr**
	2) between vowels (not necessarily in the same word), like **z** in razor	z	**casa** **as aves**	**kah**zer erz **ah**versh
	3) when final, or before **c**, **f**, **p**, **q**, **t**, like **sh** in **sh**ut	sh	**país**	per**eesh**
	4) elsewhere, like **s** in plea**s**ure	zh	**cisne**	**seezh**ner
x	1) generally like **sh** in **sh**ut	sh	**baixo**	**bigh**shoo
	2) in **ex-** before a vowel, like **z** in ra**z**or	z	**exacto**	i**zah**too
z	1) when initial or between vowels like **z** in ra**z**or	z	**zero**	**zeh**roo
	2) when final or before **c**, **f**, **p**, **q**, **s** or **t**, like **sh** in **sh**ut	sh	**feliz**	fer**leesh**
	3) elsewhere like **s** in plea**s**ure	zh	**luz da**	loozh der

Vowels

a	1) when stressed (see under "Stressing") it is like a mixture of the **u** in c**u**t and the **a** in p**a**rty	ah	**nado**	**nah**dhoo
	2) when unstressed or before **m**, **n** or **nh** but not in the same syllable like **a** in **a**bout	er*	**porta**	**por**ter
e	1) when stressed generally like **e** in g**e**t	eh	**pertu**	**pehr**too
	2) when stressed sometimes like **a** in l**a**te	ay	**cabelo**	ker**bhay**loo
	3) when unstressed, like **er** in oth**er**	er*	**pesado**	per**zah**dhoo
	4) at the beginning of a word, and in certain other cases, like **i** in h**i**t	i	**antes** **exacto**	**ern**tish i**zah**too
é	like **e** in g**e**t	eh	**café**	ker**feh**
ê	like **a** in l**a**te	ay	**mês**	maysh
i	1) when stressed like **ee** in s**ee**d	ee	**riso**	**ree**zoo
	2) when unstressed, like **i** in com**i**ng	i	**final**	fi**nahl**
o	1) when stressed, like **o** in r**o**d	o	**fora**	**for**er
	2) when unstressed, usually like **oo** in f**oo**t	oo	**caso**	**kah**zoo
	3) sometimes when stressed or unstressed, like **o** in n**o**te (most common o-sound)	oa	**voltar** **Lisboa**	voal**tahr** lizh**voa**er
ô, ou	like **o** in n**o**te	oa	**pôs**	poash
u	1) generally like **oo** in s**oo**n	oo	**número**	**noo**merroo
	2) silent in **gu** and **qu** before e or **i**		**querer**	ker**rayr**

* The **r** should not be pronounced when reading this transcription.

Diphthongs

A diphthong is two vowels pronounced as a single vowel sound, e.g., in English **boy** there is a diphthong consisting of **o** plus a weak **i** sound. In Portuguese diphthongs, **a**, **e** and **o** are strong vowels and **i** and **u** are weak vowels. In diphthongs the strong vowels are pronounced with more stress (louder) than the weak ones, e.g., **ai** is pronounced like **igh** in s**igh**, and **au** like **ow** in h**ow**. Sometimes the weak vowels can combine to make a diphthong. Apart from these generalizations the exact pronunciation of Portuguese diphthongs is not easy to predict.

Nasal vowels

These are pronounced through the mouth and through the nose at the same time, just as in the French nasal vowels (e.g., in the French **bon**) and quite similar to the nasal twang heard in some areas of America and Britain.

ã, am, an	something like **ung** in l**ung**, or like **an** in French d**ans**	ahng	**maçã**	mer**sahng**
em, en	something like **ing** in s**ing**, but recalling also the **a** in l**a**te	ayng	**cento**	**sayng**too
im, in	a nasalized version of the **ea** in l**ea**rn	eeng	**cinco**	**seeng**koo
õ, om, on	like **orn** in c**orn**cob or like **on** in French b**on**	awng	**bom**	bawng
um, un	something like a North of England pronunciation of **ung** in l**ung** (a nasalized version of **u** in p**u**t)	oong	**um**	oong

Semi-nasalized diphthongs

In these, the first element is nasalized and combined with a weak **i** (pronounced like **y** in **y**et) or **u** pronounced like **w** in **w**as).

ãe, ãi, êm, final en, usually final em	pronounced as **ã** followed by **y** in **y**et	ahng^{y}	**mãe** **sêm**	mahng^{y} sahng^{y}
ão, final unstressed am	pronounced as **ã** followed by **w** in **w**as	ahng^{w}	**mão**	mahng^{w}
õe, oi	pronounced as **õ** followed by **y** in **y**et	awng^{y}	**põe**	pawng^{y}
ui	like nasal vowel **u** followed by **y** in **y**et	oong^{y}	**muito**	**moong**^{y}too

Stressing

1) If a word ends with **a**, **e** or **o**, the stress falls on the next to the last syllable, e.g., **rosa** (pronounced **roa**zer). Plural endings **m** and **s** are generally disregarded.

2) All other words are stressed on the last syllable, e.g., **animal** (pronounced ernee**mahl**).

Words not stressed in accordance with these rules have an accent (´ or `) over the vowel of the stressed syllable.

Some basic expressions

Yes.	**Sim.**	seeng
No.	**Não.**	nahng^{w}
Please.	**Por favor.**	poor fer**voar**
Thank you.	**Obrigado.**	obree**g̊ah**dhoo
Thank you very much.	**Muito obrigado.**	**moong^{y}**too obree**g̊ah**dhoo
That's all right.	**Não tem de quê.**	nahng^{w} tayng der kay

Greetings

Good morning.	**Bom dia.**	bawng **dee**er
Good afternoon.	**Boa tarde.**	**boa**er **tahr**der
Good evening.	**Boa noite.**	**boa**er **noy**ter
Good night.	**Boa noite.**	**boa**er **noy**ter
Good-bye.	**Adeus.**	er**dheh**oosh
See you later.	**Até logo.**	er**tay loa**g̊oo
This is Mr. . . .	**Apresento-lhe o Senhor . . .**	erprer**zayn**toolyer oo say**ñoar**
This is Mrs. . . .	**Apresento-lhe a Senhora . . .**	erprer**zayn**toolyer er say**ñoa**rer
This is Miss . . .	**Apresento-lhe a Menina . . .**	erprer**zayn**toolyer er mer**nee**ner
I'm very pleased to meet you.	**Muito prazer em conhecê-lo.**	**moong^{y}**too prer**thehr** ayng kooñer**thay**loo
How are you?	**Como está?**	**koa**moo ish**tah**
Very well, thank you.	**Muito bem, obrigado.**	**moong^{y}**too bayng obree**g̊ah**dhoo
And you?	**E você?**	ee vo**say**
Fine.	**Bem.**	bayng
Excuse me.	**Desculpe.**	dehsh**kool**per

Questions

Where?	**Onde?**	**on**der
Where is . . . ?	**Onde está . . . ?**	**on**der ish**tah**
Where are . . . ?	**Onde estão . . . ?**	**on**der ish**tahng^{w}**

When?	**Quando?**	**kwahn**doo
What?	**O quê?**	oo kay
How?	**Como?**	**koa**moo
How much?	**Quanto?**	**kwahn**too
How many?	**Quantos?**	**kwahn**toosh
Who?	**Quem?**	kayng
Why?	**Porquê?**	poor**kay**
Which?	**Qual?**	kwahl
What do you call this?	**Como se chama isto?**	**koa**moo ser **sher**mer **eesh**too
What do you call that?	**Como se chama aquilo?**	**koa**moo ser **sher**mer er**kee**loo
What does this mean?	**Que significa isto?**	kay seeg**nee**feeker **eesh**too
What does that mean?	**Que significa aquilo?**	kay seeg**nee**feeker er**kee**loo

Do you speak ...?

Do you speak English?	**Fala inglês?**	**fah**ler eeng**glaysh**
Do you speak German?	**Fala alemão?**	**fah**ler erler**mahng**ʷ
Do you speak French?	**Fala francês?**	**fah**ler frahng**saysh**
Do you speak Spanish?	**Fala espanhol?**	**fah**ler ishper**ñol**
Do you speak Italian?	**Fala italiano?**	**fah**ler eeterl**yah**noo
Could you speak more slowly, please?	**Pode falar mais devagar, por favor?**	**poah**dher fer**lahr** mighsh derver**gahr** poor fer**voar**
Please point to the phrase in the book.	**Por favor, indique-me a frase no livro.**	poor fer**voar** een**dee**ker-mer er **frah**zer noo **leev**roo
Just a minute. I'll see if I can find it in this book.	**Um momento por favor, vou ver se posso encontrá-la neste livro.**	oong moo**mayng**too poor fer**voar** voa vayr ser **poss**soo ingkon**trahr**ler **nehs**ter **leev**roo
I understand.	**Compreendo.**	kawngpri**ayng**doo
I don't understand.	**Não compreendo.**	nahngʷ kawngpri**ayng**doo

Can . . . ?

Can I have . . . ?	**Pode dar-me?**	**poa**dher **dahr**mer
Can we have . . . ?	**Pode dar-nos . . . ?**	**poa**dher **dahr**noosh
Can you show me . . . ?	**Pode mostrar-me . . . ?**	**poa**dher mooshtrahrmer
Can you tell me . . . ?	**Pode dizer-me . . . ?**	**poa**dher dee**zehr**mer
Can you help me, please?	**Pode ajudar-me, por favor?**	**poa**dher erzhoo**dhahr**mer poor fer**voar**

Wanting

I'd like . . .	**Queria . . .**	ker**ree**er
We'd like . . .	**Queríamos . . .**	ker**ree**ermoosh
Please give me . . .	**Por favor, dê-me . . .**	poor fer**voar day**mer
Give it to me, please.	**Dê-mo, por favor.**	**day**moo poor fer**voar**
Please bring me . . .	**Por favor, traga-me . . .**	poor fer**voar trah**g̊ermer
Bring it to me, please.	**Traga-mo, por favor.**	**trah**g̊er moo poor fer**voar**
I'm hungry.	**Tenho fome.**	**teh**ñoo **fo**mer
I'm thirsty.	**Tenho sede.**	**teh**ñoo **seh**dher
I'm tired.	**Estou cansado.**	ish**toa** kern**sah**dhoo
I'm lost.	**Estou perdido.**	ish**toa** perr**dhee**dhoo
It's important.	**É importante.**	eh impoor**tahn**ter
It's urgent.	**É urgente.**	eh oor**zhehn**ter
Hurry up!	**Depressa!**	der**preh**ser

It is/There is . . .

It is/It's . . .	**É . . .**	eh
Is it . . . ?	**É . . . ?**	eh
It isn't . . .	**Não é . . .**	nahng^{w} eh
There is/There are . . .	**Há . . .**	ah
Is there/Are there . . . ?	**Há . . . ?**	ah

There isn't/There aren't...	**Não há...**	nawng^{w} ah
There isn't any/ There aren't any.	**Não há nenhum/ Não há nenhuns (Não há nenhuma/ Não há nenhumas).**	nawng^{w} ah ni**ñoong**/ nawng^{w} ah ni**ñoongsh** (nawng^{w} ah ni**ñoong**mer/ nawng^{w} ah ni**ñoong**mersh)

A few common words

big/small	**grande/pequeno**	**grahn**der/per**keh**noo
quick/slow	**rápido/lento**	**rah**peedhoo/**lehn**too
early/late	**cedo/tarde**	**seh**dhoo/**tahr**der
cheap/expensive	**barato/caro**	ber**rah**too/**kah**roo
near/far	**perto/longe**	**pehr**too/**lawng**zher
hot/cold	**quente/frio**	**kehn**ter/**free**oo
full/empty	**cheio/vazio**	**shay**oo/ver**zee**oo
easy/difficult	**fácil/difícil**	**fah**seel/der**fee**seel
heavy/light	**pesado/leve**	per**zah**dhoo/**leh**ver
open/shut	**aberto/fechado**	er**behr**too/fer**shah**dhoo
right/wrong	**certo/errado**	**sehr**too/ehr**rah**dhoo
old/new	**velho/novo**	**vehl**yoo/**noa**voo
old/young	**idoso/jovem**	ee**dhoa**zoo/**zho**vayng
beautiful/ugly	**belo/feio**	**beh**loo/**fay**oo
good/bad	**bom/mau**	bawng/mow
better/worse	**melhor/pior**	mil**yor**/pee**or**

Some prepositions and a few more useful words

at	**a**	ah
on	**sobre**	**soa**brer
in	**em**	ayng
to	**para**	**per**rer
from	**de**	der
inside	**dentro**	**dehn**troo
outside	**fora**	**fo**rer
up	**em cima**	ayng **see**mer
down	**em baixo**	ayng **bigh**shoo
before	**antes**	**ern**tish
after	**depois**	der**poysh**
with	**com**	kawng
without	**sem**	sayng
through	**através**	ertrer**vehsh**
towards	**para**	**per**rer
until	**até**	er**teh**
during	**durante**	doo**rahn**ter

and	**e**	ee
or	**ou**	oa
not	**não**	nawng^{w}
nothing	**nada**	**nah**dher
none	**nenhum**	ning**ñoong**
very	**muito**	**moong^{y}**too
also	**também**	tahng**bayng**
soon	**em breve**	ayng **breh**ver
perhaps	**talvez**	tahl**vaysh**
here	**aqui**	er**kee**
there	**ali**	er**lee**
now	**agora**	er**g̊o**rer
then	**depois**	der**poysh**

Arrival

Your passport, please.	**O passaporte, por favor.**	oo pahser**por**ter poor fer**voar**
Here it is.	**Aqui está.**	er**kee** ish**tah**
Have you anything to declare?	**Tem alguma coisa declarar?**	tayng ahl**g̊oo**mer **koy**zer er dherkler**rahr**
No, nothing at all.	**Não, nada.**	nawng^{w} **nah**dher
Porter!	**Bagageiro!**	berg̊er**zhay**roo
Can you help me with my luggage, please?	**Pode levar-me a bagagem, por favor?**	**poa**dher ler**vahr**mer er ber**gah**zhayng poor fer**voar**
That's my suitcase.	**Esta é a minha mala.**	**ehsh**ter eh er **mee**ñer **mah**ler
Where's the bus to the centre of town, please?	**Onde posso apanhar o autocarro para o centro da cidade, por favor?**	**on**der **pos**soo erper**ñahr** oo owtoo**kahr**roo **per**rer oo **sehn**troo der see**dhah**dher poor fer**voar**
This way, please.	**Por aqui, por favor.**	poor er**kee** poor fer**voar**

Changing money

Can you change a traveller's cheque, please?	**Pode cambiar-me um cheque de viagem, por favor?**	**poa**dher kerm**byahr**mer oong shehk der vyah**zhayng** poor fer**voar**
Where's the nearest bank, please?	**Onde fica o banco mais próximo, por favor?**	**on**der **fee**ker oo **bahng**koo mighsh **pro**seemoo poor fer**voar**

Car rental

I'd like a car.	**Queria alugar um carro.**	ker**ree**er erloo**ğahr** oong **kahr**roo
For how long?	**Por quanto tempo?**	poor **kwahn**too **tayng**poo
A day/Four days/ A week/Two weeks	**Um dia/Quatro dias/Uma semana/ Duas semanas.**	oong **dee**er/**kwah**troo **dee**ersh/**oo**mer ser**mah**-ner/**doo**ersh ser**mah**nersh

Taxi

Where can I get a taxi?	**Onde posso encontrar um táxi?**	**on**der **poss**soo ingkon-**trahr** oong **tahk**see
What's the fare to . . . ?	**Qual é o preço do percurso para . . . ?**	kwahl ay oo **preh**soo doo perr**koor**soo **per**rer
Take me to this address, please.	**Leve-me a esta morada, por favor.**	**leh**vermer er **ehsh**ter moo**rah**dher poor fer**voar**
I'm in a hurry.	**Estou com pressa.**	ish**toa** kawng **preh**ser
Could you drive more slowly, please?	**Pode ir mais devagar, por favor?**	**poa**dher eer mighsh der-ver**ğahr** poor fer**voar**

Hotel and other accommodation

My name is . . .	**O meu nome é . . .**	oo **meh**oo **noa**mer eh
Have you a reservation?	**Reservou?**	rerzerr**voa**
Yes, here's the confirmation.	**Sim, aqui está a confirmação.**	seeng er**kee** ish**tah** er kawngfeermer**sahng**^{w}
I'd like . . .	**Quero . . .**	**keh**roo
I'd like a single room/a double room.	**Quero um quarto de uma cama/um quarto de casal.**	**keh**roo oong **kwahr**too der **oo**mer **ker**mer/oong **kwahr**too der ker**zahl**
a room with a bath/with a shower	**um quarto com banho/com chuveiro**	oong **kwahr**too kawng **bah**ñoo/kawng shoo**vay**roo

How much?

What's the price per night/per week/per month?	**Qual é o preço por noite/por semana/ por mês?**	kwahl eh oo **preh**soo poor **noy**ter/poor ser**mah**ner/poor maysh
May I see the room?	**Posso ver o quarto?**	**poss**soo vehr oo **kwahr**too

I'm sorry, I don't like it.	**Lamento, mas não gosto.**	ler**mehn**too mersh nahng^{w}**gosh**too
Yes, that's fine. I'll take it.	**Sim, está bem. Fico com ele.**	seeng ish**tah** bayng. **fee**koo kawng **eh**ler
What's my room number, please?	**Qual é o número do meu quarto, por favor?**	kwahl eh oo **noo**merroo doo **meh**oo **kwahr**too poor fer**voar**
Number 123.	**Número 123.**	**noo**merroo 123.

Service, please

Who is it?	**Quem é?**	kayng eh
Just a minute.	**Um momento.**	oong moo**mehn**too
Come in! The door's open.	**Entre! A porta está aberta.**	**ehn**trer er **por**ter ish**tah** er**behr**ter
May we have breakfast in our room?	**Podemos ter o pequeno almoço no quarto?**	poo**dheh**moosh tehr oo per**keh**noo ahl**mo**soo noo**kwahr**too

Breakfast

I'll have ...	**Tomo ...**	**to**moo
I'll have some fruit juice.	**Tomo sumo de fruta.**	**to**moo **soo**moo der **froo**ter
a boiled egg	**um ovo kozido**	oong **o**voo koo**zee**dhoo
a fried egg	**um ovo estrelado**	oong **o**voo ishtrer**lah**dhoo
some bacon/some ham	**toucinho/presunto**	toa**see**ñoo/prer**zoon**too
some toast	**torradas**	toor**rah**dhersh
a pot of tea	**um bule de chá**	oong **boo**ler der shah
a cup of tea	**uma chávena de chá**	**oo**mer **shah**verner der shah
some coffee	**café**	ker**feh**
some chocolate	**chocolate**	shookoo**lah**ter
more butter	**mais manteiga**	mighsh mern**tay**g̊er
some hot water	**água quente**	**ah**gwer **kayn**ter

Difficulties

The central heating doesn't work.	**O aquecimento central não funciona.**	oo erkehsee**mehn**too sehn**trahl** nahng^{w} foon**syoa**ner
the light/the socket	**a luz/a tomada**	er loosh/er too**mah**dher
the tap/the toilet	**a torneira/a casa de banho**	er toor**nay**rer/er **kah**zer der **bah**ñoo

PORTUGUESE

There's no hot water.	**Não há água quente.**	nahng^w ah **ah**g̊wer **kayn**ter
May I see the manager, please?	**Posso falar com o director, por favor?**	**poss**soo fer**lahr** kawng oo dee**reh**toar poor fer**voar**

Telephone—Mail

There's a call for you.	**Há uma chamada para si.**	ah **oo**mer sher**mah**dher **per**rer see
Hold the line, please.	**Aguarde um momento, por favor.**	er**gwahr**der oong moo**mehn**too poor fer**voar**
Operator, I've been cut off.	**Telefonista, cortaram-me a ligação.**	terlerfoo**neesh**ter koor**tah**rermmer er leeger**sahng**^{w}
Did anyone telephone me?	**Alguém me chamou?**	ahl**gayng** mer sher**moa**
Is there any mail for me?	**Há correio para mim?**	ah koor**ray**oo **per**rer meeng
Are there any messages for me?	**Há alguma mensagem para mim.**	ah ahl**goo**mer mayng**sah**zhayng **per**rer meeng

Checking out

May I have my bill, please?	**Pode dar-me a conta, por favor?**	**poa**dher **dahr**mer er **kon**ter poor fer**voar**
We're in a great hurry.	**Temos muita pressa.**	**tay**moosh **moong**^{y}ter **preh**ser
It's been a very enjoyable stay.	**Tivemos uma óptima estadia.**	tee**veh**moosh **oo**mer **o**teemer ishter**dhee**er

Eating out

Good evening, sir/Good evening, madam.	**Boa noite, Senhor/Boa noite, Senhora.**	**boa**er **noy**ter sayñ**oar**/**boa**er **noy**ter sayñ**oa**rer
Good evening. I'd like a table for two, please.	**Boa noite. Desejo uma mesa para dois, por favor.**	**boa**er **noy**ter. der**zeh**zhoo **oo**mer **may**zer **per**rer doysh poor fer**voar**
Do you have a fixed-price menu?	**Tem um menu de preço fixo?**	tayng oong meh**noo** der **preh**soo **feek**soo
May I see the à la carte menu?	**Pode dar-me o menu?**	**poa**dher **dahr**mer oo meh**noo**

May we have an ashtray, please?	**Pode-nos dar um cinzeiro, por favor?**	**poa**dhernoosh dahr oong seen**zay**roo poor fer**voar**
some bread	**pão**	pahng^{w}
a fork	**um garfo**	oong **gahr**foo
a knife	**uma faca**	**oo**mer **fah**ker
a spoon	**uma colher**	**oo**mer koo**lyehr**
a plate	**um prato**	oong **prah**too
a glass	**um copo**	oong **ko**poo
a napkin	**um guardanapo**	oong gwerrder**nah**poo
another chair	**outra cadeira**	**oa**trer ker**dhay**rer
Where's the gentlemen's toilet (men's room)?	**Onde é a casa de banho dos cavalheiros?**	**on**der eh er **kah**zer der **bah**ñoo doosh kerver**lyay**roosh
Where's the ladies' toilet (ladies' room)?	**Onde é a casa de banho das senhoras?**	**on**der eh er **kah**zer der **bah**ñoo dersh say**ñoa**rersh

Appetizers

I'd like some ...	**Queria ...**	ker**ree**er
I'd like some assorted appetizers.	**Queria uns acepipes variados.**	ker**ree**er oongsh erser**pee**persh ver**ryah**doosh
orange juice	**um sumo de laranja**	oong **soo**moo der ler**rahng**zher
ham	**fiambre**	**fyahng**brer
melon	**melão**	mer**lahng^{w}**
pâté	**pâté**	pah**tay**
smoked salmon	**salmão fumado**	sahl**mahng^{w}** foo**mah**dhoo
shrimps (shrimp)	**camarões**	kermer**rawng^{y}sh**

Soup

Have you any ... ?	**Tem ... ?**	tayng
Have you any chicken soup?	**Tem caldo de galinha?**	tayng **kahl**doo der ger**lee**ñer
vegetable soup	**sopa de legumes**	**soa**per der ler**ĝoo**mersh
onion soup	**sopa de cebola**	**soa**per der cer**boa**ler

Fish

I'd like some ...	**Queria ...**	ker**ree**er
I'd like some fish.	**Queria peixe.**	ker**ree**er **pay**sher
sole	**linguado**	ling**gwah**dhoo
trout	**truta**	**troo**ter
lobster	**lagosta**	ler**ĝoash**ter
crayfish	**caranguejo**	kerrerng**gay**zhoo
prawns	**lagostins**	lergoosh**teengsh**

I'd like it...	**Quero-o...**	**keh**roooo
I'd like it steamed.	**Quero-o cozido a vapor.**	**keh**roooo koo**zee**dhoo er ver**poar**
grilled	**grelhado**	gril**yah**dhoo
boiled	**cozido**	koo**zee**dhoo
baked	**no forno**	noo **foar**noo
fried	**frito**	**free**too

Meat—Poultry—Game

I'd like some...	**Queria...**	ker**ree**er
I'd like some beef.	**Queria carne de vaca.**	ker**ree**er **kahr**ner der **vah**ker
a beef steak	**um bife**	oong **bee**fer
some roast beef	**rósbife**	**roz**beefer
a veal cutlet	**uma costeleta de vitela**	**oo**mer kooshter**lay**ter der vee**teh**ler
mutton	**carneiro**	kerr**nay**roo
lamb	**borrego**	boo**ray**g̊oo
a pork chop	**uma costeleta de porco**	**oo**mer kooshter**lay**ter der **poar**koo
roast pork	**porco assado**	**poar**koo er**sah**dhoo
hare	**lebre**	**leh**brer
chicken	**frango**	**frahng**goo
roast chicken	**frango assado**	**frahng**goo er**sah**dhoo
duck	**pato**	**pah**too
How do you like your meat?	**Como deseja a carne?**	**koa**moo der**zay**zher er **kahr**ner
rare	**mal passada**	mahl per**sah**dher
medium	**médio**	**meh**dyoo
well done	**bem passada**	bayng per**sah**dher

Vegetables

What vegetables have you got?	**Que legumes tem?**	ker ler**g̊oo**mersh tayng
I'd like some...	**Queria...**	ker**ree**er
I'd like some asparagus.	**Queria espargos.**	ker**ree**er ish**pahr**goosh
green beans	**feijão verde**	fay**zhahng**^{w} **vehr**der
mushrooms	**cogumelos**	koog̊oo**meh**loosh
carrots	**cenouras**	si**noa**rersh
onions	**cebolas**	ser**boa**lersh
red cabbage	**repolho**	rer**poa**lyoo
spinach	**espinafres**	ishpee**nahf**rersh

rice	**arroz**	er**roash**
peas	**ervilhas**	err**vee**lyersh
tomatoes	**tomates**	too**mah**tersh
green salad	**salada de alface**	ser**lah**dher der ahl**fah**ser
potatoes	**batatas**	ber**tah**tersh

Desserts

Nothing more, thanks.	**Mais nada, obrigado.**	mighsh **nah**dher obree**ĝah**dhoo
Just a small portion, please.	**Muito pouco, por favor.**	**moong^y**too **poa**koo poor fer**voar**
Have you any ice-cream?	**Tem gelados?**	tayng zher**lah**doosh
fruit salad	**salada de frutas**	ser**lah**der dher **froo**tersh
fresh fruit	**fruta fresca**	**froo**ter **fraysh**ker
cheese	**queijo**	**kay**zhoo

Drink

What would you like to drink?	**Que deseja tomar?**	ker der**zay**zher too**mahr**
I'll have a beer, please.	**Queria uma cerveja, por favor.**	ker**ree**er **oo**mer serr**vay**zher poor fer**voar**
I'll have a whisky, please.	**Queria um whisky, por favor.**	ker**ree**er oong **weesh**kee poor fer**voar**

Wine

I'd like a bottle of wine.	**Queria uma garrafa de vinho.**	ker**ree**er **oo**mer ger**rah**fer der **vee**ñoo
red wine	**vinho tinto**	**vee**ñoo **teen**too
rosé wine	**vinho rosé**	**vee**ñoo ro**zay**
white wine	**vinho branco**	**vee**ñoo **brahng**koo
Cheers!	**Saúde!**	ser**oo**dher

The bill (check)

May I have the bill (check) please?	**Pode dar-me a conta, por favor?**	**poa**dher **dahr**mer er **kon**ter poor fer**voar**
Is service included?	**O serviço está incluído?**	oo serr**vee**soo ish**tah** eengkloo**ee**dhoo

PORTUGUESE

Everything's included.	**Tudo incluído.**	**too**dhoo eengkloo**ee**dhoo
Thank you, that was a very good meal.	**Obrigado, foi uma boa refeição.**	obree**gah**dhoo foy **oo**mer **boa**er rerfay**sahng**^{w}

Travelling

Where's the railway station, please?	**Onde é a estação de caminho de ferro, por favor?**	**on**der eh er ishter**sahng**^{w} der ker**mee**ñoo der **feh**roo poor fer**voar**
Where's the ticket office, please?	**Onde é a bilheteira, por favor?**	**on**der eh er beelyer**tay**rer poor fer**voar**
I'd like a ticket to ...	**Queria um bilhete para ...**	ker**ree**er oong bee**lyay**ter **per**rer
First or second class?	**De primeira ou segunda classe?**	der pree**may**rer oa ser**goon**der **klah**ser
First class, please.	**De primeira, por favor.**	der pree**may**rer poor fer**voar**
Single or return (one way or round-trip)?	**Uma ida ou ida e volta?**	**oo**mer **ee**der oa **ee**der ee **vol**ter
Do I have to change trains?	**Devo mudar de comboio?**	**day**voo moo**dahr** der koam**boy**oo
What platform does the train leave from?	**De que cais parte o comboio?**	der ker kighsh **pahr**ter oo koam**boy**oo
Where's the nearest underground (subway) station?	**Onde é a estação de metro mais próxima?**	**on**der eh er ishter**sahng**^{w} der **meh**troo mighsh **pro**seemer
Where's the bus station, please?	**Onde é a estação dos autocarros?**	**on**der eh er ishter**sahng**^{w} doosh owtoo**kah**roosh
When's the first bus to ... ?	**A que horas parte o primeiro autocarro para ... ?**	er ker **o**rersh **pahr**ter oo pree**may**roo owtoo**kah**roo **per**rer
the last bus	**o último autocarro**	oo **ool**timoo owtoo**kah**roo
the next bus	**o próximo autocarro**	oo **pro**seemoo owtoo**kah**roo
Please let me off at the next stop.	**Por favor, deixe-me sair na próxima paragem.**	poor fer**voar** **day**shermer ser**eer** ner **pro**seemer per**rah**zhayng

Relaxing

What's on at the cinema (movies)?	**O que há no cinema?**	oo ker ah noo see**nay**mer

What's on at the theatre?	**O que há no teatro?**	oo ker ah noo ti**ah**troo
What time does the film begin? And the play?	**A que horas começa o filme? E a peça?**	ah ker **o**rersh koo**meh**ser oo **feel**mer. ee er **peh**ser
Are there any tickets for tonight?	**Há bilhetes para esta noite?**	ah bee**lyay**tersh **per**rer **ehsh**ter **noy**ter
Where can we go dancing?	**Onde podemos ir dançar?**	**on**der poo**dheh**moosh eer dahn**sahr**
Would you like to dance?	**Quer dançar?**	kehr dahn**sahr**

Introductions

How do you do?	**Bom dia.**	bawng **dee**er
How are you?	**Como está?**	**koa**moo ish**tah**
Very well, thank you. And you?	**Muito bem, obrigado. E você?**	**moong**^{y}too bayng obree**gah**dhoo. ee vo**say**
May I introduce Miss Philips?	**Apresento-lhe a Menina Philips.**	erprer**zayn**toolyer er mer**nee**ner Philips
My name is ...	**O meu nome é ...**	oo **meh**oo **noa**mer eh
I'm very pleased to meet you.	**Tenho muito prazer em conhecê-lo.**	**tay**ñoo **moong**^{y}too prer**zehr** ayng kooñer**say**loo
How long have you been here?	**Há quanto tempo está cá?**	ah **kwahn**too **tayng**poo ish**tah** kah
It was nice meeting you.	**Tive muito prazer em conhecê-lo.**	**tee**ver **moong**^{y}too prer**zehr** ayng kooñer**say**loo

Dating

Would you like a cigarette?	**Quer um cigarro?**	kehr oong see**gah**roo
May I get you a drink?	**Posso oferecer-lhe uma bebida?**	**poss**soo oferrer**sehr**lyer **oo**mer ber**bee**dher
Do you have a light, please?	**Tem lume, por favor?**	tayng **loo**mer poor fer**voar**
Are you waiting for someone?	**Espera alguém?**	ish**pay**rer ahl**gayng**
Are you free this evening?	**Está livre esta noite?**	ish**tah** **lee**vrer **ehsh**ter **noy**ter
Where shall we meet?	**Onde nos podemos encontrar?**	**on**der noosh poo**dheh**moosh ingkoan**trahr**

What time shall I meet you?	**A que horas posso encontra-la?**	er ker **o**rersh **poss**soo ingkoan**trah**ler
May I take you home?	**Posso leva-la a casa?**	**poss**soo ler**vah**ler er **kah**zer
Thank you, it's been a wonderful evening.	**Obrigado por esta noite tão agradável.**	obree**gah**dhoo poor **ehsh**-ter **noy**ter tahng[w] ergrer-**dhah**vehl
What's your telephone number?	**Qual é o seu número de telefone?**	kwahl eh oo **seh**oo **noo**merroo de terler**fo**ner
Do you live alone?	**Vive só?**	**vee**ver so
What time is your last train?	**A que horas é o seu último comboio?**	er ker **o**rersh eh oo **seh**oo **ool**timoo koam**boy**oo
Good-night...	**Boa noite...**	**boa**er **noy**ter

Banks

Where's the nearest bank, please?	**Onde é o Banco mais próximo, por favor?**	**on**der eh oo **bahng**koo mighsh **pro**seemoo poor fer**voar**
Where can I cash some traveller's cheques?	**Onde posso trocar alguuns cheques de viagem?**	**on**der **poss**soo troo**kahr** ahl**g̊oongsh** shehks der vyah**zhayng**
What time does the bank open? What time does it close?	**A que horas abre o Banco? A que horas fecha?**	er ker **o**rersh **ah**brer oo **bahng**koo? er ker **o**rersh **feh**sher
I'm expecting some money from home. Has it arrived?	**Aguardo dinheiro da familia. Já chegou?**	er**gwahr**dhoo di**ñay**roo der fer**mee**lyer. zhah sher**goa**
Can you give me some small change, please?	**Pode dar-me alguns trocos, por favor?**	**poa**dher **dahr**mer ahl-**goongsh tro**koosh poor fer**voar**

Shops, stores and services

Where is the nearest chemist's (pharmacy)?	**Onde é a farmácia mais próxima?**	**on**der eh er ferr**mah**seeer mighsh **pro**seemer
the nearest hairdresser's	**o cabeleireiro mais próximo**	o kerberlee**ray**roo mighsh **pro**seemoo
the photo shop	**a loja de artigos fotográficos**	er **lo**zher der err**tee**g̊oosh footoo**grah**feekoosh
the jeweller's	**a ourivesaria**	er oareevser**ree**er
the department store	**o armazém**	oo ahrmer**zayng**

the police station	**o posto de policia**	oo **posh**too der poo**lee**-seeer
the garage	**a garagem**	er ger**rah**zhayng
How do I get there?	**Como vou lá ter?**	**koa**moo voa lah tehr
Is it within walking distance?	**Pode-se ir a pé?**	**poa**dherser eer ah peh

Service

Can you help me, please?	**Pode ajudar-me, por favor?**	**poa**dher erzhoo**dhahr**mer poor fer**voar**
Can you show me this? And that, too.	**Pode mostrar-me isto? e aquilo também.**	**poa**dher moosh**trahr**mer **eesh**too ee er**kee**loo tahm**bayng**
It's too expensive/ too big/too small.	**É muito caro/muito grande/muito pequeno.**	eh **moong**^{y}too **kah**roo/ **moong**^{y}too **grahn**der/ **moong**^{y}too per**keh**noo
Can you show me some more?	**Pode mostrar-me mais alguns?**	**poa**dher moosh**trahr**mer mighsh ahl**g̊oongsh**
something better	**algo melhor**	**ahl**g̊oo mi**lyoar**
something cheaper	**algo mais barato**	**ahl**g̊oo mighsh ber**rah**too
How much is this? And that?	**Quanto custa isto? E aquilo?**	**kwahn**too **koosh**ter **eesh**-too? ee er**kee**loo
It's not quite what I want.	**Não é exatamente o que quero.**	nahng^{w} eh izahter**mehn**ter oo ker **keh**roo
I like it.	**Gosto disto.**	**gosh**too **deesh**too

Chemist's (Pharmacy)

I'd like something for a cold/for a cough/for travel sickness.	**Queria qualquer coisa para a constipação/para a tosse/para o enjôo de viagem.**	ker**ree**er kwahl**kehr** **koy**zer **per**rer er **kawng**shtipersahng^{w}/**per**rer er **to**ser/**per**rer oo ayng-**zhoa**oo der vyah**zhayng**
Can you recommend something for hay-fever/for sunburn?	**Pode indicar-me algo para a alergia do polen/para queimaduras do sol?**	**poa**dher eendee**kahr**mer **ahl**g̊oo **per**rer er erler-**zhee**er doo **po**layn/**per**rer kaymer**dhoo**rersh doo sol

Toiletry

May I have some razor blades?	**Pode dar-me lâminas de barbear?**	**poa**dher **dahr**mer **lah**meenersh der berr**byahr**
some shaving cream	**creme para a barba**	**kreay**mer **per**rer er **bahr**ber
some toothpaste	**uma pasta de dentes**	**oo**mer **pahsh**ter der **dehn**tish
I'd like some soap.	**Queria um sabonete.**	ker**ree**er oom serboo**neh**ter
some suntan oil	**um óleo para bronzear**	oong **o**lyoo **per**rer bronzee**ahr**

At the barber's

I'd like a haircut, please.	**Quero cortar o cabelo, por favor.**	**keh**roo koor**tahr** oo ker**bay**loo poor fer**voar**
Short/Leave it long.	**Curto/Deixe-o comprido.**	**koor**too/**day**sheroo kom**pree**doo
A razor cut, please.	**A navalha, por favor.**	er ner**vah**lyer poor fer**voar**

At the hairdresser's

I'd like a shampoo and set, please.	**Queria um champô e mise, por favor.**	ker**ree**er oong shahm**poa** ee **mee**zer poor fer**voar**
I'd like a bleach.	**Queria aloirar o cabelo.**	ker**ree**er erloy**rahr** oo ker**bay**loo
a permanent	**fazer uma permanente**	fer**zehr** **oo**mer pehrmer**nehn**ter
a colour rinse	**pintar o cabelo**	peen**tahr** oo ker**bay**loo
a manicure	**uma manicura**	**oo**mer mer**nee**koorer

Photography

I'd like a film for this camera.	**Queria um rolo para esta máquina fotográfica.**	ker**ree**er oong **roa**loo **per**rer **ehsh**ter **mah**keener footoo**grah**feeker
This camera doesn't work.	**Esta máquina não funciona bem.**	**ehsh**ter **mah**keener nahng^{w} foon**syoa**ner bayng

At the post office

Where's the nearest post office, please?	**Qual é o correio mais próximo, por favor?**	kwahl eh oo koo**ray**oo mighsh **pro**seemoo poor fer**voar**
I'd like to send this by express (special delivery)/by air mail.	**Queria enviar isto por expresso/por avião.**	ker**ree**er ayngvee**ahr** **eesh**too poor ish**preh**soo/ poor ervee**ahng**ʷ

Service stations

Where is the nearest service station, please?	**Qual é a estação de serviço mais próxima, por favor?**	kwahl eh er ishter**sahng**ʷ der serr**vee**soo mighsh **pro**seemer poor fer**voar**
Fill her up, please.	**Encha o depósito, por favor.**	**ayng**sher oo der**po**zeetoo poor fer**voar**
Check the oil, please.	**Verifique o óleo, por favor.**	verree**fee**ker oo **o**lyoo poor fer**voar**
Would you check the tyres?	**Pode verificar os pneus?**	**poa**dher verreefee**kahr** oosh **pneh**oosh

Street directions

Can you show me on the map where I am?	**Pode mostrar-me no mapa onde me encontro?**	**poa**dher **moosh**trahrmer noo **mah**per **on**der mer ayng**kon**troo
You're on the wrong road.	**Está na estrada errada.**	ish**tah** ner ish**trah**dher er**rah**dher
Go back to ...	**Volte atrás até ...**	**vol**ter er**trahsh** er**teh**
Go straight ahead.	**Sempre em frente.**	**saym**prer ayng **frayn**ter
It's on the left/on the right.	**É à esquerda/à direita.**	eh ah ish**kehr**der/ah di**ray**ter

Accidents

May I use your telephone?	**Posso telefonar?**	**poss**soo terlerfoo**nahr**
Call a doctor quickly.	**Chame um médico depressa.**	**sher**mer oong **may**deekoo der**preh**ser
Call an ambulance.	**Chame uma ambulância.**	**sher**mer **oo**mer ermboo**lahng**seeer
Please call the police.	**Chame a polícia, por favor.**	**sher**mer er poo**lee**seeer poor fer**voar**

Numbers

one	**um**	oong
two	**dois**	doysh
three	**três**	traysh
four	**quatro**	**kwah**tro
five	**cinco**	**seeng**koo
six	**seis**	saysh
seven	**sete**	**seh**ter
eight	**oito**	**oy**too
nine	**nove**	**no**ver
ten	**dez**	dehsh
eleven	**onze**	**awng**zer
twelve	**doze**	**doa**zer
thirteen	**treze**	**tray**zer
fourteen	**catorze**	ker**toar**zer
fifteen	**quinze**	**keen**zer
sixteen	**dezasseis**	derzer**saysh**
seventeen	**dezassete**	derzer**seh**ter
eighteen	**dezoito**	der**zoy**too
nineteen	**dezanove**	derzer**no**ver
twenty	**vinte**	**veen**ter
twenty-one	**vinte e um**	**veen**ter ee oong
thirty	**trinta**	**treen**ter
forty	**quarenta**	kwer**rehn**ter
fifty	**cinquenta**	seeng**kwehn**ter
sixty	**sessenta**	ser**sehn**ter
seventy	**setenta**	ser**tehn**ter
eighty	**oitenta**	oy**tehn**ter
ninety	**noventa**	noo**vehn**ter
one hundred	**cem**	sayng
one thousand	**mil**	meel
ten thousand	**dez mil**	dehsh meel

Days

It's Sunday.	**É domingo.**	eh doo**meeng**goo
Monday	**segunda-feira**	ser**goon**der **fay**rer
Tuesday	**terça-feira**	**tehr**ser **fay**rer
Wednesday	**quarta-feira**	**kwahr**ter **fay**rer
Thursday	**quinta-feira**	**keen**ter **fay**rer
Friday	**sexta-feira**	**saysh**ter **fay**rer
Saturday	**sábado**	**sah**berdhoo
yesterday	**ontem**	**awng**tayng
today	**hoje**	**oa**zher
tomorrow	**amanhã**	ahmer**ñahng**
morning/afternoon	**manhã/tarde**	mer**ñahng**/**tahr**der
evening/night	**noite/noite**	**noy**ter/**noy**ter

Months

January	**Janeiro**	zher**nay**roo
February	**Fevereiro**	ferver**ray**roo
March	**Março**	**mahr**soo
April	**Abril**	er**breel**
May	**Maio**	**migh**oo
June	**Junho**	**zhoo**ñoo
July	**Julho**	**zhoo**lyoo
August	**Agosto**	er**goash**too
September	**Setembro**	ser**tayng**broo
October	**Outubro**	oa**too**broo
November	**Novembro**	noo**vayng**broo
December	**Dezembro**	der**zayng**broo
Merry Christmas!	**Feliz Natal/Feliz**	fer**leesh** ner**tahl**/fer**leesh**
Happy New Year!	**Ano Novo!**	**ah**noo **no**voo

RUSSIAN

Guide to Pronunciation

Letter	Approximate pronunciation	Symbol	Example	
Vowels				
а	between the **a** in c**a**t and the **ar** in c**ar**t	ah	**как**	kahk
е	like **ye** in **ye**t	yeh	**где**	gdyeh
ё	like **yo** in **yo**nder	yo	**мёд**	myod
и	like **ee** in s**ee**	ee	**синий**	**see**nyee
й	like **y** in ga**y** or bo**y**	y	**бой**	boy
о	like **o** in h**o**t	o	**стол**	stol
у	like **oo** in b**oo**t	oo	**улица**	**oo**leetsah
ы	similar to **i** in h**i**t	i	**вы**	vi
э	like **e** in m**e**t	eh	**эта**	**eh**tah
ю	like **u** in d**u**ke	yoo	**юг**	yoog
я	like **ya** in **ya**rd	yah	**мясо**	**myah**sah

Consonants

б	like **b** in **b**it	b	**был**	bil
в	like **v** in **v**ine	v	**ваш**	vahsh
г	like **g** in **g**o	g	**город**	**go**rahd
д	like **d** in **d**o	d	**да**	dah
ж	like **s** in plea**s**ure	zh	**жаркий**	**zhahr**kee
з	like **z** in **z**oo	z	**за**	zah
к	like **k** in **k**itten	k	**карта**	**kahr**tah
л	like **l** in **l**ose	l	**лампа**	**lahm**pah
м	like **m** in **m**y	m	**масло**	**mahss**lah
н	like **n** in **n**ot	n	**нет**	nyeht
п	like **p** in **p**ot	p	**парк**	pahrk
р	like **r** in **r**un	r	**русский**	**rooss**kee
с	like **s** in **s**ee	s/ss	**слово**	**slo**vah
т	like **t** in **t**ip	t	**там**	tahm
ф	like **f** in **f**ace	f	**ферма**	**fyehr**mah
х	like **ch** in Scottish lo**ch**	kh	**хлеб**	kh lyehb
ц	like **ts** in si**ts**	ts	**цена**	tsee**nah**
ч	like **ch** in **ch**ip	ch	**час**	chahss
ш	like **sh** in **sh**ut	sh	**ваша**	**vah**shah
щ	like **sh** followed by **ch**	shch	**щётка**	**shchyot**kah

Other letters

ь gives a "soft" pronunciation to the preceding consonant. A similar effect can be produced by pronouncing **y** as in **y**et—but very, very short—after the consonant. In our transcription we shall show this with an apostrophe (') after the soft consonant.

ъ is sometimes used between two parts of a compound word, when the second part begins with **я**, **ю**, or **е**, to show that the pronunciation of the word should incorporate a clear separation of the two parts.

Diphthongs

ай	like **igh** in s**igh**	igh	**чай**	chigh
яй	like the previous sound, but preceded by the **y** in **y**es	yigh	**негодяй**	nyehgo**dyigh**
ой	like **oy** in b**oy**	oy	**вой**	voy
ей	like **ya** in **Ya**tes	yay	**соловей**	solo**vyay**
ый	like **i** in b**i**t followed by the **y** in **y**es	iy	**красивый**	krah**see**viy
уй	like **oo** in g**oo**d followed by the **y** in **y**es	ooy	**дуй**	dooy
юй	like the previous sound, but preceded by the **y** in **y**es	yooy	**плюй**	plyooy

The effects of non-stress

If a vowel or diphthong is not stressed, it often changes its pronunciation. This could be called a weakening of the sound.

о	unstressed, is pronounced like Russian **a**	ah	**отец**	ah**tyehts**
е, я, и, ой, ей, ий	unstressed, are pronounced like a short **yee** sound	yee or ee	**теперь** **английский**	tyee**pyehr'** ahn**glee**skee

The alphabet

The column at the left shows printed capital and small letters while the centre column shows handwritten capital and small letters. The right-hand column will help you to pronounce the names of these letters in Russian.

А	**а**	*А*	*а*	ah
Б	**б**	*Б*	*б*	beh
В	**в**	*В*	*в*	veh
Г	**г**	*Г*	*г*	geh
Д	**д**	*Д*	*д*	deh
Е	**е**	*Е*	*е*	yeh
Ё	**ё**	*Ё*	*ё*	yoh
Ж	**ж**	*Ж*	*ж*	zheh
З	**з**	*З*	*з*	zeh
И	**и**	*И*	*и*	ee
Й	**й**	*Й*	*й*	ee **kraht**koyeh
К	**к**	*К*	*к*	kah
Л	**л**	*Л*	*л*	ehl
М	**м**	*М*	*м*	ehm
Н	**н**	*Н*	*н*	ehn
О	**о**	*О*	*о*	o
П	**п**	*П*	*п*	peh
Р	**р**	*Р*	*р*	ehr
С	**с**	*С*	*с*	ehs
Т	**т**	*Т*	*т*	teh
У	**у**	*У*	*у*	oo
Ф	**ф**	*Ф*	*ф*	ehf
Х	**х**	*Х*	*х*	khah
Ц	**ц**	*Ц*	*ц*	tseh
Ч	**ч**	*Ч*	*ч*	chah
Ш	**ш**	*Ш*	*ш*	shah
Щ	**щ**	*Щ*	*щ*	shchah
Ъ	**ъ**		*ъ*	**tvyor**diy znahk
Ы	**ы**		*ы*	yeh**ree**
Ь	**ь**		*ь*	**myah**kee znahk
Э	**э**	*Э*	*э*	eh obo**rot**noyeh
Ю	**ю**	*Ю*	*ю*	yoo
Я	**я**	*Я*	*я*	yah

Some basic expressions

Yes.	**Да.**	dah
No.	**Нет.**	nyeht
Please.	**Пожалуйста.**	pah**zhah**loostah
Thank you.	**Спасибо.**	spah**see**bah
Thank you very much.	**Большое спасибо.**	bahl'**sho**yee spahs**ee**bah
That's all right.	**Не за что.**	nyee zah **shto**

Greetings

Good morning.	**Доброе утро.**	dobrahyee **oo**tro
Good afternoon.	**Добрый день.**	dobri **dyehn'**
Good evening.	**Добрый вечер.**	dobri **vyeh**chyeer
Good night.	**Спокойной ночи.**	spah**koy**nigh **no**chee
Good-bye.	**До свидания.**	dah svee**dah**neeyah
See you later.	**До встречи.**	dah **vstryeh**chee
This is Mr. ...	**Это господин ...**	ehtah gahspah**deen**
This is Mrs. ...	**Это госпожа ...**	ehtah gahspah**zhah**
This is Miss ...	**Это госпожа ...**	ehtah gahspah**zhah**
I'm very pleased to meet you.	**Очень приятно.**	**o**chyeen' pree**yaht**nah
How are you?	**Как дела?**	kahk dyeh**lah**
Very well, thank you. And you?	**Спасибо, хорошо. Как у Вас?**	spah**see**bah khahrah**sho** kahk oo **vahs**
Fine.	**Прекрасно.**	pryee**krahs**nah
Excuse me.	**Простите.**	prahs**tee**tyee

Questions

Where?	**Где?**	gdyeh
Where is ... ?	**Где ... ?**	gdyeh
Where are ... ?	**Где ... ?**	gdyeh
When?	**Когда?**	kahg**dah**
What?	**Что?**	shto
How?	**Как?**	kahk
How much?	**Сколько?**	**skol**'kah
How many?	**Сколько?**	**skol**'kah

Who?	**Кто?**	kto
Why?	**Почему?**	pahchyee**moo**
Which?	**Какой?**	kah**koy**
What do you call this?	**Как это называется?**	kahk **eh**tah nahzi**vah**yeetsah
What do you call that?	**Как это называется?**	kahk **eh**tah nahzi**vah**yeetsah
What does this mean?	**Что это значит?**	shto **eh**tah **znah**cheet
What does that mean?	**Что это значит?**	shto **eh**tah **znah**cheet

Do you speak . . . ?

Do you speak English?	**Вы говорите по-английски?**	vi gahvah**ree**tyee pah ahn**glee**skee
Do you speak German?	**Вы говорите по-немецки?**	vi gahvah**ree**tyee pah nyee**myeht**skee
Do you speak French?	**Вы говорите по-французски?**	vi gahvah**ree**tyee pah frahn**tsoo**skee
Do you speak Spanish?	**Вы говорите по-испански?**	vi gahvah**ree**tyee pah ees**pahn**skee
Do you speak Italian?	**Вы говорите по-итальянски?**	vi gahvah**ree**tyee pah eetah**l'yahn**skee
Could you speak more slowly, please?	**Могли-бы вы говорить медленнее?**	mah**glee**bi **vi** gahvah**reet'** **myeh**dlyeenyehyee
Please point to the phrase in the book.	**Покажите мне, пожалуйста, фразу в книге.**	pahkah**zhee**tyee mnyeh pah**zhah**loostah **frah**zoo v **knee**gyee
Just a minute. I'll see if I can find it in this book.	**Минуточку. Я посмотрю, смогу ли я её найти в книжке.**	mee**noo**tahchkoo **yah** pahsmah**tryoo** smah**goo**lee yah yee**yo** nigh**tee** v **knee**zhkyee
I understand.	**Я понимаю.**	**yah** pahnyee**mah**yoo
I don't understand.	**Я не понимаю.**	**yah** nyee pahnyee**mah**yoo

Can . . . ?

Can I have . . . ?	**Можно . . . ?**	**mo**zhnah
Can we have . . . ?	**Можно . . . ?**	**mo**zhnah
Can you show me . . . ?	**Вы мне можете показать . . . ?**	vi mnyeh **mo**zhyeetyee pahkah**zaht'**

Can you tell me . . . ?	**Вы мне можете сказать . . . ?**	vi mnyeh **mo**zhyeetyee skah**zaht'**
Can you help me, please?	**Пожалуйста помогите мне.**	pah**zhah**loostah pahmah**ghee**tyee mnyeh

Wanting

I'd like . . .	**Я хотел бы . . .**	yah khah**tyehl** bi
We'd like . . .	**Мы хотели бы . . .**	mi khah**tyeh**lee bi
Please give me . . .	**Дайте мне, пожалуйста, . . .**	**digh**tyee **mnyeh** pah**zhah**loostah
Give it to me, please.	**Дайте мне это, пожалуйста.**	**digh**tyee mnyeh **eh**tah pah**zhah**loostah
Please bring me . . .	**Принесите мне, пожалуйста . . .**	preenyee**see**tyee **mnyeh** pah**zhah**loostah
Bring it to me, please.	**Принесите мне это, пожалуйста.**	preenyee**see**tyee **mnyeh** **eh**tah pah**zhah**loostah
I'm hungry.	**Я голодный.**	**yah** gah**lo**dni
I'm thirsty.	**Мне хочется пить.**	**mnyeh** khochyeetsah **peet'**
I'm tired.	**Я устал.**	**yah** oostahl
I'm lost.	**Я заблудился.**	**yah** zahbloodeelsah
It's important.	**Это важно.**	**eh**tah **vahzh**nah
It's urgent.	**Это срочно.**	**eh**tah **sroch**nah
Hurry up!	**Скорее!**	skah**ryeh**yee

It is/There is . . .

The words "it is/there is" are often dropped in Russian. For example, the word холодно (**kho**lahdnah) alone conveys the idea "It is cold".

It is/It's . . .	**Это . . .**	**eh**tah
Is it . . . ?	**Это . . . ?**	**eh**tah
It isn't . . .	**Это не . . .**	**eh**tah **nyeh**
There is/There are . . .	**Есть . . .**	yehst'
Is there/Are there . . . ?	**Есть-ли . . . ?**	**yehst'** lee
There isn't/There aren't . . .	**Нет ли . . .**	nyeht lee
There isn't any/ There aren't any.	**Нет ли.**	nyeht lee

RUSSIAN

A few common words

big/small	большой/маленький	bahl'**shoy/mah**lyeen'kee
quick/slow	быстро/медленно	**bi**strah/**myeh**dlyeenah
early/late	рано/поздно	**rah**nah/**poz**nah
cheap/expensive	дёшево/дорого	**dyo**shyeevah/**do**rahgah
near/far	близко/далеко	**blees**kah/dahlyee**ko**
hot/cold	горячо/холодно	gah**ryah**chyo/**kho**lahdnah
full/empty	полный/пустой	**pol**ni/poo**stoy**
easy/difficult	легко/трудно	lyeekh**ko**/**trood**nah
heavy/light	тяжёлый/легкий	tyee**zho**li/**lyokh**kee
open/shut	открыто/закрыто	ah**tkri**tah/zah**kri**tah
right/wrong	верно/неверно	**vyehr**nah/nyee**vyehr**nah
old/new	старый/новый	**stah**riy/**no**vi
old/young	старый/молодой	**stah**ri/mahlah**doy**
beautiful/ugly	красиво/уродливо	krah**see**vah/oo**rod**leevah
good/bad	хорошо/плохо	khahrah**sho**/**plo**khah
better/worse	лучше/хуже	**loo**chyee/**khoo**zhyee

RUSSIAN

Some prepositions and a few more useful words

at	в	v
on	на	nah
in	в	v
to	к	k
from	от	ot
inside	внутри	vnoo**tree**
outside	снаружи	snah**roo**zhee
up	вверх	vvyehrkh
down	вниз	vnees
before	до	do
after	после	**po**slyee
with	с	s
without	без	byehss
through	через	**chyeh**ryeess
towards	к	k
until	до	do
during	во время	vah **vryeh**myee
and	и	ee
or	или	**ee**lee
not	не	nyeh
nothing	ничего	neechyee**vo**
none	ни один	nyeh ah**deen**

very	**очень**	**o**chyeen'
also	**тоже**	**to**zhyee
soon	**скоро**	**sko**rah
perhaps	**может быть**	**moz**hyeet bit'
here	**здесь**	zdyehs'
there	**там**	tahm
now	**теперь**	tyee**pyehr**'
then	**тогда**	tahg**dah**

Arrival

Your passport, please.	**Ваш паспорт, пожалуйста.**	vahsh **pahs**pahrt pah**zhah**loostah
Here it is.	**Пожалуйста.**	pah**zhah**loostah
Have you anything to declare?	**У Вас есть что-либо заявить для таможни?**	oo vahs yehst' **shto**leebah zahyah**veet**' dlyah **tah**mahzhnyee
No, nothing at all.	**Нет, ничего.**	nyeht nyeechee**vo**
Porter!	**Носильщик!**	nah**seel**'shcheek
Can you help me with my luggage, please?	**Пожалуйста возьмите мой багаж.**	pah**zhah**loostah vahz**mee**tyeh moy bah**gahzh**
That's my suitcase.	**Это мой чемодан.**	**eh**tah moy cheemah**dahn**
Where's the tourist office?	**Где бюро Интуриста?**	gdyeh bjoo**ro** eentoo**ree**stah
This way, please.	**Сюда, пожалуйста.**	syoo**dah** pah**zhah**loostáh

RUSSIAN

Changing money

Can you change a traveller's cheque, please?	**Можете ли Вы разменять аккредитив?**	**mo**zhehtyeh lee vi rahzmyeh**nyaht**' ahkryehdyee**tyeev**
Where's the nearest bank, please?	**Где ближайший банк?**	gdyeh blee**zhigh**sheey bahnk

Car rental

I'd like a car.	**Мне нужна машина.**	mnyeh noozh**nah** mah**shee**nah
For how long?	**На какое время?**	nah kah**ko**yeh **vryeh**myah
A day/Four days/ A week/Two weeks.	**На день/на четыре дня/на неделю/на две недели.**	**nah** dyehn'/nah chyeh**ti**ryeh dnyah/nah nyeh**dyeh**lyoo/nah dvyeh nyeh**dyeh**lee

Taxi

Where can I get a taxi?	**Где я могу поймать такси?**	gdyeh yah mah**goo** pigh**maht'** tahk**see**
What's the fare to . . . ?	**Сколько стоит доехать до . . . ?**	**skol'**kah **sto**eet dah**yeh**-khaht' dah
Take me to this address, please.	**Довезите меня по этому адресу, пожалуйста.**	dahvee**zee**tyeh myeh**nyah** pah **eh**tahmoo **ah**-dryehsoo pah**zhah**loostah
I'm in a hurry.	**Я спешу.**	yah spee**shoo**
Could you drive more slowly, please?	**Могли бы Вы ехать медленнее?**	mahg**lee** bi vi **yeh**khaht' **myehd**lyehnnyehyeh

Hotel and other accommodation

My name is . . .	**Моя фамилия . . .**	mah**yah** fah**mee**leeyah . . .
Have you a reservation?	**Вы зарезервировали номер?**	vi zahryehzyehr**veer**ahvahlee **no**myehr
Yes, here's the confirmation.	**Да, вот подтверждение.**	dah vot pahdtvyehr**zhdyeh**nyeeyeh
We reserved a single room/ a double room.	**Мы забронировали одинарный / двойной номер.**	mi zahbra**nyee**rahvahlee ahdyee**nahr**niy/dvigh**noy** **no**myehr
a room with a bath/with a shower	**номер с ванной/с душем**	**no**myehr s **vahn**nigh/ s **doo**shahm
What's my room number, please?	**Какой у меня номер комнаты?**	kah**koy** oo myeh**nyah** **no**myehr **kom**nahti
Number 123.	**Номер 123.**	**no**myehr 123

Service, please

Who is it?	**Кто там?**	**kto** tahm
Just a minute, please.	**Одну минуту, пожалуйста.**	ahd**noo** mee**noo**too pah**zhah**loostah
Come in! The door's open.	**Войдите! Дверь открыта.**	vigh**dyee**tyeh! dvyehr' aht**kri**tah
May we have breakfast in our room?	**Можно получить завтрак в нашей комнате?**	**mozh**nah pahloo**cheet'** **zah**vtrahk v **nah**shay **kom**nahtyeh

Breakfast

I'll have . . .	**Я хотел бы . . .**	yah khah**tyehl** bi
I'll have some fruit juice.	**Я хотел бы фруктовый сок.**	yah khah**tyehl** bi frook**to**viy sok
a boiled egg	**варёное яйцо**	vah**ryo**nahyeh yigh**tso**
a fried egg	**яичницу**	yah**yeech**nyeetsoo
some bacon/some ham	**бекон/ветчину**	**byeh**kon/veechee**noo**
some toast	**тост**	tost
a pot of tea	**чай в чайничке**	chigh v **chigh**nyeechkyeh
a cup of tea	**чашку чая**	**chahsh**koo **chah**yah
some coffee	**кофе**	**ko**fyeh
some chocolate	**шоколад**	shahkah**lahd**
more butter	**больше масла**	**bol**'sheh **mahs**lah
some hot water	**горячей воды**	gah**ryah**chyay vah**di**

Difficulties

The central heating doesn't work.	**Центральное отопление не работает.**	tsehn**trahl**'nahyeh ahtah**plyeh** nyeeyeh nyeh rah**bo**tahyeht
the light/the socket	**свет/штепсель**	svyeht/**shtehp**sehl'
the tap/the toilet	**кран/туалет**	krahn/tooah**lyeht**
There's no hot water.	**Нет горячей воды.**	nyeht gah**ryah**chyay vah**di**
May I see the manager, please?	**Можно поговорить с администратором?**	**mozh**nah pahgahvah**reet**' s ahdmeenyee**strah**tahrom

Telephone—Mail

There's a call for you.	**Вас к телефону.**	vahs k tyehlyeh**fo**noo
Hold the line, please.	**Подождите у телефона.**	pahdahzh**dyee**tyeh oo tyehlyeh**fonah**
Operator, I've been cut off.	**Девушка, нас прервали.**	**dyeh**vooshkah nahs pryeh**rvah**lee
Did anyone telephone me?	**Мне кто-нибудь звонил?**	mnyeh **kto**nyeebood' zvah**nyeel**
Is there any mail for me?	**Есть для меня почта?**	yehst' dlyah myeh**nyah** **poch**tah
Are there any messages for me?	**Мне никто не оставил записки?**	mnyeh nyee**kto** nyeh ah**stah**veel zah**pees**kee

Checking out

May I have my bill, please?	**Могу ли я получить счёт?**	mah**goo** lee yah pahloo**cheet**' shchyot
We're in a great hurry.	**Мы очень спешим.**	mi **o**chehn' spee**shim**
It's been a very enjoyable stay.	**Пребывание было очень приятным.**	preebi**vah**nyeeyeh **bi**lah **o**chehn' pree**yaht**nim

Eating out

Good evening, sir/ Good evening, madam.	**Добрый вечер, господин/ Добрый вечер госпожа.**	**do**briy **vyeh**chehr gahspah**dyeen**/**do**briy **vyeh**chehr gahspah**zhah**
Good evening, I'd like a table for two, please.	**Добрый вечер. Я хотел бы столик на двоих.**	**do**briy **vyeh**chehr. yah khah**tyehl** bi **sto**leek nah dvah**yeekh**
Do you have a fixed-price menu?	**У Вас есть меню?**	oo vahs yehst' meh**nyoo**
May I see the à la carte menu?	**У Вас есть обеденное меню?**	oo vahs yehst' ah**byeh**-dyehnnahyeh meh**nyoo**
May we have an ashtray, please?	**Можно попросить пепельницу?**	**mozh**nah pahprah**seet**' **pyeh**pyehl'nyee tsoo
some bread	**хлеб**	khlyehb
a fork	**вилку**	**veel**koo
a knife	**нож**	nozh
a spoon	**ложку**	**lozh**koo
a plate	**тарелку**	tah**ryehl**koo
a glass	**стакан**	stah**kahn**
a napkin	**салфетку**	sahl**fyeht**koo
another chair	**другой стул**	droo**goy** stool
Where's the gentlemen's toilet (men's room)?	**Где мужской туалет?**	gdyeh moozh**skoy** tooah-**lyeht**
Where's the ladies' toilet (ladies' room)?	**Где женский туалет?**	gdyeh **zhehn**skeey tooah-**lyeht**

Appetizers

I'd like some . . .	**Я хотел бы . . .**	yah khah**tyehl** bi
I'd like some assorted appetizers.	**Я хотел бы ассорти.**	yah khah**tyehl** bi ahsor-**tyee**

orange juice	**апельсиновый сок**	ahpyehl'**see**nahviy sok
ham	**ветчину**	veechee**noo**
melon	**дыню**	**di**nyoo
pâté	**паштет**	pah**shtyeht**
smoked salmon	**сёмгу**	**syom**goo
shrimps (shrimp)	**креветок**	kryeh**vyeh**tahk

Soup

Have you any ...?	**Есть у Вас ...?**	yehst' oo vahs
Have you any chicken soup?	**Есть у Вас суп с курицей?**	yehst' oo vahs soop s **koo**reetsay
vegetable soup	**овощной суп**	ovahshch**noy** soop
onion soup	**луковый суп**	**loo**kahviy soop

Fish

I'd like some ...	**Я хотел бы ...**	yah khah**tyehl** bi
I'd like some fish.	**Я хотел бы рыбу.**	yah khah**tyehl** bi **ri**boo
sole	**морской язык**	mahr**skoy** yah**zik**
trout	**форель**	fah**rehl'**
lobster	**омаров**	o**mah**rahv
crayfish	**лангуст**	lahn**goost**
prawns	**креветок**	kryeh**vyeh**tahk
I'd like it ...	**Я бы хотел это ...**	yah bi khah**tyehl eh**tah
I'd like it steamed.	**Я бы хотел это паровое.**	yah bi khah**tyehl eh**tah pahrah**vo**yeh
grilled	**жареное на рашпере.**	**zhah**ryehnahyeh nah rahsh**pyeh**ryeh
boiled	**отварное**	ahtvahr**no**yeh
baked	**печёное**	pyeh**chyo**nahyeh
fried	**жареное**	**zhah**ryehnahyeh

Meat—Poultry—Game

I'd like some ...	**Я бы хотел ...**	yah bi khah**tyehl**
I'd like some beef.	**Я бы хотел говядину.**	yahbi khah**tyehl** gah**vyah**dyeenoo
a beef steak	**бифштекс**	beef**shtehks**
some roast beef	**ростбиф**	rost**beef**
a veal cutlet	**телячью котлету**	tyeh**lyah**chyoo kaht**lyeh**too

RUSSIAN

mutton	**баранину**	bah**rah**nyeenoo
lamb	**мясо барашка**	**myah**sah bah**rahsh**kah
a pork chop	**свиную котлету**	svee**noo**yoo kaht**lyeh**too
roast pork	**жареную свинину**	**zhah**ryehnooyoo svee**nyee**noo
hare	**зайца**	**zigh**tsah
chicken	**цыплёнка**	tsip**lyon**kah
roast chicken	**жареного цыплёнка**	**zhah**ryehnahvah tsip**lyon**kah
duck	**утку**	**oot**koo

Vegetables

What vegetables have you got?	**Какие овощи у Вас есть?**	kah**kee**yeh **o**vahshchee oo vahs yehst'
I'd like some...	**Я бы хотел...**	yah bi khah**tyehl**
I'd like some asparagus.	**Я бы хотел спаржу.**	yah bi khah**tyehl** **spahr**zhoo
green beans	**бобы**	**bo**bi
mushrooms	**грибы**	gree**bi**
carrots	**морковь**	mahr**kov'**
onions	**лук**	look
red cabbage	**красную капусту**	**krahs**nooyoo kah**poo**stoo
spinach	**шпинат**	shpee**naht**
rice	**рис**	rees
peas	**горох**	gah**rokh**
tomatoes	**помидоры**	pahmee**do**ri
green salad	**зелёный салат**	zyeh**lyo**niy sah**laht**
potatoes	**картофель**	kahr**to**fyehl'

Desserts

Nothing more, thanks.	**Больше ничего, спасибо.**	**bol'**sheh nyeechyeh**vo** spah**see**bah
Just a small portion, please.	**Маленькую порцию, пожалуйста.**	**mah**lyehn'kooyoo **por**tsiyoo pah**zhah**loostah
Have you any ice-cream?	**У Вас есть мороженое?**	oo vahs yehst' mah**ro**zhehnahyeh
fruit salad	**салат из фруктов**	sah**laht** eez **frook**tahv
fresh fruit	**свежие фрукты**	**svyeh**zhiyeh **frook**ti
cheese	**сыр**	sir

Drink

What would you like to drink?	**Что бы вы хотели выпить?**	shto bi vi khah**tyeh**lee **vi**peet'
I'll have a beer, please.	**Пиво, пожалуйста.**	**pee**vah pah**zhah**loostah
I'll have a whisky, please.	**Виски, пожалуйста.**	**vee**skee pah**zhah**loostah

Wine

I'd like a bottle of wine.	**Я бы хотел бутылку вина.**	yah bi khah**tyehl** boo**til**koo vee**nah**
red wine	**красного вина**	**krahs**nahvah vee**nah**
rosé wine	**розового вина**	**ro**zahvahvah vee**nah**
white wine	**белого вина**	**byeh**lahvah vee**nah**
Cheers!	**На здоровье!**	nah zdah**ro**vyeh

The bill (check)

May I have the bill (check) please?	**Пожалуйста счёт!**	pah**zhah**loostahs-chyot
Is service included?	**Обслуживание включено?**	ahb**sloo**zhivahnyeeyeh vklyoocheh**no**
Everything's included.	**Всё включено.**	vsyo vklyoocheh**no**
Thank you, that was a very good meal.	**Спасибо, всё было очень вкусно.**	spah**see**bah, vsyo **bi**lah **o**chehn' **vkoos**nah

Travelling

Where's the railway station, please?	**Извините, где вокзал?**	eezvee**nee**tyeh gdyeh vahk**zahl**
Where's the ticket office, please?	**Извините, где касса?**	eezvee**nee**tyeh gdyeh **kah**sah
I'd like a ticket to ...	**Мне нужен билет до ...**	mnyeh **noo**zhehn bee**lyeht** dah
First or second class?	**Первый или второй класс?**	**pyehr**viy **ee**lee vtah**roy** klahss
First class, please.	**Первый класс, пожалуйста.**	**pyehr**viy klahss pah**zhah**loostah
Single or return (one way or round-trip)?	**В один или оба конца?**	v ah**dyeen ee**lee **o**bah kahn**tsah**

RUSSIAN

Do I have to change trains?	**Мне надо будет делать пересадку?**	mnyeh **nah**dah **boo**dyeht **dyeh**laht' peeree**sahd**koo
What platform does the train leave from?	**С какой платформы отправляется поезд?**	s kah**koy** plaht**for**mi ahtprahv**lyah**yehtsah **po**yehzd
Where's the nearest underground station?	**Где ближайшая станция метро?**	gdyeh blee**zhigh**shahyah **stahn**tsiyah myeh**tro**
Where's the bus station, please?	**Г де автобусная остановка?**	gdyeh ahv**to**boosnahyah ahstah**nov**kah
When's the first bus to . . . ?	**Когда идёт первый автобус в . . . ?**	kahg**dah** ee**dyot** **pyehr**viy ahv**to**boos v
the last bus	**последний автобус**	pah**slyehd**nyeey ahv**to**boos
the next bus	**следуюший автобус**	**slyeh**doosshcheey ahv**to**boos
Please let me off at the next stop.	**Дайте мне выйти на следуюшей остановке, пожалуйста.**	**digh**tyeh mnyeh **viy**tee nah **slyeh**dooshchay ah-stah**nov**kee pah**zhah**loo-stah

Relaxing

What's on at the cinema (movies)?	**Что идёт в кино?**	shto ee**dyot** v kee**no**
What's on at the theatre?	**Что идёт в театре?**	shto ee**dyot** v tyeh**ah**tryeh
What time does the film begin?	**Когда начинается фильм?**	kahg**dah** nahchee **nah**yehtsah feel'm
And the play?	**А пьеса?**	ah **pyeh**sah
Are there any tickets for tonight?	**Есть билеты на вечер?**	yehst' bee**lyeh**ti nah **vyeh**chehr
Where can we go dancing?	**Куда можно пойти танцевать?**	koo**dah** **mozh**nah pigh**tyee** tahntsi**vaht'**
Would you like to dance?	**Хотите ли вы потанцевать?**	kha**tyee**tyeh lee vi pahtahntsi**vaht'**

Introductions

How do you do?	**Добрый день?**	**dob**riy dyehn'
How are you?	**Как поживаете?**	kahk pahzhi**vah**yehtyeh
Very well, thank you. And you?	**Спасибо, очень хорошо. А Вы?**	spah**see**bah **o**chehn' khahrah**sho**. ah vi
May I introduce Miss Philips?	**Разрешите представить Мисс Филипс.**	rahzree**shi**tyeh pryehd**stah**veet' Miss Philips
My name is . . .	**Меня зовут . . .**	myeh**nyah** zah**voot**
I'm very pleased to meet you.	**Очень приятно.**	**o**chehn' pree**yaht**nah
How long have you been here?	**Вы давно уже здесь?**	vi dahv**no** oo**zheh** zdyehs'
It was nice meeting you.	**Было очень приятно с Вами встретиться.**	**bi**lah **o**chehn' pree**yaht**-nah s **vah**mee **vstryeh**-teetsah

Dating

Would you like a cigarette?	**Хотите сигарету?**	khah**tyee**tyeh seegah**ryeh**too
May I get you a drink?	**Хотите что-нибудь выпить?**	khah**tyee**tyeh **shto**nyeebood' **vi**peet'
Do you have a light, please?	**У Вас есть спички?**	vahs yehst' **speech**kee
Are you free this evening?	**Вы свободны сегодня вечером?**	vi svah**bod**ni see**vod**nyah **vyeh**chehrahm
Where shall we meet?	**Где мы встретимся?**	gdyeh mi **vstryeh**tyeem-syah
What time shall I meet you?	**Когда я Вас встречу?**	kahg**dah** yah vahs **vstryeh**choo
Thank you, it's been a wonderful evening	**Спасибо, это был чудесный вечер.**	spah**see**bah, **eh**tah bil choo**dyehs**niy **vyeh**chehr
What time is your last train?	**Когда уходит Ваш последний поезд?**	kahg**dah** oo**kho**dyeet vahsh pah**slyehd**nyeey **po**yehzd
Good-night . . .	**Доброй ночи . . .**	**do**brigh **no**chee

Banks

Where's the nearest bank, please?	**Где ближайший банк?**	gdyeh blee**zhigh**shiy bahnk
Where can I cash some traveller's cheques?	**Где я могу обменять аккредитивы?**	gdyeh yah mah**goo** ahbmyeh**nyaht**' ahkryehdyee**tyee**vi
What time does the bank open/What time does it close?	**Когда открывается банк/когда он закрывается?**	kahg**dah** ahtkri**vah**yehtsah bahnk/kahg**dah** on zahkri**vah**yehtsah
I'm expecting some money from home. Has it arrived?	**Я жду деньги из дому. Они прибыли?**	yah zhdoo **dyehn**'ghee **eez**dahmoo. ah**nyee** **pree**bilee
Can you give me some small change, please?	**Дайте мне, пожалуйста, мелочью.**	**digh**tyeh mnyeh pah**zhah**loostah **myeh**lahchyo

Shops, stores and services

Where is the nearest chemist (pharmacy)?	**Где ближайшая аптека?**	gdyeh blee**zhigh**shahyah ahp**tyeh**kah
the nearest hairdresser's	**ближайшая парикмахерская**	blee**zhigh**shahyah pahreek**mah**khehrskahyah
the photo shop	**фотомагазин**	fotomahgah**zeen**
the jeweller's	**ювелирный магазин**	yoovee**leer**niy mahgah**zeen**
the department store	**универмаг**	oonyeevyehr**mahg**
the police station	**отделение милиции**	ahtdyeh**lyeh**nyeeyeh meel**ee**tsiee
the garage	**гараж**	gah**rahzh**
How do I get there?	**Как мне туда проехать?**	kahk mnyeh too**dah** prah**yeh**khaht'
Is it within walking distance?	**Можно дойти пешком?**	**mozh**nah digh**tyee** peesh**kom**

Service

Can you help me, please?	**Помогите мне, пожалуйста.**	pahmah**ghee**tyeh mnyeh pah**zhah**loostah
Can you show me this? And that, too.	**Покажите мне, пожалуйста, это. И то тоже.**	pahkah**zhi**tyeh mnyeh pah**zhah**loostah **eh**tah. ee to **to**zheh
It's too expensive/too big/too small.	**Это слишком дорого/слишком велико/слишком мало.**	**eh**tah **sleesh**kahm **do**rahgah/**sleesh**kahm vyehleeko/**sleesh**kahm mah**lo**.

RUSSIAN

Can you show me some more?	**Вы мне можете показать еще?**	vi mnyeh **mo**zhehtyeh pahkah**zaht**' yeh**shchyo**
something better	**Что-нибудь получше**	**shto**nyeebood' pah**looch**sheh
something cheaper	**Что-нибудь подешевле**	**shto**nyeebood' pahdyee**shehv**lee
How much is this? And that?	**Сколько стоит это? И то?**	**skol**'kah **sto**eet **eh**tah? ee to?
It's not quite what I want.	**Это не совсем то, что я хочу**	**eh**tah nyeh sahv**syehm to** shto yah khah**choo**
I like it.	**Это мне нравится.**	**eh**tah mnyeh **nrah**veetsah

Chemist's (Pharmacy)

I'd like something for a cold/for a cough/for travel sickness.	**Я хотел бы что-нибудь от простуды/от кашля/от морской болезни.**	yah khah**tyehl** bi **shto**nyeebood' aht prah**stoo**di/aht **kahsh**lyah/ aht mar**skoy** bal'**yeh**zni
Can you recommend something for hay-fever/for sunburn?	**Что Вы мне можете порекомендовать от сенной лихорадки/ от ожогов?**	shto vi mnyeh **mo**zhehtyeh pahryehkahmy-ehndah**vaht'** aht **syehn**nigh leekhah**rahd**kee/ aht a**zho**gav

Toiletry

May I have some razor blades?	**У Вас есть лезвия для бритья?**	oo vahs yehst' **lyehz**-veeyah dlyah bree**tyah**
some shaving cream	**крем для бритья**	kryehm dlyah bree**tyah**
some toothpaste	**зубная паста**	zoob**nah**yah **pah**stah
I'd like some soap.	**Мне нужно мыло.**	mnyeh **noo**zhnah **mi**lah
some suntan oil	**крем для загара**	kryehm dlyah zah**gah**rah

At the barber's

I'd like a haircut, please.	**Я хотел бы постричься.**	yah khah**tyehl** bi pah**streech**syah
Short/Leave it long.	**Коротко/оставьте длинные.**	**ko**rahtkah/ah**stahv**'tyeh **dleen**niyeh
A razor cut, please.	**Бритвой, пожалуйста.**	**breet**vigh pah**zhah**loostah

RUSSIAN

At the hairdresser's

I'd like a shampoo and set, please.	**Помойте голову и сделайте укладку, пожалуйста.**	pah**moy**tyeh **go**lahvoo ee **sdyeh**lightyeh oo**klahd**koo pah**zhah**loostah
I'd like a bleach.	**Мне нужно обесцвечивание.**	mnyeh **noozh**nah ahbyeh-**stsvyeh**cheevahnyeeyeh.
a permanent	**перманент**	pyehrmah**nyehnt**
a colour rinse	**оттеночное полоскание**	aht**tyeh**nahchnahyeh pahlahs**kah**nyeeyeh
a manicure	**маникюр**	mahnyee**kyoor**

Photography

I'd like a film for this camera.	**Мне нужна плёнка для этого фотоаппарата**	mnyeh noozh**nah** **plyon**kah diyah **eh**tahvah fotahahpah**rah**tah
This camera doesn't work.	**Этот фотоаппарат не работает.**	**eh**taht fotahahpah**raht** nyeh rah**bo**tahyeht

At the post office

Where's the nearest post office, please?	**Где ближайшая почта?**	gdyeh blee**zhigh**shahyah **poch**tah
I'd like to send this by express (special delivery)/by air mail.	**Я хотел бы послать это срочно/авиапочтой.**	yah khah**tyehl** bi pah**slaht' eh**tah **sroch**nah/ahveeah**poch**tigh

Service stations

Where is the nearest service station, please?	**Где ближайшая станция обслуживания?**	gdyeh blee**zhigh**shahyah **stahn**tsiyah ahb**sloo**zhi-vahnyeeyah
Fill her up, please.	**Полный, пожалуйста.**	**pol**niy pah**zhah**loostah
Check the oil, please.	**Проверьте масло, пожалуйста.**	prah**vyehr**'tyeh **mahs**lah pah**zhah**loostah
Would you check the tyres?	**Проверьте шины, пожалуйста.**	prah**vyehr**'tyeh **shi**ni pah**zhah**loostah

Street directions

Can you show me on the map where I am?	**Вы мне можете показать на карте, где я?**	vi mnyeh **mo**zhehtyeh pahkah**zaht'** nah **kahr**tyeh gdyeh yah
You're on the wrong road.	**Вы едете неверно.**	vi **yeh**dyehtyeh nyeh**vyehr**nah
Go back to ...	**Вернитесь назад к ...**	vyehr**nyee**tyehs' nah**zahd** k
Go straight ahead.	**Вам надо прямо.**	vahm **nah**dah **pryah**mah
It's on the left/on the right.	**Это слева/справа.**	**eh**tah **slyeh**vah/**sprah**vah

Accidents

May I use your telephone?	**Можно позвонить по Вашему телефону?**	**mozh**nah pahzvah**nyeet'** pah **vah**shehmoo tyehlyeh**fo**noo
Call a doctor quickly.	**Быстро вызовите доктора.**	**bis**trah **vi**zahveetyeh **dok**tahrah
Call an ambulance.	**Вызовите скорую помощь**	**vi**zahveetyeh **sko**rooyoo **po**mahshch'
Please call the police.	**Вызовите милицию.**	**vi**zhaveetyeh mee**lee**tsiyoo

Numbers

one	**один**	ah**dyeen**
two	**два**	dvah
three	**три**	tree
four	**четыре**	chee**ti**ryeh
five	**пять**	pyaht'
six	**шесть**	shehst'
seven	**семь**	syehm'
eight	**восемь**	**vo**syehm'
nine	**девять**	**dyeh**vyaht'
ten	**десять**	**dyeh**syaht'
eleven	**одиннадцать**	ah**dyee**nahtsaht'
twelve	**двенадцать**	dvee**nah**tsaht'
thirteen	**тринадцать**	tree**naht**tsaht'
fourteen	**четырнадцать**	chyeh**tir**nahtsaht'
fifteen	**пятнадцать**	pyaht**nah**tsaht'
sixteen	**шестнадцать**	shehst'**nah**tsaht'
seventeen	**семнадцать**	syehm**nah**tsaht'
eighteen	**восемнадцать**	vahseem**nah**tsaht'

nineteen	девятнадцать	dyehvyaht**nah**tsaht'
twenty	двадцать	**dvah**tsaht'
twenty-one	двадцать один	**dvah**tsaht' ah**dyeen**
thirty	тридцать	**tree**tsaht'
forty	сорок	**so**rahk
fifty	пятвдесят	peedyee**syaht**
sixty	шестьдесят	shehs'dyeh**syaht**
seventy	семьдесят	**syehm**'dyehsyaht
eighty	восемьдесят	**vo**syehm'dyehsyaht
ninety	девяносто	dyehvyah**no**stah
one hundred	сто	sto
one thousand	тысяча	**ti**syahchah
ten thousand	десять тысяч	**dyeh**syaht' **ti**syahch

Days

It's Sunday.	**Сегодня воскресенье.**	see**vod**nyah vahskryeh**syehn**'yeh
Monday	**понедельник**	pahnyee**dyehl**'nyeek
Tuesday	**вторник**	**vtor**nyeek
Wednesday	**среда**	sryeh**dah**
Thursday	**четверг**	chyeht**vyehrg**
Friday	**пятница**	**pyaht**nyeetsah
Saturday	**суббота**	soo**bo**tah
yesterday	вчера	vchyeh**rah**
today	сегодня	syeh**vod**nyah
tomorrow	завтра	**zahv**trah
morning/afternoon	утро/после обеда	**oo**trah/**po**slyeh ah**byeh**dah
evening/night	вечер/ночь	**vyeh**chyehr/noch'

Months

January	январь	yahn**vahr**'
February	февраль	fyeh**vrahl**'
March	март	mahrt
April	апрель	ah**pryehl**'
May	май	migh
June	июнь	ee**yoon**'
July	июль	ee**yool**'
August	август	**ahv**goost
September	сентябрь	syehn**tyahbr**'
October	октябрь	ahk**tyahbr**'
November	ноябрь	nah**yahbr**'
December	декабрь	dyeh**kahbr**'
Happy New Year!	**с Новым годом!**	s **no**vim **go**dahm

SERBO-CROATIAN

Guide to Pronunciation

Note that Serbo-Croatian has some diacritical letters—with accent marks—which we do not know in English. On the other hand, **q**, **w**, **x** and **y** do not exist in Serbo-Croatian. A basic rule for handling Serbo-Croatian might be: pronounce it as it's written—every letter is pronounced, and its pronunciation is always the same, regardless of its position in a word.

Letter	Approximate pronunciation	Symbol	Example	
Consonants				
b	like **b** in **b**rother	b	**brat**	braht
c	like **ts** in **tse-tse**	ts	**cesta**	**tsehss**tah
č	like **ch** in **ch**urch	ch	**čuti**	**choo**tee
ć	like **ch** in **ch**eap (a little further forward in the mouth than **č**; called a "soft" **č**)	ch	**ćerka**	**chehr**kah
d	like **d** in **d**own	d	**dole**	**do**leh

dž	like **j** in **J**une	j	**džem**	jehm
dj	like **j** in **j**eep (a "soft" **dž**); also written **đ**	j	**djak**	jahk
f	like **f** in **f**ather	f	**figura**	fee**goo**rah
g	like **g** in **g**o	g	**gde**	gdeh
h	like **h** in **h**ouse	h	**hleb**	hlehb
j	like **y** in **y**oke	y	**ja**	yah
k	like **k** in **k**ey	k	**kuća**	**koo**chah
l	like **l** in **l**ip	l	**lep**	lehp
lj	like **l** in fai**lu**re	l^y	**ljubav**	**l^yoo**bahv
m	like **m** in **m**outh	m	**most**	most
n	like **n** in **n**ot	n	**ne**	neh
nj	like **ni** in o**ni**on	ñ	**njegov**	**ñeh**gov
p	like **p** in **p**ut	p	**policija**	po**lee**tseeyah
r	like **r** in **r**ope	r	**reka**	**reh**kah
s	like **s** in **s**ister	s/ss	**sestra**	**sehss**trah
š	like **sh** in **sh**ip	sh	**šta**	shtah
t	like **t** in **t**op	t	**tamo**	**tah**mo
v	like **v** in **v**ery	v	**vrlo**	**ver**lo
z	like **z** in **z**ip	z	**zvezda**	**zvehz**dah
ž	like **s** in plea**s**ure	zh	**želim**	**zheh**leem

Note: The letter **r** can also act as a vowel, as for example, in the word **vrlo** or in the name of the island **Krk**; in this case, it should be pronounced rather like a Scottish **r**, e.g., **Krk** is pronounced kerk.

Vowels

a	like **a** in car	ah	**sat**	saht
e	like **e** in get	eh	**svet**	sveht
i	like **i** in **it**	ee	**iz**	eez
o	like **o** in hot	o	**ovde**	**ov**deh
u	like **oo** in boom	oo	**put**	poot

SERBO-CROATIAN

The alphabet

Two different alphabets are used in Yugoslavia. Our Roman alphabet is in use in Slovenia and Croatia; elsewhere the Cyrillic alphabet (more or less like the Russian one) is dominant. Given below are the characters which the Cyrillic alphabet, as used in Yugoslavia, comprises. The column at left shows the printed capital and small letters while written letters are shown in the center column. At right the corresponding letters are shown in the Roman alphabet which we're using in this book.

А	а	*А*	*а*	**a**
Б	б	*Б*	*б*	**b**
Ц	ц	*Ц*	*ц*	**c**
Ч	ч	*Ч*	*ч*	**č**
Ћ	ћ	*Ћ*	*ћ*	**ć**
Д	д	*Д*	*д*	**d**
Џ	џ	*Џ*	*џ*	**dž** (cap. **Dž**)
Ђ	ђ	*Ђ*	*ђ*	**dj** or **đ** (cap. **Dj** or **Đ**)
Е	е	*Е*	*е*	**e**
Ф	ф	*Ф*	*ф*	**f**
Г	г	*Г*	*г*	**g**
Х	х	*Х*	*х*	**h**
И	и	*И*	*и*	**i**
Ј	ј	*Ј*	*ј*	**j**
К	к	*К*	*к*	**k**
Л	л	*Л*	*л*	**l**
Љ	љ	*Љ*	*љ*	**lj** (cap. **Lj**)
М	м	*М*	*м*	**m**
Н	н	*Н*	*н*	**n**
Њ	њ	*Њ*	*њ*	**nj** (cap. **Nj**)
О	о	*О*	*о*	**o**
П	п	*П*	*п*	**p**
Р	р	*Р*	*р*	**r**
С	с	*С*	*с*	**s**
Ш	ш	*Ш*	*ш*	**š**
Т	т	*Т*	*т*	**t**
У	у	*У*	*у*	**u**
В	в	*В*	*в*	**v**
З	з	*З*	*з*	**z**
Ж	ж	*Ж*	*ж*	**ž**

Some basic expressions

Yes.	**Da.**	dah
No.	**Ne.**	neh
Please.	**Molim.**	**mo**leem
Thank you.	**Hvala.**	**hvah**lah
Thank you very much.	**Hvala Vam mnogo.**	**hvah**lah vahm **mno**go
That's all right.	**Molim.**	**mo**leem

Greetings

Good morning.	**Dobro jutro.**	**do**bro **yoo**tro
Good afternoon.	**Dobar dan.**	**do**bahr dahn
Good evening.	**Dobro veče.**	**do**bro **veh**cheh
Good night.	**Laku noć.**	**lah**koo noch
Good-bye.	**Zbogom.**	**zbo**gom
See you later.	**Dovidjenja.**	dovee**jehn**yah
This is Mr.	**Ovo je Gospodin ...**	ovo yeh go**spo**deen
This is Mrs.	**Ovo je Gospodja ...**	ovo yeh **go**spojah
This is Miss ...	**Ovo je Gospodjica ...**	ovo yeh **go**spojeetsa
I'm very pleased to meet you.	**Milo mi je da sam Vas upoznao.**	**mee**lo mee yeh dah **sahm** vahss **oo**poznaho
How are you?	**Kako ste?**	**kah**ko steh
Very well, thank you.	**Hvala, vrlo dobro.**	**hvah**lah **ver**lo **do**bro
And you?	**A Vi?**	ah vee
Fine.	**Dobro.**	**do**bro
Excuse me.	**Izvinite.**	eez**veeh**neehteh

Questions

Where?	**Gde?**	gdeh
Where is ... ?	**Gde je ... ?**	gdeh yeh
Where are ... ?	**Gde su ... ?**	gdeh soo
When?	**Kad?**	kahd
What?	**Šta?**	shtah

How?	**Kako?**	**kah**ko
How much?	**Koliko?**	ko**lee**ko
How many?	**Koliko?**	ko**lee**ko
Who?	**Ko?..**	ko
Why?	**Zašto?**	**zah**shto
Which?	**Koji/Koja/Koje?**	**ko**yee/**ko**yah/**ko**yeh
What do you call this?	**Kako se ovo zove?**	**kah**ko seh **o**vo **zo**veh
What do you call that?	**Kako se zove ono?**	**kah**ko seh **zo**veh **o**no
What does this mean?	**Šta ovo znači?**	shtah **o**vo **znah**chee
What does that mean?	**Šta ono znači?**	shtah **o**no **znah**chee

Do you speak ... ?

Do you speak English?	**Govorite li engleski?**	**go**voreeteh lee **ehn**glehskee
Do you speak German?	**Govorite li nemački?**	**go**voreeteh lee **ne**hmahchkee
Do you speak French?	**Govorite li francuski?**	**go**voreeteh lee **frahn**-tsooskee
Do you speak Spanish?	**Govorite li španski?**	**go**voreeteh lee **shpahn**skee
Do you speak Italian?	**Govorite li italijanski?**	**go**voreeteh lee eetah**lee**yahnskee
Could you speak more slowly. please?	**Možete li govoriti sporije molim Vas?**	**mo**zhehteh lee go**vor**eetee **spo**reeyeh **mo**leem vahss
Please point to the phrase in the book.	**Pokažite mi molim Vas tu frazu u knjizi.**	po**kah**zheeteh mee **mo**leem vahss too **frah**zoo oo **kñee**zee
Just a minute. I'll see if I can find it in this book.	**Samo trenutak. Vi-deću da li mogu da je nadjem u knjizi.**	**sah**mo treh**noo**tahk. **vee**-dehchoo dah lee **mo**goo dah yeh **nah**jehm oo **kñee**zee
I understand.	**Razumem.**	rah**zoo**mehm
I don't understand.	**Ne razumem.**	neh rah**zoo**mehm

Can . . . ?

Can I have . . . ?	**Mogu li dobiti . . . ?**	**mo**goo lee **do**beetee
Can we have . . . ?	**Možemo li dobiti . . . ?**	**mo**zhehmo lee **do**beetee
Can you show me . . . ?	**Možete li mi pokazati . . . ?**	**mo**zhehteh lee mee po**kah**zahtee
Can you tell me . . . ?	**Možete li mi reći . . . ?**	**mo**zhehteh lee mee **reh**chee
Can you help me, please?	**Možete li mi pomoći molim Vas?**	**mo**zhehteh lee mee **po**mochee **mo**leem vahss

Wanting

I'd like . . .	**Želeo bih . . .**	**zheh**leho beeh
We'd like . . .	**Želeli bismo . . .**	**zheh**lehlee **beess**mo
Please give me . . .	**Molim Vas dajte mi . . .**	**mo**leem vahss **dahy**teh mee
Give it to me, please.	**Dajte mi to molim Vas.**	**dahy**teh mee to **mo**leem vahss
Please bring me . . .	**Molim Vas donesite mi . . .**	**mo**leem vahss do**neh**seeteh mee
Bring it to me, please.	**Donesite mi to molim Vas.**	do**neh**seeteh mee to moleem vahss
I'm hungry.	**Gladan sam.**	**glah**dahn sahm
I'm thirsty.	**Žedan sam.**	**zheh**dahn sahm
I'm tired.	**Umoran sam.**	**oo**morahn sahm
I'm lost.	**Zalutao sam.**	zah**loo**taho sahm
It's important.	**Važno je.**	**vahzh**no yeh
It's urgent.	**Hitno je.**	**heet**no yeh
Hurry up!	**Požurite!**	po**zhoo**reeteh

It is/There is . . .

It is/It's . . .	**To je . . .**	to yeh
Is it . . . ?	**Da li je to . . . ?**	dah lee yeh to
It isn't . . .	**To nije . . .**	to **nee**yeh
There is/There are . . .	**Ima . . .**	**ee**mah
Is there/Are there . . . ?	**Ima li . . . ?**	**ee**mah lee

There isn't/There aren't . . .	**Nema . . .**	**neh**mah
There isn't any/ There aren't any.	**Nema.**	**neh**mah

A few common words

big/small	**veliko/malo**	**veh**leeko/**mah**lo
quick/slow	**brzo/sporo**	**ber**zo/**spo**ro
early/late	**rano/kasno**	**rah**no/**kah**sno
cheap/expensive	**jeftino/skupo**	**yehf**teeno/**skoo**po
near/far	**blizu/daleko**	**blee**zoo/dah**leh**ko
hot/cold	**vruće/hladno**	**vroo**cheh/**hlah**dno
full/empty	**puno/prazno**	**poo**no/**prah**znoh
easy/difficult	**lako/teško**	**lah**ko/**tehsh**ko
heavy/light	**teško/lako**	**tehsh**ko/**lah**ko
open/shut	**otvoreno/zatvoreno**	**ot**vorehno/**zaht**vorehno
right/wrong	**tačno/pogrešno**	**tahch**no/**pog**reshno
old/new	**staro/novo**	**stah**ro/**no**vo
old/young	**star/mlad**	stahr/mlahd
beautiful/ugly	**lepo/ružno**	**leh**po/**roo**zhno
good/bad	**dobro/loše**	**do**bro/**lo**sheh
better/worse	**bolje/lošije**	**bo**l^{y}eh/**lo**sheeyeh

Some prepositions and a few more useful words

at	**kod**	kod
on	**na**	nah
in	**u**	oo
to	**ka**	kah
from	**od**	od
inside	**unutra**	oo**noo**trah
outside	**napolju**	**nah**pol^{y}oo
up	**gore**	**go**reh
down	**dole**	**do**leh
before	**pre**	preh
after	**posle**	**po**sleh
with	**sa**	sah
without	**bez**	behz
through	**kroz**	kroz
towards	**prema**	**preh**mah
until	**do**	do
during	**za vreme**	zah **vreh**meh
and	**i**	ee
or	**ili**	**ee**lee
not	**ne**	neh
nothing	**ništa**	**neesh**tah

none	**ni jedan**	nee **yeh**dahn
very	**vrlo**	**ver**lo
also	**takodje**	**tah**kojeh
soon	**uskoro**	**ooss**koro
perhaps	**možda**	**mo**zhdah
here	**ovde**	**ov**deh
there	**tamo**	**tah**mo
now	**sada**	**sah**dah
then	**tada**	**tah**dah

Arrival

Your passport, please.	**Vaš pasoš, molim Vas.**	vahsh **pah**sosh **mo**leem vahss
Here it is.	**Izvolite.**	eez**vo**leeteh
Have you anything to declare?	**Imate li nešto za carinu?**	ee**mah**teh lee **neh**shto zah **tsah**reenoo
No, nothing at all.	**Ne, nemam ništa.**	neh **neh**mahm **nee**shtah
Porter!	**Nosač!**	**no**sahch
Can you help me with my luggage, please?	**Možete li mi poneti prtljag, molim Vas?**	**mo**zhehteh lee mee **po**nehtee **pert**l^{y}ahg **mo**leem vahss
That's my suitcase.	**To je moj kofer.**	to yeh moy **ko**fehr
Where's the bus to the centre of town, please?	**Gde je autobus zà centar grada, molim Vas?**	gdeh yeh ahoo**to**booss zah **tsehn**tar **grah**dah **mo**leem vahss
This way, please.	**Ovuda, izvolite.**	**o**voodah eez**vo**leeteh

Changing money

Can you change a traveller's cheque, please?	**Možete li promeniti putni ček, molim Vas?**	**mo**zhehteh lee pro**meh**neetee **poot**nee chehk **mo**leem vahss
Where's the nearest bank, please?	**Gde je najbliža banka, molim Vas?**	gdeh yeh **nahy**bleezhah **bahn**kah **mo**leem vahss

Car rental

I'd like a car.	**Želeo bih kola.**	**zheh**leho beeh **ko**lah
For how long?	**Za koliko dugo?**	zah ko**lee**ko **doo**go
A day/Four days/ A week/Two weeks.	**Jedan dan/Četiri dana/Nedelju dana/Dve nedelje.**	**yeh**dahn dahn/**cheh**teeree **dah**nah/**neh**dehl^y oo **dah**nah/dveh **neh**dehl^{y}eh

Taxi

Where can I get a taxi?	**Gde mogu da dobijem taksi?**	gdeh **mo**goo dah **do**beeyehm **tahk**see
What's the fare to . . . ?	**Koliko staje do . . . ?**	ko**lee**ko **stah**yeh do
Take me to this address, please.	**Odvezite me na ovu adresu, molim Vas.**	od**veh**zeeteh meh nah **o**voo ah**dreh**ssoo **mo**leem vahss
I'm in a hurry.	**Žurim se.**	**zhoo**reem seh
Could you drive more slowly, please?	**Da li biste mogli da vozite malo sporije, molim Vas?**	dah lee **bee**steh **mo**glee dah **vo**zeeteh **mah**lo **spo**reeyeh **mo**leem vahss

Hotel and other accommodation

My name is . . .	**Ja se zovem . . .**	yah seh **zo**vehm
Have you a reservation?	**Imate li rezervaciju?**	ee**mah**teh lee rehzehr**vah**tseeyoo
Yes, here's the confirmation.	**Da, izvolite potvrdu.**	dah eez**vo**leeteh **pot**verdoo
I'd like . . .	**Želeo bih . . .**	**zheh**leho beeh
I'd like a single room/a double room.	**Želeo bih sobu sa jednim krevetom/sa dva kreveta.**	**zheh**leho beeh **so**boo sah **yeh**dneem **kreh**vehtom/ sah dvah **kreh**vehtah
a room with a bath/ with a shower	**sobu sa kupatilom/ sa tušem**	**so**boo sah koo**pah**teelom/ sah **too**shehm

How much?

What's the price per night/per week/per month?	**Koliko staje za jednu noć/jednu nedelju/mesec?**	ko**lee**ko **stah**yeh zah **yeh**dnoo noch/**yeh**dnoo **neh**dehl^{y}oo/**meh**ssehts
May I see the room?	**Mogu li da vidim sobu?**	**mo**goo lee dah **vee**deem **so**boo
I'm sorry, I don't like it.	**Nažalost ne dopada mi se.**	**nah**zhahlost neh **do**pahdah mee seh
Yes, that's fine. I'll take it.	**Da, dobra je, uzeću je.**	dah **do**brah yeh **oo**zehchoo yeh
What's my room number, please?	**Koji je broj moje sobe?**	**ko**yee yeh broy **mo**yeh **so**beh
Number 123.	**Broj 123.**	broy 123

Service, please

Who is it?	**Ko je?**	ko yeh
Just a minute.	**Samo jedan trenutak.**	**sah**mo **yeh**dahn treh**noo**tahk
Come in! The door's open.	**Udjite! Vrata su otvorena.**	**oo**jeeteh. **vrah**tah soo **o**tvorehnah
May we have breakfast in our room?	**Možemo li dobiti doručak u sobi?**	mozhehmo lee **do**beetee **do**roochahk oo **so**bee

Breakfast

I'll have ...	**Želeo bih ...**	**zheh**leho beeh
I'll have some fruit juice.	**Želeo bih voćni sok.**	**zheh**leho beeh **voch**nee sok
a boiled egg	**jedno kuvano jaje**	**yeh**dno **koo**vahno **yah**yeh
a fried egg	**jedno prženo jaje**	**yeh**dno **per**zhehno **yah**yeh
some bacon/some ham	**slaninu/šunku**	**slah**neenoo/**shoon**koo
some toast	**tost**	tost
a pot of tea	**lonče čaja**	**lon**cheh **chah**yah
a cup of tea	**šoljicu čaja**	**shol**^{y}eetsoo **chah**yah
some coffee	**hafu**	**kah**foo
some chocolate	**čokoladu**	choko**lah**doo
more butter	**još malo putera**	yosh **mah**lo **poo**tehrah
some hot water	**vruće vode**	**vroo**cheh **vo**deh

Difficulties

The central heating doesn't work.	**Centralno grejanje ne radi.**	**tsen**trahlno **greh**yahñeh neh **rah**dee
the light/the socket	**svetlo/utikač**	**sveh**tlo/oo**tee**kahch
the tap/the toilet	**slavina (pipa)/toalet**	**slah**veenah (**pee**pah)/ toah**leht**
There's no hot water.	**Nema tople vode.**	**neh**mah **to**pleh **vo**deh
May I see the manager, please?	**Želeo bih da govorim sa šefom, molim Vas.**	**zheh**leho beeh dah **go**voreem sah **sheh**fom **mo**leem vahss

Telephone—Mail

There's a call for you.	**Imate telefonski poziv.**	ee**mah**teh teh**leh**fonskee **po**zeev
Hold the line, please.	**Ostanite na telefonu, molim Vas.**	**o**stahneeteh nah tehleh**fo**noo **mo**leem vahss

Operator, I've been cut off.	**Gospodjice, veza se prekinula.**	**goss**pojeetseh **veh**zah seh **preh**keenoolah
Did anyone telephone me?	**Da li me neko tražio telefonom?**	dah lee meh **neh**ko **trah**zheeo tehleh**fo**nom
Is there any mail for me?	**Ima li pošte za mene?**	**ee**mah lee **po**shteh zah **meh**neh
Are there any messages for me?	**Ima li neka poruka za mene?**	**ee**mah lee **neh**kah **po**rookah zah **meh**neh

Checking out

May I have my bill, please?	**Molim Vas račun.**	**mo**leem vahss **rah**choon
We're in a great hurry.	**Jako se žurimo.**	**yah**ko seh **zhoo**reemo
It's been a very enjoyable stay.	**Boravak je bio vrlo prijatan.**	**bo**rahvahk yeh **bee**o **ver**lo **pree**yahtahn

Eating out

Good evening, sir/ Good evening, madam.	**Dobro veče Gospodine/Dobro veče Gospodjo.**	**do**bro **veh**cheh go**spo**deeneh/**do**bro **veh**cheh **go**spojo
Good evening. I'd like a table for two, please.	**Dobro veče. Hteo bih sto za dvoje molim Vas.**	**do**bro **veh**cheh. **hteh**o beeh sto zah **dvo**yeh **mo**leem vahss
Do you have a fixed-price menu?	**Imate li meni?**	ee**mah**teh lee **meh**nee
May I see the à la carte menu?	**Mogu li da dobijem jelovnik?**	**mo**goo lee dah **do**beeyehm yeh**lov**neek
May we have an ashtray, please?	**Molim Vas pepeljaru.**	**mo**leem vahss peh**pehl**^{y}ahroo
some bread	**hleb**	hlehb
a fork	**viljušku**	**veel**^{y}ooshkoo
a knife	**nož**	nozh
a spoon	**kašiku**	**kah**sheekoo
a plate	**tanjir**	**tah**ñeer
a glass	**čašu**	**chah**shoo
a napkin	**salvetu**	sahl**veh**too
another chair	**još jednu stolicu**	yosh **yeh**dnoo **sto**leetsoo
Where's the gentlemen's toilet (men's room)?	**Gde je toalet za muškarce?**	gdeh yeh toah**leht** zah moosh**kahr**tseh
Where's the ladies' toilet (ladies' room)?	**Gde je toalet za žene?**	gdeh yeh toah**leht** zah **zheh**neh

Appetizers

I'd like some ...	**Hteo bih ...**	**hteh**o beeh
I'd like some assorted appetizers.	**Hteo bih mešano predjelo.**	**hteh**o beeh **meh**shahno **prehd**yehlo
orange juice	**sok od pomorandže**	sok od po**mo**rahnjeh
ham	**šunku**	**shoon**koo
melon	**dinju**	**dee**ñoo
pâté	**paštetu**	pah**shteh**too
smoked salmon	**dimljenog lososa**	**deem**l^y^ehnog **lo**ssossah
shrimps (shrimp)	**račiće**	**rah**cheecheh

Soup

Have you any ... ?	**Imate li ... ?**	ee**mah**teh lee
Have you any chicken soup?	**Imate li pileću čorbu?**	ee**mah**teh lee **pee**lehchoo **chor**boo
vegetable soup	**čorbu od povrća**	**chor**boo od **po**verchah
onion soup	**čorbu od luka**	**chor**boo od **loo**kah

Fish

I'd like some ...	**Hteo bih ...**	**hteh**o beeh
I'd like some fish.	**Hteo bih ribu.**	**hteh**o beeh **ree**boo
sole	**tabinju**	**tah**beeñoo
trout	**pastrmku**	**pah**stermkoo
lobster	**jastoga**	**yah**stogah
crayfish	**rak**	rahk
prawns	**kozice**	**ko**zeetseh
I'd like it ...	**Želeo bih ...**	**zheh**leho beeh
I'd like it steamed.	**Spremljenu na pari.**	**sprehm**l^y^ehnoo nah **pah**ree
grilled	**na roštilju**	nah ro**shtee**l^y^oo
boiled	**kuvanu**	**koo**vahnoo
baked	**pečenu**	**peh**chehnoo
fried	**prženu**	**per**zhehnoo

Meat—Poultry—Game

I'd like some ...	**Želeo bih ...**	**zheh**leho beeh
I'd like some beef.	**Želeo bih govedinu.**	**zheh**leho beeh **go**vehdeenoo
a beef steak	**govedju šniclu**	**go**vehjoo **shneets**loo
some roast beef	**govedje pečenje**	**go**vehjeh peh**cheh**ñeh

a veal cutlet	**teleći kotlet**	**teh**lehchee **kot**leht
mutton	**ovčetinu**	**ov**chehteenoo
lamb	**jagnjetinu**	**yahg**ñehteenoo
a pork chop	**svinjski kotlet**	**sveeñ**skee **kot**leht
roast pork	**svinjsko pečenje**	**sveeñ**sko peh**cheh**ñeh
hare	**zečetinu**	**zeh**chehteenoo
chicken	**piletinu**	**pee**lehteenoo
roast chicken	**pečenu piletinu**	**peh**chehnoo **pee**lehteenoo
duck	**patku**	**paht**koo
How do you like your meat?	**Kako pečeno želite meso?**	**kah**ko **peh**chehno **zheh**leeteh **meh**sso
rare	**polu-pečeno**	**po**loo **peh**chehno
medium	**srednje pečeno**	**srehd**ñeh **peh**chehno
well done	**dobro pečeno**	**do**bro **peh**chehno

Vegetables

What vegetables have you got?	**Kakvo povrće imate?**	**kahk**vo **po**vercheh ee**mah**teh
I'd like some...	**Želeo bih...**	**zheh**leho beeh
I'd like some asparagus.	**Želeo bih špargle.**	**zheh**leho beeh **shpahr**gleh
green beans	**boraniju (mahune)**	bo**rah**neeyoo (**mah**hooneh)
mushrooms	**pečurke**	**peh**choorkeh
carrots	**šargarepu**	shahrgah**reh**poo
onions	**luk**	look
red cabbage	**crveni kupus**	**tser**vehnee **koo**pooss
spinach	**spanać (špinat)**	**spah**nahch (**shpee**naht)
rice	**pirinač (rižu)**	**pee**reenahch (**ree**zhoo)
peas	**grašak**	**grah**shahk
tomatoes	**paradajz**	pahrah**dahyz**
green salad	**zelenu salatu**	**zeh**lehnoo sah**lah**too
potatoes	**krompir**	**krom**peer

Desserts

Nothing more, thanks.	**Ništa više, hvala lepo.**	**nee**shtah **vee**sheh **hvah**lah **leh**po
Just a small portion, please.	**Jednu malu porciju, molim.**	**vehd**noo **mah**loo **por**tseeyoo **mo**leem
Have you any ice-cream?	**Imate li sladoleda?**	ee**mah**teh lee **slah**dolehdah
fruit salad	**voćnu salatu**	**voch**noo sah**lah**too
fresh fruit	**sveže voće**	**sveh**zheh **vo**cheh
cheese	**sir**	seer

Drink

What would you like to drink?	**Šta biste želeli da pijete?**	shtah **bee**steh **zheh**lehlee dah **pee**yehteh
I'll have a beer, please.	**Ja bih pivo, molim.**	yah beeh **pee**vo **mo**leem
I'll have a whisky, please.	**Ja bih viski, molim.**	yah beeh **vee**skee **mo**leem

Wine

I'd like a bottle of wine.	**Hteo bih jednu flašu vina.**	**hteh**o beeh **yeh**dnoo **flah**shoo **vee**nah
red wine	**crvenog vina**	**tser**vehnog **vee**nah
rosé wine	**ružice**	**roo**zheetseh
white wine	**belog vina**	**beh**log **vee**nah
Cheers!	**Živeli.**	**zhee**vehlee

The bill (check)

May I have the bill (check) please?	**Molim Vas račun.**	**mo**leem vahss **rah**choon
Is service included?	**Da li je servis uračunat?**	dah lee yeh **sehr**veess **oo**rahchoonaht
Everything's included.	**Sve je uračunato.**	sveh yeh **oo**rahchoonahto
Thank you, that was a very good meal.	**Hvala lepo, jelo je bilo vrlo dobro.**	**hvah**lah **leh**po **yeh**lo yeh **bee**lo **ver**lo **do**bro

Travelling

Where's the railway station, please?	**Gde je železnička stanica (kolodvor), molim Vas?**	gdeh yeh **zheh**lehzneechkah **stah**neetsah (**ko**lodvor) **mo**leem vahss
Where's the ticket office, please?	**Gde je šalter za karte, molim Vas?**	gdeh yeh **shahl**tehr zah **kahr**teh **mo**leem vahss
I'd like a ticket to ...	**Želeo bih kartu do ...**	**zheh**leho beeh **kahr**too do
First or second class?	**Prvu ili drugu klasu?**	**per**voo **ee**lee **droo**goo **klah**ssoo
First class, please.	**Prvu klasu molim.**	**per**voo **klah**ssoo **mo**leem
Single or return (one way or roundtrip)?	**U jednom pravcu ili povratnu?**	oo **yehd**nom **prahv**tsoo **ee**lee **po**vrahtnoo

SERBO-CROATIAN

Do I have to change trains?	**Moram li presedati?**	**mo**rahm lee **preh**-sehdahtee
What platform does the train leave from?	**Sa koga perona polazi voz (vlak)?**	sah **ko**gah pehr**o**nah **po**lahzee voz (vlahk)
Where's the nearest underground (subway) station?	**Gde je najbliža stanica podzemne železnice?**	gdeh yeh **nahy**bleezhah **stah**neetsah **pod**zehmneh **zheh**lehzneetseh
Where's the bus station, please?	**Gde je autobuska stanica, molim Vas?**	gdeh yeh ahoo**to**booskah **stah**neetsah **mo**leem vahss
When's the first bus to ...?	**Kad polazi prvi autobus za ...?**	kahd **po**lahzee **per**vee ahoo**to**booss zah
the last bus	**poslednji autobus**	**po**slehdñee ahoo**to**booss
the next bus	**sledeći autobus**	**sleh**dehchee ahoo**to**booss
Please let me off at the next stop.	**Sišao bih na sledećoj stanici.**	**see**shaho beeh nah **sleh**dehchoy **stah**neetsee

Relaxing

What's on at the cinema (movies)?	**Šta se daje u bioskopu (kinu)?**	shtah seh **dah**yeh oo **bee**oskopoo (**kee**noo)
What's on at the theatre?	**Šta se daje u pozorištu (kazalištu)?**	shtah seh **dah**yeh oo **po**zoreeshtoo (**kah**zahleeshtoo)
What time does the film begin?	**U koliko sati počinje film?**	oo ko**lee**ko **sah**tee **po**cheeñeh feelm
And the play?	**A komad?**	ah **ko**mahd
Are there any tickets for tonight?	**Ima li karata za večeras?**	**ee**mah lee **kah**rahtah zah veh**cheh**rahss
Where can we go dancing?	**Gde možemo da idemo na ples?**	gdeh **mo**zhehmo dah **ee**dehmo nah plehss
Would you like to dance?	**Želite li da igrate (plešete)?**	**zheh**leeteh lee dah **ee**grahteh (**pleh**shehteh)

Introductions

How do you do?	**Dobar dan.**	**do**bahr dahn
How are you?	**Kako ste?**	**kah**ko steh
Very well, thank you. And you?	**Hvala, vrlo dobro. A Vi?**	**hvah**lah **ver**lo **do**bro. ah vee
May I introduce Miss Philips?	**Mogu li da Vam predstavim Gospodjicu Filips.**	**mo**goo lee dah vahm **prehd**stahveem **go**spojeetsoo Philips

My name is ...	**Ja se zovem ...**	yah seh **zo**vehm
I'm very pleased to meet you.	**Drago mi je da sam Vas upoznao.**	**drah**go mee yeh dah sahm vahss **oo**poznaho
How long have you been here?	**Od kad ste ovde?**	od **kah**dah steh **ov**deh
It was nice meeting you.	**Bilo mi je zadovoljstvo.**	**bee**lo mee yeh zahdo**vol**ʸstvo

Dating

Would you like a cigarette?	**Želite li cigaretu?**	**zheh**leeteh lee tseegah**reh**too
May I get you a drink?	**Da li Vam mogu doneti jedno piće?**	dah lee vahm **mo**goo **do**nehtee **yehd**no **pee**cheh
Do you have a light, please?	**Imate li šibicu, molim Vas?**	ee**mah**teh lee **shee**beetsoo **mo**leem vahss
Are you waiting for someone?	**Da li čekate nekoga?**	dah lee **cheh**kahteh **neh**kogah
Are you free this evening?	**Da li ste slobodni večeras?**	dah lee steh **slo**bodnee veh**cheh**rahss
Where shall we meet?	**Gde ćemo se sastati?**	gdeh **cheh**mo seh **sah**stahtee
What time shall I meet you?	**Kad ćemo se videti?**	kahd **cheh**mo seh **vee**dehtee
May I take you home?	**Smem li Vas otpratiti kući?**	smehm lee vahss **ot**prahteetee **koo**chee
Thank you, it's been a wonderful evening.	**Hvala Vam, bilo je divno veče.**	**hvah**lah vahm **bee**lo yeh **deev**no **veh**cheh
What's your telephone number?	**Koji je broj Vašeg telefona?**	**ko**yee yeh broy **vah**shehg tehleh**fo**nah
Do you live alone?	**Da li živite sami?**	dah lee **zhee**veeteh **sah**mee
What time is your last train?	**Kad ide Vaš poslednji voz (vlak)?**	kahd **ee**deh vahsh **po**slehdnee voz (vlahk)
Good-night ...	**Laku noć ...**	**lah**koo noch

Banks

Where's the nearest bank, please?	**Gde je najbliža banka, molim Vas?**	gdeh yeh **nahy**bleezhah **bahn**kah **mo**leem vahss
Where can I cash some traveller's cheques?	**Gde mogu da unovčim putne čekove?**	gdeh **mo**goo dah **oo**novcheem **poot**neh **cheh**koveh

What time does the bank open/What time does it close?	**Kad se banka otvara/Kad se zatvara?**	kahd seh **bahn**kah **o**tvahrah/kahd seh **zah**tvahrah
I'm expecting some money from home. Has it arrived?	**Očekujem novac od kuće. Da li je stigao?**	o**cheh**kooyehm **no**vahtss od **koo**cheh. dah lee yeh **stee**gaho
Can you give me some small change, please?	**Možete li mi dati malo sitnine, molim Vas?**	**mo**zhehteh lee mee **dah**tee **mah**lo seet**nee**neh **mo**leem vahss

Shops, stores and services

Where is the nearest chemist's (pharmacy)?	**Gde je najbliža apoteka?**	gdeh yeh **nahy**bleezhah ahpo**teh**kah
the nearest hair-dresser's	**najbliži frizer**	**nahy**bleezhee **free**zehr
the photo shop	**radnja sa foto materijalom**	**rahd**ñah sah **fo**to mahtehree**yah**lom
the jeweller's	**juvelir**	yoo**veh**leer
the department store	**robna kuća**	**rob**nah **koo**chah
the police station	**policijska stanica**	po**lee**tseeyskah **stah**neetsah
the garage	**garaža**	gah**rah**zhah
How do I get there?	**Kako mogu da dodjem do tamo?**	**kah**ko **mo**goo dah **do**jehm do **tah**mo
Is it within walking distance?	**Da li se tamo može stići pešice?**	dah lee seh **tah**mo **mo**zheh **stee**chee **peh**-sheetseh

Service

Can you help me, please?	**Možete li mi pomoći, molim Vas?**	**mo**zhehteh lee mee **po**mochee **mo**leem vahss
Can you show me this? And that, too.	**Možete li mi pokazati ovo? I ono takodje.**	**mo**zhehteh lee mee po**kah**zahtee **o**vo? ee **o**no tah**ko**jeh
It's too expensive/ too big/too small.	**To je suviše skupo/suviše veliko/suviše malo.**	to yeh **soo**veesheh **skoo**po/**soo**veesheh **veh**-leeko/**soo**veesheh **mah**lo
Can you show me some more?	**Možete li mi pokazati još nekoliko?**	**mo**zhehteh lee mee po**kah**zahtee yosh **neh**koleeko
something better	**nešto bolje**	**neh**shto **bol**^{y}eh
something cheaper	**nešto jevtinije**	**neh**shto **yehv**teeneeyeh

How much is this? And that?	**Koliko staje ovo? A ono?**	ko**lee**ko **stah**yeh **o**vo? ah **o**no
It's not quite what I want.	**To baš nije ono što ja želim.**	to bahsh **nee**yeh **o**no shto yah **zheh**leem
I like it.	**Dopada mi se.**	**do**pahdah mee seh

Chemist's (Pharmacy)

I'd like something for a cold/for a cough/for travel sickness.	**Imate li nešto za nazeb/kašalj/putnu bolest?**	ee**mah**teh lee **neh**shto zah **nah**zehb/**kah**shahl^{y}/**poot**noo **bo**lehst
Can you recommend something for hay-fever/for sunburn?	**Možete li preporučiti nešto za polensku groznicu/za opekotine od sunca?**	**mo**zhehteh lee prehpo**roo**cheetee **neh**shto zah **po**lehnskoo **groz**neetsoo/zah o**peh**koteeneh od **soon**tsah

Toiletry

May I have some razor blades?	**Molim Vas žilete.**	**mo**leem vahss zhee**leh**teh
some shaving cream	**pastu za brijanje**	**pah**stoo zah **bree**yahñeh
some toothpaste	**pastu za zube**	**pah**stoo zah **zoo**beh
I'd like some soap.	**Molim Vas sapun.**	**mo**leem vahss **sa**poon
some suntan oil	**ulje za sunčanje**	**oo**l^{y}eh zah **soon**chahñeh

At the barber's

I'd like a haircut, please.	**Šišanje, molim Vas.**	**shee**shahñeh **mo**leem vahss
Short/Leave it long.	**Kratko/Ostavite malo duže.**	**kraht**ko/**o**stahveeteh **mah**lo **doo**zheh
A razor cut, please.	**Šišanje, molim, brijačem.**	**shee**shahñeh **mo**leem bree**yah**chehm

At the hairdresser's

I'd like a shampoo and set, please.	**Operite mi kosu i počešljajte me, molim Vas.**	o**peh**reeteh mee **ko**soo ee po**cheh**shl^{y}ahyteh meh **mo**leem vahss

I'd like a bleach.	**Molim Vas blajhanje.**	**mo**leem vahss **blahy**hahñeh
a permanent	**trajnu ondulaciju**	**trahy**noo ondoo**lah**tseeyoo
a colour rinse	**preliv**	**preh**leev
a manicure	**manikir**	mah**nee**keer

Photography

I'd like a film for this camera.	**Hteo bih film za ovaj aparat.**	**hteh**o beeh feelm zah **o**vahy ah**pah**raht
This camera doesn't work.	**Ovaj aparat je pokvaren.**	**o**vahy ah**pah**raht yeh **po**kvahrehn

At the post office

Where's the nearest post office, please?	**Gde je najbliža pošta, molim Vas?**	gdeh yeh **nahy**bleezhah **po**shtah **mo**leem vahss
I'd like to send this by express (special delivery)/by air mail.	**Želeo bih da pošaljem ovo ekspres/avionom.**	**zheh**leho beeh dah **po**shahl^{y}ehm **o**vo ehks**prehss**/ahvee**o**nom

Service stations

Where is the nearest service station, please?	**Gde je najbliža servisna stanica?**	gdeh yeh **nahy**bleezhah **sehr**veessnah **stah**neetsah
Fill her up, please.	**Napunite rezervoar, molim Vas.**	**nah**pooneeteh rehzehr**vo**ahr **mo**leem vahss
Check the oil, please.	**Proverite ulje, molim Vas.**	**pro**vehreeteh **ool**^{y}eh **mo**leem vahss
Would you check the tyres?	**Da li biste hteli da proverite gume?**	dah lee **bee**steh **hteh**lee dah **pro**vehreeteh **goo**meh

Street directions

Can you show me on the map where I am?	**Možete li mi pokazati na karti gde se nalazim?**	**mo**zhehteh lee mee po**kah**zahtee nah **kahr**tee gdeh seh **nah**lahzeem
You're on the wrong road.	**Vi ste na pogrešnom putu.**	vee steh nah **po**grehshnom **poo**too
Go back to ...	**Vratite se do ...**	**vrah**teeteh seh do
Go straight ahead.	**Idite pravo napred.**	**ee**deeteh **prah**voo **nah**prehd
It's on the left/on the right.	**Na levoj je strani/na desnoj.**	nah **leh**voy yeh **strah**nee/nah **deh**snoy

Accidents

May I use your telephone?	**Mogu li se poslužiti Vašim telefonom?**	**mo**goo lee seh po**sloo**zheetee **vah**sheem tehleh**fo**nom
Call a doctor quickly.	**Pozovite brzo doktora.**	po**zo**veeteh **ber**zo **dok**torah
Call an ambulance.	**Pozovite kola za hitnu pomoć.**	po**zo**veeteh **ko**lah zah **heet**noo **po**moch
Please call the police.	**Pozovite, molim Vas, policiju.**	po**zo**veeteh **mo**leem vahss po**lee**tseeyoo

Numbers

zero	**nula**	**noo**lah
one	**jedan**	**yeh**dahn
two	**dva**	dvah
three	**tri**	tree
four	**četiri**	**cheh**teeree
five	**pet**	peht
six	**šest**	shehst
seven	**sedam**	**seh**dahm
eight	**osam**	**o**ssahm
nine	**devet**	**deh**veht
ten	**deset**	**deh**seht
eleven	**jedanaest**	yeh**dah**nahehst
twelve	**dvanaest**	**dvah**nahehst
thirteen	**trinaest**	**tree**nahehst
fourteen	**četrnaest**	cheh**ter**nahehst
fifteen	**petnaest**	**peht**nahehst
sixteen	**šesnaest**	**shehss**nahehst
seventeen	**sedamnaest**	seh**dahm**nahehst
eighteen	**osamnaest**	o**sahm**nahehst
nineteen	**devetnaest**	deh**veht**nahehst
twenty	**dvadeset**	**dvah**dehseht
twenty-one	**dvadeset jedan**	**dvah**dehseht **yeh**dahn
thirty	**trideset**	**tree**dehseht
forty	**četrdeset**	chehter**deh**seht
fifty	**pedeset**	peh**deh**seht
sixty	**šezdeset**	shehz**deh**seht
seventy	**sedamdeset**	sehdahm**deh**seht
eighty	**osamdeset**	osahm**deh**seht
ninety	**devedeset**	dehveh**deh**seht
one hundred	**sto**	sto
one thousand	**hiljadu**	**heel**^{y}ahdoo
ten thousand	**deset hiljada**	**deh**seht **heel**^{y}ahdah

Days

It's Sunday.	**Nedelja je.**	**neh**dehl^{y}ah yeh
Monday	**ponedeljak**	po**neh**dehl^{y}ahk
Tuesday	**utorak**	**oo**torahk
Wednesday	**sreda**	**sreh**dah
Thursday	**četvrtak**	cheht**ver**tahk
Friday	**petak**	**peh**tahk
Saturday	**subota**	**soo**botah
yesterday	**juče**	**yoo**cheh
today	**danas**	**dah**nahss
tomorrow	**sutra**	**soo**trah
morning/afternoon	**jutro/posle podne**	**yoo**tro/**po**sleh **po**dneh
evening/night	**veče/noć**	**veh**cheh/noch

Months

January	**januar**	**yah**nooahr
February	**februar**	**feh**brooahr
March	**mart**	mahrt
April	**april**	**ah**preel
May	**maj**	mahy
June	**jun**	yoon
July	**juli**	**yoo**lee
August	**avgust**	**ahv**goost
September	**septembar**	sehp**tehm**bahr
October	**oktobar**	ok**to**bahr
November	**novembar**	no**vehm**bahr
December	**decembar**	deh**tsehm**bahr
Merry Christmas!	**Srećan Božić!**	**sreh**chahn **bo**zheech!
Happy New Year!	**Srećna Nova godina!**	**sreh**chnah **no**vah **go**deenah

SPANISH

Guide to Pronunciation

Letter	Approximate pronunciation	Symbol	Example	
Consonants				
f, k, l, m, n, p, t, x, y	as in English			
b	1) generally as in English	b	**bueno**	**bway**noa
	2) between vowels, a sound between **b** and **v**	bh	**bebida**	bay**bhee**dhah
c	1) before **e** and **i** like **th** in **th**in	th	**centro**	**thayn**troa
	2) otherwise, like **k** in **k**it	k	**como**	**koa**moa
ch	as in English	ch	**mucho**	**moo**choa
d	1) generally as in **d**og, although less decisive	d	**donde**	**don**day
	2) between vowels and at the end of a word, like **th** in **th**is	dh	**edad**	ay**dhahdh**

g	1) before **e** and **i**, like **ch** in Scottish lo**ch**	kh	**urgente**	oor**khayn**tay
	2) between vowels and sometimes inside a word, a weak, voiced version of the **ch** in lo**ch**	g̊	**agua**	**ah**g̊wah
	3) otherwise, like **g** in **g**o	g	**ninguno**	neeng**goo**noa
h	always silent		**hombre**	**om**bray
j	like **ch** in Scottish lo**ch**	kh	**bajo**	**bah**khoa
ll	like **lli** in mi**lli**on	ly	**lleno**	**lyay**noa
ñ	like **ni** in o**ni**on	ñ	**señor**	say**ñor**
qu	like **k** in **k**it	k	**quince**	**keen**thay
r	more strongly trilled (like a Scottish **r**), especially at the beginning of a word	r	**río**	**ree**oa
rr	strongly trilled	rr	**arriba**	ahr**ree**bhah
s	always like the **s** in **s**it, often with a slight lisp	s/ss	**vista** **cuantos**	**bee**stah **kwahn**toass
v	1) tends to be like **b** in **b**ad, but less tense	b	**viejo**	**byay**khoa
	2) between vowels, more like English **v**	bh	**rival**	ree**bhahl**
z	like **th** in **th**in	th	**brazo**	**brah**thoa

SPANISH

Vowels

a	like **a** in c**a**r, but fairly short	ah	**gracias**	**grah**thyahss
e	1) sometimes like **a** in l**a**te	ay	**de**	day
	2) less often, like **e** in g**e**t	eh	**llover**	lyoa**bhehr**
i	like **ee** in f**ee**t	ee	**si**	see
o	1) sometimes fairly like **o** in rope	oa	**sopa**	**soa**pah
	2) sometimes like **o** in g**o**t	o	**dos**	doss
u	like **oo** in l**oo**t	oo	**una**	**oo**nah
y	only a vowel when alone or at the end of a word; like **ee** in f**ee**t	ee	**y**	ee

N.B. 1) In forming diphthongs, **a**, **e**, and **o** are strong vowels, and **i** and **u** are weak vowels. This means that in diphthongs the strong vowels are pronounced more strongly than the weak ones. If two weak vowels form a diphthong, the second one is pronounced more strongly.
2) The acute accent (´) is used to indicate a syllable that is stressed, e.g., *río* = **ree**oa.
3) In words ending with a consonant, the last syllable is stressed, e.g., *señor* = say**nor**.
4) In words ending with a vowel, the next to the last syllable is stressed, e.g., *mañana* = mah**ñah**nah.

Some basic expressions

Yes.	**Sí.**	see
No.	**No.**	noa
Please.	**Por favor.**	por fah**bhor**
Thank you.	**Gracias.**	**grah**thyahss
Thank you very much.	**Muchas gracias.**	**moo**chahss **grah**thyahss
That's all right.	**No hay de qué.**	noa igh day kay

Greetings

Good morning.	**Buenos días.**	**bway**noass **dee**ahss
Good afternoon.	**Buenas tardes.**	**bway**nahss **tahr**dhayss
Good evening.	**Buenas tardes.**	**bway**nahss **tahr**dhayss
Good night.	**Buenas noches.**	**bway**nahss **noa**chayss
Good-bye.	**Adiós.**	ah**dhyoss**
See you later.	**Hasta luego.**	**ahss**tah **lway**goa
This is Mr....	**Este es el Señor...**	**ayss**tay ayss ehl say**ñor**
This is Mrs....	**Esta es la Señora...**	**ayss**tah ayss lah say**ñoa**rah
This is Miss...	**Esta es la Señorita...**	**ayss**tah ayss lah sayñoa**ree**tah
I'm very pleased to meet you.	**Encantado de conocerle.**	ayngkahn**tah**dhoa day koanoa**thayr**lay
How are you?	**¿Cómo está usted?**	**koa**moa ayss**tah** ooss**taydh**
Very well, thank you. And you?	**Muy bien, gracias. ¿Y usted?**	mwee byayn **grah**thyahss. ee ooss**taydh**
Fine. Thank you.	**Bien. Gracias.**	byayn **grah**thyahss
Excuse me.	**Dispénseme.**	deess**payn**saymay

Questions

Where?	**¿Dónde?**	**don**day
Where is...?	**¿Dónde está...?**	**don**day ayss**tah**
Where are...?	**¿Dónde están...?**	**don**day ayss**tahn**
When?	**¿Cuándo?**	**kwahn**doa

What?	**¿Qué?**	kay
How?	**¿Cómo?**	**koa**moa
How much?	**¿Cuánto?**	**kwahn**toa
How many?	**¿Cuántos?**	**kwahn**toass
Who?	**¿Quién?**	kyayn
Why?	**¿Por qué?**	por kay
Which?	**¿Cuál?**	kwahl
What do you call this?	**¿Cómo se llama esto?**	**koa**moa say **lyah**mah **ayss**toa
What do you call that?	**¿Cómo se llama eso?**	**koa**moa say **lyah**mah **ay**soa
What does this mean?	**¿Qué quiere decir esto?**	kay **kyay**ray day**theer** **ayss**toa
What does that mean?	**¿Qué quiere decir eso?**	kay **kyay**ray day**theer** **ay**soa

Do you speak . . . ?

Do you speak English?	**¿Habla usted inglés?**	**ah**bhlah ooss**taydh** eeng**glayss**
Do you speak German?	**¿Habla usted alemán?**	**ah**bhlah ooss**taydh** ahlay**mahn**
Do you speak French?	**¿Habla usted francés?**	**ah**bhlah ooss**taydh** frahn**thayss**
Do you speak Spanish?	**¿Habla usted español?**	**ah**bhlah ooss**taydh** aysspah**ñol**
Do you speak Italian?	**¿Habla usted italiano?**	**ah**bhlah ooss**taydh** eetah**lyah**noa
Could you speak more slowly, please?	**¿Puede usted hablar más despacio, por favor?**	**pway**dhay ooss**taydh** ah**bhlahr** mahss day**spah**thyoa por fah**bhor**
Please point to the phrase in the book.	**Por favor, señale la frase en el libro.**	por fah**bhor** say**ñah**lay lah **frah**say ayn ehl **lee**bhroa
Just a minute. I'll see if I can find it in this book.	**Un momento. Veré si lo puedo encontrar en este libro.**	oon moa**mayn**toa. bay**ray** see loa **pway**dhoa ayngkon**trahr** ayn **ayss**tay **lee**broa
I understand.	**Comprendo.**	kom**prayn**doa
I don't understand.	**No comprendo.**	noa kom**prayn**doa

Can . . . ?

Can I have . . . ?	**¿Puede darme . . . ?**	**pway**dhay **dahr**may
Can we have . . . ?	**¿Puede darnos . . . ?**	**pway**dhay **dahr**noss
Can you show me . . . ?	**¿Puede usted enseñarme . . . ?**	**pway**dhay oos**taydh** aynsay**ñahr**may
Can you tell me . . . ?	**¿Puede usted decirme . . . ?**	**pway**dhay oos**taydh** day**theer**may
Can you help me, please?	**¿Puede usted ayudarme, por favor?**	**pway**dhay oos**taydh** ahyoo**dhahr**may por fah**bhor**

Wanting

I'd like . . .	**Quisiera . . .**	kee**syay**rah
We'd like . . .	**Quisiéramos . . .**	kee**syay**rahmoss
Please give me . . .	**Por favor, déme . . .**	por fah**bhor day**may
Give it to me, please.	**Démelo, por favor.**	**day**mayloa por fah**bhor**
Please bring me . . .	**Por favor, tráigame . . .**	por fah**bhor trigh**gahmay
Bring it to me, please.	**Tráigamelo, por favor.**	**trigh**gahmayloa por fah**bhor**
I'm hungry.	**Tengo hambre.**	**tayng**goa **ahm**bray
I'm thirsty.	**Tengo sed.**	**tayng**goa saydh
I'm tired.	**Estoy cansado.**	ayss**toy** kahn**sah**dhoa
I'm lost.	**Me he perdido.**	may ay pehr**dhee**dhoa
It's important.	**Es importante.**	ayss eempoar**tahn**tay
It's urgent.	**Es urgente.**	ayss oor**khayn**tay
Hurry up!	**¡Dése prisa!**	**day**say **pree**sah

It is/There is . . .

It is/It's . . .	**Es . . .**	ayss
Is it . . . ?	**¿Es . . . ?**	ayss
It isn't . . .	**No es . . .**	noa ayss
There is/There are . . .	**Hay . . .**	igh
Is there/Are there . . . ?	**¿Hay . . . ?**	igh

There isn't/There aren't . . .	**No hay . . .**	noa igh
There isn't any/ There aren't any.	**No hay ninguno/No hay ningunos (No hay ninguna/No hay ningunas).**	noa igh neeng**goo**noa/noa igh neeng**goo**noss (noa igh neeng**goo**nah/noa igh neeng**goo**nahss)

A few common words

big/small	**grande/pequeño**	**grahn**day/pay**kay**ñoa
quick/slow	**rápido/lento**	**rah**peedhoa/**layn**toa
early/late	**temprano/tarde**	taym**prah**noa/**tahr**dhay
cheap/expensive	**barato/caro**	bah**rah**toa/**kah**roa
near/far	**cerca/lejos**	**thehr**kah/**lay**khoass
hot/cold	**caliente/frío**	kah**lyayn**tay/**free**oa
full/empty	**lleno/vacío**	**lyay**noa/bah**thee**oa
easy/difficult	**fácil/difícil**	**fah**theel/dee**fee**theel
heavy/light	**pesado/ligero**	pay**sah**dhoa/lee**khay**roa
open/shut	**abierto/cerrado**	ah**bhyehr**toa/thayr**rah**dhoa
right/wrong	**correcto/incorrecto**	kor**rehk**toa/eengkor**rehk**toa
old/new	**viejo/nuevo**	**byay**khoa/**nway**bhoa
old/young	**anciano/joven**	ann**thya**noa/**khoa**bhayn
beautiful/ugly	**bonito/feo**	boa**nee**toa/**fay**oa
good/bad	**bueno/malo**	**bway**noa/**mah**loa
better/worse	**mejor/peor**	meh**khor**/pay**or**

Some prepositions and a few more useful words

at	**a**	ah
on	**sobre**	**soa**bhray
in	**en**	ayn
to	**para**	**pah**rah
from	**desde**	**dayz**day
inside	**dentro**	**dayn**troa
outside	**fuera**	**fway**rah
up	**arríba**	ahr**ree**bhah
down	**abajo**	ah**bhah**khoa
before	**antes**	**ahn**tayss
after	**después**	dayss**pwayss**
with	**con**	kon
without	**sin**	seen
through	**a través**	ah trah**bhayss**
towards	**hacia**	**ah**thyah
until	**hasta**	**ahss**tah
during	**durante**	doo**rahn**tay
and	**y**	ee
or	**o**	oa

not	**no**	noa
nothing	**nada**	**nah**dhah
none	**ninguno**	neeng**goo**noa
very	**muy**	mwee
also	**también**	tahm**bhyayn**
soon	**pronto**	**pron**toa
perhaps	**tal vez**	tal bayth
here	**aquí**	ah**kee**
there	**allí**	ah**lyee**
now	**ahora**	ah**o**rah
then	**entonces**	ayn**ton**thayss

Arrival

Your passport, please.	**Su pasaporte, por favor.**	soo pahsah**por**tay por fah**bhor**
Here it is.	**Aquí está.**	ah**kee** ayss**tah**
Have you anything to declare?	**¿Tiene usted algo que declarar?**	**tyay**nay ooss**taydh ahl**goa kay dayklah**rahr**
No, nothing at all.	**No, nada en absoluto.**	noa **nah**dhah ayn ahbsoa**loo**toa
Porter!	**¡Mozo!**	**moa**thoa
Can you help me with my luggage, please?	**¿Puede usted ayudarme con mi equipaje, por favor?**	**pway**dhay ooss**taydh** ahyoo**dhahr**may kon mee aykee**pah**khay por fah**bhor**
That's my suitcase.	**Esa es mi maleta.**	**ay**sah ayss mee mah**lay**tah
Where's the bus to the centre of town, please?	**¿Dónde está el autobús que va al centro, por favor?**	**don**day ayss**tah** ehl owtoa**booss** kay bah ahl **thayn**troa por fah**bhor**
This way, please.	**Por aquí, por favor.**	por ah**kee** por fah**bhor**

Changing money

Can you change a traveller's cheque, please?	**¿Puede usted cambiarme un traveller's cheque, por favor?**	**pway**dhay ooss**taydh** kahm**byahr**may oon "traveller's cheque" por fah**bhor**
Where's the nearest bank, please?	**¿Dónde está el banco más cercano, por favor?**	**don**day ayss**tah** ehl **bahng**koa mahss thehr**kah**noa por fah**bhor**

SPANISH

Car rental

I'd like a car.	**Quisiera un coche.**	kee**syay**rah oon **koa**chay
For how long?	**¿Para cuánto tiempo?**	**pah**rah **kwahn**toa **tyaym**poa
A day/Four days/ A week/Two weeks.	**Un día/Cuatro días/Una semana/ Dos semanas.**	oon **dee**ah/**kwah**troa **dee**ahss/**oo**nah say**mah**nah/doss say**mah**nahss

Taxi

Where can I get a taxi?	**¿Dónde puedo coger (conseguir) un taxi?**	**don**day **pway**dhoa ko**khehr** (koansay**geer**) oon **tahk**see
What's the fare to . . . ?	**¿Cuál es la tarifa a . . .?**	kwahl ayss lah tah**ree**fah ah
Take me to this address, please.	**Lléveme a esta dirección, por favor.**	**lyay**bhaymay ah **ayss**tah deerehğ**thyon** por fah**bhor**
I'm in a hurry.	**Tengo mucha prisa.**	**tayng**goa **moo**chah **pree**sah
Could you drive more slowly, please?	**¿Puede usted ir más despacio, por favor?**	**pway**dhay ooss**taydh** eer mahss dayss**pah**thyoa por fah**bhor**

Hotel and other accommodation

My name is . . .	**Me llamo . . .**	may **lyah**moa
Have you a reservation?	**¿Ha hecho usted una reserva?**	ah **ay**choa ooss**taydh** **oo**nah rreh**sehr**bhah
Yes, here's the confirmation.	**Sí, aquí está la confirmación.**	see ah**kee** ayss**tah** lah konfeermah**thyon**
I'd like . . .	**Quisiera . . .**	kee**syay**rah
I'd like a single room/a double room.	**Quisiera una habitación sencilla/una habitación doble.**	kee**syay**rah **oo**nah ahbheetah**thyon** sayn**thee**lyah/**oo**nah ahbheetah**thyon** **doa**bhlay
a room with a bath/ with a shower	**una habitación con baño/con ducha**	**oo**nah ahbheetah**thyon** kon **bah**ñoa/kon **doo**chah

How much?

What's the price per night/per week/per month?	**¿Cuánto cuesta por noche/por semana/ por mes?**	**kwahn**toa **kwayss**tah por **noa**chay/por say**mah**nah/ por mayss

May I see the room?	**¿Puedo ver la habitación?**	**pway**dhoa bayr lah ahbheetah**thyon**
I'm sorry, I don't like it.	**Lo siento, no me gusta.**	loa **syayn**toa noa may **gooss**tah
Yes, that's fine. I'll take it.	**Muy bien, la tomaré.**	mwee byayn lah toamah**ray**
What's my room number, please?	**¿Cuál es el número de mi habitación, por favor?**	kwahl ayss ehl **noo**mayroa day mee ahbheetah**thyon** por fah**bhor**
Number 123.	**Número 123.**	**noo**mayroa 123.

Service, please

Who is it?	**¿Quién es?**	kyayn ayss
Just a minute.	**Un momento, por favor.**	oon moa**mayn**toa por fah**bhor**
Come in! The door's open.	**¡Adelante! la puerta está abierta.**	ahdhay**lahn**tay! lah **pwehr**tah ayss**tah** ah**bhyehr**tah
May we have breakfast in our room?	**¿Podemos desayunar en nuestra habitación?**	poa**dhay**moass daysahyoo**nahr** ayn **nwayss**trah ahbheetah**thyon**

Breakfast

I'll have ...	**Quisiera ...**	kee**syay**rah
I'll have some fruit juice.	**Quisiera un zumo de fruta.**	kee**syay**rah oon **thoo**moa day **froo**tah
a boiled egg	**un huevo cocido**	oon **way**bhoa koa**thee**dhoa
a fried egg	**un huevo frito**	oon **way**bhoa **free**toa
some bacon/some ham	**un poco de tocino/un poco de jamón**	oon **poa**koa day toa**thee**noa/oon **poa**koa day khah**mon**
some toast	**un poco de pan tostado**	oon **poa**koa day pahn toass**tah**dhoa
a pot of tea	**una tetera de té**	**oo**nah tay**tay**rah day tay
a cup of tea	**una taza de té**	**oo**nah **tah**thah day tay
some coffee	**un poco de café**	oon **poa**koa day kah**fay**
some chocolate	**un poco de chocolate**	oon **poa**koa day choakoa**lah**tay
more butter	**más mantequilla**	mahss mahntay**kee**lyah
some hot water	**un poco de agua caliente**	oon **poa**koa day **ah**g̊wah kah**lyayn**tay

Difficulties

The central heating doesn't work.	**La calefacción central no funciona.**	lah kahlayfahk**thyon** thayn**trahl** noa foon**thyoa**nah
the light/the socket	**la luz/el enchufe**	lah looth/ehl ayn**choo**fay
the tap/the toilet	**el grifo/el water**	ehl **gree**foa/ehl **vah**tehr
There's no hot water.	**No hay agua caliente.**	noa igh **ah**g̊wah kah**lyayn**tay
May I see the manager, please?	**¿Puedo ver al director, por favor?**	**pway**dhoa behr ahl deerehk**tor** por fah**bhor**

Telephone—Mail

There's a call for you.	**Hay una llamada para usted.**	igh **oo**nah lyah**mah**dhah **pah**rah oos**taydh**
Hold the line, please.	**Espere un momento, por favor.**	ayss**pay**ray oon moa**mayn**toa por fah**bhor**
Operator, I've been cut off.	**Telefonista, me han cortado.**	taylayfoa**neess**tah may ahn kor**tah**dhoa
Did anyone telephone me?	**¿Me ha llamado alguien?**	may ah lyah**mah**dhoa ahl**gyayn**
Is there any mail for me?	**¿Hay correo para mí?**	igh kor**ray**oa **pah**rah mee
Are there any messages for me?	**¿Hay algún recado para mí?**	igh ahl**goon** ray**kah**dhoa **pah**rah mee

Checking out

May I have my bill, please?	**¿Puede darme mi cuenta, por favor?**	**pway**dhay **dahr**may mee **kwayn**tah por fah**bhor**
We're in a great hurry.	**Tenemos mucha prisa.**	tay**nay**moss **moo**chah **pree**sah
It's been a very enjoyable stay.	**Ha sido una estancia muy agradable.**	ah **see**dhoa **oo**nah ayss**tahn**thyah mwee ahgrah**dhah**bhlay

Eating out

Good evening, sir/Good evening, madam.	**Buenas noches, señor/Buenas noches, señora.**	**bway**nahss **noa**chayss say**ñor** **bway**nahss **noa**chayss say**ñoa**rah
Good evening. I'd like a table for two, please.	**Buenas noches. Quisiera una mesa para dos, por favor.**	**bway**nahss **noa**chayss. kee**syay**rah **oo**nah **may**sah **pah**rah doss por fah**bhor**

Do you have a fixed-price menu?	**¿Tiene usted un menú de precio fijo?**	**tyay**nay oss**taydh** oon may**noo** day **pray**thyoa **fee**khoa
May I see the à la carte menu?	**¿Puedo ver la carta?**	**pway**dhoa behr lah **kahr**-tah
May we have an ashtray, please?	**¿Nos puede traer un cenicero, por favor?**	noss **pway**dhay trah**ehr** oon thaynee**thay**roa por fah**bhor**
some bread	**un poco de pan**	oon **poa**koa day pan
a fork	**un tenedor**	oon taynay**dhor**
a knife	**un cuchillo**	oon koo**chee**lyoa
a spoon	**una cuchara**	**oo**nah koo**chah**rah
a plate	**un plato**	oon **plah**toa
a glass	**un vaso**	oon **bah**soa
a napkin	**una servilleta**	**oo**nah sehrbhee**lyay**tah
another chair	**otra silla**	**oa**tra **see**lyah
Where's the gentlemen's toilet (men's room)?	**¿Dónde está el lavabo de caballeros?**	**don**day ayss**tah** ehl lah-**bhah**bhoa day kahbhah**lyay**ross
Where's the ladies' toilet (ladies' room)?	**¿Dónde está el lavabo de señoras?**	**don**day ayss**tah** ehl lah-**bhah**bhoa day say**ñoa**rahss

Appetizers

I'd like some ...	**Quisiera ...**	kee**syay**rah
I'd like some assorted appetizers.	**Quisiera unos entremeses variados.**	kee**syay**rah **oo**noss ayn-tray**may**sayss bahree**ah**-dhoss
orange juice	**un jugo de naranja**	oon **khoo**ǧoa day nah**rahn**khah
ham	**jamón**	khah**mon**
melon	**melón**	may**lon**
pâté	**pastel de carne**	pahss**tehl** day **kahr**nay
smoked salmon	**salmón ahumado**	sahl**mon** ahoo**mah**dhoa
shrimps (shrimp)	**quisquillas**	keess**kee**lyahss

Soup

Have you any ... ?	**¿Tiene usted ... ?**	**tyay**nay oss**taydh**
Have you any chicken soup?	**¿Tiene usted sopa de pollo?**	**tyay**nay oss**taydh** **soa**pah day **poa**lyoa
vegetable soup	**sopa de verduras**	**soa**pah day behr**dhoo**-rahss
onion soup	**sopa de cebollas**	**soa**pah day thay**bhoa**-lyahss

Fish

I'd like some . . .	**Quisiera . . .**	kee**syay**rah
I'd like some fish.	**Quisiera pescado.**	kee**syay**rah payss**kah**dhoa
sole	**lenguado**	layng**gwah**dhoa
trout	**trucha**	**troo**chah
lobster	**langosta**	lang**goss**tah
crayfish	**cangrejos**	kahng**gray**khoss
prawns	**gambas**	**gahm**bahss
I'd like it . . .	**Me gustaría . . .**	may goosstah**ree**ah
I'd like it steamed.	**Me gustaría al vapor.**	may goosstah**ree**ah ahl bah**por**
grilled	**a la parrilla**	ah lah pah**ree**lyah
boiled	**cocido**	koa**thee**dhoa
baked	**asado**	ah**sah**dhoa
fried	**frito**	**free**toa

Meat—Poultry—Game

I'd like some . . .	**Quisiera . . .**	kee**syay**rah
I'd like some beef.	**Quisiera carne de vaca.**	kee**syay**rah **kahr**nay day **bah**kah
a beef steak	**un bistec**	oon beess**tehk**
some roast beef	**rosbif**	rroz**bheef**
a veal cutlet	**una chuleta de ternera**	**oo**nah choo**lay**tah day tehr**nay**rah
mutton	**carnero**	kahr**nay**roa
lamb	**cordero**	kor**dhay**roa
a pork chop	**una chuleta de cerdo**	**oo**nah choo**lay**tah day **thehr**dhoa
roast pork	**cerdo asado**	**thehr**dhoa ah**sah**dhoa
hare	**liebre**	**lyay**bhray
chicken	**pollo**	**poa**lyoa
roast chicken	**pollo asado**	**poa**lyoa ah**sah**dhoa
duck	**pato**	**pah**toa
How do you like your meat?	**¿Cómo le gusta la carne?**	**koa**moa lay **goos**stah lah **kahr**nay
rare	**poco asada**	**poa**koa ah**sah**dhah
medium	**medio asada**	**may**dhyoa ah**sah**dhah
well done	**bien hecha**	byayn **ay**chah

Vegetables

What vegetables have you got?	**¿Qué verduras tiene usted?**	kay behr**dhoo**rahss **tyay**nah ooss**taydh**
I'd like some . . .	**Quisiera . . .**	kee**syay**rah

I'd like some asparagus.	**Quisiera unos espárragos.**	kee**syay**rah **oo**noss ayss-**pahr**rahg̊oss
green beans	**unas judías verdes**	**oo**nahss **khoo**dhyahss **behr**dhayss
mushrooms	**unas setas**	**oo**nahss **say**tahss
carrots	**unas zanahorias**	**oo**nahss thahnah**o**ryahss
onions	**unas cebollas**	**oo**nahss thay**bhoa**lyahss
red cabbage	**lombarda**	loam**bahr**dhah
spinach	**unas espinacas**	**oo**nahss aysspee**nah**kahss
rice	**un poco de arroz**	oon **poa**koa day ahr**roth**
peas	**unos guisantes**	**oo**nos gee**sahn**tayss
tomatoes	**unos tomates**	**oo**nos toa**mah**tayss
green salad	**ensalada de lechuga**	aynsah**lah**dhah day lay-**choo**g̊ah
potatoes	**unas patatas**	**oo**nahss pah**tah**tahss

Desserts

Nothing more, thanks.	**Nada más, gracias.**	**nah**dhah mahss **grah**-thyahss
Just a small portion, please.	**Una pequeña porción, por favor.**	**oo**nah pay**kay**ñah por-**thyon** por fah**bhor**
Have you any ice-cream?	**¿Tiene usted helado?**	**tyay**nay oos**staydh** ay**lah**-dhoa
fruit salad	**ensalada de fruta**	aynsah**lah**dhah day **froo**tah
fresh fruit	**fruta fresca**	**froo**tah **frayss**kah
cheese	**queso**	**kay**soa

Drink

What would you like to drink?	**¿Qué le gustaría beber?**	kay lay goosstah**ree**ah bay**bhayr**
I'll have a beer, please.	**Tomaré una cerveza, por favor.**	toamah**ray** **oo**nah thehr-**bhay**thah por fah**bhor**
I'll have a whisky, please.	**Tomaré un whisky, por favor.**	toamah**ray** oon **wee**skee por fah**bhor**

Wine

I'd like a bottle of wine.	**Quisiera una botella de vino.**	kee**syay**rah **oo**nah boa**tay**lyah day **bee**noa
red wine	**vino tinto**	**bee**noa **teen**toa
rosé wine	**vino clarete**	**bee**noa klah**ray**tay
white wine	**vino blanco**	**bee**noa **blahng**koa
Cheers!	**¡A su salud!**	ah soo sah**loodh**

The bill (check)

May I have the bill (check) please?	**¿Podría darme la cuenta, por favor?**	poa**dhree**ah **dahr**may lah **kwayn**tah por fah**bhor**
Is service included?	**¿Está incluido el servicio?**	ayss**tah** eengklooe**e**dhoa ehl sehr**bhee**thyoa
Everything's included.	**Todo está incluido.**	**toa**dhoa ayss**tah** eengklooe**e**dhoa
Thank you, that was a very good meal.	**Gracias. Ha sido una comida muy buena.**	**grah**thyahss. ah **see**dhoa **oo**nah koa**mee**dhah mwee **bway**nah

SPANISH

Travelling

Where's the railway station, please?	**¿Dónde está la estación de ferrocarril, por favor?**	**don**day ayss**tah** lah ayss-tah**thyon** day fehrro**kahr**reel por fah**bhor**
Where's the ticket office, please?	**¿Dónde está la taquilla, por favor?**	**don**day ayss**tah** lah tah**kee**lyah por fah**bhor**
I'd like a ticket to ...	**Quisiera un billete para ...**	kee**syay**rah oon bee**lyay**tay **pah**rah
First or second class?	**¿Primera o segunda clase?**	pree**may**rah o say**goon**dah **klah**say
First class, please.	**Primera clase, por favor.**	pree**may**rah **klah**say por fah**bhor**
Single or return (one way or round-trip)?	**¿Ida, o ida y vuelta?**	**ee**dhah o **ee**dhah ee **bwehl**tah
Do I have to change trains?	**¿Tengo que hacer transbordo?**	**tayng**goa kay ah**thehr** trahnz**bhoar**dhoa
What platform does the train leave from?	**¿De qué andén sale el tren?**	day kay ahn**dayn** **sah**lay ehl trayn
Where's the nearest underground (subway) station?	**¿Dónde está la próxima estación de metro?**	**don**day ayss**tah** lah **proǧ**seemah aysstah**thyon** day **may**troa

Where's the bus station, please?	**¿Dónde está la estación de autobuses, por favor?**	**don**day ayss**tah** lah ayss-tah**thyon** day owtoa-**boss**ayss por fah**bhor**
When's the first bus to . . . ?	**¿Cuándo sale el primer autobús para . . . ?**	**kwahn**doa **sah**lay ehl pree**mehr** owtoa**booss** **pah**rah
the last bus	**el último autobús**	ehl **ool**teemoa owtoa-**booss**
the next bus	**el próximo autobús**	ehl **proĝ**seemoa owtoa-**booss**
Please let me off at the next stop.	**Por favor, pare en la próxima parada.**	por fah**bhor** **pah**ray ayn lah **proĝ**seemah pah**rah**-dhah

Relaxing

What's on at the cinema (movies)?	**¿Qué dan en el cine?**	kay dahn ayn ehl **thee**nay
What's on at the theatre?	**¿Qué dan en el teatro?**	kay dahn ayn ehl tay**ah**-troa
What time does the film begin? And the play?	**¿A qué hora empieza la película? ¿Y la obra?**	ah kay **oa**rah aym**pyay**-thah lah pay**lee**koolah? ee lah **oabh**rah
Are there any tickets for tonight?	**¿Quedan entradas para esta noche?**	**kay**dhahn ayn**trah**dhahss **pah**rah **ayss**tah **noa**chay
Where can we go dancing?	**¿Dónde se puede ir a bailar?**	**don**day say **pway**dhay eer ah bigh**lahr**
Would you like to dance?	**¿Quiere usted bailar?**	**kyay**ray ooss**taydh** bigh**lahr**

Introductions

How do you do?	**Buenos días.**	**bway**noss **dee**ahss
How are you?	**¿Cómo está usted?**	**koa**moa ayss**tah** ooss-**taydh**
Very well, thank you. And you?	**Muy bien, gracias. ¿Y usted?**	mwee byayn **grah**thyahss. ee ooss**taydh**
May I introduce Miss Philips?	**¿Me permite presentarle la Señorita Philips?**	may pehr**mee**tay pray-sayn**tahr**lay lah sayñoa-**ree**tah Philips
My name is . . .	**Me llamo . . .**	may **lyah**moa
I'm very pleased to meet you.	**Tanto gusto (en conocerle).**	**tahn**toa **gooss**toa (ayn koanoa**thehr**lay)

SPANISH

How long have you been here?	**¿Cuánto tiempo lleva usted aquí?**	**kwahn**toa **tyaym**poa **lyay**-bhah oos**taydh** ah**kee**
It was nice meeting you.	**Ha sido un placer conocerle.**	ah **see**dhoa oon plah-**thehr** koanoa**thehr**lay

Dating

Would you like a cigarette?	**¿Quiere usted un cigarrillo?**	**kyay**ray oos**taydh** oon theegah**ree**lyoa
May I get you a drink?	**¿Me permite invitarlo a una bebida?**	may pehr**mee**tay een-bhee**tahr**loa ah **oo**nah bay**bhee**dhah
Do you have a light, please?	**¿Tiene usted fuego, por favor?**	**tyay**nay oos**taydh** **fway-g̊oa** por fah**bhor**
Are you waiting for someone?	**¿Está usted esperando a alguien?**	ayss**tah** oos**taydh** ayss-pay**rahn**doa ah ahl**gyayn**
Are you free this evening?	**¿Está usted libre esta noche?**	ayss**tah** oos**taydh** **lee**-bhray **ayss**tah **noa**chay
Where shall we meet?	**¿Dónde quedamos citados?**	**don**day kay**dhah**moss thee**tah**dhoss
What time shall I meet you?	**¿A qué hora puedo verla?**	ah kay **oa**rah **pway**dhoa **behr**lah
May I take you home?	**¿Puedo acompañarla a su casa?**	pwaydhoa ahkoampah-**ñahr**lah ah soo **kah**sah
Thank you, it's been a wonderful evening.	**Gracias, he pasado una velada maravillosa.**	**grah**thyahss ay pah**sah**-dhoa **oo**na bay **lah**dhah mahrahbhee**lyoa**sah
What's your telephone number?	**¿Cuál es su número de teléfono?**	kwahl ayss soo **noo**may-roa day tay**lay**foanoa
Do you live alone?	**Vive usted sola?**	**bee**bhay oos**taydh** **soa**lah
What time is your last train?	**¿A qué hora sale su último tren?**	ah kay **oa**rah **sah**lay soo **ool**teemoa trayn
Good-night . . .	**Buenas noches . . .**	**bway**nahss **noa**chayss

Banks

Where's the nearest bank, please?	**¿Dónde está el banco más cercano, por favor?**	**don**day ayss**tah** ehl **bahng**koa mahss thehr-**kah**noa por fah**bhor**
Where can I cash some traveller's cheques?	**¿Dónde puedo cambiar unos traveller's cheques?**	**don**day **pway**dhoa kahm-**byahr** **oo**noss "traveller's cheques"

What time does the bank open/What time does it close?	**¿A qué hora abren el banco/A qué hora lo cierran?**	ah kay **oa**rah **ah**brayn ehl **bahng**koa/ah kay **oa**rah loa **thyehr**rahn
I'm expecting some money from home. Has it arrived?	**Estoy esperando dinero de casa. ¿Ha llegado?**	ayss**toy** aysspay**rahn**doa dee**nay**roa day **kah**sah. ah yay**ğah**doa
Can you give me some small change, please?	**¿Puede usted darme algún dinero suelto, por favor?**	**pway**dhay ooss**taydh dahr**may ahl**goon** dee**nay**roa **swehl**toa por fah**bhor**

Shops, stores and services

Where is the nearest chemist (pharmacy)?	**¿Dónde está la farmacia más cercana?**	**don**day ayss**tah** lah fahrmah**thee**ah mahss thehr**kah**nah
the nearest hairdresser's	**la peluquería más cercana**	lah paylookay**ree**ah mahss thehr**kah**nah
the photo shop	**la tienda fotográfica**	lah **tyayn**dha foatoa**ğrah**feekah
the jeweller's	**la joyería**	lah khoayay**ree**ah
the department store	**los grandes almacenes**	loss **grahn**dayss ahlmah**thay**nayss
the police station	**la comisaría**	lah koameesah**ree**ah
the garage	**el garaje**	ehl gah**rah**khay
How do I get there?	**¿Cómo podría ir allí?**	**koa**moa poa**dhree**ah eer ah**lyee**
Is it within walking distance?	**¿Se puede ir andando?**	say **pway**dhay eer ahn**dahn**doa

Service

Can you help me, please?	**¿Puede usted atenderme, por favor?**	**pway**dhay ooss**taydh** ahtayn**dehr**may por fah**bhor**
Can you show me this? And that, too.	**¿Puede usted enseñarme esto? ¿Y aquello también?**	**pway**dhay ooss**taydh** aynsay**ñahr**may **ayss**toa? ee ah**kway**lyoa tahm**byyayn**
It's too expensive/too big/too small.	**Es demasiado caro/demasiado grande/demasiado pequeño.**	ayss daymah**syah**dhoa **kah**roa/daymah**syah**dhoa **grahn**day/daymah**syah**dhoa pay**kay**ñoa
Can you show me some more?	**¿Puede usted enseñarme algo más?**	**pway**dhay ooss**taydh** aynsay**ñahr**may **ahl**goa mahss
something better	**algo mejor**	**ahl**goa may**khor**
something cheaper	**algo más barato**	**ahl**goa mahss bah**rah**toa

How much is this? And that?	**¿Cuánto cuesta éste? ¿Y ése?**	**kwahn**toa **kwayss**tah **ayss**tay? ee **ay**say
It's not quite what I want.	**No es exactamente lo que quiero.**	noa ayss ehg̊sahktah**mayn**tay loa kay **kyay**roa
I like it.	**Me gusta.**	may **gooss**tah

Chemist's (Pharmacy)

I'd like something for a cold/for a cough/for travel sickness.	**Desearía algo para el catarro/para la tos/contra el mareo.**	daysayah**ree**ah **ahl**goa **pah**rah ehl kah**tahr**roa/ **pah**rah lah toss/**kon**trah ehl mah**ray**oa
Can you recommend something for hay-fever/for sunburn?	**¿Podría recomendarme algo para la fiebre del heno/ para las quemaduras del sol?**	poa**dhree**ah raykoamayn**dahr**may **ahl**goa **pah**rah lah **fyay**bhray dehl **ay**noa/**pah**rah lahss kaymah**dhoo**rahss dehl sol

Toiletry

May I have some razor blades?	**¿Puede darme unas cuchillas para afeitar?**	**pway**dhay **dahr**may **oo**nahss koo**chee**lyahss **pah**rah ahfay**tahr**
some shaving cream	**una crema para afeitar**	**oo**nah **kray**mah **pah**rah ahfay**tahr**
some toothpaste	**una pasta de dientes**	**oo**nah **pahss**tah day **dyayn**tayss
I'd like some soap.	**Quisiera jabón.**	kee**syay**rah khah**bhon**
some suntan oil	**aceite bronceador**	ah**thay**tay bronthayah**dhor**

At the barber's

I'd like a haircut, please.	**Quisiera cortarme el pelo, por favor.**	kee**syay**rah kor**tahr**may ehl **pay**loa por fah**bhor**
Short/Leave it long.	**Corto/Déjemelo largo.**	**kor**toa/**day**khaymayloa **lahr**goa
A razor cut, please.	**Un corte a navaja, por favor.**	oon **kor**tay ah nah**bhah**khah por fah**bhor**

At the hairdresser's

I'd like a shampoo and set, please.	**Quiero un lavado y marcado por favor.**	**kyay**roa oon lah**bhah**dhoa ee mahr**kah**dhoa por fah**bhor**

I'd like a bleach.	**Desearía un aclarado.**	daysayah**ree**ah oon ahklah**rah**dhoa
a permanent a colour rinse a manicure	**una permanente un reflejo una manicura**	**oo**nah pehrmah**nayn**tay oon ray**flay**khoa **oo**nah mahnee**koo**rah

Photography

I'd like a film for this camera.	**Desearía un carrete para esta máquina.**	daysayah**ree**ah oon kahr**ray**tay **pah**rah **ayss**tah **mah**keenah
This camera doesn't work.	**Esta cámera no funciona.**	**ayss**tah **kah**mayrah noa foon**thyoa**nah

At the post office

Where's the nearest post office, please?	**¿Dónde está la oficina de correos más cercana, por favor?**	**don**day ayss**tah** lah oafee**thee**nah day kor**reh**oss mahss thehr**kah**nah por fah**bhor**
I'd like to send this by express (special delivery)/by air mail.	**Quisiera enviar esto por correo urgente/ por avión.**	kee**syay**rah ay**bhyahr** **ayss**toa por kor**reh**oa oor**khayn**tay/ por ah**bhyon**

Service stations

Where is the nearest service station, please?	**¿Dónde está la estación de servicio más cercana?**	**don**day ayss**tah** lah ayss-tah**thyon** day sehr**bhee**thyoa mahss thehr**kah**nah
Fill her up, please.	**Llénemelo por favor.**	**lyay**naymayloa por fah**bhor**
Check the oil, please.	**Compruebe el aceite, por favor.**	kom**prway**bhay ehl ah**thay**tay por fah**bhor**
Would you check the tyres?	**¿Quiere comprobar los neumáticos?**	**kyay**ray komproa**bhahr** loss nehw**mah**teekoss

Street directions

Can you show me on the map where I am?	**¿Puede enseñarme en el mapa dónde estoy?**	**pway**dhay aynsay**ñahr**may ayn ehl **mah**pah **don**day ayss**toy**
You're on the wrong road.	**Está usted equivocado de camino.**	ayss**tah** ooss**taydh** aykee-bhoa**kah**dhoa day kah**mee**noa

SPANISH

Go back to ...	**Vuelva a ...**	**bwehl**bha a
Go straight ahead.	**Siga todo derecho.**	**see**ğah **toa**dhoa day**ray**choa
It's on the left/on the right.	**Está a la izquierda/ a la derecha.**	ayss**tah** ah lah eeth**kyehr**dhah/ah lah day**ray**chah

Accidents

May I use your telephone?	**¿Puedo utilizar su teléfono?**	**pway**dhoa ooteelee**thar** soo tay**lay**foanoa
Call a doctor quickly.	**Llame a un médico rápidamente.**	**lyah**may ah oon **may**deekoa **rah**peedhamayntay
Call an ambulance.	**Llame a una ambulancia.**	**lyah**may ah **oo**nah ahmboo**lahn**thyah
Please call the police.	**Llame a la policía, por favor.**	**lyah**may ah lah polee**thee**ah por fah**bhor**

Numbers

zero	**cero**	**thay**roa
one	**uno**	**oo**noa
two	**dos**	doss
three	**tres**	trayss
four	**cuatro**	**kwah**troa
five	**cinco**	**theeng**koa
six	**seis**	**seh**eess
seven	**siete**	**syay**tay
eight	**ocho**	**oa**choa
nine	**nueve**	**nway**bhay
ten	**diez**	dyayth
eleven	**once**	**on**thay
twelve	**doce**	**doa**thay
thirteen	**trece**	**tray**thay
fourteen	**catorce**	kah**tor**thay
fifteen	**quince**	**keen**thay
sixteen	**dieciséis**	dyehthee**seh**eess
seventeen	**diecisiete**	dyehthee**syay**tay
eighteen	**dieciocho**	dyehthee**oa**choa
nineteen	**diecinueve**	dyehthee**nway**bhay
twenty	**veinte**	**bayn**tay
twenty-one	**veintiuno**	bayntio**o**noa
thirty	**treinta**	**trayn**tah
forty	**cuarenta**	kwah**rayn**tah
fifty	**cincuenta**	theeng**kwayn**tah
sixty	**sesenta**	say**sayn**tah
seventy	**setenta**	say**tayn**tah

eighty	**ochenta**	oa**chayn**tah
ninety	**noventa**	noa**bhayn**tah
one hundred	**cien**	thyayn
one thousand	**mil**	meel
ten thousand	**diez mil**	dyayth meel

Days

It's Sunday.	**Es domingo.**	ayss doa**meeng**goa
Monday	**lunes**	**loo**nayss
Tuesday	**martes**	**mahr**tayss
Wednesday	**miércoles**	**myehr**koalayss
Thursday	**jueves**	**khway**bhayss
Friday	**viernes**	**byehr**nayss
Saturday	**sábado**	**sah**bhahdhoa
yesterday	**ayer**	ah**yehr**
today	**hoy**	oy
tomorrow	**mañana**	mah**ñah**nah
morning/afternoon	**mañana/media tarde**	mah**ñah**nah/**may**dhyah **tahr**dhay
evening/night	**tarde/noche**	**tahr**dhay/**noa**chay

Months

January	**enero**	ay**nay**roa
February	**febrero**	fay**bhray**roa
March	**marzo**	**mahr**thoa
April	**abril**	ah**bhreel**
May	**mayo**	**mah**yoa
June	**junio**	**khoo**nyoa
July	**julio**	**khoo**lyoa
August	**agosto**	ah**goss**toa
September	**septiembre**	sayp**tyaym**bray
October	**octubre**	ok**too**bhray
November	**noviembre**	noa**bhyaym**bray
December	**diciembre**	dee**thyaym**bray
Merry Christmas!	**¡Felices Pascuas!**	fay**lee**thayss **pahss**kwahss!
Happy New Year!	**¡Feliz Año Nuevo!**	fay**leeth ah**ñoa **nway**bhoa

SPANISH

SWEDISH

Guide to Pronunciation

Letter	Approximate pronunciation	Symbol	Example	
Consonants				
b, c, d, f, h, l, m, n, p, v, w, x	as in English			
ch	at the beginning of words borrowed from French, like **sh** in **sh**ut	sh	**chef**	shayf
g	1) before stressed **i**, **e**, **y**, **ä**, **ö** and sometimes after **l** or **r**, like **y** in **y**et	y	**genast**	**yay**nahst
	2) before **e** and **i** in many words of French origin, like **sh** in **sh**ut	sh	**generös**	shaynerr**urss**
	3) elsewhere, generally like **g** in **g**o	g	**gammal**	**gah**mahl
j, dj, gj, lj	like **y** in **y**et	y	**ja**	yar
k	1) before stressed **i**, **e**, **y**, **ä**, **ö**, generally like **ch** in Scottish lo**ch**, but pronounced in the front of the mouth	kh	**köpa**	**khur**pah
	2) elsewhere, like **k** in **k**it	k	**kål**	koal

kj	like **ch** in Scottish lo**ch**, but pronounced in the front of the mouth	kh	**kjol**	khool
qu	like **k** in **k**it followed by **v** in **v**at	kv	**Lindquist**	**lind**kvist
r	slightly rolled near the front of the mouth	r	**råd**	road
s	1) in the ending **-sion** like **sh** in **sh**ut	sh	**mission**	mi**shoon**
	2) elsewhere, like **s** in **s**o	s/ss	**smak**	smark
	3) the groups **sch**, **skj**, **stj** are pronounced like **sh** in **sh**ut	sh	**schema**	**shay**mah
sk	1) before stressed **e**, **i**, **y**, **ä**, **ö**, like **sh** in **sh**ut	sh	**skepp**	shehp
	2) elsehwere, like **sk** in **sk**ip	sk	**handske**	**hahnd**sker
t	1) **ti** in the ending **-tion**, is pronounced like **sh** in **sh**ut or like	sh	**station**	stah**shoon**
	ch in **ch**at	tsh	**nation**	nah**tschoon**
	2) elsehwere, like **t** in **t**op	t	**talk**	tahlk
tj	like **ch** in Scottish lo**ch**, but pronounced in the front of the mouth; sometimes with a **t**-sound at the beginning	kh	**tjäna**	**khai**nah
z	like **s** in **s**o	s	**zon**	soon

N.B. In the groups **rd**, **rl**, **rn**, **rs** and **rt**, the letter **r** is generally not pronounced but influences the pronunciation of the **d**, **l**, **n**, **s** or **t**, which is then pronounced with the end of the tongue *not* on the upper front teeth, but behind the gums of the upper teeth.

SWEDISH

Vowels

Vowels in stressed syllables are long if followed at most by one consonant, but are short if followed by two or more consonants. Vowels in unstressed syllables are short.

a	1) when long, like **a** in c**a**r	ar*	**dag**	darg
	2) when short, something like the **u** in c**u**t or **o** in American c**o**llege	ah	**tack**	tahk
e	1) when long, like **ay** in s**ay**, but a *pure* vowel, not a diphthong	ay	**blek**	blayk
	2) in the stressed prefix er-, like **a** in m**a**n, but longer	ææ	**erfara**	**ææar**farrah
	3) when short, like **e** in g**e**t	eh	**penna**	**peh**na
	4) when unstressed, like **a** in **a**bout	er*	**betala**	ber**tar**lah

* The **r** should not be pronounced when reading this transcription.

ej	like **a** in m**a**te	ay	**nej**	nay
i	1) when long, like **ee** in b**ee**	ee	**vit**	veet
	2) when short, between **ee** in m**ee**t and **i** in h**i**t	i	**bild**	bild
o	1) when long, often like **oo** in s**oo**n, but with the lips more tightly rounded, and with a puff of breath at the end	oo	**sko**	skoo
	2) the same sound can be short	oo	**ost**	oost
	3) when long, it is also sometimes pronounced like **oa** in m**oa**n	oa	**son**	soan
	4) when short, sometimes like **o** in h**o**t	o	**socker**	**sok**kerr
u	1) when long, like Swedish **y**, but with the tongue a little lower in the mouth, and with a puff of breath at the end	ew	**hus**	hewss
	2) when short, a little more like the **u** of p**u**t; a very difficult sound	ew	**ung**	ewng
y	pronounce the **ee** of b**ee** and then round your lips without moving your tongue; the sound can be long or short	ew	**vy** **syster**	vew **sew**sterr
å	1) when long, like **aw** in r**aw**, but with the tongue a little higher in the mouth	oa	**gå**	goa
	2) when short, like **o** in h**o**t	o	**sång**	song
ä	1) when followed by **r**, like **a** in m**a**n, long or short	ææ æ	**ära** **värka**	**ææ**rah **vær**kah
	2) elsewhere, like **e** in g**e**t; long or short	ai eh	**läsa** **bäst**	**lai**sah behst
ö	like **u** in f**u**r, long or short; when followed by **r**, it is pronounced with the mouth a little more open	ur*	**röd** **höst** **öra**	rurd hurst **ur**rah

N.B. The principal stress is generally on the *first* syllable of a word, unless it comes from Latin or French.

Throughout the pronunciation section you will notice that some letters are placed in parentheses [e.g. **mew**ker(t)]. In absolutely correct Swedish you should pronounce all the sounds indicated. However, in current usage most Swedes omit the sounds that are shown in parentheses.

* The **r** should not be pronounced when reading this transcription.

Some basic expressions

Yes.	**Ja.**	yar
No.	**Nej.**	nay
Please.	**Varsågod.**	**vahr**soagood
Thank you.	**Tack.**	tahk
Thank you very much.	**Tack så mycket.**	tahk soa **mew**ker(t)
That's all right.	**Ingen orsak.**	**ing**ern **oor**shark

Greetings

Good morning.	**God morgon.**	goo **mo**ron
Good afternoon.	**God middag.**	goo **mid**dah(g)
Good evening.	**God afton.**	goo **ahf**ton
Good night.	**God natt.**	goo naht
Good-bye.	**Adjö.**	ah**yur**
See you later.	**Vi ses.**	vee sayss
This is Mr....	**Det här är herr...**	day hæær æær hær
This is Mrs....	**Det här är fru...**	day hæær æær frew
This is Miss...	**Det här är fröken...**	day hæær æær **frur**kern
I'm very pleased to meet you.	**Angenämt.**	ahnyer**nehmt**
How are you?	**Hur står det till?**	hewr stoar deht til
Very well, thank you. And you?	**Tack bara bra. Och Ni själv?**	tahk **bar**rah brar. o(k) nee shehlv
Fine.	**Fint.**	fint
Excuse me.	**Förlåt.**	furr**loat**

Questions

Where?	**Var?**	varr
Where is...?	**Var är...?**	varr ai
Where are...?	**Var är...?**	varr ai
When?	**När?**	næær
What?	**Vad?**	vard
How?	**Hur?**	hewr
How much?	**Hur mycket?**	hewr **mew**ker(t)
How many?	**Hur många?**	hewr **mon**gah

Who?	**Vem?**	vaym
Why?	**Varför?**	**vahr**furr
Which?	**Vilken?**	**vil**kern
What do you call this?	**Vad heter det här?**	vard **hay**terr day hææ
What do you call that?	**Vad heter det där?**	vard **hay**terr day dææ
What does this mean?	**Vad betyder det här?**	vard ber**tew**derr day hææ
What does that mean?	**Vad betyder det där?**	vard ber**tew**derr day dææ

Do you speak . . . ?

Do you speak English?	**Talar Ni engelska?**	**tar**lahr nee **ehng**erlskah
Do you speak German?	**Talar Ni tyska?**	**tar**lahr nee **tew**skah
Do you speak French?	**Talar Ni franska?**	**tar**lahr nee **frahn**skah
Do you speak Spanish?	**Talar Ni spanska?**	**tar**lahr nee **spahn**skah
Do you speak Italian?	**Talar Ni italienska?**	**tar**lahr nee itahli**ehn**skah
Could you speak more slowly, please?	**Kan Ni vara snäll och tala lite långsammare?**	kahn nee **var**rah snehl o **tar**lah **lee**ter **long**-sahmahrer
Please point to the phrase in the book.	**Var snäll och peka på meningen i boken.**	**varr** snehl o **pay**kah poa **may**ningern ee **boo**kern
Just a minute. I'll see if I can find it in this book.	**Ett ögonblick, så ska jag se om jag hittar det i den här boken.**	eht **ur**gonblik soa skar jar(g) say om yar(g) **hi**tahr day ee dehn hææ **boo**kern
I understand.	**Jag förstår.**	yar(g) furr**shtoar**
I don't understand.	**Jag förstår inte.**	yar(g) furr**shtoar in**ter

Can . . . ?

Can I have . . . ?	**Kan jag få . . . ?**	kahn yar(g) foa
Can we have . . . ?	**Kan vi få . . . ?**	kahn vee foa

Can you show me . . . ?	**Kan Ni visa mig . . . ?**	kahn nee **vee**sah may
Can you tell me . . . ?	**Kan Ni säga mig . . . ?**	kahn nee **sai**gah may
Can you help me, please?	**Kan Ni vara snäll och hjälpa mig?**	kahn nee **var**rah snehl o **yehl**pah may

Wanting

I'd like . . .	**Jag skulle vilja ha . . .**	yar(g) **skew**ller **vil**yah har
We'd like . . .	**Vi skulle vilja ha . . .**	vee **skew**ller **vil**yah har
Please give me . . .	**Var snäll och ge mig . . .**	varr snehl o yay may
Give it to me, please.	**Var snäll och ge mig den.**	varr snehl o yay may dehn
Please bring me . . .	**Var snäll och hämta . . .**	varr snehl o **hehm**tah
Bring it to me, please.	**Var snäll och hämta den.**	varr snehl o **hehm**tah dehn
I'm hungry.	**Jag är hungrig.**	yar(g) ææ**r** **hewng**ri(g)
I'm thirsty.	**Jag är törstig.**	yar(g) æær **turr**shti(g)
I'm tired.	**Jag är trött.**	yar(g) æær trurt
I'm lost.	**Jag har gått vilse.**	yar(g) harr got **vil**ser
It's important.	**Det är viktigt.**	day æær **vik**tikt
It's urgent.	**Det är brådskande.**	day æær **bro**skahnder
Hurry up!	**Skynda på!**	**shewn**dah poa

It is/There is . . .

It is/It's . . .	**Det är . . .**	day ai
Is it . . . ?	**Är det . . . ?**	ai day
It isn't . . .	**Det är inte . . .**	day ai **in**ter
There is/There are . . .	**Det finns . . .**	day finss
Is there/Are there . . . ?	**Finns det . . .**	finss day
There isn't/There aren't . . .	**Det finns inte . . .**	day finss **in**ter
There isn't any/ There aren't any.	**Det finns ingen/Det finns inga.**	day finss **ing**ern/day finss **ing**ah

A few common words

big/small	**stor/liten**	stoor/**lee**tern
quick/slow	**snabb/långsam**	snahb/**long**sahm
early/late	**tidig/sen**	**tee**di(g)/sayn
cheap/expensive	**billig/dyr**	**bil**li(g)/dewr
near/far	**nära/avlägsen**	**nai**rah/**ahv**lehgsern
hot/cold	**varm/kall**	vahrm/kahl
full/empty	**full/tom**	fewl/toom
easy/difficult	**lätt/svår**	leht/svoar
light/heavy	**lätt/tung**	leht/tewng
open/shut	**öppen/stängd**	**ur**pern/stehngd
right/wrong	**rätt/fel**	reht/fayl
old/new	**gammal/ny**	**gah**mahl/new
old/young	**gammal/ung**	**gah**mahl/ewng
beautiful/ugly	**vacker/ful**	**vah**kerr/fewl
good/bad	**god/dålig**	good/**doa**li(g)
better/worse	**bättre/sämre**	**beh**trer/**sehm**rer

Some prepositions and a few more useful words

at	**vid**	veed
on	**på**	poa
in	**i**	ee
to	**till**	till
from	**från**	froan
inside	**inne**	**in**ner
outside	**ute**	**ew**ter
up	**upp**	ewp
down	**ner**	nayr
before	**före**	**fur**rer
after	**efter**	**ehf**terr
with	**med**	mayd
without	**utan**	**ew**tahn
through	**genom**	**yay**nom
towards	**mot**	moot
until	**till dess**	til dehss
during	**under**	**ewn**derr
and	**och**	ok
or	**eller**	**ehl**lerr
not	**inte**	**in**ter
nothing	**ingenting**	**ing**ernting
none	**ingen**	**ing**ern
very	**mycket**	**mew**ker(t)
also	**också**	ok**soa**
soon	**snart**	snahrt

SWEDISH

perhaps	**kanske**	**kahn**sher
here	**här**	hææer
there	**där**	dææer
now	**nu**	new
then	**då**	doa

Arrival

Your passport, please.	**Passet, tack.**	**pah**sert tahk
Here it is.	**Varsågod.**	**vahr**soagood
Have you anything to declare?	**Har Ni någonting att förtulla?**	harr nee **noa**gonting aht **furr**tewlah
No, nothing at all.	**Nej, ingenting alls.**	nay **ing**ernting ahlss
Porter!	**Bärare!**	**bææ**rahrer
Can you help me with my luggage, please?	**Kan Ni vara snäll och hjälpa mig med mitt bagage?**	kahn nee **var**rah snehl o **yehl**pah may mayd mit bah**garsh**
That's my suitcase.	**Det där är min väska.**	day dææer ai meen **vehss**kah
Where's the bus to the centre of town, please?	**Var är bussen som går till centrum?**	varr ai **bewss**ern soam goar til **sehn**troom
This way, please.	**Den här vägen.**	dehn hææer **vai**gern

Changing money

Can you change a traveller's cheque, please?	**Kan Ni växla in en resecheck?**	kahn nee **vehks**lah in ayn **ray**ssershehk
Where's the nearest bank, please?	**Var ligger närmaste bank?**	varr **lig**gerr **nææer**mahsster bahnk

Car rental

I'd like a car.	**Jag skulle vilja hyra en bil.**	yar(g) **skew**ller **vil**yah **hew**rah ayn beel
For how long?	**Hur länge?**	hewr **lehng**er
A day/Four days/ A week/Two weeks.	**En dag/Fyra dagar/ En vecka/Två veckor.**	ayn darg/**few**rah **dar**-gahr/ayn **veh**kah/tvoa **veh**kor

Taxi

Where can I get a taxi?	**Var kan jag få tag på en taxi?**	varr kahn yar(g) foa targ poa ayn **tahk**si
What's the fare to ...?	**Vad kostar det till ...?**	vard **koss**tahr day til
Take me to this address, please.	**Var snäll och kör mig till den här adressen.**	varr snehl o khurr may til dehn hæær ah**drehss**ern
I'm in a hurry.	**Jag har bråttom.**	yar(g) harr **brot**tom
Could you drive more slowly, please?	**Skulle Ni kunna köra litet långsammare?**	**skewl**ler nee **kewn**nah **khur**rah **lee**tert **long**-sahmahrer

Hotel and other accommodation

My name is ...	**Mitt namn är ...**	mit nahmn ai
Have you a reservation?	**Har Ni reserverat?**	harr nee raysæær**vay**raht
Yes, here's the confirmation.	**Ja, här är bekräftelsen.**	yar hæær ai ber**krehf**terl-sern
I'd like ...	**Jag skulle vilja ha ...**	yar(g) **skewl**ler **vil**yah har
I'd like a single room/a double room.	**Jag skulle vilja ha ett enkelrum/ett dubbelrum.**	yar(g) **skewl**ler **vil**yah har eht **ehng**kerlrewm/eht **dewb**berlrewm
a room with a bath/with a shower	**ett rum med bad/ med dusch**	eht rewm mayd bard/ med dewsh

How much?

What's the price per night/per week/per month?	**Hur mycket kostar det per natt/per vecka/per månad?**	hewr **mew**ker(t) **koss**tahr day pær naht/pær **veh**kah/pær **moa**nahd
May I see the room?	**Kan jag få se på rummet?**	kahn yar(g) foa say poa **rew**mert
I'm sorry, I don't like it.	**Tyvärr, men jag tycker inte om det.**	tew**vær** mayn yar(g) **tewk**-kerr **in**ter om day
Yes, that's fine. I'll take it.	**Ja, det här var bra. Jag tar det.**	yar day hæær varr brar. yar(g) tarr day
What's my room number, please?	**Vilket rumsnummer har jag?**	**vil**kert **rewmss**newmerr har yar
Number 123.	**Nummer 123.**	**new**merr 123.

SWEDISH

Service, please

Who is it?	**Vem är det?**	vaym ai day
Just a minute.	**Ett ögonblick.**	eht **ur**gonblik
Come in! The door's open.	**Kom in. Dörren är öppen.**	kom in **dur**rern ai **urp**pern
May we have breakfast in our room?	**Kan vi få frukost på rummet?**	kahn vee foa **frew**kost poa **rew**mert

Breakfast

I'll have ...	**Jag ska be att få ...**	yar(g) skar bay aht foa
I'll have some fruit juice.	**Jag ska be att få juice.**	yar(g) skar bay aht foa yooss
a boiled egg	**ett kokt ägg**	eht kookt ehg
a fried egg	**ett stekt ägg**	eht staykt egh
some bacon/some ham	**bacon/skinka**	**bay**kon/**shing**kah
some toast	**rostat bröd**	**ross**taht brurd
a pot of tea	**en kanna te**	ayn **kah**nah tay
a cup of tea	**en kopp te**	ayn kop tay
some coffee	**kaffe**	**kahf**fer
some chocolate	**choklad**	shoo**klard**
more butter	**mera smör**	**may**rah smurr
some hot water	**lite hett vatten**	**lee**ter heht **vah**tern

Difficulties

The central heating doesn't work.	**Centralvärmen fungerar inte.**	sehn**trarl**værmern fewng**gay**rahr **in**ter
the light/the socket	**ljuset/kontakten**	**yew**sert/kon**tahk**tern
the tap/the toilet	**vattenkranen/toaletten**	**vah**ternkrarnern/twah**leh**tern
There's no hot water.	**Det finns inget varmvatten.**	day finss **in**gert **vahrm**vahtern
May I see the manager, please?	**Kan jag få tala med direktören, tack?**	kan yar(g) foa **tar**lah mayd direhk**tur**rern tahk

Telephone—Mail

There's a call for you.	**Det är telefon till Er.**	day ai taylay**foan** til ayr
Hold the line, please.	**Var god dröj.**	varr good **drury**

Operator, I've been cut off.	**Fröken, linjen är bruten.**	**frur**kern **lin**yern ai **brew**tern
Did anyone telephone me?	**Har någon ringt mig?**	harr **noa**gon ringt may
Is there any mail for me?	**Finns det post till mig?**	finss day post til may
Are there any messages for me?	**Finns det några meddelanden till mig.**	finss day **noa**gra meh**day**lahndern til may

Checking out

May I have my bill, please?	**Kan jag få räkningen, tack?**	kahn yar(g) foa **rehk**ningern tahk
We're in a great hurry.	**Vi har mycket bråttom.**	vee harr **mew**ker(t) **brot**tom
It's been a very enjoyable stay.	**Det har varit mycket trevligt att bo här.**	day har **var**rit **mew**ker(t) **trayv**ligt aht boo hææ̈r

Eating out

Good evening. I'd like a table for two, please.	**God afton. Jag skulle vilja ha ett bord för två.**	goo **ahf**ton. yar(g) **skew**leh **vil**yah har eht boord furr tvoa
Do you have a fixed-price menu?	**Har Ni en meny?**	harr nee ayn may**new**
May I see the à la carte menu?	**Kan jag få se på à la carte matsedeln?**	kahn yar(g) foa say poa ah lah kahrt **mart**serderln
May we have an ashtray, please?	**Kan vi få en askkopp, tack?**	kahn vee foa ayn **ahsk**kop tahk
some bread	**litet bröd**	**lee**ter(t) brurd
a fork	**en gaffel**	ayn **gah**ferl
a knife	**en kniv**	ayn kneev
a spoon	**en sked**	ayn shayd
a plate	**en tallrik**	ayn **tahl**rik
a glass	**ett glas**	eht glarss
a napkin	**en servett**	ayn sær**veht**
another chair	**en stol till**	ayn stool til
Where's the gentlemen's toilet (men's room)?	**Var är herrtoaletten?**	varr ai **hær**twahlehtern

Where's the ladies' toilet (ladies' room)?	**Var är damtoaletten?**	varr ai **darm**twahlehtern

Appetizers

I'd like some ...	**Jag ska be att få ...**	yar(g) skar bay aht foa
I'd like some assorted appetizers.	**Jag ska be att få några smårätter.**	yar(g) skar bay aht foa **noa**grah **smoa**rehterr
orange juice	**apelsinjuice**	**ah**perlseenyooss
ham	**skinka**	**shing**kah
melon	**melon**	may**loon**
pâté	**pastej**	pass**tayy**
smoked salmon	**rökt lax**	rurkt lahks
shrimps (shrimp)	**räkor**	**rai**koor

Soup

Have you any ... ?	**Har Ni ... ?**	harr nee
Have you any chicken soup?	**Har Ni kycklingsoppa?**	harr nee **khewk**lingsopah
vegetable soup	**grönsakssoppa**	**grurn**sahkssopah
onion soup	**löksoppa**	**lurk**sopah

Fish

I'd like some ...	**Jag ska be att få ...**	yar(g) skar bay aht foa
I'd like some fish.	**Jag ska be att få en fiskrätt.**	yar(g) skar bay aht foa ayn **fisk**reht
sole	**sjötunga**	**shur**tewngah
trout	**forell**	fo**rehl**
lobster	**hummer**	**hew**merr
crayfish	**kräftor**	**krehf**toor
prawns	**räkor**	**rai**koor
I'd like it ...	**Jag skulle vilja ha den ...**	yar(g) **skew**ler **vil**yah har dehn
I'd like it steamed.	**Jag skulle vilja ha den ångkokt.**	yar(g) **skew**ler **vil**yah har dehn **ong**kookt
grilled	**grillad**	**gri**lahd
boiled	**kokt**	kookt
baked	**ugnsstekt**	**ewngns**staykt
fried	**stekt**	staykt

SWEDISH

Meat—Poultry—Game

I'd like some...	**Jag ska be att få...**	yar(g) skar bay aht foa
I'd like some beef.	**Jag ska be att få oxkött.**	yar(g) skar bay aht foa **ooks**khurt
a beef steak	**en biff**	ahn bif
some roast beef	**rostbiff**	**rost**bif
a veal cutlet	**en kalvkotlett**	ahn **kahlv**kotleht
lamb	**lammkött**	**lahm**khurt
a pork chop	**en fläskkotlett**	ahn **flehsk**kotleht
roast pork	**grisstek**	**greess**stayk
hare	**hare**	**har**rer
chicken	**kyckling**	**khewk**ling
roast chicken	**stekt kyckling**	staykt **khewk**ling
duck	**anka**	**ahng**kah
How do you like your meat?	**Hur vill Ni ha köttet tillagat?**	hewr vil nee har **khur**tert ti**lar**gaht
rare	**blodig**	**bloo**dig
medium	**lagom**	**lar**gom
well done	**genomstekt**	**yay**nomstaykt

Vegetables

What vegetables have you got?	**Vad för grönsaker finns det?**	vard furr **grurn**sarkerr finss day
I'd like some...	**Jag ska be att få...**	yar(g) ska bay aht foa
I'd like some asparagus.	**Jag ska be att få sparris.**	yar(g) ska bay aht foa **spah**riss
green beans	**haricots verts**	hahreekoa**væær**
mushrooms	**svamp**	svahmp
carrots	**morötter**	moo**rur**terr
onions	**lök**	lurk
red cabbage	**rödkål**	**rurd**koal
lettuce	**grönsallad**	**grurn**sahlahd
spinach	**spenat**	spay**nart**
rice	**ris**	**reess**
peas	**ärtor**	**ær**toor
tomatoes	**tomater**	too**mar**terr
green salad	**grönsallad**	**grurn**sahlahd
potatoes	**potatis**	poo**tar**tiss

Desserts

Nothing more, thanks.	**Ingenting mer, tack.**	**ing**ernting mayr tahk
Just a small portion, please.	**Bara en liten portion, tack.**	**bar**rah ehn **lee**tern por**choon** tahk

SWEDISH

Have you any ice-cream?	**Har Ni glass?**	har nee glahss
fruit salad	**fruktsallad**	**frewkt**sahlahd
fresh fruit	**färsk frukt**	færshk frewkt
cheese	**ost**	oost

Drink

What would you like to drink?	**Vad vill Ni ha att dricka?**	vard vil nee har aht **dri**kah
I'll have a beer, please.	**Jag tar en öl, tack.**	yar(g) tarr ehn url tahk
I'll have a whisky, please.	**Jag ska be att få en whisky, tack.**	yar(g) skar bay aht foa ehn **wiss**kew tahk

Wine

I'd like a bottle of wine.	**Jag ska be att få en flaska vin.**	yar(g) skar bay aht foa ehn **flahss**kah veen
red wine	**rödvin**	**rurd**veen
rosé wine	**rosévin**	roa**say**veen
white wine	**vitt vin**	vit veen
Cheers!	**Skål!**	skoal

The bill (check)

May I have the bill (check) please?	**Får jag be om notan, tack?**	foar yar(g) bay om **noo**tahn tahk
Is service included?	**Ingår servis?**	in**goar surr**viss
Everything's included.	**Allt ingår.**	ahlt in**goar**
Thank you, that was a very good meal.	**Tack, det var en mycket god måltid.**	tahk day varr ehn **mew**ker(t) goo **moal**teed

Travelling

Where's the railway station, please?	**Var är järnvägs-stationen?**	varr ai **yærn**vehgsstah**shoo**nern
Where's the ticket office, please?	**Var är biljettluckan?**	varr ai bil**yeht**lewkahn
I'd like a ticket to ...	**Jag ska be att få en biljett till ...**	yar(g) skar bay aht foa ehn bil**yeht** til
First or second class?	**Första eller andra klass?**	**furr**shtah **eh**lerr **ahn**drah klahss

First class, please.	**Första klass, tack.**	**furr**shtah klahss tahk
Single or return (one way or round-trip)?	**Enkel eller tur och retur?**	**ehng**kerl **eh**lerr tewr o(k) re**tewr**
Do I have to change trains?	**Måste jag byta tåg?**	**moss**ter yar **bew**tah toag
What platform does the train leave from?	**Från vilken perrong avgår tåget?**	froan **vil**kern pæ**rong** ahv**goar toa**gert
Where's the nearest underground (subway) station?	**Var ligger närmaste tunnelbanestation?**	varr **lig**ger **nææ**rmahster **tew**nerlbarnerstah**shoon**
Where's the bus station, please?	**Var är buss-stationen?**	varr ai **bewss**stah-shoonern
When's the first bus to . . . ?	**När går första bussen till . . . ?**	nææ**r** goar **furr**shtah **bew**ssern til
the last bus the next bus	**sista bussen/** **nästa buss**	**sis**stah **bew**ssern/ **nehss**tah bewss
Please let me off at the next stop.	**Var god och låt mig gå av vid nästa hållplats.**	varr goo o(k) loat may goa ahv veed **nehss**tah **hol**plahts

Relaxing

What's on at the cinema (movies)?	**Vad går det på bio?**	vard goar day poa **bee**oo
What's on at the theatre?	**Vad ger man på teatern?**	vard yayr mahn poa tay**ar**terrn
What time does the film begin?	**När börjar filmen?**	nææ**r** **burr**yarr **fil**mern
And the play?	**Och teaterföreställningen?**	o tay**ar**terrfurrerstehl-ningern
Are there any tickets for tonight?	**Finns det några biljetter till i kväll?**	finss day **noa**grah bil**yeh**terr til ee kvehl
Where can we go dancing?	**Var kan vi gå och dansa?**	varr kahn vee goa o(k) **dahn**sah
Would you like to dance?	**Får jag lov?**	foar yar(g) loav

Introductions

How do you do?	**Goddag.**	goo**dar(g)**
How are you?	**Hur står det till?**	hewr stoar day til
Very well, thank you. And you?	**Tack bara bra. Och Ni själv?**	tahk **bar**rar brar. o(k) nee shehlv

SWEDISH

May I introduce Miss Philips?	**Får jag presentera fröken Philips?**	foar yar(g) praysern**tay**rah **frur**kern Philips
My name is . . .	**Mitt namm är . . .**	mit nahmn æær
I'm very pleased to meet you.	**Roligt att lära känna Er.**	**roo**ligt aht **læ**ærah **kheh**nah ayr
How long have you been here?	**Hur länge har Ni varit här?**	hewr **lehng**er harr nee **var**rit hæær
It was nice meeting you.	**Det var trevligt att träffas.**	day varr **trayv**ligt aht **treh**fahss

Dating

Would you like a cigarette?	**Vill Ni ha en cigarrett?**	vil nee har ehn sigah**reht**
May I get you a drink?	**Vill Ni ha något att dricka?**	vil nee har **noa**got aht **dri**kar
Do you have a light, please?	**Har Ni möjligen eld?**	harr nee **mury**liggern ayld
Are you waiting for someone?	**Väntar Ni på någon?**	**væn**tahr nee poa **noa**gon
Are you free this evening?	**Är Ni ledig i kväll?**	ai nee **lay**dig ee kvehl
Where shall we meet?	**Var ska vi träffas?**	varr skar vee **treh**fahss
What time shall I meet you?	**När ska vi träffas?**	næær skar vee **treh**fahss
May I take you home?	**Får jag följa Er hem?**	foar yar(g) **fur**lyah ayr haym
Thank you, it's been a wonderful evening.	**Tack, det har varit en underbar kväll.**	tahk day har **var**rit ehn **ewn**derrbarr kvehl
What's your telephone number?	**Vad har Ni för telefonnummer?**	vard harr nee furr taylay**foan**newmerr
Do you live alone?	**Bor Ni ensam?**	boor nee **ayn**sahm
What time is your last train?	**När går sista tåget?**	næær goar **sis**tah **toa**get
Good-night . . .	**God natt . . .**	goo naht

Banks

Where's the nearest bank, please?	**Var ligger närmaste bank?**	varr **lig**ger **nææer**mahster bahnk

Where can I cash some traveller's cheques?	**Var kan jag växla in några resecheckar?**	varr kahn yar(g) **vehks**lah in **noa**grah **ray**ssershehkahr
What time does the bank open/What time does it close?	**När öppnar banken/När stänger den?**	næær **urp**nahr **bahn**kern/næær **stehng**err dehn
I'm expecting some money from home. Has it arrived?	**Jag väntar pengar hemifrån. Har de kommit?**	yar(g) **vehn**tahr **pehng**ahr **hay**mifron. harr day **kom**mit
Can you give me some small change, please?	**Kan jag få litet växel, tack?**	kahn yar(g) foa **lee**ter(t) **vehk**serl tahk

Shops, stores and services

Where is the nearest chemist's (pharmacy)?	**Var finns närmaste apotek?**	varr finss **næær**mahster ahpoo**tayk**
the nearest hairdresser's	**närmaste hårfrisörska**	**næær**mahster **hoar**frisurrshkah
the photo shop	**fotoaffär**	**foo**tooahfair
the jeweller's	**juvelerare**	yewver**lay**rahrer
the department store	**varuhus**	**var**rewhewssert
the police station	**polisstation**	poo**leess**stahshoon
the garage	**garage**	gah**rar**sher
How do I get there?	**Hur kommer jag dit?**	hewr **kom**merr yar(g) deet
Is it within walking distance?	**Kan man gå dit?**	kahn mahn **goa** deet

Service

Can you help me, please?	**Kan Ni vara snäll och hjälpa mig?**	kahn nee **var**rah snehl o(k) **yehl**pah may
Can you show me this? And that, too.	**Kan Ni visa mig den här? Och den där också.**	kahn nee **vee**sah may dehn hæær? o(k) dehn dæær ok**soa**
It's too expensive/too big/too small.	**Den är för dyr/för stor/för liten.**	dehn ai furr dewr/furr stoor/furr **lee**tern
Can you show me some more?	**Kan Ni visa mig något mer?**	kahn nee **vee**sah may **noa**got mayr
something better	**någonting bättre**	**noa**gonting **beh**trer
something cheaper	**någonting billigare**	**noa**gonting **bi**ligahrer
How much is this? And that?	**Hur mycket kostar den här? Och den där?**	hewr **mew**ker(t) **koss**tar dehn hæær? o(k) dehn dæær

It's not quite what I want.	**Det är inte precis vad jag tänkt mig.**	day ai **in**ter pray**sseess** vard yar(g) tehnkt may
I like it.	**Jag tycker om den.**	yar(g) **tew**kerr om dehn

Chemist's (Pharmacy)

I'd like something for a cold/for a cough/for travel sickness.	**Jag skulle vilja ha någonting mot förkylning/mot hosta/mot ressjuka.**	yar(g) **skew**ler **vil**yah har **noa**gonting moot furr**khewl**ning/moot **hoo**stah/ moot **rayss**shewkah
Can you recommend something for hay-fever/for sunburn?	**Kan Ni rekommendera någonting mot hösnuva/mot solsveda?**	kahn nee raykomehn**day**rah **noa**gonting moot **hur**snewvah/moot **sool**svaydah

Toiletry

May I have some razor blades?	**Kan jag få några rakblad?**	kahn yar(g) foa **noa**grah **rark**blahd
some shaving cream	**rakkräm**	**rark**krehm
some toothpaste	**tandkräm**	**tahnd**krehm
I'd like some soap.	**Jag ska be att få en tvål.**	yar(g) skar bay aht foa ayn tvoal
some suntan oil	**sololja**	**sool**olyah

At the barber's

I'd like a haircut, please.	**Jag skulle vilja ha håret klippt.**	yar(g) **skew**ler **vil**yah har **hoa**rert klipt
Short/Leave it long.	**Kort/Låt det vara långt.**	kort/loat day **var**rah longt
A razor cut, please.	**Klippning med rakblad, tack.**	**klip**ning mayd **rark**blahd tahk

At the hairdresser's

I'd like a shampoo and set, please.	**Jag ska be att få håret tvättat och lagt.**	yar(g) skar bay aht foa **hoa**rert **tveh**taht o(k) lahgt
I'd like a bleach.	**Jag skulle vilja ha det blekt.**	yar(g) **skew**ler **vil**yah har day blaykt
a permanent	**permanentat**	pærmah**nehn**taht
a colour rinse	**tonat**	**too**naht
a blow dry	**fönat**	**fur**naht

SWEDISH

Photography

I'd like a film for this camera.	**Jag ska be att få en film till den här kameran.**	yar(g) skar bay aht foa ayn film til dehn hæær **kar**mayrahn
This camera doesn't work.	**Den här kameran fungerar inte.**	dehn hæær **kar**mayrahn fewng**gay**rahr **in**ter

At the post office

Where's the nearest post office, please?	**Var ligger närmaste postkontor?**	var **lig**gerr **nææ**rmahster **posst**kontoor
I'd like to send this by express (special delivery)/by air mail.	**Jag skulle vilja skicka det här express/med flygpost.**	yar(g) **skew**ler **vil**yah **shi**kar day hææ r ehks**prehss**/mayd **flewg**posst

Service stations

Where is the nearest service station, please?	**Kan Ni säga mig var närmaste bensinstation ligger?**	kahn nee **sai**gah may varr **nææ r**mahster behn**seen**stahshoon **lig**gerr
Fill her up, please.	**Full tank, tack.**	fewl tahnk tahk
Check the oil, please.	**Kontrollera oljan, tack.**	kontro**lay**rah **ol**yahn tahk
Would you check the tyres?	**Skulle Ni vilja kontrollera däcken?**	**skew**ler nee **vil**yah kontro**lay**rah **deh**kern

Street directions

Can you show me on the map where I am?	**Kan Ni visa mig på kartan var jag är?**	kahn nee **vee**sah may poa **kahr**tahn varr yar(g) ai
You're on the wrong road.	**Ni är på fel väg.**	nee ai poa fayl vaig
Go back to ...	**Kör tillbaka till ...**	khurr til**bar**kah til
Go straight ahead.	**Kör rakt fram.**	khurr rahkt frahm
It's on the left/on the right.	**Det är till vänster/till höger.**	day ai til **vehn**sterr/til **hur**ger

Accidents

May I use your telephone?	**Kan jag få låna Er telefon?**	kahn yar(g) foa **loa**nah ayr taylay**foan**

Call a doctor quickly.	**Ring genast efter en läkare.**	ring **yay**nahst **ehf**terr ayn **lai**kahrer
Call an ambulance.	**Ring på ambulansen.**	ring poa ahmbew**lahn**sern
Please call the police.	**Var snäll och ring polisen.**	varr snehl o(k) ring poo**lee**ssern

Numbers

zero	**noll**	nol
one	**en, ett**	ayn/eht
two	**två**	tvoa
three	**tre**	tray
four	**fyra**	**few**rah
five	**fem**	fehm
six	**sex**	sehks
seven	**sju**	shew
eight	**åtta**	**o**tah
nine	**nio**	**nee**oo
ten	**tio**	**tee**oo
eleven	**elva**	**ehl**vah
twelve	**tolv**	tolv
thirteen	**tretton**	**treh**ton
fourteen	**fjorton**	**fyoor**ton
fifteen	**femton**	**fehm**ton
sixteen	**sexton**	**sehks**ton
seventeen	**sjutton**	**shew**ton
eighteen	**arton**	**arr**ton
nineteen	**nitton**	**nit**ton
twenty	**tjugo**	**khew**goo
twenty-one	**tjugoett**	**khew**gooeht
thirty	**trettio**	**treh**tioo
forty	**fyrtio**	**fewr**tioo
fifty	**femtio**	**fehm**tioo
sixty	**sextio**	**sehks**tioo
seventy	**sjuttio**	**shew**tioo
eighty	**åttio**	**o**tioo
ninety	**nittio**	**nit**tioo
one hundred	**hundra**	**hewn**drah
one thousand	**tusen**	**tew**sern
ten thousand	**tio tusen**	**tee**oo **tew**ssern

Days

It's Sunday.	**Det är söndag.**	day ai **surn**dar(g)
Monday	**måndag**	**moan**dar(g)
Tuesday	**tisdag**	**tiss**dar(g)
Wednesday	**onsdag**	**oons**dar(g)

SWEDISH

Thursday	**torsdag**	**toorsh**dar(g)
Friday	**fredag**	**fray**dar(g)
Saturday	**lördag**	**lurr**dar(g)
yesterday	**i går**	ee goar
today	**i dag**	ee dar(g)
tomorrow	**i morgon**	ee **mo**ron
morning/afternoon	**förmiddag/eftermiddag**	**furr**middar(g)/**ehf**termiddar(g)
evening/night	**kväll/natt**	kvehl/naht

Months

January	**januari**	yahnew**ar**ri
February	**februari**	faybrew**ar**ri
March	**mars**	mahrsh
April	**april**	ah**preel**
May	**maj**	migh
June	**juni**	**yew**ni
July	**juli**	**yew**li
August	**augusti**	ahew**gew**sti
September	**september**	sehp**tehm**berr
October	**oktober**	ok**too**berr
November	**november**	no**vehm**berr
December	**december**	day**sehm**berr
Merry Christmas! Happy New Year!	**God Jul! Gott Nytt År!**	goo(d) yewl! got newt oar

Reference section

Weight conversion

The figure in the middle stands for both kilograms and pounds, e.g., 1 kilogram = 2.205 lb. and 1 pound = 0.45 kilograms.

Kilograms (kg.)		Avoirdupois pounds
0.45	**1**	2.205
0.90	**2**	4.405
1.35	**3**	6.614
1.80	**4**	8.818
2.25	**5**	11.023
2.70	**6**	13.227
3.15	**7**	15.432
3.60	**8**	17.636
4.05	**9**	19.840
4.50	**10**	22.045
6.75	**15**	33.068
9.00	**20**	44.889
11.25	**25**	55.113
22.50	**50**	110.225
33.75	**75**	165.338
45.00	**100**	220.450

1 kilogram or kilo (kg) = 1000 grams (g)

100 g = 3.5 oz.	½ kg = 1.1 lb.
200 g = 7.0 oz.	1 kg = 2.2 lb.

1 oz. = 28.35 g
1 lb. = 453.60 g

Metres and feet

The figure in the middle stands for both metres and feet, e.g., 1 metre = 3.281 ft. and 1 foot = 0.30 m.

Metres		Feet
0.30	**1**	3.281
0.61	**2**	6.563
0.91	**3**	9.843
1.22	**4**	13.124
1.52	**5**	16.403
1.83	**6**	19.686
2.13	**7**	22.967
2.44	**8**	26.248
2.74	**9**	29.529
3.05	**10**	32.810
3.35	**11**	36.091
3.66	**12**	39.372
3.96	**13**	42.635
4.27	**14**	45.934
4.57	**15**	49.215
4.88	**16**	52.496
5.18	**17**	55.777
5.49	**18**	59.058
5.79	**19**	62.339
6.10	**20**	65.620
7.62	**25**	82.023
15.24	**50**	164.046
22.86	**75**	246.069
30.48	**100**	328.092

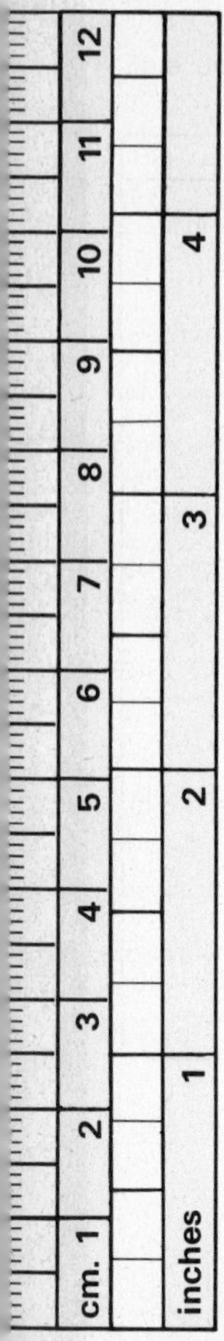

Centimetres and inches

To change centimetres into inches, multiply by .39.

To change inches into centimetres, multiply by 2.54.

	in.	feet	yards
1 mm	0,039	0,003	0,001
1 cm	0,39	0,03	0,01
1 dm	3,94	0,32	0,10
1 m	39,40	3,28	1,09

	mm	cm	m
1 in.	25,4	2,54	0,025
1 ft.	304,8	30,48	0,304
1 yd.	914,4	91,44	0,914

(32 metres = 35 yards)

Temperature

To convert Centigrade into degrees Fahrenheit, multiply Centigrade by 1.8 and add 32.

To convert degrees Fahrenheit into Centigrade, subtract 32 from Fahrenheit and divide by 1.8.

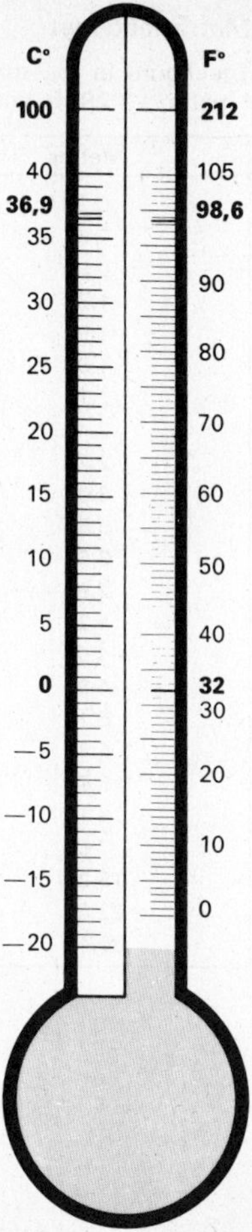

The car

Miles into kilometres										
1 mile=1.609 kilometres (km)										
miles	10	20	30	40	50	60	70	80	90	100
km	16	32	48	64	80	97	113	129	145	161

Kilometres into miles													
1 kilometre (km)=0.62 miles													
km	10	20	30	40	50	60	70	80	90	100	110	120	130
miles	6	12	19	25	31	37	44	50	56	62	68	75	81

Tire pressure

lb./sq. in.	kg/cm²	lb./sq. in.	kg/cm²
10	0.7	26	1.8
12	0.8	27	1.9
15	1.1	28	2.0
18	1.3	30	2.1
20	1.4	33	2.3
21	1.5	36	2.5
23	1.6	38	2.7
24	1.7	40	2.8

Fluid measures

litres	imp. gal.	U.S. gal.	litres.	imp. gal.	U.S. gal.
5	1.1	1.3	30	6.6	7.8
10	2.2	2.6	35	7.7	9.1
15	3.3	3.9	40	8.8	10.4
20	4.4	5.2	45	9.9	11.7
25	5.5	6.5	50	11.0	13.0

1 litre (l) = 0.88 imp. quarts = 1.06 U.S. quarts

1 imp. quart = 1.14 l
1 imp. gallon = 4.55 l

1 U.S. quart = 0.95 l
1 U.S. gallon = 3.81 l

This is your size

Ladies

	Dresses/suits					
American	10	12	14	16	18	20
British	32	34	36	38	40	42
Continental	38	40	42	44	46	48

	Stockings						Shoes			
American / British	8	8½	9	9½	10	10½	6	7	8	9
Continental	0	1	2	3	4	5	36	38	38½	40

Gentlemen

	Suits/overcoats						Shirts					
American / British	36	38	40	42	44	46	14	15	15½	16	16½	17
Continental	46	48	50	52	54	56	36	38	39	41	42	43

	Shoes						
American / British	5	6	7	8	9	10	11
Continental	38	39	41	42	43	44	45

In Europe sizes vary somewhat from country to country, so the above must be taken as an approximate guide.

REFERENCE SECTION

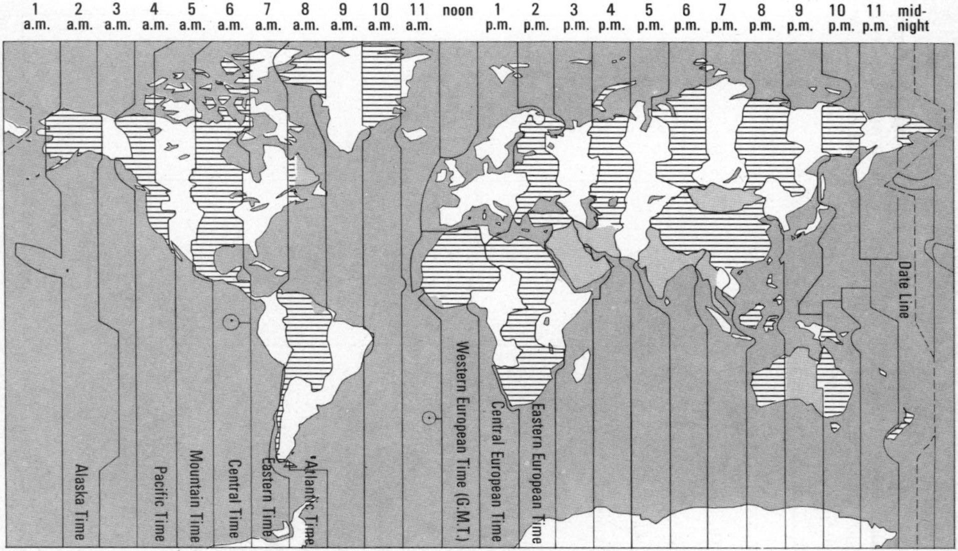

Countries which have adopted a time differing from that in the corresponding time zone. Note that also in the USSR, official time is one hour ahead of the time in each corresponding time zone. In summer, numerous countries advance time one hour ahead of standard time.

Currency converter

In a world of fluctuating currencies, we can offer no more than this handy do-it-yourself chart. You can get information about exchange rates from banks, travel agents and tourist offices. Why not fill in this chart too, for handy reference?

	£1	**$1**
Austria (shillings)		
Belgium (francs)		
Croatia (dinars)		
Denmark (crowns)		
Finland (marks)		
France (francs)		
Germany (marks)		
Greece (drachmas)		
Italy (lire)		
Netherlands (guilders)		
Norway (crowns)		
Poland (zlotys)		
Portugal (escudos)		
Russia (roubles)		
Spain (pesetas)		
Sweden (crowns)		
Switzerland (francs)		
Yugoslavia (dinars)		